Northwestern University STUDIES IN *Phenomenology & Existential Philosophy*

Signs

Maurice Merleau-Ponty

Translated, with an Introduction by

Signs

RICHARD C. McCLEARY

NORTHWESTERN UNIVERSITY PRESS

1964

Signes was first published by
Librairie Gallimard, Paris, in 1960.

Library of Congress Catalog Card Number: 64–19455
Printed in the United States of America
Second Printing, 1969
SBN: 8101-0253-6

TRANSLATOR'S Preface

MAURICE MERLEAU-PONTY was a philosopher who made men wonder. Convinced that his thought had a role to play in present history, he sought and found a journalistic and an academic audience, yet scarcely tried to win a following. He was well enough known in the cosmopolitan world he comments on in *Signs,* but the studied wall of solitude he built about him made it hard for even intimates to know him. Although he was more involved politically than his friend Sartre when they founded *Les Temps Modernes,* and never stopped speaking out for political freedom and lucidity, his aesthetic fascination with the visible and his metaphorical multiplication of perspectives subsequently led Sartre to ask whether he had not adopted the politically ineffectual position of contemplating them all without choosing any. His former friends in the French Communist Party were more blunt, calling him a dangerous idealist and challenging him to admit his errors. Instead of snarling back, he confessed his differences with apparent candor, kept insisting that the Communists be represented in French political life, and then answered his accusers with disarming questions of his own. He kept his distance.

Yet from that distance he made men wonder. His studied anonymity became at times intensely personal. He moved men. Seeing him as their *semblable,* their *frère,* they saw into the mirror of themselves; and what had been so conveniently remote and queer became as touching, strange, and problematic as their own uncertain lives. They responded to his indirect appeal to freedom and truth. Abandoned to the primal wonders of their suddenly evasive world, they even turned in awe and open adulation toward this "miracle," this "monster," for support. He kept his distance, but now it was their distance too and they communicated—obliquely.

This is the lot of the philosopher who seeks to be (as Merleau-

Ponty in a self-revealing passage said Montaigne perhaps had learned to be) simultaneously "ironic and solemn, faithful and free." Can he also say without presumption that his lot should be every man's goal? He knows his stage is a shifting world, which he sees according to his own lights on the edge of the dark pit of non-sense, and that the very brightness of his vision all too often blinds him to the darkness without which his world would become invisible. If he tries to be a spy of God who looks on high into the universal essence of mankind, he may discover foolishly that he has lost the tie that links him to the world in an "inextricable confusion," the carnal bond that is his only point of contact with the universal. Ironically, he may be forced to recognize that a remote pursuit of abstract objectivity has really made of him the proud, narrow slave to the life-denying he once shrugged off as a blind world's defensive caricature. Then the roles are reversed—the world becomes the questioning philosopher.

But the true philosopher, in Merleau-Ponty's view, counts on such reversals. He willingly admits that he is simply trying to express more clearly the experience he shares with other men, who cannot put it into words and yet are vital to his effort. Convinced that "it is easier to write books than to live," he knows that men whose formal speech is blurred can sometimes master in their style of life a tacit, universal language which "speaks without saying." He knows that he may fail where they succeed. Although he is indeed distinguished from his fellow men by his awareness of the risk of reason and the need to take it, he can never do without them. It is their quizzical awareness of his folly which provides him with what is perhaps his sole assurance—men do have an idea of the truth, and only the exchange of mutual questioning can ever hope to call it from its inarticulate shadows.

Merleau-Ponty is a wondering philosopher who tries to remain free to pursue the "rumination" of his life without losing contact with its source in the living present. Through the span of years we glimpse here in *Signs,* we see him searching for himself by questioning his world. We hear him learning "to speak with his own voice." Across the growing distance which embodies him in history, he speaks from his time of his times—difficult times, and less and less opportunity to question them. In the mature thought of *Signs,* time and distance mingle in the shadow of approaching death. When the times are an agony, time itself can be so. Yet in his Introduction, Merleau-Ponty can reproach his alter ego Sartre for his despair, since he believes that there is only time and (in the "callings and responses" of succeeding generations) always time. There is no "new being"; it is like the "myth of the Androgynes." No man is ever "wholly saved or damned." Since our only hope—human questioning and creative response—is never wholly lost, "men never should despair."

The hope and promise—and confusions—which arise from the times and their crises are confirmed in Merleau-Ponty's own philosophy. His philosophy is a phenomenology. In its origins, its tasks and goals, and its essential characteristics, it is inseparable from history and time. It came to pass (but came to be) when Edmund Husserl sought a way beyond the "crisis of the European sciences." According to the classical thought in terms of which these sciences developed, scientific concepts were the sole means of gaining objective knowledge of phenomena and of the things which underlay them as the invariant "order of nature." The "crisis of the European sciences" arose when turn-of-the-century developments in mathematics and physics proved to be incompatible with classical thought. In Husserl's view, this crisis revealed the "artificial" character of the "scientific attitude" and the need to seek the phenomenological origins of the classical ontology. According to Husserl's central concept of "intentionality," there is always an inseparable correlation between the "intentions" of "constituting" consciousness—the source or origin of the *meaning* of our experience—and the objective, "constituted" meaning-structures they intend and are united in. Consciousness has constituted many "worlds" of objective meaning-structures. Vietà, Galileo, and Descartes, in their search for absolute and certain bases of all knowledge, constituted the world of classical ontology. Since this ontology had proved untenable, Husserl thought the classical search must be begun again on the basis of the unreflected "natural" attitude of consciousness, from which the special worlds constituted by our "theoretical" attitude arise.

Merleau-Ponty's first book, *The Structure of Behavior,* is an effort to explore the crisis in the classical foundations of the sciences of man. According to the classical ontology of the judging subject and objective things, the living body had become an object, other persons inferred existences, and behavior a mechanical process in which a consciousness seated somehow "in" the body was acted upon causally by external agents. This doctrine of the "little man within man" implied that consciousness is really the theoretical consciousness of the scientific observer, the overarching viewer of the world who alone is not embodied in the system he observes. In the Husserlian tradition, but in terms of the empirical findings of contemporary psychologies, Merleau-Ponty tries to show that the classical doctrine and its underlying ontology are not only inadequate to our effective experience of behavior, but are in fact particular theoretical derivatives of it. Since all scientific experience is only a more explicit form of a natural, perceptual experience from which it arises but for whose appearance it cannot provide a justification, there can be no "objective science of subjectivity." The scientific universe is not a self-contained one, and our natural perception is not an event in this universe.

Although this first work of Merleau-Ponty's might be considered "theoretical philosophy," he has always tried to draw the vital as well as the intellectual conclusions of an absolutist reason in a state of crisis. His phenomenology does call for a critical revision of an abstract reason which endangers understanding by obscuring "living reason," but it also demands awareness of the way in which a failure to revise endangers living reasoners. For "the War did take place," and the place that it took in the lives of the generation Merleau-Ponty speaks of still with feeling in his Introduction to *Signs* was both enormous and irremediable. While he was developing his academic thesis in *The Structure of Behavior*, this generation slowly wove the web of an "anonymous adversity" which fell upon them with suffocating force with the Fall of France. The subsequent events which wrenched them from their childish dreams of "strolling on the lawns of peace" and made them men, and the revolutionary ambiance they lived in during the Occupation, led Merleau-Ponty to attempt to draw upon the thought of Marx as well as Husserl in his search for vital infrastructures. The crises of our thought and history had taught him that "nature *is not* geometrical in itself; it only seems so to a careful observer who sticks to macroscopic data. Human society *is not* a community of reasonable minds; it was only able to be understood as such in favored countries in which economic and vital equilibrium had obtained locally for a while. The experience of chaos, on the speculative level as on the other, invites us to look at rationalism in an historical perspective from which it claimed in principle to escape, to look for a philosophy which will make us understand the surging forth of reason in a world it has not made, and which will prepare the vital infrastructure without which reason and freedom become empty and decompose." As the essays published here in *Signs* not only state but show, Merleau-Ponty's version of phenomenology developed and defined itself through his "perpetual beginning" of the effort to revive a living reason muffled in forgetfulness, a reason which he thought had to be rendered present if our abstract calculations and established ideologies were to make some sense within the context of our total knowledge and experience.

In its insistence upon the ontological and epistemological primacy of our perceptual experience, his philosophy was first and always a phenomenology of perception. Perception is the "primordial operation which impregnates sensible being with a meaning, and which all logical mediation as well as all psychological causality presupposes." Merleau-Ponty's phenomenology tries to make us look at what we see, and ask ourselves just what it means to see. In the process we are led to ask ourselves as well just what it means to be incarnate in our times and time—to have a history—and speak. His philosophy is a phenomenology of "perception, history, expression." It is Husserl's celebrated "return to the things themselves" as they appear contextually in our pre-theoretical perceptual experience; that is, as "natural" meaning-structures basic to our "artificial" logics—the structures which the later Husserl called the "Logos of the aesthetic world." As Merleau-Ponty summed it up in his *Phenomenology of Perception,* his is a philosophy which has taken up the challenge offered by the crisis in the classical foundations of Western thought "to return to the life-world this side of the objective world; . . . to give the thing its concrete physiognomy, to organisms their own manner of handling the world, to subjectivity its historical inherence; to rediscover phenomena, the layer of living experience through which others and things are first given to us . . . ; to arouse perception and reveal the ruse by which it lets itself be forgotten as a fact and as perception in favor of the object it reveals to us and of the rational tradition it founds."

Pursuing these aims in his *Phenomenology of Perception,* Merleau-Ponty shows that our fundamental and original perceptual experience is always of "a *world,* that is . . . an indefinite and open multiplicity in which relations are relations of reciprocal implication. . . ." Our perceptual "field of presence" is always structured in terms of objects and their relatively but never fully constituted horizons, linked together in a pre-objective order of their own by a constituting consciousness "which makes explicit and thematizes what was previously presented as only an undetermined horizon." Consciousness is always perspectival and essentially incapable of the total synthesis of horizons which would enable us to be aware of something from all times and places—that is, at the limit and as an example, from the overarching view presupposed in the classical ontology. Yet as a consequence of reason's "presumption" to a total synthesis, and of the "retrospective illusion" by which we take the perceived objects constituted by our perceiving consciousness as pre-existent causes *of* perception, we normally pass from our experience of a world to that of "*a universe,* that is, of a finished, explicit totality in which the relations are those of reciprocal determination."

In *Signs,* the origins and consequences of our claim to bring our world to total visibility and rid it wholly of its shadows are explored in the behavioral sciences and psychoanalysis, in literature and painting, in politics and history, and in philosophy itself. For since in Merleau-Ponty's thought it is perception which "opens" us to reality and forms the basis for our understanding, reason's presumption to a total synthesis—the retrospective illusion by which our constituted universes lead us to deny the life-world and the perceptual origins of all reason—is the fundamental philosophic problem. In order to attempt to solve this problem we must first describe the life-world we perceive and then reflexively determine the essential meaning-structures of the self in its relations to itself, to other persons, and to the world. The central problem, Merleau-Ponty once said (and the other side, so to speak, of the problem of reason's presumption), is to understand how we can simultaneously constitute the meaning-structures of experience and find that it is always already constituted in terms of meanings we have not bestowed upon it. How is it that the past and the world (as the horizons of our present) can be both immanent in our experience as a matter of principle and as a matter of fact transcend it? In the Husserlian language of the *Phenomenology of Perception,* the central problem is to understand how "I can be open to phenomena which go beyond me, and which nevertheless exist only to the extent I take them up and live them; *how the presence to myself (Urpräsenz) which defines me and conditions all alien presence is at the same time depresentation (Entgegenwärtigung) and throws me outside myself.*"

Through its very efforts to establish the *essential* structures of the reflective presence of the self to itself which forms the basis of all thought, Merleau-Ponty's phenomenology of perception necessarily becomes a dialectical philosophy of *existence.* For this experiencing of the world as always already constituted yet always still to be constituted by our active and spontaneous involvement in it is precisely what it means to him to "exist," to "be present to the world" as an "existential field." Sometimes Merleau-Ponty speaks of "existence" in terms of the nonrepresentational, implicit "operating" intentionality of pre-objective consciousness; sometimes in terms of the explicit intentions and creative acts in which we represent and then assume our situation by our projects and commitments. But it is always what he calls a "thought in act"—our unending assumption of already constituted facts and hazards in a meaning-giving act of constitution which does not exist before or without that assumption. Existential self-awareness is awareness that our consciousness in essence is involvement in an already meaningful world as the creative negation of it, which is to say that it is the dialectic of assumption and transcendence of an existential field of presence which transforms the meaning-structures of that field.

To understand the essence of consciousness and the experiential meaning-structures it constitutes and is constituted by, we must therefore understand our existence as temporal beings. Consciousness is essentially the intentional transcendence of a field of presence toward another, future field of presence. Time is essentially the vector or polarization which characterizes the intentionality of consciousness. Consequently, the basis for whatever has a meaning or (more precisely) "makes sense" is temporality. The characteristic common to all the usages of "sense"—perception, direction, meaning, understanding—is for Merleau-Ponty just this constituting, meaning-giving intentional transcendence.

Like every other being, the self exists, takes place, or comes to be as a "temporalization." It is a being which expresses itself and makes itself be what it is in intention in a single gesture of existence which takes up the past, incorporates it into the present, and links this present to a future. In so doing, it opens a whole cycle of time in which "acquired" meanings will remain present as dimensions of experience that (at least "for a time") do not have to be called into question. Although reason's presumption and the retrospective illusion tend to obscure the fact, such "objective" time and being clearly have their roots in an historical time and an intentional being—the "living present . . . torn between a past which it takes up and a future it projects." Time and being become present only from a certain point of view through the intentionality of consciousness. Since the world and things are thus the linking of perspectives, they exist only as lived and constituted by some subject.

Yet they simultaneously transcend all perspectives precisely because this linking is temporal and thus leaves horizons of undetermined or "latent" meaning which I have not constituted. In fact, they have not been constituted by any subject, in the sense that all men are embodied in a natural world and time which they are not the authors of. "The world is inseparable from the subject, but from a subject who is nothing but a project of the world; and the subject is inseparable from the world, but from a world which he himself projects." As Merleau-Ponty points out in *Signs,* the "presence to myself which defines me and conditions all alien presence" is simultaneously presence to a compresent world which always bears me "somewhere else" and so requires me to assume once more the search to constitute the bases of my thought and existence. "There is time for me only because I am situated in it, that is, only because I find myself already committed in it, only because not all of being is given to me in person, and finally, only because a sector of being is so close to me that it is not even spread out in front of me and I cannot *see* it, as I cannot see my face. There is time for me because I have a present. . . . It is in communicating with the world that we communicate with ourselves." There is time and meaning for me only because I am incarnate.

Since we are fundamentally and originally conscious of our world and times only because we are literally and metaphysically "embodied" in them, we may say that Merleau-Ponty's phenomenology of perception, existence, and time is above all a phenomenology of incarnation. The invisible sector of being which forms the "anchorage" of my present and the basic source of time and meaning for me is my carnal being. My own body is "the unperceived point towards which all objects turn their side"; and "I know that objects have several sides because I am able to go around them, and in this sense I am conscious of the world by means of my body." From the start, and constantly, Merleau-Ponty sought to follow out the fundamental network of implications constituted not by the explicit acts of constituting consciousness but by the existential relationships between my body as an "I am able to" (the motor power of operating intentionality) and the "properties" of things which it reveals because (and only because) it is situated in the visible world as an absolute here and now which forms the inalienable source of distances and times and meanings. "I comprehend the world because there is for me near and far, foreground and horizon, and because it thus spreads out and takes on a meaning for me; that is to say, finally, because I am situated in it and it comprehends me."

This fundamental network of incarnate implications is not of course the analytic, causal system of reciprocal determination and objective co-variation constituted retrospectively by our theoretical consciousness. It is the life-world's open unity of implication, based upon the body's "awareness" of itself as simultaneously perceiving and perceived, which is prior experientially and metaphysically to any theoretical reflection. Nor is the body which presents me to the world and time the constituted object of our theoretical analyses. It is the body as this present body which I call "my body." Neither thing nor concept, my body in its fundamental self-awareness is my consciousness incarnate or (reciprocally) my animate body—what Merleau-Ponty calls in *Signs* the "vinculum" between my self and things, my "flesh."

In a strict sense, my primordial perception as incarnate self-awareness is not even "my" perception. I am always conscious on the basis of my natural, cultural, already acquired "pre-personal" body, whose functional infrastructure of operating intentions constitutes the relatively invariant, established horizons of my perceptual field. My carnal world has a "pre-given" meaning which I do not personally constitute. My body moves, and a world spreads out, takes shape, and becomes visible and meaningful. The synthesis of horizons which connects the stages of my exploration of an aspect of the world, the changing aspects of the world perceived, and the two series to each other is constituted by the transition which my flesh effects from one stage of its movement to another. Corporeal perception is originally and fundamentally our presence to a world in which the active and the passive and the visible and the invisible are so little distinguishable that all our traditional categories become indefinite. Far from being able to demarcate a perceiving subject and the object he perceives, we can no longer tell precisely who is seen and who is seeing. That is why those masters of perception, painters, often say that what they look at looks at them. As the body's self-awareness as projecting project of the world, consciousness is basically the anonymous, pre-personal life of the flesh.

Carnal self-awareness is the Archimedian point of Merleau-Ponty's philosophy; for the body's presence to itself as both perceiving and perceived provides us with our fundamental knowledge of the consciousness in terms of which the self, the world, and other men are constituted. I can perceive something objectively only if I can perceive it simultaneously from more than one perspective. Since I am actually embodied at each moment of my experience in a particular perspective, the basis for objectivity must be the simultaneous presence of others and their perspectives in my field of presence. Theoretically, I cannot conceive of other persons (or of myself as an other person). To be conscious is to constitute, and I could not posit another person as another myself without thereby constituting him as constituting in respect to the very act through which I constitute him. Only my body provides me with a way between the possible and the necessary toward the real. As my fundamental and original experience of a being which is inseparably both constituting and constituted, my body teaches me what I cannot learn in any other way.

My body teaches me to know the simultaneous presence of multiple perspectives because the body as perceived in self-awareness and the body as perceiving motor power are linked in "coexistence" or "compresence" as the visible and constituted and the invisible, constituting aspects of a single existential world. Suppose, as Merleau-Ponty puts it, that my left hand begins to touch my right while my right is touching it. Through the "sort of reflection" effected in this carnal self-perception, the operating intentions of my body as perceiving motor power (the right hand constituting the left as a perceived thing) are suddenly "encroached" upon by the constituting intentions of my left hand, which set about in turn to constitute my perceiving body. My body has become a "subject-object" or "perceiving thing," an experience of the constituting and the constituted which provides me with a sort of premonition of a common world in which my self and others are embodied as reciprocally perceiving and perceived.

In the life-world which arises from my carnal self-awareness, the visible world and the world of my motor projects are in an open, dialectical relationship of meaningful exchange. Although my moving body is aware of itself as a part of the visible world in terms of which it is constituted, it is simultaneously aware that the world visible to it is constituted by its power to move itself. The "properties" of a perceived thing are there before my flesh only because their manifest visibility is paralleled by and echoed in my body's hidden visibility—its intentional structure as an "I am able to"—which forms the internal equivalent or carnal formula of the bodily presence of things. Yet my body's existence as simultaneously seeing and aware of itself as seeing enables it to recognize in what it sees the "other side" of its power to see—the still visible trace of its invisible motor power. In my bodily perception of the "Moses," the tension of his body becomes visible as it is constituted by my body's motor power; and simultaneously it forms a visible trace of previous relationships between my body and the world, which reinvokes that motor power and makes it visible to my flesh in the flesh of the world.

My body as the self-awareness of an "I am able to" is thus a sort of "intersection" of perceiving and perceived within an existential system of exchanges and "equivalences," in which the flesh of sensible being both reflects and forms the counterpart of my own incarnation. In the presence of another man as flesh, my flesh extends this coexistence of perceiving and perceived through an intentional encroachment similar to the one which originally constituted it as a perceiving thing. My body as an "I am able to" is faced with something visible whose behavior evokes my body's motor possibilities as if it were my body's own behavior. This alien behavior thus becomes not just the visible and constituted "other side" but the *constituting* "other side" of the intentions of my body. My intentions are in "circuit" with its own, and pass through them toward the public meaning-structures of a common world. Like the reflecting mirror which is its technical amplification, carnal self-awareness draws my flesh outside me into the public world of carnal intersubjectivity. I am embodied in the world as one dimension of that primordial, all-comprehending Being of "many foci" which Merleau-Ponty describes as being coming to be through the fundamental "We" of the evolving human community. In the "absolute of presence" of carnal intersubjectivity, flesh meets flesh in the flesh of the world, and man can now become a living mirror for his fellow man.

A mirror full of moving shadows; for even though a world which can arise from carnal gestures is a "magic" one, the wondrous creatures of our vision always drag along reluctant flesh. Although visible being is indeed present to the eye of the body "in person," and not as represented being, it is always present from across the distance of its latent meaning for my body's hidden motor power. To see, for Merleau-Ponty, is to have at a distance, to be present at a world both hidden and revealed—a "chiaroscuro" world whose being becomes visible only in terms of its invisibility.

This "ambiguity" of carnal intersubjectivity is as insurmountable as the dialectical relationship of synthesis and tension between my already constituted and my always constituting and still to be constituted body that it springs from. It cannot be dissipated by any theoretical reflection, but is an essential characteristic of what Merleau-Ponty calls in *Signs* "the fundamental." The term itself may well be a pun on "*Fundierung*," the Husserlian concept according to which "the founding term—time, the unreflected, fact, language, perception—is primary in the sense that the founded is given as a determination or an explicit form of the founding, which prevents the founded from ever absorbing the founding; and yet the founding is not primary in the empiricist sense and the founded is not simply derived from it, because it is through the founded that the founding is manifested." In Merleau-Ponty's thought, logical objectivity and carnal intersubjectivity are related as the founded and the founding.

On the one hand, the "pre-given" meanings constituted by the body as projecting project of the world are the founding source of any subsequent meaning-structures our reflective consciousness may produce, and thus cannot be derived from any theoretical source. Reason and order are in this sense a fundamental *fact* of our experience—the Logos of the aesthetic world which, as the perceptually revealed basis of all further explanation and itself incapable of any further explanation, may literally be called the "mystery" of rationality. On the other hand, this fundamental reason is insurmountably presumptive; for it is essential to the operating intentions of the constituting body to seek a stable equilibrium in founded meaning-structures or acquired horizons which approximate the permanence and false eternity of nature. The body can constitute stable horizons of meaning only by "forgetting" or repressing the pluridimensional ambiguity which always characterizes its field of presence. In order to establish objective horizons of meaning, it must "invest" the complementary dimensions of the life-world's existential system of equivalences in its hidden motor power, where they continue to lead a "latent" existence as "sedimented" meaning-structures which are present as the past horizons of a new objective field of presence. Thus the pre-objective order of our carnal intersubjectivity, which is both the founding source of logical objectivity and the measure of its value, begins to exist fully only in the objective order that it founds, which is itself the culmination of the advent of the pre-objective meanings of perceptual experience to explicit existence.

Philosophers who try to find the fundamental "signs" or pre-objective, sedimented meaning-structures at the basis of the several worlds of human life and thought, in order to reconstitute experience as meaningful in terms of them, must thus subject acquired, established meaning-structures to an endless "questioning" and seek with fine sophistication to regain the naivete of carnal intersubjectivity. In the world of present things, "more ancient than all fabricated things" —of things which stand "upright" before our eyes, "flaying our glance with their edges"—such men must try to find a new birth of "wonder," which is as old as our philosophy itself. The only "solution" to the problem of reason's presumption and the retrospective illusion which conceals its existential origins is to constantly reveal the problematic nature of human existence. In our reflective search to discover the fundamental bases of all meaning, we do have to try to recall sedimented meaning-structures to explicit consciousness and bring to light the pre-objective as well as the explicit intentions which constituted them. We are interested in describing these structures and their advent, and in determining their essential characteristics and relationships. But reflective consciousness is itself based upon the body and its dialectic of the constituting and the constituted, and is thus "a creative operation which itself participates in the facticity of the unreflected." All reflection is situational, none can be total, and the essences which we determine are justified only by the experience they clarify and are thus always subject to revision. Our incarnation in a present body of our own is simultaneously the inalienable alienation of the flesh and the fundamental basis for our power to find a meaning for existence and to gain some measure of fulfillment through the self-expression which expresses what is valuable and true.

Indeed, "perception already stylizes," and Merleau-Ponty's phenomenology of incarnate and carnal perception is inseparably a phenomenology of expression as well. To begin with, a phenomenology of language—a philosophy of "speaking" language—becomes the privileged way to the "fundamental." Then increased concern with what Freud called the "archeology" of reason leads Merleau-Ponty to dig beneath language for the pre-objective, latent meaning-structures of expression. As the search for carnal sources of expression makes it clear that speech arises from a hidden silent sea, his phenomenology of expression turns into a raid on the inarticulate. In ever deeper forays he attempts to sound the silent voices in the visible invisibility of painting, in hopes that he may surface a primordial model for what Nathalie Sarraute has called "*sous-conversations*," and Merleau-Ponty's friend the psychoanalyst Lacan has called an "eros of the eye." We are led beneath established rules and languages, toward their sources in expressive flesh, until we are confronted with the mute and shifting, polymorphous radiance of meaning in the shadows of a world at Marienbad. Although this world in genesis seems almost timeless in its simultaneous evocation of multiple perspectives, Merleau-Ponty shows us through the studies he has made in *Signs* of physics, painting, literature, psychoanalysis, and history that it is in every sense our "present" one.

Merleau-Ponty's view of the relationship between the science of linguistics and the phenomenology of language parallels and is based upon his view of the relationship between logical objectivity and carnal intersubjectivity. The series of fortuitous developments which linguistics reveals as causal factors modifying spoken language in the "empirical order of events" owes its fundamental meaning to its incorporation in a speaking language, whose series of fields of presence (with their existential systems of equivalences and their sedimented meanings) are united by the "advent" of new meaning. Like the carnal intersubjectivity that is its ever-present source, speaking language is a moving equilibrium governed by the present and incarnate logic of existence. Confronted with a world to be expressed, and with the random factors and events which people it, speaking men assume their past horizons of linguistic meaning without representing them, and in a series of existential acts connect them to the present they perceive by bringing them to new expression. And yet the existential systems of equivalences which they thus define are always open to the brute events and latent shifts of meaning which arise historically in the empirical order of events, the province of linguistics. The objective science of language turns toward the past of already established language and already acquired meanings. The phenomenology of language seeks to unveil the field of presence of the speaking subject and the "differentiation" and convergence of linguistic gestures he effects in his unending efforts to bring the implicit meaning-structures of experience to explicit expression. In their autonomy, science and philosophy mutually envelop one another within the dialectic of the constituted and the constituting.

Like the creative expression of the painter, whose body with its carnal eye preceives the world in person and expresses it with gestures of its carnal hand, speaking language and communication have their fundamental basis in the pre-objective order of the flesh. Every spoken word appears to me as a visible trace of the invisible significative intention which is constituting it, and I comprehend and respond to it by means of my own significative intentions. In my dialogue with other speaking men, expression and communication are polarized about significative intentions which converge through reciprocal encroachments in spoken words. Since these signifying words are visible traces of corporeal intentions, they are always surrounded by a corona of latent significations. No established meaning of a term ever exhausts its meaning. Expression is never total but must always be sought for anew. Although creative vision and expression are perhaps brought to perfection in painting, all living expression is, as Merleau-Ponty puts it, a "continuous birth," in the sense that a man is born when what was visible only in the depths of the maternal body becomes visible to itself and others in a single act.

As in the case of flesh and the expressive gestures which our common world of carnal intersubjectivity emerges from, the universal forms of signification in language do not arise from theoretical constructions or reside in dictionaries. Men whose languages are different are able to communicate because they find within themselves a speaking power which lets them pass into the style of another language which encroaches on their own. In the process, we may attain to a "lateral" universal which consists in the convergence of two different styles toward a common meaning; but we do so only on the basis of their common carnal presence as autonomous but mutually enveloping dimensions of what is now an extended existential and expressive system of equivalences. (As witness to these truths one might evoke the parallel example of the psychoanalytic dialogue, or more appropriately the countless epigrams and counsels of despair of every translator; but this one is "content" to point to *Signes* and *Signs*, and leave the question of covergence to others—only betting that a look at Merleau-Ponty's style will let them guess how much "translation" is a matter of an existential "transformation"!)

What is true of foreign languages is equally true of all forms of creative expression, which after all are always alien to our already established languages. In speaking language, in painting, and in perception, creative expression is a thought in act which learns to express only by drawing upon the past expression present in the body's hidden motor power and making its intended meanings visible. Expression is always a sort of schema of the carnal other side of the flesh of the intersubjective world, exposed for the first time to the public eye as a visible trace of the indirect, symbolic texture of the invisible reality which constitutes it. As Merleau-Ponty's own metaphorical style attests, the speaking language which attempts to liberate the hidden meanings captive in the present world must bend itself to fit the indirections and "allusive logic" of that world itself. In creative expression, the real and the imaginary, the public and the private, and the multiple fields of presence all coexist in the advent of truth.

For the truth is brought to be by our taking up already speaking expressions, opening new fields of understanding through our search to express, and bringing this commerce with ourselves, the world, and other men to a conclusion by making it converge in a new view of experience as the visible expression of what we were all seeking to signify. In our creative expression of the truth, we confront "brute being" (the never yet expressed "other side" of visible being) and, drawing upon our "wild-flowering mind" (the hidden, spontaneous power of expression which is the source of the lateral universal that links us to all men), partially realize and at the same time extend the project to retrieve the world as meaningful which began with man's first expressive gestures and now speaks within and to our act. By encountering past and alien projects and freeing what was there to be known but never before expressed, creative expression opens up an inner personal and interpersonal communication with the past and present which transforms an experience into its meaning and establishes it as the present truth of all the other attempts to know about it.

Speaking language clearly has its roots in an expressive power through which men communicate beneath their cultural boundaries. And Merleau-Ponty saw (and indicates in several essays in *Signs*) that his phenomenology of language could be taken as a general model for a phenomenology of culture. In particular, the much-discussed works of the cultural anthropologist Claude Lévi-Strauss provided an illustration of the fundamental importance of the life-world to cultural understanding, and the belligerent pseudo-Marxist claim to derive philosophy causally from historical infrastructures an occasion for insisting upon that importance. Both are salient examples of the theoretical and practical problems arising from the fact that cultural phenomena are both already constituted things to be understood through impartial observation, objective analysis, and causal explanation, and significations to be understood in terms of the life-world from which they arise.

As he does in his phenomenology of language, Merleau-Ponty maintains in his phenomenology of culture that the cultural "metastructures" revealed by our constructed scientific models can be understood only in terms of the "infrastructures" of implicit meaning constituted by pre-objective systems of exchanges and equivalences between individual and society. Cultural anthropology seems to him to show that the scientist can communicate with alien cultures and discover the concretely human meaning of his constructed variables only by combining objective analysis and lived experience. In involving himself in a critical dialogue between an alien culture and his own, the scientist must both understand himself as a lived, internalized system of the structures of his own culture and reconstruct himself until he regains possession of that primordial region of himself (unincorporated in his own culture) where his wild-flowering mind encounters brute being—and the alien culture as a variant relationship to being. By thus gaining access to the existential field where all men coexist through the lateral relationships of cultures in the same historical life-world, he can communicate with fellow men in an alien culture and attain knowledge of a cross-cultural complementarity of incompatible but inseparable views upon which he can meaningfully construct his inclusive theoretical models. As is the case for linguistics and the phenomenology of language, the cultural sciences and the philosophy of culture reciprocally envelop one another.

And the truths both arrive at are inescapably situational. The phenomenology of culture reminds both philosopher and scientist of something their presumption to total synthesis leads them to forget: both are situated within an historical dialogue as beings who construct their conceptual universes on the basis of their thought's "anchorage" in a certain historical situation of its own. Since the self, whose presence to itself is the basis of all understanding, is linked essentially to its own and other fields of presence by the "primordial historicity" of its incarnate existence, Merleau-Ponty can say of culture, as he does of perception and language, that it is at the heart of our present situation that we find the means of understanding all other presents.

He must also insist for the same reasons that this understanding is necessarily partial, that is, both partisan and incomplete. In our most objectively established knowledge, we always discover that the objects of our reflection have laminated horizons of sedimented meanings. To understand the empirical order of events, we must reconstitute their horizons and trace out the advent of new meaning-structures within them. The significance of the empirical history which seeks a causal explanation of events is ultimately based upon the "intentional history" which seeks to reveal the a-causal "genesis of meaning" and advent of truth constituted by men's existential assumption of pre-objective meaning-structures in the contingency of their situation. Yet this history too, since it is known through our imaginative variation of our present knowledge and experience, is insurmountably perspectival and unfinished.

Since neither science nor philosophy can justifiably claim to have absolute or disembodied knowledge, neither can reduce philosophy to its historical origins. Philosophy is no more just a constituted thing and a causal result than language is. All philosophies are creative expressions of meanings which advene in the socio-historical order of events. As "discriminants" of new kinds of thinking and symbolizing which transform these implicit meanings into the order of explicit meanings and truth, philosophies open a field which is incommensurable with their origins.

But how can a philosophy which rejects all claims to an absolute point of view and which insists upon the situational character of all truth still meaningfully seek the truth? According to Merleau-Ponty, it can do so because it knows that the center of philosophy is "everywhere and nowhere," in the sense that truth and the whole are in the first philosophy and every subsequent one, but as a task to be accomplished and thus not yet there. It is true that all philosophies and cultures are human creations and particular variants of the historical life-world. As such, they are all on an equal footing, and each must confront all the others in order to overcome its bias and get a clearer view of the meaning of human life. Yet as is the case in cross-cultural understanding, a philosopher can attain to a lateral universality when the limitations which stem from his particular situation in the empirical order of events are invested in an intentional history of the advent of meaning, which transforms that situation into a means of understanding his own and other situations, and which establishes—through the philosophical dialogue it opens up—an indirect unity of convergence with all other philosophies.

Furthermore, Western thought and culture have an *historically* privileged position among men's creations. The West has invented an idea of truth which requires examination of all other cultures in an effort to incorporate them as aspects of a total truth, and a technology capable one day of sustaining a world culture. Consequently it has the historical task and destiny of re-examining all things (in terms of their source in the historical life-world) in order to face up to the crises of human culture by revealing its primordial unity and to achieve the new creations of effective cross-cultural unity which are the only justification for its privileged position.

Like all thought in act, this task is open-ended; that is (like philosophy itself), both liberal and endless. Philosophy must be a continuing confrontation of fact with essence and essence with fact which seeks to untie knots of meaning, eliminate false problems, and open the way to new truths and solutions—for the times and for a time. In its essential openness to all meaningful experience, it cannot exclude such indirect or imaginative modes of expression as painting, literature, or religion. They are modes of human self-transcendence which have a truth-value measured by the lateral universality they enable us to attain to. And yet philosophy is compelled to recognize that this truth-value differs from and conflicts with the value such modes of expression may have for thought in terms of our fundamental choice of a way of life.

Since Merleau-Ponty's own philosophy required him to define a truth in his present situation which would unite these two values, his phenomenology of culture was logically involved in the problems of political philosophy and the philosophy of history. The logic was a present logic whose meanings were structured by his existential exchanges with his changing times. Historically, the problems were raised in the empirical order of twentieth century events in an acute and intensely personal way. In the political and historical "adventure" and advent of meaning Merleau-Ponty and his generation lived through, traditional distinctions were blurred and institutions overthrown; and they were faced with life-and-death questions concerning the "fundamental."

Merleau-Ponty gives us indications in *Signs* of the way in which the events and advents of his times outmoded more than one philosophy of history and politics. But the crucial victim in this decade was his a-communism of the immediate post-war period. He tells us more specifically in *The Adventures of the Dialectic* than he does in his introduction to *Signs* how the events of the fifties made him realize that he could no longer be content with affirming communism's truth-value as a valid critique of capitalism, but had to decide whether he was for or against communism as a committed way of life. Yet *Signs* does make it clear that as he became increasingly concerned with events in underdeveloped countries, he recognized that communism was no more adequate than capitalism to express and cope with the problems of transition from the "old world" of meaning-structures polarized in terms of communism versus capitalism, to the "new world" of meaning-structures which took the life-worlds of emergent nations into account and which constituted for him the central advent of political and historical meaning in our time. It is equally evident in *Signs* that he had reached the philosophical conclusion that there is a dialectical and essential relation of tension and complementarity between past and present, the "objective" and the "subjective," and thought and action—and that subject and object, consciousness and history, present and future can no longer have a vital meaning if this relation is not effectively maintained in political practice. In its idealistic appeal to universal human rights defined in terms of present interests, a "juridical politics" had disregarded historical infrastructures. But had communism, which had certainly explored them better than any other philosophy, swung historically to the other extreme? What is raised as a question in the earliest essays in *Signs* is clearly answered in the affirmative in subsequent ones. Contemporary communism buries class consciousness and the evolution of the present underneath a praise of economic growth and an exhortation to advance a revolution written in the pseudo-history of myth. Realizing that the "spoken language" of Communist régimes could not conceal its contradictions with their underlying "speaking language," Merleau-Ponty was faced with contingency and the need for a new style in a manner he had not experienced since World War II had fallen wrathfully upon his generation.

Since Merleau-Ponty had never believed that "history, like a fan, is going to fold in upon itself," the actual practice of Marxist humanism did not lead him (as it did so many disillusioned members of his generation) to betray himself or others in a burst of desperate idiocy. Yet he had fought and hoped for the Liberation, and thought in Marxian terms of man's universal recognition of his fellow man. Now when a man in his mid-forties is deprived of the language he has been learning to speak for twenty years, and must suffer the further losses of former friends who now speak against him in that language, he may well apply "the severe rule of death" to his life. There are passages in *Signs* hinting at a personal crisis which was in its own way as painful as the one Sartre has been revealing in his mordant autocriticisms. But Merleau-Ponty's Introduction makes it equally clear he realized that a whole age was dying with the fifties; and it was not just he but his fellow men as well who needed "reasons for living." The question of the basis for the unity of theory and practice which these losses raised was inseparably individual and collective.

Merleau-Ponty's personal dilemma is best summed up in the twin quotations which preface his essay, "Reading Montaigne"—"I commit myself with difficulty" and "We must live among the living." In its personal dimension, the problem of finding a guideline for intelligent commitment to the stupidly, the cruelly disordered world we are inescapably involved in is one of reason and passion. To commit ourselves is to believe passionately that (as Sartre had once said and both Communists and anti-Communists were still saying) we choose the good of all men in choosing our own. It is just this belief which is indefensible. If we are passionate, we act beyond reason. We sacrifice the wisdom of "resolving to be irresolute," which is wisdom because we know that the world's comedy is not divine but all too human and deprived of any final justification, and that our efforts to know involve us in the comedy of reason's endless contradictions.

But if we give up our impossible search for the complete and absolute understanding that a God's-eye view supposedly provides—and recognize that total self-possession is illusion and presumption, and our only recourse human passions and opinions—then the fact that there is an appearance of the good and true becomes the Archimedian point for a true skepticism, which is a movement toward truth and a critique of false passions. We can act upon the world from a distance in a non-partisan fashion; and when it seems to us that our lives are at stake in the lives of others, we can commit ourselves passionately to their just cause without abandoning the critical honesty which compels us to search out our own faults and our enemies' merits. In this way we can hope to be simultaneously "ironic and solemn, faithful and free."

Since we are fundamentally temporal and social beings, our personal commitments always have collective historical dimensions. We are historical actors who live our present as future history yet must search the past for the true meaning of our actions, even though these actions themselves bring past undertakings to a conclusion. To unify theory and practice intelligently, we must understand our past in terms of our present and make our present experience and the practical options it offers us benefit from our comprehension of the past.

The essence of history (as it is revealed in the primordial historicity of our field of presence) is to be indefinite in the present—to be "dream or nightmare"—and to become completely real only as a spectacle to posterity's "responding generations," who alone can judge the truth of our own "calling generation." Our present generation must make its understanding of history a methodical extension of its experience of the present by attempting to reconstruct the origins of past "fundamental choices" which, in contact with the contingencies of the empirical order of events, brought about the advent of historical meaning and a common situation. As thinking actors inescapably embodied in our times, we must expect from future generations a fulfillment different than the one which we intended. Yet this different fulfillment is also the same one. The men whose thought in act brings our own to a different close can do so only because they are linked to us (as we are to our past) through the "public duration" of that network of callings and responses which is constituted by the "We" of man's primordial historicity—and which makes all generations fellow men who can communicate. Whether we contemplate history as a spectacle or assume it as a responsibility, the distinction only reveals the inseparability of thought and action in the single, open, and indefinite history of man's untamed but often suppressed freedom.

Our relation to history, like our more fundamental perceptual opening to the world, has inseparable positive and negative dimensions. In the various studies of Communist, capitalist, and colonial societies which appear in *Signs,* Merleau-Ponty tries to establish the relation of these societies to our own times and the human community by seeing how their past fundamental choices have become explicit as an advent of meaning, and how they have been measured according to their own criteria in the empirical order of events. Since his own and others' situational view is always subject to error and future correction, however, he realizes that there can be no final solution—human or superhuman—to the problems of men, whose essential ambiguity and freedom make history insurmountably contingent. We can only hope to eliminate past mistakes and create more rational solutions in the future. History, like the men who make it, must be a "mixture" of hope and despair, progress and regress, sense and non-sense.

The way in which the study of past history can provide positive criteria for judging present politics is perhaps best illustrated in *Signs* by the essay, "A Note on Machiavelli." Extending his responding generation's experience of a present adventure to a Renaissance which called for it as a possible conclusion, Merleau-Ponty opens up a dialogue with Machiavelli concerning the nature of political power and virtue in a political life-world which is simultaneously truthful and propagandistic, peaceful and warlike; which admits the ambiguity of all causes; and whose every act has both a manifest and a latent meaning. The conclusions Merleau-Ponty reaches give a good indication of the criteria he established to distinguish between just and unjust political causes.

Just as human behavior is never pure thought or mechanical reaction, but is always incarnate expression, political power is never based merely upon the rational persuasion of a juridical politics nor upon a power politics' cynical coercion, but upon an underlying struggle for power. Since those who win power can maintain it only if they avoid the contempt and hatred of those they rule, they must alternate tension and relaxation, repression and legality, in an effort to thwart those who threaten their power. All political power requires at least the tacit acceptance of the ruled, and can never be absolute. Although the violence of struggle underlying all political life can never be eliminated, the need to attain the pre-objective acceptance of the ruled which sustains all political power requires the rulers to go beyond the struggle.

Political violence itself initiates a self-transcending dialectic. Since each man is in interpersonal circuit with his fellow men (including his enemies) as alter egos, his struggle against other men becomes a struggle against himself and a recognition of his inescapable dependence upon others. Then he realizes that power thwarts better if it appeals to freedom. Without those in power being wholly aware of it, and by the sole fact that they try to win others in order to consolidate their power, a human community emerges politically and historically from collective life.

As it did, for example, in Hungary, East Germany, Indochina, and Algeria, the fundamental and original struggle always threatens to reappear. In view of the world's contingency and man's freedom—of the human situation beyond ultimate hope or despair—Merleau-Ponty cannot help recognizing a fundamental element of chance or anonymous, unintentional adversity in history which our errors or faults help create, which always limits our power in spite of our understanding or willing, but which never limits it necessarily, definitively, or irrevocably. Yet the same irreducible contingency and violence suggest that our best and only hope of mastering the accidents and struggles of political life lies in a politics of *virtù* and reform.

A just politics must satisfy the people—not simply because they alone are qualified to judge their personal needs, but also because they seek in the main not to practice but to avoid injustice, tyranny, and oppression. Nevertheless, the ruler must rule. The ruler who does not clearly assert his authority is as likely to be despised as the man who rules in tyrannical authority is to be hated. In his efforts to renew political life by bringing force and understanding to the aid of passion, the virtuous ruler will establish a relationship of consultation and exchange with others which makes them aware of a shared situation and unites them in the bonds of a common work and destiny by appealing to their freedom. If he allows them to come to the support of a decision which (since it is the result of an exchange) is in some respects their own, he can dissipate the ferocity of the power struggle without concealing it in mystification. Consequently, the virtuous leader will listen to the confused voice of the people, understand his times and what is humanly valuable within the possibilities of the present situation, and conceive of an historical undertaking all may support.

In our times, this undertaking must be worldwide. On the strength of his modified Husserlian-Marxian view of the West's contingent historical task and destiny of constructing a total truth and the socioeconomic means of realizing it, Merleau-Ponty insists that the only acceptable humanism today is the one which works concretely for man's effective and universal recognition by his fellow man. In order to do so, it must not only confront man with man and constitute a common bond between all men. It must also create political structures which can hold power in check without emasculating it, and find virtuous leaders who can "live history and invent what will subsequently seem to have been demanded by the times." But what are the possibilities of the moment? Many essays in *Signs* explore this question, and the answers are scarcely encouraging.

The revolutionary solution has failed; there is no face of the world proletariat behind the mask. French colonies swing from the Fascist incantation of "Al-gé-rie Fran-çaise" to the national revolutions which obscure the problems of a concrete humanism in the magic word "independence." In France herself, a "party rule" of checks and balances which is despised for its refusal to assert its authority in positive action is replaced by an authoritarian rule above parties which reinvokes outmoded provincialisms. Although Merleau-Ponty thinks that responsible reform is the only feasible solution, his final essay in *Signs*, "Tomorrow," ends with an imploring, angry "Where are the counsellors of the people, and have they nothing they can offer us but their regrets?"

Yet "men never should despair," and Merleau-Ponty's suffocated cry (like these essays themselves) is a sign of life and struggle for air. The sarcastic impatience of his earlier a-communism is replaced by controlled passion and greater humanistic depth, but he never stops affirming the central, ultimate truths he insisted upon for more than a decade. With unabated urgency and wonder, he reconfirms the world's fundamental contingency and anonymous adversity, the insuperably problematic character of human existence, the irrepressible presumption of reason's claim to dispel the "shadow" of the invisible "other side" of experience, and the consequent need for an untiring phenomenological questioning which seeks to restore the existential encounter between "wild-flowering mind" and "brute being" from which all truth and cultural renewal must and can arise. The times required him to ask himself for an answer to the question he presented to his students as a model of profundity beneath simplicity: What time is it? Yet he never abandoned his essential conception of the time we are all embodied in. In the shadow of death—"the counter-proof of life"—his insistence that our only victory over time lies in expressing time takes on a solemnity and depth approaching classic grandeur.

If Merleau-Ponty is correct, it is the common grandeur of a human task and truth so near to us we cannot see them—unless we make the effort to discern their "signs." And yet the "din and prodigality" of a world "humming like a shipyard" cannot drown out the rumors of some secret embarkation, some new adventure to the edge of the "abyss" of unknown being: "underneath the clamor a silence is growing, an expectation. Why could it not be a hope?" We must not stare at our mortal world's kaleidoscope in fascination or despair; we must watch it closely for the advent of new meanings. If we look upon man's ever-nascent community as a "caryatid of the void," we shall see that both our strength and limitations spring from our embodiment in living flesh. In our effort to re-constitute the pre-objective bases of all meaningful relations to ourselves, the world, and other men, we will always encounter a hidden, pre-constituted other side of our experience which limits our investigations. But this primordial meeting of brute being and wild-flowering mind is equally the source of that thought in act which sometimes lets us break the rhythmic monotony of our "mortal circle" and move forward into truth. Groping along the walls of fundamental being, grasping at the significant threads of living reason in our slow search to confront that "miracle," that "monster," man in his incarnate presence, we are plunged into the "labyrinth" of a chiaroscuro world. We are all embodied in this labyrinth—this "mixture" of sense and non-sense, good and evil, freedom and repression, the days of life and death—because it is ourselves and our anonymous creation. Merleau-Ponty sought to make its hidden ways more visible in hopes that we might make its goal more human. Perhaps the signs he saw will be a guideline to the problems of our times.

RICHARD CALVERTON MCCLEARY

Brussels, 1964

Contents

PART I

INTRODUCTION

How DIFFERENT—HOW DOWNRIGHT INCONGRUOUS—the philosophical essays and the ad hoc, primarily political observations which make up this volume seem! The philosopher's road may be hard, but we can at least be sure that each step points a way for those to come. In politics, one has the oppressive sensation of blazing a trail which must be endlessly reopened. It is not just a question of chance and the unforeseen. There are some errors of prognostication to be found in this volume (although frankly, fewer than were to be feared), but the situation is far worse than that. It is as if some cunning mechanism whisked events away at just the moment they appeared on the scene. Or as if history censored the dramas it is made up of and, preferring to conceal itself, gave us a glimpse of truth only in brief moments of confusion, the rest of the time taxing its ingenuity to repress all our "surpassing" deeds, re-establish the roles and formulas of its repertoire, and persuade us in short that nothing is "coming to pass." Maurras [1] used to say that he had found evident truth in politics, but never in pure philosophy. But that was because he only considered already accomplished history, and dreamed of an already established philosophy. If we take philosophy and history as they are being made, we shall see that philosophy finds its surest evidence at the moment of inception, and that history as it comes to be is dream or nightmare.

Whenever we reach the point of asking a question, whenever scattered anguishes and angers have ended up taking on an identifiable form in human space, we imagine that nothing thereafter can ever be as it was before. Questions can indeed be total; but answers, in their positive significance, cannot. Like a passion that one day just ceases, destroyed by its own duration, a question burns out and is replaced by

1. Charles Maurras, French writer and editor of the proto-Fascist *Action française*.—Trans.

an unquestioned state of affairs. A country which lay bleeding from a war or revolution stands suddenly intact and whole. The dead are implicated in this abatement: only by living could they recreate the very lack and need of them which is being blotted out. Conservative historians record Dreyfus' innocence as a self-evident truth—and are no less conservative for it. Dreyfus is not avenged; he is not even rehabilitated. Having become a commonplace, his innocence is cheap at the price of his shame. It is not inscribed in history as he was robbed of it, or as it was demanded by his defenders. History takes still more from those who have lost everything, and gives yet more to those who have taken everything. For its sweeping judgments acquit the unjust and dismiss the pleas of their victims. History never *confesses*.

The familiarity of these truths in no way diminishes the force with which they strike us every time we meet them with the shock of recognition. The main concern of our time is going to be to reconcile the old world and the new. In the face of this problem, the U.S.S.R. and its recent adversaries are perhaps on the same side, the side of the old world. Be that as it may, the end of the Cold War is in sight. The West can scarcely show up well in peaceful competition if it does not invent a democratic way of managing its economy. At present, the development of industrial society here is marked by extraordinary disorder. Capitalism haphazardly extends its giant branches, puts the economies of nations at the mercy of dominant industries which choke their towns and highways, and destroys the classical forms of the human establishment. At all levels immense problems appear; not just techniques but political forms, motives, a spirit, reasons for living need to be found.

It is in these circumstances that an army which has long been isolated from the world in colonial wars, and which has learned about the social struggle there, falls back with its full weight upon the State it is supposed to be subordinate to, and floods the times once more with the Cold War ideology they were about to rid themselves of. Someone who twenty years ago knew how to judge "élites" (especially military élites) now thinks he can construct a lasting power by isolating himself at the summit of the State, and only frees it from the harassments of parties to expose it to factions. Someone who said that no man can take the place of the people (but no doubt this was only a formulation of despair and "useless service") now separates the nation's aspirations from what he calls its standard of living. As if any fully developed nation could accept such dilemmas. As if the economy in a real society could ever be subordinate like the commissary in the army's artificial society. As if bread and wine and labor were in themselves less grave and sacred things than history books.

Perhaps it will be said that this stationary, provincial history is France's alone. But is the world at large facing any more frankly the questions which confront it? Because these questions threaten to break down the frontiers between communism and capitalism, the Church does its best to silence them, revives forgotten interdicts, condemns anew all socialism which is not democratic, attempts to reoccupy the positions of a state religion, and suppresses on all sides—beginning in its own ranks—the spirit of inquiry and confidence in the truth.

As for Communist politics, we know how many filters the air of de-Stalinization had to pass through before it reached Paris or Rome. After so many denials of "revisionism," and above all after Budapest, we need sharp eyes to see that Soviet society is getting involved in another epoch and is liquidating the spirit of social warfare along with Stalinism and orienting itself toward new forms of power. This is called officially a transition to the highest stage of communism. Does the prognostication of a spontaneous evolution toward world communism hide unchanging schemes for domination, or is it simply a decent way of saying that the effort to force such a transition has been abandoned? Or is Soviet society taking a position between two lines, ready in case of danger to fall back to the old? The real question is not a question of aims, or of the face behind the mask. Perhaps these concerted schemes count less than the human reality and the movement of the whole. Perhaps the U.S.S.R. has many faces, and it is the events themselves which are equivocal. In that case the hot peace and somber humor which entered the international theater with Khrushchev ought to be greeted as a step toward clarity. If humor, as Freud said, is the mildness of the super-ego, perhaps this is the greatest degree of relaxation that history's super-ego will allow.

What good is there in having been right yesterday against Stalinism and today against the Algerian affair, what good in patiently untying the false knots of communism and anti-communism, and in setting down in black and white what both know better than we do, if these truths of tomorrow do not exempt a young man from the adventures of fascism and communism today? What good is it if these truths are sterile to the extent they are not given political expression in that language which speaks without saying, which touches the springs of hope and anger in every man, and which will never be the prose of truth? Is it not an incredible misunderstanding that all, or almost all, philosophers have felt obliged to have a politics, whereas politics arises from the "practice of life" and escapes understanding? The politics of philosophers is what no one *practices*. Then is it politics? Are there not many other things philosophers can talk about with greater assurance? And when they map out wise perspectives about which the interested parties care nothing, are they not in fact admitting that they simply do not know what politics is all about?

* * *

These reflections are latent on all sides. We detect them in readers and writers who are or used to be Marxists and who, divided about everything else, seem to agree in *confirming* the separation of philosophy and politics. More than anyone else these men have tried to unite the two in their lives. The question is dominated by their experience and must be reconsidered in the light of it.

One thing that is certain at the outset is that there has been a political mania among philosophers which has not produced good politics or good philosophy. Since politics, as we know, is the *modern tragedy,* we have been waiting for its dénouement. Under the pretext that all human questions are found in this drama, all political anger became holy wrath, and reading the newspaper (as Hegel once said in his youth) the morning prayer of philosophy. Marxism discovered all the abstract dramas of Being and Nothingness in history. It had put down an immense metaphysical burden there—and rightly so, since it was thinking of the place of mind and matter, man and nature, and consciousness and existence in the architectonic structure of history, whose algebra or schema alone is given by philosophy. As a total reconstruction of human origins in a new future, revolutionary politics went by way of this metaphysical center.

But in the recent period, all forms of life and spirit were linked to a purely tactical politics, a discontinuous series of actions and episodes with no tomorrow. Instead of combining their virtues, philosophy and politics exchanged their vices: practice became tricky and thought superstitious. How many hours and arguments were wasted over the vote of some parliamentary group or over a drawing by Picasso; as if Universal History, Revolution, Dialectic, and Negativity were really present in these frugal Eucharistic species. In fact, these great historico-philosophical concepts—deprived of all contact with knowledge, technics, art, and changes in the economy—were bloodless. Except in the best, political strictness gave its hand to laziness, lack of curiosity, and improvisation. If this was the marriage of philosophy and politics, we are likely to think we can only be pleased with the divorce. Some Marxist writers have made their break with all this and are reconsidering their role. What could be better? And yet there is a "bad" breakup between philosophy and politics which preserves nothing and leaves both to their misery.

Listening to these writers, we occasionally sense an uneasiness.

They say at times that they are still Marxists on the essential points (without making it too clear which ones are essential or how one can be a Marxist *on certain points*), perhaps smiling among themselves at the confusion in which Marxists, Marxians, and Marxologists rub elbows. At other times, on the contrary, they say that a new doctrine, almost a new system, is needed; but they scarcely venture beyond a few borrowings from Heraclitus, Heidegger, or Sartre. The two timidities are understandable. These men have philosophized for years inside Marxism. When they were discovering the young Marx, going back upstream to his Hegelian source, and coming down again from there to Lenin, they often encountered the abstract outlines of their future drama. They know that all the necessary arms for one or several contrasting positions can be found in this tradition, and it is natural that they still think of themselves as Marxists. But since it is also Marxism which, all things considered, has long provided them with their reasons for remaining Communists and renewing communism's license as history's interpreter, it is understandable that, having "returned to the things themselves," they should want to put aside all intermediaries and demand a wholly new doctrine.

To remain faithful to what one was; to begin everything again from the beginning—each of these two tasks is immense. In order to state the precise respects in which one is still a Marxist, it would be necessary to show just what is essential in Marx and when it was lost. One would have to point out the fork at which he stood on the genealogical tree if he wanted to be a new offshoot or main branch, or if he thought of rejoining the trunk's axis of growth, or if finally he was reintegrating Marx as a whole to an older and more recent way of thought, of which Marxism was only a transitory form. In short, one would have to redefine the relationships of the young Marx to Marx, of both to Hegel, of that whole tradition to Lenin, of Lenin to Stalin and even to Khrushchev, and finally, the relationships of Hegelo-Marxism to what had gone before and followed it. This Herculean task (of which all of Lukacs' works together constitute a very guarded outline) tempted Marxists when they were in the Party because it was the only way at that time of philosophizing without seeming too evidently to do so. Now that they have left the Party, the task must seem crushing and derisory to them. And so they turn toward the sciences, art, and investigation free of Party commitments. But how upsetting it is to no longer be able to base one's calculations on the almost century-old background of Marxism, to have to *try things out* on one's own, naked, deprived of its machinery—and to do so, furthermore, in the annoying vicinity of those who have never done anything else yet were formerly dismissed rather than discussed.

And so these marginal men remain undecided between their need to be loyal and their need to make a break, without fully accepting one or the other. Sometimes they write as if Marxism had never existed, treating history for example in terms of the formalism of the theory of games. But in other respects they keep Marxism in reserve, eluding all revision. As a matter of fact, a revision is taking place; but they hide it from themselves, disguising it as a return to sources. For after all, they say, what has gone bankrupt in Marxist orthodoxy is its dogmatism, its philosophy. The true Marxism is not a philosophy, and that Marxism (which incidentally encompasses everything—Stalinism and anti-Stalinism, and the whole life of the world) is the one we hold to. Perhaps one day, after incredible detours, the proletariat will rediscover its role as the universal class, and will once more take over that universal Marxist criticism which for the moment has no historical impact or bearing.

The Marxist identity of thought and action which the present calls into question is thus postponed till a later date. The appeal to an indefinite future preserves the doctrine as a way of thinking and a point of honor at the moment it is in difficulty as a way of living. According to Marx this is precisely the vice of philosophy. But who would guess it, since at the same time it is philosophy which is made the scapegoat? Non-philosophy, which Marx taught for the profit of the revolutionary praxis, is now the refuge of uncertainty. These writers know better than anyone that the Marxist link between philosophy and politics is broken. But they act as if it were still *in principle* (and in a future—that is, an imaginary—world) what Marx said it was: philosophy simultaneously realized and destroyed in history, the saving negation and fulfilling destruction. This metaphysical operation has not taken place—and that is why these writers have abandoned communism, which so incompletely realized the abstract values it destroyed in order to institute its own. These writers are not at all sure that it will ever take place. Whereupon, instead of examining its philosophical background, they transform its audacity and resolution into hopes and dreams.

This consolation is not an innocent one, for it shuts the lid again on the debate which has begun within them and among them, and bottles up the questions which insist on being heard. To begin with, the question of knowing whether there is an operation of destruction-realization (particularly a realization of thought which makes its independent existence superfluous), or whether this schema does not presuppose an absolute positivity of nature and an absolute negativity of history (or antiphysis), which Marx thought were confirmed empirically but which are perhaps no more than philosophical assumptions that must be re-examined like any others. Next there is the question whether that "no" which is a "yes" (the philosophical formula of the revolution) does not justify an unlimited use of authority, and thereby raise the apparatus which has the historical role of the negative above any assignable criterion and any justifiable accusation of an inner "contradiction," even that of Budapest.

It is this family of interrogations concerning Marxist ontology which is cleverly eliminated if Marxism is from the start declared valid as a truth for some later date. These questions have always constituted the pathos and profound life of Marxism, which was the trial or test of the creative negation, the realization-destruction. In forgetting them, we repudiate Marxism as revolution. In any case, if we grant without debate both Marxism's claim to be not a philosophy but the expression of a single great historical fact and its criticism of all philosophy as an alibi and sin against history, and if we confirm in another connection the present lack of any proletarian movement on a worldwide scale, we retire Marxism to inactive status and define ourselves as honorary Marxists. If philosophy alone is decreed at fault in the divorce between philosophy and politics, the divorce will be a failure. For divorces as well as marriages can fail.

We are not assuming any pre-established thesis in what we say here. Above all, we are not using the fact that Marxism and communism alike reject philosophy as a pretext for lumping the two together before the absolute judgment seat of philosophy. There is a clear difference between the Marxist rule not to destroy philosophy without realizing it, and the Stalinist practice which simply destroys it. We are not even suggesting that this rule inevitably degenerates into that practice. What we are saying is that with the events of recent years Marxism has definitely entered a new phase of its history, in which it can inspire and orient analyses and retain a real heuristic value, but is certainly no longer true *in the sense it was believed to be true*.

By placing Marxism in the order of *secondary truth*, recent experience gives Marxists a new posture and almost a new method, which make it useless to call them into court. When they are asked—and ask themselves—if they are still Marxists, it is a bad question for which there are only bad answers. Not just because, as we said before, a precise answer would presuppose that an enormous labor of putting things in perspective had been accomplished, but because this task, even if it had been accomplished, could not arrive at any simple answer, since the question itself excludes a yes or a no as soon as it is asked. It would be senseless to picture recent events as one of those "crucial experiments" (which in spite of a tenacious legend do not exist even in physics) enabling us to conclude that a theory is "verified" or "refuted." It is incredible that the question should be put in these rudimentary terms, as if the "true" and the "false" were the only modes of intellectual existence. Even in the sciences, an outmoded theoretical framework can be reintegrated into the language of the one which replaced it; it remains significant, keeps *its* truth. When it is a question of re-examining the whole inner history of Marxism and its relationships to pre- and post-Marxist philosophy and history, we know from the outset that our conclusion can never be one of those platitudes heard all too often: that Marxism is "still valid" or that it is "contradicted by the facts."

Behind Marxist statements, confirmed or disconfirmed, there is always Marxism as a matrix of intellectual and historical experiences, which can always be saved from total failure by means of some additional hypotheses, just as one can always maintain on the other hand that it is not validated *in toto* by success. For a century the doctrine has inspired so many theoretical and practical undertakings; has been the laboratory for so many successful or unsuccessful experiments; and has been even for its opponents the stimulus of so many responses, obsessions, and profoundly meaningful counter-doctrines; that after all this it is simply as barbarous to speak of "refutation" as of "verification." Even though "errors" are to be found in the fundamental formulations or ontology of Marxism which we were just discussing, they are not of the type which one can simply strike out or forget. Even though there is no pure negation which is a yes or an absolute negation of itself, the "error" here is not simply the converse of truth but rather a truth that failed. There is an internal relation of the positive and the negative, which Marx had in mind even though he mistakenly restricted it to the object-subject dichotomy. This relation is operative in whole segments of his works. Under his historical analysis it opens new dimensions and enables them to stop being conclusive in Marx's sense of the term without ceasing to be sources of meaning and open to reinterpretation. Marx's theses can remain true as the Pythagorean theorem is true: no longer in the sense it was true for the one who invented it—as an immutable truth and a property of space itself—but as a property of a certain model of space among other possible spaces.

The history of thought does not summarily pronounce: This is true; that is false. Like all history, it has its veiled decisions. It dismantles or embalms certain doctrines, changing them into "messages" or museum pieces. There are others, on the contrary, which it keeps active. These do not endure because there is some miraculous adequation or correspondence between them and an invariable "reality"—such an exact and fleshless truth is neither sufficient nor necessary for the greatness of a doctrine—but because, as obligatory steps for those who want to go further, they retain an expressive power which exceeds their statements and propositions. These doctrines are the *classics*. They are recognizable by the fact that no one takes them literally, and yet new facts are never absolutely outside their province but call forth new echoes from them and reveal new lustres in them. We are saying that a re-examination of Marx would be a meditation upon a classic, and that it could not possibly terminate in a *nihil obstat* or a listing on the Index. Are you or are you not a Cartesian? The question does not make much sense, since those who reject this or that in Descartes do so only in terms of reasons which owe a lot to Descartes. We say that Marx is in the process of becoming such a secondary truth.

And we say it in the name of recent experience alone, especially that of Marxist writers. For in the last analysis, when as long-time Communists they came to leave the Party or let themselves be expelled from it, did they do so as "Marxists" or "non-Marxists"? By their actions they clearly showed that the dilemma was a verbal one, that it was necessary to move beyond it, that no doctrine could prevail against "the things themselves" or transform the suppression at Budapest into a victory for the proletariat. They did not break with orthodoxy in the name of freedom of conscience and philosophical idealism. They broke because that orthodoxy had made a proletariat decay to the point of rebellion and the harsh critique of arms, and with it the life of its unions and economy, and with its economy its inner truth and the life of art and science. Thus they made the break as Marxists. And yet in making the break they sinned against the equally Marxist rule which states that at each moment there is the camp of the proletariat and the camp of its adversaries, that every undertaking is to be evaluated in relation to this historical rift, and that one should in no case "play the enemy's game." They were not fooling themselves then and are not fooling us now when they say that they are still Marxists, but with the added stipulation that their Marxism is no longer identified with any apparatus, that it is a view of history and not the movement of history in action—that it is, in short, a philosophy. At the moment when they made the break, they went out before or overtook, in anger or despair, one of history's silent promotions; and it is they after all who have made of Marx a classic or a philosopher.

They had been told that in the last analysis every undertaking and political or non-political investigation is judged according to its political implications, the political line according to the interests of the Party, and the Party's interests according to its leaders' views. They rejected these assembly-line reductions of all proceedings and criteria to a single one. They declared that the course of history is made by different means and with a different rhythm on the level of political organization and in the proletariat, the unions, and the arts and sciences—that history has more than one focus, or more than one dimension, frame of reference, or source of meaning. Thereby they rejected a certain idea of Being as object, and of identity and difference, adopting the idea of a coherent Being of many foci or dimensions. And they say they are not philosophers?

They retort: you talk about Marxism, but are you talking about it from within or without? The question no longer means much at the moment when Marxism is perhaps bursting apart and is in any case opening up. One talks about it from within when one can, and when there is no longer any way of doing so, from without. Who does any better? When one performs for Marxism the notorious "surpassing from within" which it recommended for all doctrines, is one outside or inside? One is already outside as soon as instead of resaying things which have been said one uses them to try to understand oneself and existing things. The question of knowing whether one is within or without arises only in respect to an historical movement or a doctrine at its birth. Marxism is less and more than that. It is an immense field of sedimented history and thought where one goes to practice and to learn to think. For the man who wanted to be the operation of history put into words, it is a grievous change. But his was precisely the height of philosophical arrogance.

There are certainly many situations of class struggle throughout the world. They exist in old countries—Yves Velan's Switzerland. They exist in countries newly come to independence. It is clear that their independence will be no more than a word if the poles of their development are defined in terms of the interests of advanced countries, and that the left wing of the new nationalisms is in conflict with the local middle classes. It is certain, on the other hand, that the new economic climates and the development of industrial society in Europe, which render the old way of parliamentary and political life decrepit, make the struggle for the control and management of the new economic apparatus the order of the day. One can of course start out from Marxism to invent the categories which orient analysis of the present, and "structural imperialism" would be one of them.[2] It is even correct to say that no *long-term* policy will be appropriate to our times if it ignores these problems and the Marxist frame of reference which discloses them. This is what we were saying before in calling Marx a classic.

But is this kind of Marxism even the outline of a policy? Is the theoretical grasp of history it provides a practical one as well? In the

2. Serge Mallet, "Gaullisme et néo-capitalisme," *Esprit* (February, 1960).

Marxism of Marx the two went hand in hand. The answer was disclosed along with the question; the question was nothing but the beginning of an answer. Socialism was uneasiness—the course of capitalism itself. When we read that by uniting, the independent countries of North Africa will be in a position to control their development but "not to do without French capital, technicians, and trade outlets"; [3] that in another connection the political and syndicalist Left in France is far from having even an imperfect grasp of the new problems; that the Communist Party in particular maintains a purely negative attitude toward neo-capitalism; and finally that in the U.S.S.R., even after the Twentieth Congress, "structural imperialism" has not been abandoned; we would have to be colossal optimists to expect that "the most advanced wing of African nationalisms will soon find itself led to compare its concerns with those of the working classes of the economically dominant countries." [4] Even if this comparison took place, what policy could be drawn from it? Even if the proletariats recognized one another, what type of common action could they envisage? How could they return to the Leninist conception of the Party as such, and how could they return to it half way? We are aware of the distance between Marxism as an instrument of theoretical analysis and the Marxism which defines theory as consciousness of practice. There are situations of class struggle, and we may if we wish formulate the world situation in terms of bourgeoisie and proletariat; but this is no longer anything but a way of speaking, and the proletariat but a name for a rationalistic politics.

What we are defending here under the name of philosophy is exactly the kind of thought which the Marxists have been driven to by events. A naive rationality can be deceived daily by our times. Disclosing fundamental meaning-structures through all its many fissures, our age calls for a philosophical interpretation. Our times have not swallowed up philosophy; philosophy does not loom over our times. It is neither history's servant nor its master. The relationship between philosophy and history is less simple than was believed. It is in a strict sense an *action at a distance*, each from the depths of its difference requiring intermingling and promiscuity. We have yet to learn the proper uses of this encroachment. Above all, we have not yet learned a philosophy which is all the less tied down by political responsibilities to the extent it has its own, and all the more free to enter everywhere to the extent it does not take anyone's place (does not *play* at passions, politics, and life, or reconstruct them in imagination) but discloses exactly the Being we inhabit.

3. *Ibid.*, p. 211.
4. *Ibid.*, p. 214.

* * *

The philosopher who maintains that the "historical process" passes through his study is laughed at. He gets his revenge by settling the accounts of history's absurdities. Such is his job in a vaudeville show which is now a century old. Yet if we look farther back into the past, if we ask ourselves what philosophy can be today, we shall see that the philosophy of God-like survey was only an episode—and that it is over.

Now as before, philosophy begins with a "What is thinking?" and is absorbed in the question to begin with. No instruments or organs here. It is a pure "It seems to me that." He whom all things appear before cannot be hidden from himself. He appears to himself first of all. He is this appearance of self to self. He springs forth from nothing; no thing and no one can stop him from being himself, or help him. He always was, he is everywhere, he is king on his desert island.

But the first truth can only be a half-truth. It opens upon something different. There would be nothing if there were not that abyss of self. But an abyss is not nothing; it has its environs and edges. One always thinks of something; about, according to, in the light of something; with regard to, in contact with something. Even the action of thinking is caught up in the push and shove of being. I cannot think of identically the same thing for more than an instant. The opening is in principle immediately filled, as if lived only in a nascent state. If it holds out, it does so through and by means of the sliding movement which casts it into the latent. For that which we acquire as well as that which we forget involves a latent meaning. It is by time that my thoughts are dated. It is by time too that they make a date, open a future for thought—a cycle, a field—form a unified body of thought, are a single thought—are me. Thought does not bore through time. It follows in the wake of previous thoughts, without even exercising the power (which it presumes) of retracing that wake as we could go look at the other slope of the hill again if we wished. But why do it, since the hill is there? Why assure myself that today's thought overlaps that of the day before? I know well that it does because today I see farther. It is not because I leap out of time into an intelligible world that I am able to think, or because each time I recreate significance from nothing, but because the arrow of time draws everything along with it and causes my successive thoughts to be simultaneous in a secondary sense, or at least to encroach legitimately upon one another. Thus I function by construction. I am installed on a pyramid of time which has been me. I take up a field and invent myself (but not without my temporal equipment), just as I move about in the world (but not without the unknown mass of my body). Time is that "body of the spirit" Valéry used to talk about. Time and thought are mutually entangled. In the dark night of thought dwells a glimmering of Being.

How could thought impose any necessity upon things? How could it reduce them to pure objects of its own construction? Along with time's secret linkages, I learn those of the perceived world, its incompatible and simultaneous "faces." I see it as it is before my eyes, but also as I would see it from another situation—and not as a possibility but as an actuality, for from this moment forth it gleams *elsewhere* from many fires which are masked from me. When one says simultaneity, is it time he means or is it space? That line from me to the horizon is a rail my gaze may move upon. The house on the horizon gleams solemnly like a thing past or hoped for. And inversely, my past has its space, its paths, its nameplaces, and its monuments. Beneath the crossed but distinct orders of succession and simultaneity, beneath the train of synchronizations added onto line by line, we find a nameless network—constellations of spatial hours, of point-events. Should we even say "thing," should we say "imaginary" or "idea," when each thing exists beyond itself, when each fact can be a dimension, when ideas have their regions? The whole description of our landscape and the lines of our universe, and of our inner monologue, needs to be redone. Colors, sounds, and things—like Van Gogh's stars—are the focal points and radiance of being.

Take *others* at the moment they appear in the world's flesh. They would not exist for me, it is said, unless I recognized them, deciphering in them some sign of the presence to self whose sole model I hold within me. But though my thought is indeed only the other side of my times, of my passive and perceptible being, whenever I try to understand myself the whole fabric of the perceptible world comes too, and with it come the others who are caught in it. Before others are or can be subjected to my conditions of possibility and reconstructed in my image, they must already exist as outlines, deviations, and variants of a single Vision in which I too participate. For they are not fictions with which I might people my desert—offspring of my spirit and forever unactualized possibilities—but my twins or the flesh of my flesh. Certainly I do not live their life; they are definitively absent from me and I from them. But that distance becomes a strange proximity as soon as one comes back home to the perceptible world, since the perceptible is precisely that which can haunt more than one body without budging from its place. No one will see that table which now meets my eye; only I can do that. And yet I know that at the same moment it presses upon every glance in exactly the same way. For I see these other glances too. Within the same field with things they sketch out a dis-position of the table, linking its parts together for a new compresence. Over there, enveloped in the one I am now bringing into play, the articulation of a view of something visible is being renewed or propagated. My vision overlaps another one; or rather they function together and fall as a matter of principle upon the same Visible World. Something visible to me is becoming a viewer. I am present at the metamorphosis. From now on it is no longer one thing among others; it is in circuit with them or interposes itself between them. When I look at it, my glance no longer stops or terminates in it, as it stops or terminates in things. Through it, as through a way-point, my glance goes on toward things—the same things that I alone saw, that I alone shall ever see, but that it too, from now on, alone shall see in its way. I know that *it too* alone is itself.

Everything rests upon the insurpassable richness, the miraculous multiplication of perceptible being, which gives the same things the power to be things for more than one perceiver, and makes some of the things—human and animal bodies—have not only hidden faces but an "other side," [5] a perceiving side, *whose significance is based upon what is perceptible to me* [un autre sentir *compté à partir de mon sensible*]. Everything depends upon the fact that this table over which my glance now sweeps, probing its texture, does not belong to any "space of consciousness" and inserts itself equally well into the circuit of other bodies. Everything depends, that is, upon the fact that our glances are not "acts of consciousness," each of which claims an invariable priority, but openings of our flesh which are immediately filled by the universal flesh of the world. All depends, in short, upon the fact that it is the lot of living bodies to close upon the world and become seeing, touching bodies which (since we could not possibly touch or see without being capable of touching or seeing ourselves) are *a fortiori* perceptible to themselves. The whole enigma lies in the perceptible world, in that tele-vision which makes us simultaneous with others and the world in the most private aspects of our life.

What is it like when one of the others turns upon me, meets my gaze, and fastens his own upon my body and my face? Unless we have recourse to the ruse of speech, putting a common domain of thoughts between us as a third party, the experience is intolerable. There is nothing left to look at but a look. Seer and seen are exactly interchangeable. The two glances are immobilized upon one another. Nothing can distract them and distinguish them from one another, since things are abolished and each no longer has to do with anything but its duplicate. In terms of reflection, all we have here is two "points of view" with

5. Husserl.

nothing in common—two "I think's," each of which can believe itself the winner of the trial (for after all, if I think the other is thinking of me there is still nothing there but one of my thoughts). Vision produces what reflection will never understand—a combat which at times has no victor, and a thought for which there is from now on no titular incumbent. I look at him. He sees that I look at him. I see that he sees it. He sees that I see that he sees it. The analysis is endless; and if it were the measure of all things, glances would slip from one to another indefinitely—*there would never be but a single cogito at a time.* Well, even though in principle reflections upon reflections go on to infinity, vision is such that the obscure results of two glances adjust to each other, and there are no longer two consciousnesses with their own teleology but two mutually enfolding glances, alone in the world. Vision sketches out what is accomplished by desire when it pushes two "thoughts" out toward that line of fire between them, that blazing surface where they seek a fulfillment which will be identically the same for the two of them, as the sensible world is for everyone.

Speech, as we said, would interrupt this fascination. It would not suppress it; it would put it off, carrying it on forward. For speech takes flight from where it rolls in the wave of speechless communication. It tears out or tears apart meanings in the undivided whole of the nameable, as our gestures do in that of the perceptible. To make of language a means or a code for thought is to break it. When we do so we prohibit ourselves from understanding the depth to which words sound within us—from understanding that we have a need, a passion, for speaking and must (as soon as we think) speak to ourselves; that words have power to arouse thoughts and implant henceforth inalienable dimensions of thought; and that they put responses on our lips we did not know we were capable of, teaching us, Sartre says, our own thought. If language duplicated externally a thought which in its solitude legislates for every other possible thought, it would not be, in Freud's terms, a total "reinvestment" of our life. It would not be our element as water is the element of fishes. A parallel thought and expression would each have to be complete in its own order; the irruption of one into the other, or the interception of one by the other, would be inconceivable.

Now the very idea of a *complete* statement is inconsistent. We do not understand a statement because it is complete in itself; we say that it is complete or sufficient because we have understood. Nor is there any thought which is wholly thought and does not require of words the means of being present to itself. Thought and speech anticipate one another. They continually take one another's place. They are waypoints, stimuli for one another. All thought comes from spoken words and returns to them; every spoken word is born in thoughts and ends up in them. Between men and within each man there is an incredible growth of spoken words, whose nerve is "thoughts."

But listen, someone will say, the reason why speech is more than noise or sound is that thought has deposited a burden of meaning in it—primarily its lexical or grammatical meaning—so that there is never any contact except between thought and thought. Of course sounds only speak for thought, but that does not mean that speech is derivative or secondary. Of course the very system of language has its thinkable structure. But when we speak we do not think about it as the linguist does; we do not even think about it—we think about *what we are saying*. It is not just that we cannot think of two things at a time. It would seem that *in order to* have something signified before us (whether at emission or reception), we *must* stop picturing its code or even its message to ourselves, and make ourselves sheer operators of the spoken word. Operative language makes us think, and living thought magically finds its words. There is not *thought* and *language;* upon examination each of the two orders splits in two and puts out a branch into the other. There is sensible speech, which is called thought, and abortive speech, which is called language. It is when we do not understand that we say, "Those are words there"; and that our own discourses, in return, are pure thought for us.[6] There is an inarticulate thought (the psychologists' "*aha-Erlebnis*") and an accomplished thought, which suddenly and unaware discovers itself surrounded by words. Expressive operations take place between thinking language and speaking thought; not, as we thoughtlessly say, between thought and language. It is not because they are parallel that we speak; it is because we speak that they are parallel.

The weakness of every "parallelism" is that it provides itself with correspondences between the two orders and conceals the operations which produced these correspondences by encroachment to begin with. The "thoughts" which weave speech and make a comprehensive system of it, the fields or dimensions of thought which the great authors and our own labor have installed in us, are open wholes of available significations which we do not reactivate. They are the wake of thought which we do not retrace but follow along in. We have this acquisition as we have arms and legs. We make use of it without a thought, just as without thinking we "find" our arms and legs; and Valéry was right to call this speaking power in which expression premeditates itself the "animal of words." It cannot be understood as the union of two positive orders.

6. Jean Paulhan.

But if the sign is only a certain deviation between signs, and the signification a similar deviation between significations, thought and speech overlap one another like two reliefs. As pure differences, they are indiscernible. Expression is a matter of reorganizing things-said, affecting them with a new index of curvature, and bending them to a certain enhancement of meaning. There was that which is of itself comprehensible and sayable—notably that which more mysteriously summons all things from the depths of language beforehand as nameable. There is that which is to be said, and which is as yet no more than a precise uneasiness in the world of things-said. Expression is a matter of acting in such a way that the two gather one another in or cross one another. I would never take a step if my faraway view of the goal did not find in my body a natural art of transforming it into an approaching view. My thought could not advance a step if the horizon of meaning it opens up did not become, through speech, what is called in the theater a *real* décor.

Language can vary and amplify intercorporeal communication as much as we wish; it has the same spring and style as the latter. In language too, that which was secret must become public and almost *visible*. In intercorporeal communication as in language, significations come through in whole packages, scarcely sustained by a few peremptory gestures. In both cases I envision things and others together. Speaking to others (or to myself), I do not speak *of* my thoughts; I *speak them,* and what is between them—my afterthoughts and underthoughts. Someone will reply, "This is not *what* you say; it is what your interlocutor induces." Listen to Marivaux: "I do not dream of calling you coquettish. Those are things which are said before one dreams of saying them." Said by whom? Said to whom? Not by a mind to a mind, but by a being who has body and language to a being who has body and language, each drawing the other by invisible threads like those who hold the marionettes—*making* the other speak, *think,* and become what he is but never would have been by himself.

Thus things *are said* and *are thought* by a Speech and by a Thought which we do not have but which has us. There is said to be a wall between us and others, but it is a wall we build together, each putting his stone in the niche left by the other. Even reason's labors presuppose such infinite conversations. All those we have loved, detested, known, or simply glimpsed speak through our voice. No more than space is made of simultaneous points-in-themselves, no more than our duration can sever its adherence to a space of durations, is the communicative world a bundle of parallel consciousnesses. Our traces mix and intermingle; they make a single wake of "public durations."

We ought to think of the historical world according to this model. Why ask if history is made by men or by things, since it is obvious that human initiatives do not annul the weight of things, and the "force of things" always acts through men? It is just this failure of analysis, when it tries to bring everything down to one level, which reveals history's true milieu. There is no "last analysis," because there is a flesh of history in which (as in our own body) everything counts and has a bearing—the infrastructure, our idea of it, and above all the perpetual exchanges between the two in which the weight of things becomes a sign as well, thoughts become forces, and the balance of the two becomes events. It is asked, "*Where* is history made? Who makes it? What is this movement which traces out and leaves behind the figures of the wake?" It is of the same order as the movement of Thought and Speech, and, in short, of the perceptible world's explosion within us. Everywhere there are meanings, dimensions, and forms in excess of what each "consciousness" could have produced; and yet it is men who speak and think and see. We are in the field of history as we are in the field of language or existence.

These transformations of private into public, of events into meditations, of thought into spoken words and spoken words into thought, this echo coming from everywhere makes it such that in speaking to others we also speak to ourselves, and speak of what exists. This swarming of words behind words, thoughts behind thoughts—this universal substitution is also a kind of stability. Joubert wrote to Chateaubriand that all he had to do was "shake his talisman." Although it is harder to live than to write books, it is a fact that, given our corporeal and linguistic equipment, everything we do ultimately has a meaning and a name—even if we do not know at first which one. Ideas can no longer be considered a second positivity or second world which puts its riches on display beneath a second sun. In regaining the "vertical" world or existence—the one which stands upright before my upright body—and within it the other persons who are in it, we learn about a dimension in which ideas also obtain their true solidity. They are the secret axes or (as Stendhal said) the "pilings" of our spoken words. Ideas are the centers of our gravitation, this very definite void which the vault of language is built around, and which has actual existence only in the weight and counterweight of stones. But are the visible things of the visible world constructed any differently? They are always behind what I see of them, as horizons, and what we call visibility is this very transcendence. No thing, no side of a thing, shows itself except by actively hiding the others, denouncing them in the act of concealing them. To see is as a matter of principle to see farther than one sees, to reach a latent existence. The invisible is the outline and the depth of the visible. The visible does not admit of pure positivity any more than the invisible does.

As for the source of thoughts itself, we now know that to find it we must seek beneath statements, and especially the famous statement of Descartes. Its logical truth ("in order to think one must exist") and its signification as a statement betray it as a matter of principle. For they relate to an object of thought at the moment when access must be found to the thinker and his inborn cohesion, for which the established meanings of things and ideas are only the cue. Descartes' spoken word is the gesture which reveals in each of us that thinking thought to be discovered; it is the "Open Sesame" of fundamental thought. "Fundamental" because it is not borne by anything, but not fundamental as if with it one reached a foundation upon which one ought to base oneself and stay. As a matter of principle, fundamental thought is bottomless. It is, if you wish, an abyss. This means that it is never *with* itself, that we find it next to or setting out from things thought, that it is an opening out—the other invisible extremity of the axis which connects us to ideas and things.

Must we say that this extremity is *nothing*? If it were "nothing," the differences between the nearby and the far (the contour lines of all existence) would be effaced before it. Dimensionality and opening would no longer make any sense. The absolutely open would be applied completely to an *unrestricted being;* and through the lack of another dimension from which it would have to be distinguished, what we call "verticality"—the present—would no longer mean anything. It would be better to speak of "the visible and the invisible," pointing out that they are not contradictory, than to speak of "being and nothingness." One says invisible as one says immobile—not in reference to something foreign to movement, but to something which stays still. The invisible is the limit or degree zero of visibility, the opening of a dimension of the visible. There can be no question here of a zero in every respect or of an unrestricted being. When I speak of nothingness there is already being; thus this nothingness does not really annihilate, and this being is not self-identical and unquestioned. In a sense, the highest point of philosophy is perhaps no more than rediscovering these truisms: thought thinks, speech speaks, the glance glances. But each time between the two identical words there is the whole spread one straddles in order to think, speak, and see.

The philosophy which lays bare this chiasma of the visible is the exact opposite of a philosophy of God-like survey. It plunges into the perceptible, into time and history, toward their articulations. It does not surpass them through forces it has in its own right; it surpasses them only in their meaning. Montaigne's saying that "every movement unmasks us" was recently recalled and the conclusion rightly drawn from it that man exists only in movement.[7] Similarly the world and Being hold together only in movement; it is only in this way that all things can be together. Philosophy is a reminding of this being. Science is not concerned with it, because it conceives of the relationships of being and understanding as those of the geometrical and its projections, and forgets the being which surrounds and invests us, and could be called the topology of being.

But this philosophy which searches *beneath* science is not in turn "deeper" than passions, politics, and life. There is nothing more profound than experience which passes through the wall of being. Marivaux also wrote: "Our life is cheaper to us than ourselves, our passions. Seeing at times what goes on in our instincts on this score, one would say that it is not necessary to live in order to be, that we live only by accident, but that it is by nature that we are." Those who go by way of passion and desire up to this being know all there is to know. Philosophy does not comprehend them better than they are comprehended; it is in their experience that it learns about being. Philosophy does not hold the world supine at its feet. It is not a "higher point of view" from which one embraces all local perspectives. It seeks contact with brute being, and in any case informs itself in the company of those who have never lost that contact. It is just that whereas literature, art, and the practice of life—creating themselves with things themselves, the perceptible itself, beings themselves—can (except at their extreme limits) have and create the illusion of dwelling in the habitual and the already constituted, philosophy—which paints without colors in black and white, like copperplate engravings—does not allow us to ignore the strangeness of the world, which men confront as well as or better than it does, but as if in a half-silence.

* * *

Such in any case is the philosophy which has been essayed in parts of this volume. If we are found to speak a little bit too loftily and sagely about politics, it is clear that our philosophy is not to blame. Perhaps the truth is that one would need many lives to enter each realm of experience with the total abandon it demands.

But is this sage and lofty tone really so false? Does it have so little to recommend it? Everything we believed to be thought through, and thought through correctly—freedom and authority, the citizen against authority, the heroism of the citizen, liberal humanism, formal democracy and the real democracy which suppresses it and realizes it, revolu-

7. Jean Starobinski, "Montaigne en mouvement," *N.R.F.* (February, 1960).

tionary heroism and humanism—has all fallen into ruin. We are filled with scruples about these matters; we reproach ourselves for speaking about them too dispassionately. But we should be careful. What we call disorder and ruin, others who are younger live as the natural order of things; and perhaps with ingenuity they are going to master it precisely because they no longer seek their bearings where we took ours. In the din of demolitions, many sullen passions, many hypocrisies or follies, and many false dilemmas also disappear. Who would have hoped it ten years ago? Perhaps we are at one of those moments when history moves on. We are stunned by French affairs or diplomacy's clamorous episodes. But underneath the clamor a silence is growing, an expectation. Why could it not be a hope?

One hesitates to write these words at the moment when Sartre, in a fine recollection of our youth, has for the first time adopted the tone of despair and rebellion.[8] But this rebellion is not a recrimination and an accusation brought against the world and others, nor is it a self-absolution. It does not revel in itself; it has a complete understanding of its own limits. It is like a reflective rebellion. Exactly. It is the regret at not having begun by rebelling. It is an "I ought to have" which cannot be categorical, even in retrospect; for now as then Sartre knows perfectly well (and shows perfectly in his treatment of Nizan) that rebellion can neither remain the same nor be fulfilled in revolution. Thus he cherishes the idea of a rebellious youth, and it is a chimera; not just because there is no longer time, but because his precocious lucidity does not cut such a bad figure beside the violent delusions of others. One doubts that Sartre would have exchanged it (had he been at the age of illusions) for the illusions of wrath. It was not, as he insinuates, his natural indigence, but already the same acuteness, the same impatience with self-compromises and suspicious attitudes, the same modesty, and the same disinterestedness which have kept him from being shameless himself, and which are precisely the inspiration for the noble self-criticism we have just read. This preface to *Aden Arabie* is the mature Sartre lecturing the young Sartre, who like all young people pays no attention and persists there in our past; or more precisely, who is reborn at the turning of a page, forces his way into his judge, and speaks through his mouth; and speaks in such a decisive way that one finds it difficult to believe that he is so outmoded and blameable, and one comes to suspect what is after all likely, that there is only one Sartre.

We do not advise young readers to believe too hastily that Sartre's life is a failure because he failed to rebel, and that they can thus expect forty or fifty irreproachable years if they are only sufficiently rebellious.

8. Preface to *Aden Arabie*, F. Maspéro, ed.

Sartre offers us a debate carried on between Sartre and Sartre across the past, the present, and others. In order to make the truth manifest, he sternly confronts the Sartre of twenty and the Sartre of the Liberation and more recent years; these characters with the Nizan of twenty, Nizan the Communist, and the Nizan of September, 1939; and all those people with today's "angry young men." But we must not forget that the scenario is Sartre's. His continuing rule, since it is his freedom, is to refuse himself the excuses he gives so lavishly to others. His only fault, if it is one, is to set up this distinction between us and himself. In any case, it would be abusive of us to base our judgments upon it. Consequently, we must correct the perspective and recheck the balance sheet—on which, by the way, his cursed lucidity, in lighting up the labyrinths of rebellion and revolution, has recorded in spite of himself all we need to absolve him.

This text is no mirror dawdled down Sartre's way; it is an act of today's Sartre. We who read and recall cannot so easily separate the guilty man from his judge; we find a family likeness in them. No, the Sartre of twenty was not so unworthy of the one who now disowns him, and today's judge still resembles him in the strictness of his sentence. As an effort of an experience to understand itself; as a self-interpretation and, through that self, an interpretation of all things; this text is not written to be read passively like a report or an inventory, but to be deciphered, meditated upon, and re-read. It surely has—and this is the lot of all good literature—a richer and perhaps a different meaning than the one the author put into it.

If this were the place to do it, we would have to analyze this extraordinary remembrance (after thirty years) of men past. We would have to show what is fanciful in it. Not, certainly, that Nizan was not beneath his external appearance of elegance and the greatest talents the man whom Sartre describes—righteous, full of courage, and faithful to his endowments—but because the Sartre of those same days has no less reality or weight in our memory.

I kept telling him, Sartre says, that we are free, and the thin smile at the corner of his mouth which was his only answer said more about it than all my speeches. I did not want to feel the physical weight of my chains, or know the external causes which hid my true being from me and bound me as a point of honor to freedom. I saw nothing which could touch or threaten that freedom. Foolishly, I thought I was immortal. I found nothing worth thinking about in either death or anguish. I was aware of nothing in me which was in danger of being lost. I was saved, elected. In fact, I was a thinking or a writing subject; I was living externally; and the realm of Spirit, where I had my dwelling, was no more than my abstract condition as a student nourished at the

Prytaneum. Being ignorant of the needs and bonds in my own self, I was unaware of them in others; that is, I was unacquainted with the travail of their lives. When I saw suffering and anguish, I imputed them to complacency or even to affectation. Squabbling, panic, horror of amours and friendships, decisions to displease—in a word, the negative—could not really last; they were chosen attitudes. I believed that Nizan had decided to be the perfect Communist. Because I was outside all struggles, particularly those of politics (and when I had engaged in politics it had been to bring my decency and my constructive, conciliatory humor to bear), I had no understanding of the effort Nizan had to make in order to emerge from childhood. Or of his loneliness. Or of his quest for salvation. His hatreds sprang from his life; they were solid gold. Mine came out of my head, counterfeit.

On one point we admit that Sartre is right. It is indeed astounding that he did not see in Nizan what hit one squarely in the eye: the meditation upon death and the fragility beneath the irony and mastery. This means that there are two ways of being young, which are not easily comprehensible to one another. Some are fascinated by their childhood; it possesses them, holding them enchanted in a realm of privileged possibilities. Others, it casts out toward adult life; they believe that they have no past and are equally near to all possibilities. Sartre was one of the second type. Thus it was not easy to be his friend. The distance he put between himself and the conditions of his existence also separated him from what others have to live. No more than his own self did he allow other persons to "take hold"—to be their uneasiness or anguish before his eyes as they were secretly and shamefully in themselves. In himself and in others, he had to learn that nothing is without roots, and that the decision not to have any is another way of admitting them.

But must we say that the others, those who prolonged their childhood or wanted to preserve it in going beyond it (and who thus were seeking recipes for salvation), were right and Sartre was wrong? They had to learn that one does not go beyond what one preserves, that nothing could give them the wholeness they were nostalgic for, and that if they stubbornly persisted they would soon have no choice but to be simpletons or liars. Sartre did not join them in their quest. But could it have been public? From compromise to compromise, did it not require a chiaroscuro? And they were well aware that it did. That is why the intimate and distant relations between them and Sartre were humorous. Sartre reproaches himself for them now, but would they have put up with any other sort? The most we can say is that reserve and irony are contagious. Sartre did not understand Nizan because Nizan transformed his suffering into dandyism. His books, the sequel of his life, and (for Sartre) twenty years of experience after his death were necessary before Nizan was finally understood. But did Nizan want to be understood? Is not the suffering which Sartre is now talking about the kind of admission one would rather make to a reader than to a friend? Would Nizan have ever tolerated this confidential tone between Sartre and himself? Sartre knows the answer better than we do. But let us bring up a few minor facts.

One day while we were preparing for the Ecole Normale, we saw entering our classroom with the aura of the chosen few a former student visiting for some reason unknown to us. He was admirably dressed in dark blue, and wore the tricolor cockade of Valois. They told me it was Nizan. Nothing in his dress or carriage advertised the labors of the Khagne or of the Ecole Normale. And when our professor (who on the contrary still felt their effect) smilingly suggested that Nizan take his place with us again, he said "Why not?" in an icy voice and sat down quickly in an empty seat next to me where he buried himself impassibly in my Sophocles as if that had really been his only aim for the morning. When he came back from Aden, I found in my mail the card of Paul-Yves Nizan, who invited the conscript Merleau-Ponty, whose cousin he had known very well down there, to visit him one day soon in the pad he shared with Sartre. The meeting was according to protocol. Sartre's corner was empty and bare. Nizan in return had hung on the wall two foils crossed beneath a fencing mask, and it was against this background that the man whom I later knew had skirted suicide in Araby appeared to me. Much later, I ran into him on the back platform of bus S. He was married, a militant, and on this particular day loaded down with a heavy briefcase and untypically wearing a hat. He brought up Heidegger's name himself, and had a few words of praise for him in which I sensed a desire to show that he had not abandoned philosophy. But he spoke so coldly that I would not have dared to ask him openly.

I like to recall these little facts. They prove nothing, but they are vital. They make us feel that if Sartre did not follow too closely the travail which was going on in Nizan, Nizan for his part—by virtue of humor, reserve, and politeness—entered more than halfway into the game. I have said that Sartre would understand him only after thirty years, because Sartre was Sartre, but also because Nizan was Nizan. And above all because they both were young; that is, peremptory and timid. And perhaps after all for one final, deeper reason.

Did the Nizan Sartre reproaches himself for having misunderstood exist entirely in 1928—before his family, his books, his life as a militant, his break with the Party, and above all his death at thirty-five? Because he perfected, enclosed, and immobilized himself in these thirty-five short years, they have slid twenty years behind us in a block, and now we would have it that everything he might have been is given at their inception and in each moment of them. Feverish like a beginning, his life is also solid like an ending. He is forever young. And because on the contrary we have been given time to be mistaken more than once, and to correct our mistakes, our comings and our goings cover up our tracks. Our own youth is worn out and insignificant for us, inaccessible to us as it really was. To another life which ends too soon, I apply the standard of hope. To mine, which is perpetuated, the severe rule of death. A young man has done a lot if he has been a "perhaps." It seems to us that a mature man who is still around has done nothing. As in the things of childhood, it is in the lost comrade that I find plenitude, *either because creative faith has dried up within me, or because reality takes shape only in my memory.*[9] Another retrospective illusion, which Bergson did not speak about: no longer that of pre-existence, but that of fall from grace. Perhaps time does not flow from the future or the past. Perhaps it is distance which constitutes the reality another person has for us—above all another person who is lost. But that distance would also rehabilitate us if we could only see ourselves from there. As a balance to what Sartre writes today about himself and Nizan at twenty, what the Nizan of fifty could have said about their youth will be forever missing. For us, they were two men starting out in life, and starting out opposite one another.

What makes Sartre's account melancholy is that in it one sees the two friends slowly learning from experience what they could have learned from one another at the outset. Nizan had been confiscated by his father's image. He was possessed by the drama (older than he was) of a worker who, having left his class, discovers that his life since then has been unreal and a failure, and ends his days hating himself. Consequently, Nizan knew from the start the weight of childhood, the body, and society, as well as the interwoven ties that bind us to our parents and to history in one single anguish. He would not have put an end to this fascination with his father's image, perhaps indeed he would have aggravated it, by simply choosing marriage and the family, taking up the father's role for his own. If he wanted to re-enter the life cycle his father's life had turned him out of, he had to purify its source, break with the society which had produced their solitude, and undo what his father had done, setting out upon his road again in the opposite direction.

In proportion to the passing years, the omens multiply, the evident truth approaches. The flight to Aden is the last attempt at a solution through adventure. It would have been no more than a diversion if

9. *Swann*, I, 265.

Nizan had not found in the colonial régime (either by chance or because confusedly he was looking for this particular lesson) the clear image of our dependence in respect to the external world. So suffering has external causes; they are identifiable, have a name, can be abolished. So there is an external enemy, and we are helpless against him if we stay by ourselves. So life is war and social war.

Nizan already knew what Sartre said much later. In the beginning is not play but need. We do not keep the world, or situations, or others at the length of our gaze like a spectacle; we are intermingled with them, drinking them in through all our pores. We are what is lacking in everything else; and within us, with the nothingness which is the center of our being, a general principle of alienation is given. Before Sartre, Nizan lived this pantragism, this flood of anguish which is also the flux of history.

But for this very reason, and because he was not living in the tragic realm, Sartre understood much sooner the artifices of salvation and of the return to the positive. He was not exactly an optimist; he never equated the Good and Being. Nor was he saved, one of the elect. He was vigorous, gay, and enterprising; all things which lay before him were new and interesting. Precisely. He was *supralapsarian*, this side of tragedy and hope, and thus well equipped to tease out their secret knots. His premonitions find their factual demonstration in Nizan's experience during the ten years preceding the War; and when he tells about that experience today—when he takes it up again on his own account, profoundly and fraternally—he cannot help finding exactly what he has been telling us since then about conversions.

One day a man declares himself a Christian or a Communist. Just what does he mean? We are not completely changed in an instant. What happens is simply that in recognizing an external cause of his destiny, man suddenly gets permission and even the mission (as I believe Maritain used to say) to *live in the bosom of the faith of his natural life.* It is neither necessary nor possible for his backslidings to stop; from then on they are "consecrated." [10] His torments are now stigmata whose stamp is an immense Truth. The sickness he was dying of helps him, and helps others, to live. He is not required to renounce his talents, if he has any. On the contrary, the loosening of the anguish which had clutched his throat releases them. To live, to be happy, to write meant to give in to slumber; it was suspect and base. Now it means recovering from sin what sin presumptuously had claimed, or, as Lenin used to say, stealing from the bourgeoisie what it had stolen.

Communism sees through a glass darkly in the perspective of a new man and a new society. But for the time being, and for a whole

10. Preface to *Aden Arabie*, p. 51.

long period which is called negative, what it turns against the bourgeois State is the machinery of the State. The means it turns against evil are evil means. From now on, each thing has a double meaning, depending on whether it is judged according to its evil origin or in the perspective of the future it invokes. The Marxist is the wretch he was; he is also that wretchedness restored to its place in the total scheme of things and known in terms of its causes. As a writer in a period of "demoralization," he prolongs bourgeois decadence; but in the very process of doing so he bears witness to it and surpasses it towards a different future. Nizan the Communist "saw the world and saw himself there." [11] He was subject and he was object. As object, lost along with his times; as subject, saved along with the future.

And yet this double-entried life is only one life. Marxist man is a product of history, and he also participates from within in history as the production of a new society and a new man. How is this possible? He would have to be reintegrated as a finite being into the infinite productivity. That is why many Marxists have been tempted by Spinozism, and Nizan was one of them. As Nizan did, Sartre liked Spinoza; but in opposition to the transcendent and the reconcilers, the equivalent of whose contrivances he was quick to find in Spinoza in the form of "the affirmative plenitude of the finite mode which at the same time bursts its bonds and returns to the infinite substance." [12] In the end, Spinoza does everything to hide the labor and the peculiar virtue of the negative; and Spinozist Marxism is simply a fraudulent way of assuring us in this life of the return of the positive. The adhesion to an infinite positivity is a pseudonym for naked anguish—the pretention to have crossed the negative and reached the other shore; to have exhausted, totaled up, internalized death. "We do not have even this, not even this unmediated communication with our nothingness." [13]

Sartre found this philosophical formulation later. But he sensed at twenty-five that there is trickery and falsification when the savior counts himself out of the reckoning. Nizan wanted to stop thinking about himself and he succeeded; he had regard only for causal chains. But it was still he—the nay-sayer, the irreplaceable one—who annihilated himself in things.[14] True negativity cannot be made of two positivities joined together, my being as a product of capitalism and the affirmation of a new future through me. For there is a rivalry between them, and one or the other must win. Having become a means of edification and a professional theme, rebellion may be no longer felt,

11. *Ibid.*, p. 48.
12. *Ibid.*, p. 55.
13. *Ibid.*, p. 41.
14. *Ibid.*, p. 55.

no longer lived. Marxist man is saved by the doctrine and the movement. He sets himself up in his job. According to the old criteria, he is lost. Or (and this is what happens to the best) he does not forget or lie to himself—his wisdom is reborn from his continual suffering, and his incredulity is his faith—but he cannot say so, and in that case he must lie to others. Hence the impression we get from so many conversations with Communists: they possess the most objective thought there is, but the most anguished and, beneath its toughness, secretly slack and humid. Sartre has always known and said (and this is what has kept him from being a Communist) that the Communist negation, being positivity reversed, is not what it says it is, or that it doubletalks like a ventriloquist.

Since he understands the subterfuges of the "negative man" so well, it is astonishing that he should sometimes speak with such nostalgia of the wholly critical period prior to 1930, especially since the Revolution already had its counterfeit coin in its "constructive" period. The explanation is that Sartre has resigned himself to the inevitable, later and upon reflection, as to a lesser evil. He never simply reoccupied the positions Nizan held thirty years ago. He justifies them at one remove from them, for reasons which remain his own, in the name of an experience which led him to involvement without modifying what he has always thought of salvation. But this experience, which begins in 1939, remains to be retraced.

In 1939, Nizan is going to discover abruptly that one is not so quickly saved, that adherence to communism does not free one from dilemmas and heart-rending anguish; while Sartre, who knew it, begins that apprenticeship in history and the positive which was to lead him later on to a sort of communism from without. Thus their paths cross. Nizan returns from Communist politics to rebellion, and the a-political Sartre becomes acquainted with the social. This fine account must be read. It must be read over Sartre's shoulder, as his pen sets it forth—all mixed in with his reflections, and mixing ours in too.

Nizan, he says, had admitted that the new man and the new society did not yet exist; that perhaps he would not see them himself; and that it was necessary to dedicate oneself to that unknown future without weighing the sacrifice or constantly haggling over and contesting the Revolution's means. He said nothing about the Purge Trials. Comes another, clearer, test for him. Responsible for the foreign affairs section of a Party journal, he has explained a hundred times that the Soviet alliance would avert both fascism and war. He repeats it in July, 1939, at Marseille, where Sartre accidentally runs into him.

Here I ask permission to add a word of my own: Nizan knew that perhaps we would not avoid both fascism and war, and within himself he had accepted war if it was the only means of containing fascism. It happens that I can bear witness to this. Maybe three weeks after his meeting with Sartre, I in turn saw Nizan. It was in Corsica, at Porto, at Casanova's,[15] if I am not mistaken. He was gay and smiling, as Sartre had seen him. But (whether his friends were getting him ready for a new line or whether they were themselves being worked on from higher up I do not know) he no longer said that fascism would be brought to its knees by Fall. He says: "We will have war against Germany, but with the U.S.S.R. as an ally, and we shall win it in the end." He says it firmly, serenely (I can still hear his voice), as if he were released from himself at last.

Fifteen days later came the Nazi-Soviet pact, and Nizan left the Communist Party. Not, he explained, because of the pact, which beat Hitler's Western friends at their own game. But the French Party should have saved its dignity, pretending indignation and giving the appearance of declaring its independence. Nizan realized that to be a Communist is not to play a role one has chosen but to be caught in a drama where without knowing it one receives a different role. It is a lifetime undertaking which one carries on in faith or ends up pulling out of, but which in any case exceeds agreed-upon limits and the promises of prudence. If it is like this, and if it is true that in the Communist life as in the other nothing is ever irrevocably accomplished—if years of labor and of action can be stricken in a twinkling with derision—in that case, Nizan thinks, I cannot do it, and the answer is no.

What is Sartre thinking at the same moment? He would like to believe that Nizan has deceived him. But no, Nizan resigns. He is the one who has been deceived. They are two children in the world of politics. A harsh world where the risks cannot be calculated and where peace is perhaps given only to those who do not fear war. One acts in a show of force only if one is determined to make use of it. If one shows it fearfully, one has war and defeat. "I discovered . . . the monumental error of a whole generation . . . : we were being pushed toward massacres across a fierce prelude to war, and we thought we were strolling on the lawns of peace." [16]

Thus Sartre and Nizan were deceived in different ways, and they learned a different lesson from their deception. Nizan had accepted force and war and death for a very clear cause; events made sport of his sacrifice, and he no longer had any sanctuary but himself. Sartre,

15. Laurent Casanova, French Resistance leader and (until he lost out to the Stalinist element) high-ranking Communist official and Deputy. His wife Danielle, killed by the Nazis, became one of the most popular martyrs of the Resistance.—Trans.

16. Preface to *Aden Arabie*, p. 57.

who had believed in peace, discovered a nameless adversity which had to be clearly taken into account. A lesson he will not forget. It is the source of his pragmatism in politics. In a world bewitched, the question is not to know who is right, who follows the truest course, but who is the match for the Great Deceiver, and what action will be tough and supple enough to bring it to reason.

One can understand, then, the objections Sartre makes today to the Nizan of 1939, and why they are without weight against him. Nizan, he says, was angry. But is that anger a matter of mood? It is a mode of understanding which is not too inappropriate when fundamental meaning-structures are at stake. For anyone who has become a Communist and has acted within the Party day after day, things said and done have a weight, because he has said and done them too. In order to take the change in line of 1939 as he should, Nizan would have to have been a puppet. He would have to have been broken, and he had not become a Communist to play the skeptic. Or, again, he would have to have been only a sympathizer. But the Party is not at issue, Sartre also says. Death does not come to Nizan through the Party. "The massacre was brought to birth by the Earth, and sprang forth on all sides." [17] All right. But this is justifying the Party relatively as a fact in the Earth's history. For Nizan, who is in it, it is all or nothing.

"An impulsive act," Sartre rejoins. "If he had lived, I tell myself that the Resistance would have brought him back into the ranks as it brought others." [18] In the ranks, certainly. But in the ranks of the Party? That is another matter. It is almost the opposite: a function of authority, a mark of distinction. Even rallied to the cause, he would not have forgotten the episode. The communism he had abandoned was the sagacious doctrine for which the Revolution is both family and fatherland. He would have found an adventurous communism which played the role of the Revolution through the Resistance, after having played the role of defeatism, and in expecting to play, after the War, the role of reconstruction and compromise.

Even if he had wanted to, would Nizan have been able to follow this sequence—he who had believed in Marxism's truth? He would have been able to on the condition that he had not taken a position each time. It is one thing, from without or after the fact (which is the same thing), to justify with documents in hand the detours of communism. It is another thing to organize the deception and to be the deceiver. I recall having written from Lorraine, in October, 1939, some prophetic letters which divided the roles between us and the U.S.S.R. in a Machiavellian fashion. But I had not spent years preaching the Soviet alliance.

17. *Ibid.*, p. 60.
18. *Ibid.*, p. 58.

Like Sartre, I had no party: a good position for serenely doing justice to the toughest of parties.

We were not wrong, but Nizan was right. Communism from without has no lessons to teach Communists. Sometimes more cynical than they and sometimes less, rebellious where they give in, resigned where they refuse, it is a natural lack of comprehension of Communist life. Nizan "unlearned," but that means learning, too. If his rebellion in 1939, which was based upon his reasons for being, and for being a Communist, was a strategic withdrawal, then so was the Budapest uprising.

One starting out from anguish, the other from gaiety; one taking the road toward happiness, the other toward tragedy; both drawing near to communism, one from its classical and the other from its shadowy side; and both finally rejected by events; Nizan and Sartre have perhaps never been closer to one another than today, at the hour when their experiences mutually clarify one another in these profound pages. In order to say now what conclusions all this tends toward, we must draw out some of the sparkling words which this meditation strikes from Sartre.

What is unimpaired in Sartre is the sense of novelty and freedom: "Lost freedom will not be found except by being invented. It is forbidden to look back, even in order to determine the dimensions of our 'authentic' needs." [19] But where in the present are the arms and emblems of this true negativity, which cannot be satisfied with giving different names to the same things? Should we look to the new course of events or to new peoples for what the Russia of the October generation has not given to the world? Can we displace our radicalism? History gives no pure and simple answers. Shall we say to the young: "Be Cubans, be Russian or Chinese, according to your taste, be Africans? They will answer that it is pretty late to change extraction." [20] What perhaps is clear in China is at least implicit and confused here; the two histories do not mesh. Who would dare maintain that China, even if she has the power some day, will *liberate*, let us say Hungary or France? And where in the France of 1960 is the sense of untamed freedom to be found? A few young people maintain it in their lives, a few Diogenes in their books. Where is it, let us not even say in public life, but in the masses? Freedom and invention are in the minority, of the opposition. Man is hidden, well hidden, and this time we must make no mistake about it: this does not mean that he is there beneath a mask, ready to appear. Alienation is not simply privation of what was our own by natural right; and to bring it to an end, it will not suffice to

19. *Ibid.*, pp. 44–45.
20. *Ibid.*, p. 17.

steal what has been stolen, to give us back our due. The situation is far more serious: there are no faces underneath the masks, historical man has never been human, and yet no man is alone.

Thus we see by what right and in what sense Sartre can take up the young Nizan's claim again and offer it to the rebellious young men of today. "Nizan used to speak bitterly of the old guys who laid our women and intended to castrate us." [21] He wrote: "As long as men are not complete and free, they will dream at night." [22] He said "that love was true and they kept us from loving; that life could be true, that it could give birth to a true death, but they made us die before we were even born." [23] Thus our brother love is there, our sister life, and even our sister bodily death, as promising as childbirth. Being is there within reach; we only have to free it from the reign of the old men and the rich. Desire, be insatiable; "turn your rage upon those who have provoked it; do not try to escape your trouble; seek out its causes and smash them." [24] Alas! Nizan's story, which Sartre goes on to tell, shows clearly enough that it is not so easy to find the true causes—and *smash them* is precisely the language of a war in which the enemy is imperceptible. The complete man, the man who does not dream, who can die well because he lives well, and who can love his life because he envisages his death is, like the myth of the Androgynes, the symbol of what we lack.

It is just that since this truth would be too harsh, Sartre retranslates it into the language of the young, the language of the young Nizan. "In a society which reserves its women for the old and the rich. . . ." [25] This is the language of sons. It is the Oedipal word one hears in each generation. Sartre quite properly says that each child in becoming a father simultaneously kills his father and regenerates him. Let us add that the good father is an accessory to the immemorial childishness; he himself offers himself up to the murder which his childhood lives anew in, and which confirms him as a father. Better to be guilty than to have been impotent. Noble dodge for hiding life from children.

This bad world is the one "we have made for them." [26] These ruined lives are those "which have been made . . . which are being manufactured today for the young." [27] But that is not true. It is not true that we have at any moment been masters of things, nor that, having clear problems before us, we have botched everything by our futility. The

21. *Ibid.*, p. 29.
22. *Ibid.*, p. 30.
23. *Ibid.*, p. 45.
24. *Ibid.*, p. 18.
25. *Ibid.*, p. 29.
26. *Ibid.*, p. 18.
27. *Ibid.*, p. 61.

young will learn precisely in reading this preface that their elders have not had such an easy life. Sartre is spoiling them. Or rather, exactly following the pattern he has always followed, he is hard on the children of his spirit, who are already in their forties, but grants everything to those who follow—and starts them out again in the eternal return of rivalry.

It is Nizan who was right; there is your man; read him. I would like to add: read Sartre too. This little sentence, for example, which weighs so heavily: "The same reasons take happiness from us and render us forever incapable of possessing it." [28] Does he mean the same *causes,* and that it is not this humanity but another which will be happy? That would be, like Pascal, staking everything on a beyond. However, he says the same *reasons.* The fall is thus not an accident; its causes count us as accomplices. There is equal weakness in blaming ourselves alone and in believing only in external causes. In one way or another we will always *miss the mark* if we do. Evil is not *created* by us or by others; it is born in this web that we have spun about us—and that is suffocating us. What sufficiently tough new men will be patient enough to really re-weave it?

The remedy we seek does not lie in rebellion, but in unremitting *virtù.* A deception for whoever believed in salvation, and in a single means of salvation in all realms. Our history, where space reappears and China, Africa, Russia, and the West are not advancing at the same pace, is a fall for whoever believed that history, like a fan, is going to fold in upon itself. But if this philosophy of time was yet another reverie born of the age-old distress, why then should we judge the present from such a height in its name? There is no universal clock, but local histories take form beneath our eyes, and begin to regulate themselves, and haltingly are linked to one another and demand to live, and confirm the powerful in the wisdom which the immensity of the risks and the consciousness of their own disorder had given them. The world is more present to itself in all its parts than it ever was. In world capitalism and in world communism and between the two, more truth circulates today than twenty years ago. History never confesses, not even her lost illusions, but neither does she dream of them again.

(*February and September, 1960*)

28. *Ibid.,* p. 51.

PART II

1 / Indirect Language and the Voices of Silence

to Jean-Paul Sartre

. . . WHAT WE HAVE LEARNED from Saussure is that, taken singly, signs do not signify anything, and that each one of them does not so much express a meaning as mark a divergence of meaning between itself and other signs. Since the same can be said for all other signs, we may conclude that language is made of differences without terms; or more exactly, that the terms of language are engendered only by the differences which appear among them. This is a difficult idea, because common sense tells us that if term A and term B do not have any meaning at all, it is hard to see how there could be a difference of meaning between them; and that if communication really did go from the whole of the speaker's language to the whole of the hearer's language, one would have to know the language in order to learn it. But the objection is of the same kind as Zeno's paradoxes; and as they are overcome by the act of movement, it is overcome by the use of speech. And this sort of circle, according to which language, in the presence of those who are learning it, precedes itself, teaches itself, and suggests its own deciphering, is perhaps the marvel which defines language.

Language is learned, and in this sense one is certainly obliged to go from part to whole. The prior whole which Saussure is talking about cannot be the explicit and articulated whole of complete language as it is recorded in grammars and dictionaries. Nor does he have in mind a logical totality like that of a philosophical system, all of whose elements can (in principle) be deduced from a single idea. Since what he is doing is rejecting any other than a "diacritical" meaning of signs, he cannot base language upon a system of positive ideas. The unity he is talking about is a unity of coexistence, like that of the sections of an arch which shoulder one another.

In a unified whole of this kind, the learned parts of a language have an immediate value as a whole, and progress is made less by addition and juxtaposition than by the internal articulation of a function which is in its own way already complete. It has long been known that for a child the word first functions as a sentence, and perhaps even certain phonemes as words. But contemporary linguistics conceives of the unity of language in an even more precise way by isolating, at the origin of words—perhaps even at the origin of form and style—"oppositive" and "relative" principles to which the Saussurian definition of sign applies even more rigorously than to words, since it is a question here of components of language which do not for their part have any assignable meaning and whose sole function is to make possible the discrimination of signs in the strict sense. Now these first phonemic oppositions may well have gaps and be enriched subsequently by new dimensions, and the verbal chain may well find other means of self-differentiation. The important point is that the phonemes are from the beginning variations of a unique speech apparatus, and that with them the child seems to have "caught" the principle of a mutual differentiation of signs and at the same time to have acquired *the meaning of the sign.* For the phonemic oppositions—contemporaneous with the first attempts at communication—appear and are developed without any relation to the child's babbling. His babbling is often repressed by the oppositions, and in any case retains only a marginal existence without its materials being integrated to the new system of true speech. This lack of relation between babbling and phonemic oppositions seems to indicate that possessing a sound as an element of babbling which is addressed only to itself is not the same as possessing a sound as a stage in the effort to communicate. It can be said that beginning with the first phonemic oppositions the child *speaks,* and that only afterwards will he learn to apply the principle of speech in diverse ways.

Saussure's insight becomes more precise: with the first phonemic oppositions the child is initiated to the lateral liaison of sign to sign as the foundation of an ultimate relation of sign to meaning—in the special form it has received in the language in question. Phonologists have succeeded in extending their analysis beyond words to forms, to syntax, and even to stylistic differences because the language in its entirety as a style of expression and a unique manner of handling words is anticipated by the child in the first phonemic oppositions. The whole of the spoken language surrounding the child snaps him up like a whirlwind, tempts him by its internal articulations, and brings him *almost* up to the moment when all this noise begins to mean something. The untiring way in which the train of words crosses and recrosses itself, and the emergence one unimpeachable day of a certain phonemic scale according to which discourse is visibly composed, finally sways the child over to the side of those who speak. Only language as a whole enables one to understand how language draws the child to himself and how he comes to enter that domain whose doors, it is believed, open only from within. It is because the sign is diacritical from the outset, because it is composed and organized in terms of itself, that it has an interior and ends up laying claim to a meaning.

This meaning arising at the edge of signs, this immanence of the whole in the parts, is found throughout the history of culture. There is that moment at which Brunelleschi built the cupola of the cathedral in Florence in a definite relation to the configuration of the site. Should we say that he broke with the closed space of the Middle Ages and discovered the universal space of the Renaissance? [1] But *an* operation of art is still a long way from being a deliberate use of space as the medium of a universe. Should we say then that this space is not yet there? But Brunelleschi did make for himself a strange device [2] in which two views of the Battistero and the Palazzo della Signoria, with the streets and the squares which frame them, were reflected in a mirror, while a disc of polished metal projected the light of the sky upon the scene. Thus he had done research and had raised a question of space. It is just as difficult to say when the generalized number begins in the history of mathematics. "In itself" (that is, as Hegel would say, for us who project it into history), it is already present in the fractional number which, before the algebraic number, inserts the whole number in a continuous series. But it is there as if it were unaware of its existence; it is not there "for itself." In the same way one must give up trying to establish the moment at which Latin becomes French. Grammatical forms begin to be efficacious and outlined in a language before being systematically employed. A language sometimes remains a long time pregnant with transformations which are to come; and the enumeration of the means of expression in a language does not have any meaning, since those which fall into disuse continue to lead a diminished life in the language and since the place of those which are to replace them is sometimes already marked out—even if only in the form of a gap, a need, or a tendency.

Even when it is possible to date the emergence of a principle which exists "for itself," it is clear that the principle has been previously present in the culture as an obsession or anticipation, and that the act of consciousness which lays it down as an explicit signification is never without a residue. The space of the Renaissance will in turn be thought of later as a very particular case of possible pictorial space. Culture thus never gives us absolutely transparent significations; the genesis of

1. Pierre Francastel, *Peinture et Société*, pp. 17ff.
2. *Ibid.*

meaning is never completed. What we rightly call our truth we never contemplate except in a symbolic context which dates our knowledge. We always have to do only with sign structures whose meaning, being nothing other than the way in which the signs behave toward one another and are distinguished from one another, cannot be set forth independently of them. We do not even have the morose consolation of a vague relativism, since each stage of our knowledge is indeed a truth and will be preserved in the more comprehensive truth of the future.

As far as language is concerned, it is the lateral relation of one sign to another which makes each of them significant, so that meaning appears only at the intersection of and as it were in the interval between words. This characteristic prevents us from forming the usual conception of the distinction and the union between language and its meaning. Meaning is usually thought to transcend signs in principle (just as thought is supposed to transcend the sounds or sights which indicate it), and to be immanent in signs in the sense that each one of them, having *its* meaning once and for all, could not conceivably slip any opacity between itself and us, or even give us food for thought. Signs are supposed to be no more than monitors which notify the hearer that he must consider such and such of his thoughts. But meaning does not actually dwell in the verbal chain or distinguish itself from the chain in this way. Since the sign has meaning only in so far as it is profiled against other signs, its meaning is entirely involved in language. Speech always comes into play against a background of speech; it is always only a fold in the immense fabric of language. To understand it, we do not have to consult some inner lexicon which gives us the pure thoughts covered up by the words or forms we are perceiving; we only have to lend ourselves to its life, to its movement of differentiation and articulation, and to its eloquent gestures. There is thus an opaqueness of language. Nowhere does it stop and leave a place for pure meaning; it is always limited only by more language, and meaning appears within it only set in a context of words. Like a charade, language is understood only through the interaction of signs, each of which, taken separately, is equivocal or banal, and makes sense only by being combined with others.

For the speaker no less than for the listener, language is definitely something other than a technique for ciphering or deciphering ready-made significations. Before there can be such ready-made significations, language must first make significations exist as guideposts by establishing them at the intersection of linguistic gestures as that which, by common consent, the gestures reveal. Our analyses of thought give us the impression that before it finds the words which express it, it is already a sort of ideal text that our sentences attempt to *translate.* But the author himself has no text to which he can compare his writing, and no language prior to language. His speech satisfies him only because it reaches an equilibrium whose conditions his speech itself defines, and attains a state of perfection which has no model.

Language is much more like a sort of being than a means, and that is why it can present something to us so well. A friend's speech over the telephone brings us the friend himself, as if he were wholly present in that manner of calling and saying goodbye to us, of beginning and ending his sentences, and of carrying on the conversation through things left unsaid. Because meaning is the total movement of speech, our thought crawls along in language. Yet for the same reason, our thought moves through language as a gesture goes beyond the individual points of its passage. At the very moment language fills our mind up to the top without leaving the smallest place for thought not taken into its vibration, and exactly to the extent that we abandon ourselves to it, it passes beyond the "signs" toward their meaning. And nothing separates us from that meaning any more. Language does not *presuppose* its table of correspondence; it unveils its secrets itself. It teaches them to every child who comes into the world. It is entirely a "monstration." Its opaqueness, its obstinate reference to itself, and its turning and folding back upon itself are precisely what make it a mental power; for it in turn becomes something like a universe, and it is capable of lodging things themselves in this universe—after it has transformed them into their meaning.

Now if we rid our minds of the idea that our language is the translation or cipher of an original text, we shall see that the idea of *complete* expression is nonsensical, and that all language is indirect or allusive—that it is, if you wish, silence. The relation of meaning to the spoken word can no longer be a point for point correspondence that we always have clearly in mind. Saussure notes that the English "the man I love" expresses just as completely as the French "l'homme *que* j'aime." We say that the English does not express the relative pronoun. The truth is that instead of being expressed by a word, the relative pronoun passes into the language by means of a blank between the words. But we should not even say that it is implied. This notion of implication naively expresses our conviction that a language (generally our native tongue) has succeeded in capturing things themselves in its forms; and that any other language, if it wants to reach things themselves too, must at least tacitly use the same kind of instruments. Now the reason French seems to us to go to things themselves is certainly not that it has actually copied the articulations of being. French has a distinct word to express relation, but it does not distinguish the function of being the object of a verb by means of a special flexional ending. It could be said that French implies the declension that German expresses (and the aspect that Russian expresses, and the optative that Greek expresses). The reason French seems to us to be traced upon things is not that it is but that it gives us the illusion of being so by the internal relation of one sign to another. But "the man I love" does so just as well. The absence of a sign can be a sign, and expression is not the adjustment of an element of discourse to each element of meaning, but an operation of language upon language which suddenly is thrown out of focus towards its meaning.

To speak is not to put a word under each thought; if it were, nothing would ever be said. We would not have the feeling of living in the language and we would remain silent, because the sign would be immediately obliterated by its own meaning and because thought would never encounter anything but thought—the thought it wanted to express and the thought which it would form from a wholly explicit language. We sometimes have, on the contrary, the feeling that a thought has been *spoken*—not replaced by verbal counters but incorporated in words and made available in them. And finally, there is a power of words because, working against one another, they are attracted at a distance by thought like tides by the moon, and because they evoke their meaning in this tumult much more imperiously than if each one of them brought back only a listless signification of which it was the indifferent and predestined sign.

Language speaks peremptorily when it gives up trying to express the thing itself. As algebra brings unknown magnitudes under consideration, speech differentiates significations no one of which is known separately; and it is by treating them as known (and giving us an abstract picture of them and their interrelations) that language ends up imposing the most precise identification upon us in a flash. Language signifies when instead of copying thought it lets itself be taken apart and put together again by thought. Language bears the meaning of thought as a footprint signifies the movement and effort of a body. The empirical use of already established language should be distinguished from its creative use. Empirical language can only be the result of creative language. Speech in the sense of empirical language—that is, the opportune recollection of a pre-established sign—is not speech in respect to an authentic language. It is, as Mallarmé said, the worn coin placed silently in my hand. True speech, on the contrary—speech which signifies, which finally renders *"l'absent de tous les bouquets"* present and frees the meaning captive in the thing—is only silence in respect to empirical usage, for it does not go so far as to become a common name. It goes without saying that language is oblique and autonomous, and that its ability to signify a thought or a thing directly is only a secondary power derived from the inner life of language. Like the weaver, the writer works on the wrong side of his material. He has to do only with language, and it is thus that he suddenly finds himself surrounded by meaning.

If this account is true, the writer's act of expression is not very different from the painter's. We usually say that the painter reaches us across the silent world of lines and colors, and that he addresses himself to an unformulated power of deciphering within us that we control only after we have blindly used it—only after we have enjoyed the work. The writer is said, on the contrary, to dwell in already elaborated signs and in an already speaking world, and to require nothing more of us than the power to reorganize our significations according to the indications of the signs which he proposes to us. But what if language expresses as much by what is between words as by the words themselves? By that which it does not "say" as by what it "says"? And what if, hidden in empirical language, there is a second-order language in which signs once again lead the vague life of colors, and in which significations never free themselves completely from the intercourse of signs?

There are two sides to the act of painting: the spot or line of color put on a point of the canvas, and its effect in the whole, which is incommensurable with it, since it is almost nothing yet suffices to change a portrait or a landscape. One who, with his nose against the painter's brush, observed the painter from too close would see only the wrong side of his work. The wrong side is a feeble movement of the brush or pen of Poussin; the right side is the sunlit glade which that movement releases. A camera once recorded the work of Matisse in slow motion. The impression was prodigious, so much so that Matisse himself was moved, they say. That same brush which, seen with the naked eye, leaped from one act to another, was seen to meditate in a solemn and expanding time—in the imminence of a world's creation—to try ten possible movements, dance in front of the canvas, brush it lightly several times, and crash down finally like a lightning stroke upon the one line necessary. Of course, there is something artificial in this analysis. And Matisse would be wrong if, putting his faith in the film, he believed that he really chose between all possible lines that day and, like the God of Leibniz, solved an immense problem of maximum and minimum. He was not a demiurge; he was a man. He did not have in his mind's eye all the gestures possible, and in making his choice he did not have to eliminate all but one. It is slow motion which enumerates the possibilities. Matisse, set within a man's time and vision, looked at the still open whole of his work in progress and brought his brush toward the line which called for it in order that the painting might finally be that which it was in the process of becoming. By a simple gesture he resolved the problem which in retrospect seemed to imply an infinite number of data (as the hand in the iron filings, according to Bergson, achieves in a single stroke the arrangement which will make a place for it). Everything happened in the human world of perception and gesture; and the camera gives us a fascinating version of the event only by making us believe that the painter's hand operated in the physical world where an infinity of options is possible. And yet, Matisse's hand did hesitate. Consequently, there was a choice, and the chosen line was chosen in such a way as to observe, scattered out over the painting, twenty conditions which were unformulated and even informulable for any one but Matisse, since they were only defined and imposed by the intention of executing *this painting which did not yet exist.*

The case is no different for all truly expressive speech and thus for all language in the phase in which it is being established. Expressive speech does not simply choose a sign for an already defined signification, as one goes to look for a hammer in order to drive a nail or for a claw to pull it out. It gropes around a significative intention which is not guided by any text, and which is precisely in the process of writing the text. If we want to do justice to expressive speech, we must evoke some of the other expressions which might have taken its place and were rejected, and we must feel the way in which they might have touched and shaken the chain of language in another manner and the extent to which this particular expression was really the only possible one if that signification was to come into the world. In short, we must consider speech before it is spoken, the background of silence which does not cease to surround it and without which it would say nothing.

Or to put the matter another way, we must uncover the threads of silence that speech is mixed together with. In already acquired expressions there is a direct meaning which corresponds point for point to figures, forms, and established words. Apparently there are no gaps or expressive silences here. But the meaning of expressions which are in the process of being accomplished cannot be of this sort; it is a lateral or oblique meaning which runs between words. It is another way of shaking the linguistic or narrative apparatus in order to tear a new sound from it. If we want to understand language as an originating operation, we must pretend to have never spoken, submit language to a reduction without which it would once more escape us by referring us to what it signifies for us, *look* at it as deaf people look at those who are speaking, compare the art of language to other arts of expression, and try to see it as one of these mute arts. It is possible that the meaning of language has a decisive privilege, but it is in trying out the parallel that we will perceive what may in the end make that parallel impossible. Let us begin by understanding that there is a tacit language and that painting speaks in this way.

* * *

Malraux says that painting and language are comparable only when they are detached from what they "represent" and are brought together under the category of creative expression. It is then that they are both recognized as two forms of the same effort. Painters and writers worked for centuries without a suspicion of their relationship. But it is a fact that they experienced the same adventure. At first, art and poetry are consecrated to the city, the gods, and the sacred, and it is only in the mirror of an external power that they can see the birth of their own miracle. Later, both know a classic age which is the secularization of the sacred age; art is then the representation of a Nature that it can at best embellish—but according to formulas taught to it by Nature herself. As La Bruyère would have it, speech has no other role than finding the exact expression assigned in advance to each thought by a language of things themselves; and this double recourse to an art before art, to a speech before speech, prescribes to the work a certain point of perfection, completeness, or fullness which makes all men assent to it as they assent to the things which fall under their senses. Malraux has made a good analysis of this "objectivist" prejudice, which is challenged by modern art and literature. But perhaps he has not measured the depth to which the prejudice is rooted. Perhaps he has too swiftly abandoned the domain of the visible world. Perhaps it is this concession which has led him, contrary to what is to be seen, to define modern painting as a return to subjectivity—to the "incomparable monster"—and to bury it in a secret life outside the world. His analysis needs to be re-examined.

To begin with, oil painting seems to enjoy a special privilege. For more than any other kind of painting it permits us to attribute a distinct pictorial representative to each element of the object or of the human face and to look for signs which can give the illusion of depth or volume, of movement, of forms, of relative intensity of touch, or of different kinds of material. (Think of the patient studies which brought the representation of velvet to perfection.) These processes, these secrets augmented by each generation, seem to be elements of a general technique of *representation* which, at the limit, should reach the thing itself (or the man himself), which cannot be imagined capable of containing any element of chance or vagueness, and whose sovereign function painting should try to equal. Along this road one takes steps that cannot be retraced. The career of a painter, the productions of a school, and even the development of painting all go toward *masterpieces* in which what was sought after up until then is finally obtained; masterpieces which, at least provisorily, make the earlier attempts useless and stand out as landmarks of the progress of painting. Classical painting wants to be as convincing as things and does not think that it can reach us except as things do—by imposing an unimpeachable spectacle upon *our senses.* It relies in principle upon the perceptual apparatus, considered as a natural means and as a datum of communication between men. Don't we all have eyes, which function more or less in the same way? And if the painter has known how to discover the sufficient signs of depth or velvet, won't we all, in looking at the painting, see the same spectacle, which will rival that of Nature?

The fact remains that the classical painters were painters and that no valuable painting has ever consisted in simply representing. Malraux points out that the modern conception of painting as creative expression has been a novelty for the public much more than for the painters themselves, who have always practiced it, even if they did not construct the theory of it. That is why the works of the classical painters have a different meaning and perhaps more meaning than the painters themselves thought, why these works frequently anticipate a kind of painting that is free from their canons, and why they are still necessary mediators in any initiation to painting. At the very moment when, their eyes fixed upon the world, the classical painters thought they were asking it for the secret of a sufficient representation, they were unknowingly bringing about that *metamorphosis* which painting later became aware of. Consequently, classical painting cannot be defined by its representation of nature or by its reference to "our senses," nor modern painting by its reference to the subjective. The perception of classical painters already depended upon their culture, and our culture can still give form to our perception of the visible. It is not necessary to abandon the visible world to classical formulas or shut modern painting up in a recess of the individual. There is no choice to be made between the world and art or between "our senses" and absolute painting, for they pass into one another.

Sometimes Malraux speaks as if "sense data" had never varied throughout the centuries, and as if the classical perspective had been imperative whenever painting referred to sense data. Yet it is clear that the classical perspective is only one of the ways that man has invented for projecting the perceived world before him, and not the copy of that world. The classical perspective is an optional interpretation of spontaneous vision, not because the perceived world contradicts the laws of classical perspective and imposes others, but rather because it does not insist upon any one and is not of the order of laws. In free perception, objects spread out in depth do not have any definite "apparent size." We must not even say that the perspective "deceives us" and that the faraway objects are "bigger" for the naked eye than their projection in a drawing or a photograph would lead us to believe—at least not according to that size which is supposed to be a common measure of backgrounds and foregrounds. The size of the moon on the horizon cannot be measured by a certain number of aliquot parts of the coin that I hold in my hand; it is a question of a "size-at-a-distance," and of a kind of quality which adheres to the moon as heat and cold adhere to other objects. Here we are in the order of the "ultra-things" which H. Wallon [3] speaks about and which do not arrange themselves according to a single graduated perspective in relation to nearby objects. Once a certain size and distance have been passed, we encounter the absolute of size in which all the "ultra-things" meet; and that is why children say that the sun is as "big as a house."

If I want to come back from there to perspective, I must stop perceiving the whole freely. I must circumscribe my vision, mark (on a standard of measurement I hold) what I call the "apparent size" of the moon and of the coin, and, finally, transfer these measurements onto paper. But during this time the perceived world has disappeared along with the true simultaneity of objects, which is not their peaceful coexistence in a single scale of sizes. When I was seeing the coin and the moon together, my glance had to be fixed on one of them. Then the other one appeared to me in marginal vision—"little-object-seen-up-close" or "big-object-seen-far-away"—incommensurable with the first. What I transfer to paper is not this coexistence of perceived things as rivals in my field of vision. I find the means of arbitrating their conflict, which makes depth. I decide to make them co-possible on the same plane, and I succeed by coagulating a series of local and monocular sights, no one of which may be superimposed upon the elements of the living perceptual field. Once things disputed for my glance; and, anchored in one of them, I felt in it the solicitation of the others which made them coexist with the first—the demands of a horizon and its claim to exist. Now I construct a representation in which each thing ceases to call the whole of vision to itself, makes concessions to the other things, and no longer occupies on the paper any more than the space which they leave to it. Then my glance, running freely over

3. Henri Wallon, French professor of child psychology—until retirement at the Collège de France.—Trans.

depth, height, and width, was not subjected to any point of view, because it adopted them and rejected them in turn. Now I renounce that ubiquity and agree to let only that which could be seen from a certain reference point by an immobile eye fixed on a certain "vanishing point" of a certain "vanishing line" figure in my drawing. (A deceptive modesty, for if I renounce the world itself by precipitating the narrow perspective upon the paper, I also cease to see like a man, who is open to the world because he is situated in it. I think of and dominate my vision as God can when he considers his *idea* of me.) Then I had the experience of a world of teeming, exclusive things which could be taken in only by means of a temporal cycle in which each gain was at the same time a loss. Now the inexhaustible being crystallizes into an ordered perspective within which backgrounds resign themselves to being only backgrounds (inaccessible and vague as is proper), and objects in the foreground abandon something of their aggressiveness, order their interior lines according to the common law of the spectacle, and already prepare themselves to become backgrounds as soon as it is necessary. A perspective, in short, within which nothing holds my glance and takes the shape of a present.

The whole scene is in the mode of the completed or of eternity. Everything takes on an air of propriety and discretion. Things no longer call upon me to answer, and I am no longer compromised by them. And if I add the artifice of aerial perspective to this one, the extent to which I who paint and they who look at my landscape dominate the situation is readily felt. Perspective is much more than a secret technique for imitating a reality given as such to all men. It is the invention of a world which is dominated and possessed through and through in an instantaneous synthesis which is at best roughed out by our glance when it vainly tries to hold together all these things seeking individually to monopolize it. The faces of the classical portrait, always in the service of a character, a passion, or a love—always signifying—or the babies and animals of the classical painting, so desirous to enter the human world and so little anxious to reject it, manifest the same "adult" relation of man to the world, except when, giving in to his fortunate daemon, the great painter adds a new dimension to this world too sure of itself by making contingency vibrate within it.

Now if "objective" painting is itself a creation, the fact that modern painting seeks to be a creation no longer provides any reasons for interpreting it as a passage to the subjective and a ceremony glorifying the individual. And here Malraux' analysis seems to us to be on tenuous grounds. There is only one subject in today's painting, he says—the painter himself.[4] Painters no longer look for the velvet of peaches, as Chardin did, but, like Braque, for the velvet of the painting. The classical painters were unconsciously themselves; the modern painter wants first of all to be original, and for him his power of expression is identical to his individual difference.[5] *Because* painting is no longer for faith or beauty, it is for the individual; [6] it is "the annexation of the world by the individual." [7] The artist is thus supposed to be "in the tribe of the ambitious and the drugged," [8] and like them devoted to stubborn self-pleasure, to daemonic pleasure—that is, to the pleasure of all in man which destroys man.

It is clear, however, that it would be hard to apply these definitions to Cézanne or Klee, for example. There are two possible interpretations of that tolerance for the incomplete shown by those moderns who present sketches as paintings, and whose every canvas, as the signature of a moment of life, demands to be seen on "show" in a series of successive canvases. It may be that they have given up the *work,* and no longer look for anything but the immediate, perceived and individual—the "brute expression" as Malraux says. Or else, completion in the sense of a presentation that is objective and convincing for the *senses* may no longer be the means to or the sign of a work that is really *complete,* because henceforth expression must go from man to man across the common world they *live,* without passing through the anonymous realm of the *senses* or of Nature. Baudelaire wrote—in an expression very opportunely recalled by Malraux—"that a complete work was not necessarily finished, and a finished work not necessarily complete." [9] The accomplished work is thus not the work which exists in itself like a thing, but the work which reaches its viewer and invites him to take up the gesture which created it and, skipping the intermediaries, to rejoin, without any guide other than a movement of the invented line (an almost incorporeal trace), the silent world of the painter, henceforth uttered and accessible.

There is the improvisation of child prodigies who have not learned their own gesture and who believe, under the pretext that a painter is no more than a hand, that it suffices to have a hand in order to paint. They extract petty wonders from their body as a morose young man who observes his body with sufficient complacency can always find

4. *Le Musée imaginaire,* p. 59. These pages were already written when the definitive edition of the *Psychologie de l'Art* (*The Voices of Silence,* published by Gallimard) appeared. We quote from Skira's edition.

5. *Ibid.,* p. 79.

6. *Ibid.,* p. 83.

7. *La Monnaie de l'absolu,* p. 118.

8. *La Création esthétique,* p. 144.

9. *Le Musée imaginaire,* p. 63.

some little peculiarity in it to nourish his private religion. But there is also the improvisation of the artist who has turned toward the world that he wants to express and (each word calling for another) has finally composed for himself an acquired voice which is more his than the cry which gave birth to his search for expression. There is the improvisation of automatic writing and there is that of the *Charterhouse of Parma.* Since perception itself is never complete, since our perspectives give us a world to express and think about which envelops and exceeds those perspectives, a world which announces itself in lightning signs as a spoken word or as an arabesque, why should the expression of the world be subjected to the prose of the *senses* or of the concept? It must be poetry; that is, it must completely awaken and recall our sheer power of expressing beyond things already said or seen. Modern painting presents a problem completely different from that of the return to the individual: the problem of knowing how one can communicate without the help of a pre-established Nature which all men's senses open upon, the problem of knowing how we are grafted to the universal by that which is most our own.

This is one of the philosophies toward which Malraux' analysis may be extended. It just has to be detached from the philosophy of the individual or of death which, with it nostalgic inclination toward civilizations based upon the sacred, is at the forefront of his thought. The painter does not put his immediate self—the very nuance of feeling—into his painting. He puts his *style* there, and he has to master it as much in his own attempts as in the painting of others or in the world. How long it takes, Malraux says, before a writer learns to speak with his own voice. Similarly, how long it takes the painter—who does not, as we do, have his work spread out before him, but who creates it—to recognize in his first paintings the features of what will be his completed work, provided that he is not mistaken about himself.

Even more: he is no more capable of seeing his paintings than the writer is capable of reading his work. It is in others that expression takes on its relief and really becomes signification. For the writer or painter, there is only one's allusion to oneself in the familiarity of one's personal vibration, which is also called an inner monologue. The painter works and leaves his wake; and except when he amuses himself with earlier works by discovering what he has become, he does not like very much to look at his work. He has something better in his own possession; the language of his maturity eminently contains the feeble accent of his first works. Without turning toward them, and by the sole fact that they have fulfilled certain expressive operations, he finds himself endowed with new organs. And experiencing the excess of what is to be said over and beyond their already verified power, he is capable (unless, as it has more than once, a mysterious fatigue intervenes) of going "farther" in the same direction. It is as if each step taken called for another step and made it possible, or as if each successful expression prescribed another task to the spiritual automaton or founded an institution whose efficacy it will never stop experiencing.

This "inner schema" which is more and more imperious with each new painting—to the point that the famous chair becomes, Malraux says, "a brutal ideogram of the very name of Van Gogh"—is legible *for Van Gogh* neither in his first works, nor even in his "inner life" (for in this case Van Gogh would not need painting in order to be reconciled with himself again; he would stop painting). It is that life itself, to the extent that the life emerges from its inherence, ceases to be in possession of itself and becomes a universal means of understanding and of making something understood, of seeing and of presenting something to see—and is thus not shut up in the depths of the mute individual but diffused throughout all he sees. Before the style becomes an object of predilection for others and an object of delectation for the artist himself (to the great detriment of his work), there must have been that fecund moment when the style germinates at the surface of the artist's experience, and when an operant and latent meaning finds the emblems which are going to disengage it and make it manageable for the artist and at the same time accessible to others. Even when the painter has already painted, and even if he has become in some respects master of himself, what is given to him with his style is not a manner, a certain number of procedures or tics that he can inventory, but a mode of formulation that is just as recognizable for others and just as little visible to him as his silhouette or his everyday gestures.

Thus when Malraux writes that style is the "means of re-creating the world according to the values of the man who discovers it"; [10] or that it is "the expression of a meaning lent to the world, a call for and not a consequence of a way of seeing; [11] or finally, that it is "the reduction to a fragile human perspective of the eternal world which draws us along according to a mysterious rhythm into a drift of stars"; [12] he does not get inside the functioning of style itself. Like the public, he looks at it from the outside. He indicates some of its consequences, which are truly sensational ones—the victory of man over the world—but ones the painter has not seen in it. The painter at work knows nothing about the antithesis of man and the world, of signification and the absurd, of style and "representation." He is far too busy

10. *La Création esthétique*, p. 51.
11. *Ibid.*, p. 154.
12. *Ibid.*

expressing his communication with the world to become proud of a style which is born almost as if he were unaware of it. It is quite true that style for the moderns is much more than a means of representing. It does not have any external model; painting does not exist before painting. But we must not conclude from this, as Malraux does, that the representation of the world is only a *stylistic means* [13] for the painter, as if the style could be known and sought after outside all contact with the world, as if it were an *end*. We must see it appear in the context of the painter's perception as a painter; style is an exigency that has issued from that perception.

Malraux says so in his best passages: perception already stylizes. A woman passing by is not first and foremost a corporeal contour for me, a colored mannequin, or a spectacle; she is "an individual, sentimental, sexual expression." She is a certain manner of being flesh which is given entirely in her walk or even in the simple shock of her heel on the ground—as the tension of the bow is present in each fiber of wood—a very noticeable variation of the norm of walking, looking, touching, and speaking that I possess in my self-awareness because I am incarnate. If I am also a painter, what will be transmitted to the canvas will no longer be only a vital or sensual value. There will be in the painting not just "a woman" or "an unhappy woman" or "a hatmaker." There will also be the emblem of a way of inhabiting the world, of handling it, and of interpreting it by a face as by clothing, by agility of gesture as by inertia of body—in short, the emblem of a certain relationship to being.

But even though this truly pictorial style and meaning are not in the woman seen—for in that case the painting would be already completed—they are at least called for by her. "All style is that giving form to elements of the world which permits the orientation of these elements towards one of the essential parts of the form." There is signification when we submit the data of the world to a "coherent deformation." [14] That convergence of all the visible and intellectual vectors of the painting towards the same signification, X, is already sketched out in the painter's perception. It begins as soon as he perceives—that is, as soon as he arranges certain gaps or fissures, figures and grounds, a top and a bottom, a norm and a deviation in the inaccessible plenum of things. In other words, as soon as certain elements of the world take on the value of dimensions to which from then on we relate all the others and in whose *language* we express them. For each painter, style is the system of equivalences that he makes for himself for the work which manifests the world he sees. It is the universal index of the "coherent

13. *Ibid.*, p. 158.
14. *Ibid.*, p. 152.

deformation" by which he concentrates the still scattered meaning of his perception and makes it exist expressly. The work is not brought to fulfilment far from things and in some intimate laboratory to which the painter and the painter alone has the key. Whether he is looking at real flowers or paper flowers, he always goes back to *his* world, as if the principle of the equivalences by means of which he is going to manifest it had been buried there since the beginning of time.

Writers must not underestimate the painter's labor and study, that effort which is so like an effort of thought and which allows us to speak of a language of painting. It is true that, scarcely having drawn his system of equivalences from the world, the painter invests it again in colors and a quasi-space on a canvas. Some think that the painting does not so much *express* the meaning as the meaning impregnates the painting. "That yellow rent in the sky over Golgotha . . . is an anguish made thing, an anguish which has turned into a yellow rent in the sky, and which is immediately submerged and thickened by the qualities appropriate to things . . ." [15] More than being manifested by the painting, the meaning sinks into it and trembles around it "like a wave of heat." [16] It is "like an immense and futile effort, always arrested halfway between heaven and earth," to express what the nature of painting prevents it from expressing. For professional users of language, the preceding impression is perhaps inevitable. The same thing happens to them that happens to us when we hear a foreign language which we speak poorly; we find it monotonous and marked with an excessively heavy accent and flavor, precisely because we have not made it the principal instrument of our relations with the world. The meaning of the painting remains *captive* for those of us who do not communicate with the world through painting. But for the painter, and even for us if we set ourselves to living in the painting, the meaning is much more than a "wave of heat" at the surface of the canvas, since it is capable of demanding *that* color and *that* object in preference to all others, and since it commands the arrangement of a painting just as imperiously as a syntax or a logic. For not all the painting is in those little anguishes or local joys with which it is sown: they are only the components of a total meaning which is less moving, more *legible,* and more enduring.

Malraux is quite right to relate the anecdote of the innkeeper at Cassis who, seeing Renoir at work by the sea, comes up to him: "There were some naked women bathing in some other place. Goodness knows

15. Sartre, *Situations II,* p. 61.
16. *Ibid.,* p. 60.

what he was looking at, and he changed only a little corner." Malraux comments, "The blue of the sea had become that of the brook in *The Bathers*. His vision was less a way of looking at the sea than the secret elaboration of a world to which that depth of blue whose immensity he was recapturing pertained." [17] Nevertheless, Renoir was looking at the sea. And why did the blue of the sea pertain to the world of his painting? How was it able to teach him something about the brook in *The Bathers*? Because each fragment of the world—and in particular the sea, sometimes riddled with eddies and ripples and plumed with spray, sometimes massive and immobile in itself—contains all sorts of shapes of being and, by the way it has of joining the encounter with one's glance, evokes a series of possible variants and teaches, over and beyond itself, a general way of expressing being. Renoir can paint women bathing and a fresh water brook while he is by the sea at Cassis because he only asks the sea—which alone can teach what he asks—for its way of interpreting the liquid substance, of exhibiting it, and of arranging it. In short, because he only asks for a typical form of manifestations of water.

The painter can paint while he is looking at the world because it seems to him that he finds in appearances themselves the style which will define him in the eyes of others, and because he thinks he is spelling out nature at the moment he is recreating it. "A certain peremptory equilibrium or disequilibrium of colors and lines overwhelms the person who discovers that the half-opened door over there is that of another world." [18] *Another world*—by this we mean the same world that the painter sees and that speaks his own language, only freed from the nameless weight which held it back and kept it equivocal. How would the painter or poet express anything other than his encounter with the world? What does abstract art itself speak of, if not of a negation or refusal of the world? Now austerity and the obsession with geometrical surfaces and forms (or the obsession with infusoria and microbes; for the interdict put upon life, curiously enough, begins only with the Metazoon) still have an odor of life, even if it is a shameful or despairing life. Thus the painting always says something. It is a new system of equivalences which demands precisely this particular upheaval, and it is in the name of a *truer* relation between things that their ordinary ties are broken.

A vision or an action that is finally free throws out of focus and regroups objects of the world for the painter and words for the poet. But breaking or burning up language did not suffice to write the *Illuminations*, and Malraux profoundly remarks of modern painters that

17. *La Création esthétique*, p. 113.
18. *Ibid.*, p. 142.

"although no one of them spoke of truth, all, faced with the works of their adversaries, spoke of imposture." [19] They want nothing to do with a truth defined as the resemblance of painting and the world. They would accept the idea of a truth defined as a painting's cohesion with itself, the presence of a unique principle in it which affects each means of expression with a certain contextual value. Now when a stroke of the brush replaces a reorganization of appearances (in principle complete) which introduces us to wool or flesh, what replaces the object is not the subject—it is the allusive logic of the perceived world.

We always intend to signify something; there is always something we have to say that we succeed more or less in saying. It is just that Van Gogh's "going farther" at the moment he paints *The Crows* no longer indicates some reality one must go towards, but what still must be done in order to restore the encounter between his glance and the things which solicit it, the encounter between the man who has to be and what exists. And that relation is certainly not one of copying. "As always in art, one must lie to tell the truth," Sartre rightly says. It is said that the exact recording of a conversation which had seemed brilliant later gives the impression of indigence. The presence of those who were speaking, the gestures, the physiognomies, and the feeling of an event which is coming up and of a continuous improvisation, all are lacking in the recording. Henceforth the conversation no longer exists; it *is*, flattened out in the unique dimension of sound and all the more deceptive because this wholly auditory medium is that of a text read. In order to fill our mind as it does, the work of art—which often addresses itself to only one of our senses and never hems us in on all sides as our lived experience does—must thus be something other than frozen existence. It must be, as Gaston Bachelard [20] says, "superexistence." But it is not arbitrary or, as we say, fictional. Modern painting, like modern thought generally, obliges us to admit a truth which does not resemble things, which is without any external model and without any predestined instruments of expression, and which is nevertheless truth.

If we put the painter back in contact with his world, as we are trying to, perhaps the metamorphosis which through him transforms the world into painting, changes him into himself from his beginnings to his maturity, and, finally, gives certain works of the past a meaning in each generation that had not been perceived before will seem less enigmatic to us. When a writer considers painting and painters, he is a little in the position of readers in relation to the writer, or in that of the

19. *La Monnaie de l'absolu*, p. 125.

20. Gaston Bachelard, French philosopher, whose several works on the "psychoanalysis of the elements" had some influence on Merleau-Ponty and Sartre in the forties.—Trans.

man in love who thinks of the absent woman. Our conception of the writer begins with his work; the man in love sums up the absent woman in a few words and attitudes by which she expressed herself most purely. When he meets her again, he is tempted to repeat Stendhal's famous "What? Is this all?" When we make the writer's acquaintance, we feel foolishly disappointed at not finding, in each moment of his presence, that essence and impeccable speech that we have become accustomed to designating by his name. So that's what he does with his time? So that's the ugly house he lives in? And these are his friends, the woman with whom he shares his life? These, his mediocre concerns? But all this is only reverie—or even envy and secret hate. One admires as one should only after having understood that there are not any supermen, that there is no man who does not have a man's life to live, and that the secret of the woman loved, of the writer, or of the painter, does not lie in some realm beyond his empirical life, but is so mixed in with his mediocre experiences, so modestly confused with his perception of the world, that there can be no question of meeting it face to face apart from his life.

In reading the *Psychologie de l'Art,* we sometimes get the impression that Malraux, who certainly knows all this as a writer, forgets it where painters are concerned and dedicates the same kind of cult to them which we believe he would not accept from his readers. In short, he makes painters divine. "What genius is not fascinated by that extremity of painting, by that appeal before which time itself vacillates? It is the moment of possession of the world. Let painting go no further, and Hals the Elder becomes God." [21] This is perhaps the painter seen by others. The painter himself is a man at work who each morning finds in the shape of things the same questioning and the same call he never stops responding to. In his eyes, his work is never completed; it is always in progress, so that no one can prevail against the world. Sometimes, life escapes; the body is written off. At other times, and more sadly, it is the question spread out through the world's spectacle which is no longer heard. Then the painter is no more, or he has become an honorary painter. But as long as he paints, his painting concerns visible things. Or if he has become blind, it concerns that unimpeachable world which he has access to through his other senses and which he speaks of in terms of a man who sees. And that is why his labor, which is obscure for him, is nevertheless guided and oriented. It is always only a question of advancing the line of the already opened furrow and of recapturing and generalizing an accent which has already appeared in the corner of a previous painting or in some instant of his experience, without the painter himself ever being able to say

21. *La Création esthétique,* p. 150.

(since the distinction has no meaning) what comes from him and what comes from things, what the new work adds to the old ones, or what it has taken from the others and what is its own.

This triple resumption which makes a sort of provisory eternity of the operation of expression is not simply a metamorphosis in the fairytale sense of miracle, magic, and absolute creation in an aggressive solitude. It is also a response to what the world, the past, and the completed works demanded. It is accomplishment and brotherhood. Husserl has used the fine word *Stiftung*—foundation or establishment—to designate first of all the unlimited fecundity of each present which, precisely because it is singular and passes, can never stop having been and thus being universally; but above all to designate that fecundity of the products of a culture which continue to have value after their appearance and which open a field of investigations in which they perpetually come to life again. It is thus that the world as soon as he has seen it, his first attempts at painting, and the whole past of painting all deliver up a *tradition* to the painter—*that is,* Husserl remarks, *the power to forget origins* and to give to the past not a survival, which is the hypocritical form of forgetfulness, but a new life, which is the noble form of memory.

Malraux emphasizes the deceptive and derisory in the comedy of mind. Those rival contemporaries, Delacroix and Ingres, whom posterity recognizes as twins. Those painters who want to be classic and are only neo-classical, that is, the contrary. And those styles which escape the view of the creator and become visible only when the Museum gathers together works scattered about the earth and photography enlarges miniatures, transforms a section of a painting by its way of framing it, changes rugs, coins, and stained glass windows into paintings, and brings to painting a consciousness of itself which is always retrospective. But if expression recreates and transforms, the same was already true of times preceding ours and even of our perception of the world before painting, since that perception already marked things with the trace of human elaboration. The productions of the past, which are the data of our time, themselves once went beyond anterior productions towards a future which we are, and in this sense called for (among others) the metamorphosis which we impose upon them. One can no more inventory a painting (say what is there and what is not) than, according to the linguists, one can inventory a vocabulary—and for the same reason. In both cases it is not a question of a finite sum of signs, but of an open field or of a new organ of human culture.

We cannot deny that in painting such and such a fragment of a painting, that classical painter had already invented the very gesture of this modern. But we must not forget that he did not make it the principle of his painting and that in this sense he did not invent it, as St. Augustine did not invent the Cogito as a central thought but merely encountered it. And yet what Aron [22] called each age's dreamlike quest for ancestors is possible only because all ages pertain to the same universe. The classical and the modern pertain to the universe of conceived painting as a single task stretching from the first sketches on the walls of caves up to our "conscious" painting. No doubt one reason why our painting finds something to recapture in arts which are linked to an experience very different from our own is that it transfigures them. But it also does so because they transfigure it, because they at least have something to say to it, and because their artists, believing that they were continuing primitive terrors or those of Asia and Egypt, secretly inaugurated another history which is still ours and which makes them present to us, while the empires and beliefs to which they thought they *pertained* have disappeared long ago.

The unity of painting does not exist in the Museum alone; it exists in that single task which all painters are confronted with and which makes the situation such that one day they *will be* comparable in the Museum, and such that these fires answer one another in the night. The first sketches on the walls of caves set forth the world as "to be painted" or "to be sketched" and called for an indefinite future of painting, so that they speak to us and we answer them by metamorphoses in which they collaborate with us. There are thus two historicities. One is ironic or even derisory, and made of misinterpretations, for each age struggles against the others as against aliens by imposing its concerns and perspectives upon them. This history is forgetfulness rather than memory; it is dismemberment, ignorance, externality. But the other history, without which the first would be impossible, is constituted and reconstituted step by step by the *interest* which bears us toward that which is not us and by that life which the past, in a continuous exchange, brings to us and finds in us, and which it continues to lead in each painter who revives, recaptures, and renews the entire undertaking of painting in each new work.

Malraux often subordinates this cumulative history, in which paintings join each other by what they affirm, to cruel history, in which paintings oppose each other because they deny. For him, reconciliation takes place only in death, and it is always in retrospect that one perceives the single problem to which rival paintings are responding

22. Raymond Aron, French political philosopher, perhaps best known in the United States for his *The Century of Total War*, but also one of the first to make German phenomenology known in France.—Trans.

and which makes them contemporaneous. But if the problem were really not already present and operative in the painters—if not at the center of their consciousness, at least at the horizon of their labors—what could the Museum of the future derive it from? What Valéry said of the priest applies pretty well to the painter: he leads a double life, and half of his bread is consecrated. He is indeed that irascible and suffering man for whom all other painting is a rival. But his angers and hatreds are the waste-product of a work. Wherever he goes, this poor wretch enslaved by his jealousy brings along an invisible double who is free from his obsessions—his self as he is defined by his painting—and he can easily recognize the filiations or kinships manifested by what Péguy called his "historical inscription" if only he consents not to take himself for God and not to venerate each gesture of his brush as unique.

Malraux shows perfectly that what makes "a Vermeer" for us is not the fact that this canvas which one day was painted has come from Vermeer the man. It is the fact that the painting observes the system of equivalences according to which each of its elements, like a hundred pointers on a hundred dials, marks the same deviation—the fact that it speaks the language of Vermeer. And if the counterfeiter succeeded in recapturing not only the processes but the very style of the great Vermeers, he would no longer be a counterfeiter; he would be one of those painters who painted for the Old Masters in their studios. It is true that such counterfeiting is impossible: one cannot spontaneously paint like Vermeer after centuries of other painting have gone by and the meaning of the problem of painting itself has changed. But the fact that a painting has been copied in secret by one of our contemporaries qualifies him as a counterfeiter only to the extent that it prevents him from truly reproducing the style of Vermeer.

The fact is that the name of Vermeer and of each great painter comes to stand for something like an institution. And just as the business of history is to discover, behind "Parliament under the *ancien régime*" or "the French Revolution," what they really signify in the dynamics of human relations and what modulation of these relations they represent; and as it must designate this as accessory and that as essential in order to accomplish its task; so a true history of painting must seek beyond the immediate aspect of the canvases attributed to Vermeer for a structure, a style, and a meaning against which the discordant details (if there are any) that fatigue, circumstance, or self-imitation has torn from his brush cannot prevail. The history of painting can judge the authenticity of a canvas only by examining the painting, not simply because we lack information concerning origins, but also because the complete catalogue of the work of a master does not suffice to tell us what is really *his,* because he himself is a certain speech in the discourse of painting which awakens echoes from the past and future to the exact degree that it does not look for them, and because he is linked to all other attempts to the exact degree that he busies himself resolutely with his world. Retrospection may well be indispensable for this true history to emerge from empirical history, which is attentive only to events and remains blind to advents, but it is traced out to begin with in the total will of the painter. History looks toward the past only because the painter first looked toward the work to come; there is a fraternity of painters in death only because they live the same problem.

In this respect the Museum's function, like the Library's, is not entirely beneficent. It certainly enables us to see dead productions scattered about the world and engulfed in cults or civilizations they sought to ornament as unified aspects of a single effort. In this sense our consciousness of painting as painting is based upon the Museum. But painting exists first of all in each painter who works, and it is there in a pure state, whereas the Museum compromises it with the somber pleasures of retrospection. One should go to the Museum as the painters go there, in the sober joy of work; and not as we go there, with a somewhat spurious reverence. The Museum gives us a thieves' conscience. We occasionally sense that these works were not after all intended to *end up* between these morose walls, for the pleasure of Sunday strollers or Monday "intellectuals." We are well aware that something has been lost and that this self-communion with the dead [recueillement de nécropole] is not the true *milieu* of art—that so many joys and sorrows, so much anger, and so many labors were not *destined* to reflect one day the Museum's mournful light.

By transforming efforts into "works," the Museum makes a history of painting possible. But perhaps it is essential to men to attain greatness in their works only when they do not look for it too hard. Perhaps it is not bad that the painter and the writer do not clearly realize that they are establishing a human community. Perhaps, finally, they have a truer and more vital feeling for the history of art when they carry it on in their work than when they make "art lovers" of themselves in order to contemplate it in the Museum. The Museum adds a false prestige to the true value of the works by detaching them from the chance circumstances they arose from and making us believe that the artist's hand was guided from the start by fate. Whereas the style of each painter throbbed in his life like his heart beat, and was just what enabled him to recognize every effort which differed from his own, the Museum converts this secret, modest, non-deliberated, involuntary, and, in short, living historicity into official and pompous history.

The imminence of a regression gives our liking for such and such a painter a nuance of pathos which was quite foreign to him. He *labored* the whole lifetime of a man; we see his work like flowers on the brink of a precipice. The Museum makes the painters as mysterious for us as octopi or lobsters. It transforms these works created in the fever of a life into marvels from another world, and in its pensive atmosphere and under its protective glass, the breath which sustained them is no more than a feeble flutter on their surface. The Museum kills the vehemence of painting as the Library, Sartre said, changes writings which were originally a man's gestures into "messages." It is the historicity of death. And there is a historicity of life of which the Museum provides no more than a fallen image. This is the historicity which lives in the painter at work when with a single gesture he links the tradition that he recaptures and the tradition that he founds. It is the historicity which in one stroke welds him to all which has ever been painted in the world, without his having to leave his place, his time, or his blessed or accursed labor. The historicity of life reconciles paintings insofar as each one expresses the whole of existence—insofar as they are all successful—instead of reconciling them insofar as they are all finished and like so many futile gestures.

If we put painting back into the present, we shall see that it does not admit the barriers between the painter and others, and between the painter and his own life, that our purism would like to multiply. Even if the innkeeper at Cassis does not understand Renoir's transmutation of the blue of the Mediterranean into the water of *The Bathers*, it is still true that he wanted to see Renoir work. That *interests* him too—and after all, nothing stops him from discovering the path that the cave dwellers one day opened without tradition. Renoir would have been quite wrong to ask his advice and try to please him. In this sense, he was not painting for the innkeeper. By his painting, he himself defined the conditions under which he intended to be approved. But he did paint; he questioned the visible and made something visible. It was the world, the water of the sea, that he asked to reveal the secret of the water of *The Bathers;* and he opened the passage from one to the other for those who were caught up in the world with him. As Vuillemin[23] says, there was no question of speaking their language, but of expressing them in expressing himself.

And the painter's relation to his own life is of the same order: his style is not the style of his life, but he draws his life toward expression too. It is understandable that Malraux does not like psychoanalytic *explanations* in painting. Even if St. Anne's cloak is a vulture, even if

23. Jules Vuillemin. French philosopher of science, successor to Merleau-Ponty in the chair of philosophy at the Collège de France.—Trans.

one admitted that while da Vinci painted it as a cloak, a second da Vinci in da Vinci, head tilted to one side, deciphered it as a vulture like a reader of riddles (after all, it is not impossible: in the life of da Vinci there is a frightening taste for mystification which could very well inspire him to enshrine his monsters themselves, and precisely in a work of art), no one would speak about this vulture any more if the painting did not have another meaning. The explanation only accounts for the details; at most for the materials. Admitting that the painter likes to handle colors (the sculptor, clay) because he is an "anal erotic," this does not always tell us what it is to paint or sculpt.[24] But the contrary attitude, the artists' devotion which forbids us to know anything about their life and places their work beyond private or public history and outside the world like a miracle, hides their true greatness from us. The reason why Leonardo is something other than one of the innumerable victims of an unhappy childhood is not that he has one foot in the great beyond, but that he succeeded in making a means of interpreting the world out of everything he lived—it is not that he did not have a body or sight, but that he constituted his corporeal or vital situation in language.

When one goes from the order of events to the order of expression, one does not change the world; the same circumstances which were previously submitted to now become a signifying system. Hollowed out, worked from within, and finally freed from that weight upon us which makes them painful or wounding, they become transparent or even luminous, and capable of clarifying not only the aspects of the world which resemble them but the others too; yet transformed as they may be, they still do not cease to exist. The knowledge of them we may gain will never replace our experience of the work itself. But it helps measure the creation and it teaches us about that immediate surpassing of one's situation which is the only irrevocable surpassing. If we take the painter's point of view in order to be present at that decisive moment when what has been given to him to live as corporeal destiny, personal adventures or historical events crystallizes into "the motive," we will recognize that his work, which is never an effect, is always a response to these data, and that the body, the life, the landscapes, the schools, the mistresses, the creditors, the police, and the revolutions which might suffocate painting are also the bread his work consecrates. To live in painting is still to breathe the air of this world—above all for the man who sees something in the world to paint. And there is a little of him in every man.

24. Besides, Freud never said that he explained da Vinci by the vulture; he said in effect that analysis stops where painting begins.

* * *

To get to the bottom of the problem. Malraux meditates upon miniatures and coins in which photographic enlargement miraculously reveals the very same style that is found in full-sized works; or upon works uncovered beyond the limits of Europe, far from all "influences," in which moderns are astonished to find the same style which a conscious painter has reinvented somewhere else. If one shuts art up in the most secret recess of the individual, he can explain the convergence of separate works only by invoking some destiny which rules over them. ". . . As if an imaginary spirit of art pushed forward from miniature to painting and from fresco to stained-glass window in a single conquest which it suddenly abandoned for another, parallel or suddenly opposed, as if a subterranean torrent of history unified all these scattered works by dragging them along with it, . . . a style known in its evolution and metamorphoses becomes less an idea than the illusion of a living fatality. Reproduction, and reproduction alone, has brought into art those imaginary superartists who have an indistinct birth, a life with its conquests and concessions to the taste for wealth or seduction, and a death-agony and resurrection—and who are called styles." [25] Thus Malraux meets, at least metaphorically, the idea of a History which reunites the most scattered efforts, of a painting which works behind the painter's back, and of a Reason in history of which he is the instrument. These Hegelian monstrosities are the antithesis and complement of Malraux's individualism. What do they become when the theory of perception makes the painter dwell once more in the visible world and once more lays bare the body as spontaneous expression?

Let us begin with the simplest fact (which we have already clarified in part). The magnifying glass reveals the very same style in a medallion or miniature as the one found in full-sized works because one's hand has its own ubiquitous style, which is undivided in one's gesture and does not need to lean heavily upon each point of the tracing in order to mark the material with its stripe. Our handwriting is recognized whether we trace letters on paper with three fingers of our hand or in chalk on the blackboard at arm's length; for it is not a purely mechanical movement of our body which is tied to certain muscles and destined to accomplish certain materially defined movements, but a general motor power of formulation capable of the transpositions which constitute the constancy of style.

Or rather, there is not even any transposition; we simply do not write in space "in itself" with a thing-hand and a thing-body for which

25. *Le Musée imaginaire*, p. 52.

each new situation presents new problems. We write in perceived space, where results with the same form are immediately analogous—if we ignore differences of scale—just as the same melody played at different pitches is immediately identified. And the hand with which we write is a phenomenon-hand which possesses, in the formula of a movement, something like the effectual law of the particular cases in which it may have to realize itself. The whole marvel of a style already present in the invisible elements of a work thus comes down to the fact that, working in the human world of perceived things, the artist comes to put his stamp upon even the inhuman world revealed by optical instruments—just as the swimmer unknowingly skims over a whole buried universe which would frighten him if he looked at it with undersea goggles; or as Achilles, in the simplicity of one step, effects an infinite summation of spaces and instants.

There is no doubt that this marvel, whose strangeness the word *man* should not hide from us, is a very great one. But we can at least recognize that this miracle is natural to us, that it begins with our incarnate life, and that there is no reason to look for its explanation in some Spirit of the World which allegedly operates within us without our knowledge and perceives in our place, beyond the perceived world, on a microscopic scale. Here, the spirit of the world is ourselves, as soon as we know how to *move ourselves* and *look*. These simple acts already enclose the secret of expressive action. As the artist makes his style radiate into the very fibers of the material he is working on, I move my body without even knowing which muscles and nerve paths should intervene, nor where I must look for the instruments of that action. I want to go over there, and here I am, without having entered into the inhuman secret of the bodily mechanism or having adjusted that mechanism to the givens of the problem. For example: without having adjusted the bodily mechanism to the position of a goal defined by its relation to some system of coordinates, I look at the goal, I am drawn by it, and the bodily apparatus does what must be done in order for me to be there. For me, everything happens in the human world of perception and gesture, but my "geographical" or "physical" body submits to the demands of this little drama which does not cease to arouse a thousand natural marvels in it.

Just my glance toward the goal already has its own miracles. It too takes up its dwelling in being with authority and conducts itself there as in a conquered country. It is not the object which obtains movements of accommodation and convergence from my eyes. It has been shown that on the contrary I would never see anything clearly, and there would be no object for me, if I did not use my eyes in such a way as to make a view of a single object possible. And it is not the mind which takes the place of the body and anticipates what we are going to see. No; it is my glances themselves—their synergy, their exploration, and their prospecting—which bring the imminent object into focus; and our corrections would never be rapid and precise enough if they had to be based upon an actual calculation of effects.

We must therefore recognize that what is designated by the terms "glance," "hand," and in general "body" is a system of systems devoted to the inspection of a world and capable of leaping over distances, piercing the perceptual future, and outlining hollows and reliefs, distances and deviations—a meaning—in the inconceivable flatness of being. The movement of the artist tracing his arabesque in infinite matter amplifies, but also prolongs, the simple marvel of oriented locomotion or grasping movements. Already in its pointing gestures the body not only flows over into a world whose schema it bears in itself but possesses this world at a distance rather than being possessed by it. So much the more does the gesture of expression, which undertakes through expression to delineate what it intends and make it appear "outside," retrieve the world. But already with our first oriented gesture, *someone's* infinite relationships to his situation had invaded our mediocre planet and opened an inexhaustible field to our behavior. All perception, all action which presupposes it, and in short every human use of the body is already *primordial expression.* Not that derivative labor which substitutes for what is expressed signs which are given elsewhere with their meaning and rule of usage, but the primary operation which first constitutes signs as signs, makes that which is expressed dwell in them through the eloquence of their arrangement and configuration alone, implants a meaning in that which did not have one, and thus—far from exhausting itself in the instant at which it occurs—inaugurates an order and founds an institution or a tradition.

Now if the presence of style in miniatures which no one had ever seen (*and in a sense no one had ever made*) is one with the fact of our corporeality and does not call for any occult explanation, it seems to us that one can say as much of the singular convergences which, outside all influences, make works which *resemble one another* appear from one end of the world to another. We ask for a cause which explains these resemblances, and we speak of a Reason in history or of Super-artists who guide artists. But to begin with, to speak of resemblances is to put the problem badly. Resemblances are, after all, of little importance in respect to the innumerable differences and varieties of cultures. The probability, no matter how slight, of a reinvention without guide or model suffices to account for these exceptional recurrences. The true problem is to understand why such different cultures become involved in the same search and have the same task in view (and when the opportunity arises, encounter the same modes of expression). We must understand why what one culture produces has meaning for another culture, even if it is not its original meaning; why we take the trouble to transform fetishes into art. In short, the true problem is to understand why there is *a* history or *a* universe of painting.

But this is a problem only if we have begun by placing ourselves in the geographical or physical world, and by placing works of art there as so many separate events whose resemblance or mere connection then becomes improbable and calls for an explanatory principle. We propose on the contrary to consider the order of culture or meaning an original order of *advent*,[26] which should not be derived from that of mere events, if they exist, or treated as simply the effect of extraordinary conjunctions. If it is characteristic of the human gesture to signify beyond its simple existence in fact, to inaugurate a meaning, it follows that every gesture is *comparable* to every other. They all arise from a single syntax. Each is both a beginning and a continuation which, insofar as it is not walled up in its singularity and finished once and for all like an event, points to a continuation or recommencements. Its value exceeds its simple presence, and in this respect it is allied or accompliced in advance to all other efforts of expression.

The difficult and essential point here is to understand that in positing a field distinct from the empirical order of events, we are not positing a Spirit of Painting which is already in possession of itself on the other side of the world that it is gradually manifested in. There is not, above and beyond the causality of events, a second causality which makes the world of painting a "suprasensible world" with its own laws. Cultural creation is ineffectual if it does not find a vehicle in external circumstances. But if circumstances lend themselves in the least to creation, a preserved and transmitted painting develops a suggestive power in its inheritors which is without proportion to what it is—not only as a bit of painted canvas, but even as a work endowed by its creator with a definite signification. This significance which the work has in excess of the painter's deliberate intentions involves it in a multitude of relationships which are only faintly reflected in short histories of painting and even in psychological studies of the painter, just as the body's gesture toward the world introduces it into an order of relations that pure physiology and biology do not have the slightest idea of. Despite the diversity of its parts, which makes it fragile and vulnerable, the body is capable of gathering itself into a gesture which for a time dominates their dispersion and puts its stamp upon every-

26. The expression is Paul Ricoeur's. (Paul Ricoeur, younger and extremely versatile contemporary of Merleau-Ponty and perhaps the leading phenomenologist in France, has probably done as much as any other man to make phenomenology known there and in the United States.—Trans.)

thing it does. In the same way, we may speak of a unity of human style which transcends spatial and temporal distances to bring the gestures of all painters together in one single effort to express, and their works in a single cumulative history—a single art. The enveloping movement which the unity of culture extends beyond the limits of the individual life is of the same type as that which unites all the moments of the individual life itself in advance at the moment of its institution or birth, when a consciousness is, as we say, sealed up into a body and a new being appears in the world. We do not know what will come to pass in this new life. We only know that from now on something cannot fail to come to pass, even if it is only the end of this life which has barely begun.

Analytic thought interrupts the perceptual transition from one moment to another, and then seeks in the mind the guarantee of a unity which is already there when we perceive. Analytic thought also interrupts the unity of culture and then tries to reconstitute it from the outside. After all, it says, there are only the works themselves—which in themselves are a dead letter—and the individuals who freely give them a meaning. How is it then that works resemble one another and that individuals understand one another? It is then that the Spirit of Painting is introduced. But just as we must recognize the existential spanning of diversity, and in particular the bodily possession of space, as a fundamental fact; and just as our body, insofar as it *lives* and makes itself gesture, sustains itself only through its effort to be in the world, holds itself upright because its inclination is towards the top and because its perceptual fields draw it towards that risky position, and could not possibly receive this power from a separate spirit; so the history of painting, which runs from one work to another, rests upon itself and is borne only by the caryatid of our efforts, which converge by the sole fact that they are efforts to express.

The intrinsic order of meaning is not eternal. Although it does not follow each zigzag of empirical history, it sketches out, it calls for, a series of successive steps. For it is not (as we stated provisionally) defined simply by the family relationship which all of its moments bear to one another within a single task. Precisely because these moments are all moments of painting, each one of them (if it is preserved and transmitted) modifies the situation of the undertaking and requires precisely that those which come after it be different from it. Two cultural gestures may be identical only if they are unaware of one another. It is thus essential to art to develop; that is, both to change and, in Hegel's words, to "return to itself," and thus to present itself as history. The meaning of the expressive gesture upon which we have based the unity of painting is in principle a meaning in genesis.

Advent is a promise of events. The domination of the many by the one in the history of painting, like that domination which we have encountered in the use of the perceiving body, does not consummate succession in an eternity. On the contrary, it insists upon succession; it needs it at the same time that it establishes its signification. And there is not simply a question of an *analogy* between the two problems; it is the expressive operation of the body, begun by the smallest perception, which is amplified into painting and art. The first sketch on the walls of caves founded one tradition only because it was gleaned from another—the tradition of perception. The quasi-eternity of art is of a piece with the quasi-eternity of incarnate existence; and in the use of our body and our senses, insofar as they involve us in the world, we have the means of understanding our cultural gesticulation insofar as it involves us in history. The linguists sometimes say that since there is strictly no means of marking the date in history when, for example, Latin ends and French begins, there is only one single language and almost only one single tongue unceasingly at work. Let us say more generally that the continued attempt at expression founds one single history, as the hold our body has upon every possible object founds one single space.

Thus understood, history would escape—here we can only indicate how—the confused discussions it is the object of today and become once more what it should be for the philosopher: the center of his reflections. Not, certainly, as a *"nature simple,"* absolutely clear in itself, but on the contrary as the place of all our questionings and wonderments. Whether it be to worship it or to hate it, we conceive of history and the dialectic of history today as an external Power. Consequently, we are forced to choose between this power and ourselves. To choose history means to devote ourselves body and soul to the advent of a future man not even outlined in our present life. For the sake of that future, we are asked to renounce all judgment upon the means of attaining it; and for efficaciousness' sake, all judgment of value and all "self-consent to ourselves." This history-idol secularizes a rudimentary conception of God, and it is not by accident that contemporary discussions return so willingly to a parallel between what is called the "horizontal transcendence" of history and the "vertical transcendence" of God.

The fact is that we doubly misstate the problem when we draw such a parallel. The finest encyclicals in the world are powerless against the fact that for at least twenty centuries Europe and a good part of the world have renounced so-called vertical transcendence. And it is a little too much to forget that Christianity is, among other things, the recognition of a mystery in the relations of man and God, which stems precisely from the fact that the Christian God wants nothing to do with a vertical relation of subordination. He is not simply a principle of which we are the consequence, a will whose instruments we are, or even a model of which human values are only the reflection. There is a sort of impotence of God without us, and Christ attests that God would not be fully God without becoming fully man. Claudel goes so far as to say that God is not above but beneath us—meaning that we do not find Him as a suprasensible idea, but as another ourself which dwells in and authenticates our darkness. Transcendence no longer hangs over man: he becomes, strangely, its privileged bearer.

Furthermore, no philosophy of history has ever carried all the substance of the present over into the future or *destroyed* the self to make room for the other person. Such a neurotic attitude toward the future would be exactly non-philosophy, the deliberate refusal to know what one believes in. No philosophy has ever consisted in choosing between transcendences—for example between that of God and that of a human future. They have all been concerned with mediating them (with understanding, for example, how God makes himself man or how man makes himself God) and with elucidating that strange enveloping movement which makes the choice of means already a choice of ends and the self become world cultural history, but which makes the culture decline at the same time it does. According to Hegel, as is endlessly repeated, all that is real is rational, and thus justified—but justified sometimes as a true acquisition, sometimes as a pause, and sometimes as an ebbing withdrawal for a new surge. In short, all is justified relatively as a moment in total history on condition that this history be made, and thus in the sense that our errors themselves are said to carry weight and that our progress is our mistakes understood—which does not erase the difference between growth and decline, birth and death, regression and progress.

It is true that in Hegel's works the theory of the state and the theory of war seem to reserve judgment of historical works for the absolute knowledge of the philosopher and take it away from all other men. This is not a reason for forgetting that even in the *Philosophy of Right* Hegel rejects judging action by its results alone as well as judging it by its intention alone. "The principle of not taking consequences into account in action, and that other of judging actions according to what follows from them and of taking these consequences as the measure of what is just and good, both pertain to abstract understanding." [27] The twin abstractions which Hegel wishes to avoid are lives so separated that one can limit the responsibilities of each to the deliberate and necessary

27. *Principles of the Philosophy of Right*, para. 118.

consequences of what it has dreamed of, and a History which is one of equally unmerited failures and successes, and which consequently brands men glorious or infamous in terms of the external accidents which have come to deface or embellish what they have done. What he has in mind is the moment when the internal becomes external, that turning or veering by which we merge with others and the world as the world and others merge with us. In other words, action.

By action, I make myself responsible for everything; I accept the aid of external accidents just as I accept their betrayals—"the transformation of necessity into contingence and vice versa." [28] I claim to be master not only of my intentions, but also of what events are going to make of them. I take the world and others as they are. I take myself as I am and I answer for all. *"To act is . . . to deliver oneself up to this law."* [29] Action makes the event its own to such an extent that the botched crime is punished more lightly than the successful one, and Oedipus thinks of himself as a parricide and an incestuous person, even though he is so in fact only.

Confronted with the folly of action, which assumes responsibility for the course of events, one may be tempted to conclude with equal justice that there are only the guilty—since to act or even to live is already to accept the risk of infamy along with the chance for glory—and that there are only the innocent—since nothing, not even crime, has been willed *ex nihilo,* no one having chosen to be born. But beyond these philosophies of the internal and the external before which all is equivalent, what Hegel suggests (since when all is said and done there is a difference between the valuable and the non-valuable, and between what we accept and what we refuse) is a judgment of the attempt, of the undertaking, or of the *work.* Not a judgment of the intention or the consequences only, but of the use which we have made of our good will, and of the way in which we have evaluated the factual situation. A man is judged by neither intention nor fact but by his success in making values become facts.

When this happens, the meaning of the action does not exhaust itself in the situation which has occasioned it, or in some vague judgment of value; the action remains as an exemplary type and will survive in other situations in another form. It opens a field. Sometimes it even institutes a world. In any case it outlines a future. History according to Hegel is this maturation of a future in the present, not the sacrifice of the present to an unknown future; and the rule of action for him is not to be efficient at any cost, but to be first of all fecund.

The polemics against "horizontal transcendence" in the name of

28. *Ibid.*
29. *Ibid.*

"vertical transcendence" (admitted or simply regretted) are thus no less unjust toward Hegel than toward Christianity. And by throwing overboard along with history not only what they consider a blood-smeared idol but also the duty of carrying principles over into events, they have the inconvenience of reintroducing a false simplicity which is no remedy for the abuses of the dialectic. Today as always one another's accomplice, both the pessimism of the neo-Marxists and the laziness of non-Marxist thought present the dialectic—within and without us—as a power of lying and failure, a transformation of good into evil, and an inevitable deception. According to Hegel, this is only one side of the dialectic. It is also something like a grace in events which draws us away from evil toward the good, and which, for example, throws us toward the universal when we think we are pursuing only our own interest. The dialectic is, Hegel said approximately, *a movement which itself creates its course and returns to itself*—and thus a movement which has no other guide but its own initiative and which nevertheless does not escape outside itself but cuts across itself again and confirms itself at long intervals.

So the Hegelian dialectic is what we call by another name the phenomenon of expression, which gathers itself up and launches itself again through the mystery of rationality. And we would undoubtedly recover the concept of history in the true sense of the term if we were to get used to modeling it after the example of the arts and language. For the fact that each expression is closely connected within one single order to every other expression brings about the junction of the individual and the universal. The central fact to which the Hegelian dialectic returns in a hundred ways is that we do not have to choose between the *pour soi* and the *pour autrui,* between thought according to us and according to others, but that at the moment of expression the other to whom I address myself and I who express myself are incontestably linked together. The others such as they are (or will be) are not the sole judges of what I do. If I wanted to deny myself for their benefit, I would deny them too as "Selves." They are worth exactly what I am worth, and all the powers I give them I give simultaneously to myself. I submit myself to the judgment of another *who is himself worthy of that which I have attempted,* that is to say, in the last analysis, to the judgment of a peer whom I myself have chosen.

History is the judge—not history as the Power of a moment or of a century, but history as the inscription and accumulation, beyond the limits of countries and epochs, of what (account taken of situations) we have done and said that is most true and valuable. Others will judge what I have done, because I painted in the realm of the visible and spoke for those who have ears; but neither art nor politics consists in pleasing or flattering them. What they expect of the artist or of the politician is that he draw them toward values in which they will only later recognize their values. The painter or the politician moulds others much more often than he follows them. The public he aims at is not given; it is precisely the one which his works will elicit. The others he thinks of are not empirical "others," defined by what they expect of him at this moment. He thinks even less of *humanity* conceived of as a species which possesses "human dignity" or "the honor of being a man" as other species have a carapace or an air-bladder. No, his concern is with others become such that he is able to live with them. The history that the writer participates in (and the less he thinks about "making history"—about making his mark in the history of letters—and honestly produces *his* work, the more he will participate) is not a power before which he must bend his knee. It is the perpetual conversation carried on between all spoken words and all valid actions, each in turn contesting and confirming the other, and each recreating all the others. The appeal to the judgment of history is not an appeal to the complacency of the public (and even less, it must be said, an appeal to the secular arm). It is inseparable from the inner certainty of having said what waited to be said in the particular situation and what consequently could not fail to be understood by X. "I shall be read in one hundred years," Stendhal thinks. This means that he wants to be read, but also that he is willing to wait a century, and that his freedom invites a world as yet in limbo to become as free as he is by recognizing as acquired what he has had to invent.

This unvarnished appeal to history is an invocation of truth, which is never created by what is inscribed in history, but which, insofar as it is truth, requires that inscription. It dwells not only in literature or art but also in every undertaking of life. Except perhaps in the case of some wretched men who think only of winning or of being right, all action and all love are haunted by the expectation of an account which will transform them into their truth. In short, they are haunted by the expectation of the moment at which it will finally be known just what the situation was. Was it one person's shyness hiding under an apparent respect for others which one day definitively rejected the other, who thought about him a hundred times thereafter; or were the chips down from that moment on and that love impossible? Perhaps this expectation will always be in some way disappointed. Men borrow from one another so constantly that each movement of our will and thought takes flight from other men, so that in this sense it is impossible to have any more than a rough idea of what is due to each individual man. It is nevertheless true that this desire for a total manifestation animates life as it does literature, and that beneath the petty motives it is this desire which makes the writer want to be read, which makes man sometimes become a writer, and which in any case makes man speak and everyone want to account for himself in the eyes of X—which means that everyone thinks of his life and all lives as something that can in every sense of the word be told as a "story."

True history thus gets its life entirely from us. It is in our present that it gets the force to refer everything else to the present. The other whom I respect gets his life from me as I get mine from him. A philosophy of history does not take away any of my rights or initiatives. It simply adds to my obligations as a solitary person the obligation to understand situations other than my own and to create a path between my life and that of others, that is, to express myself. Through the action of culture, I take up my dwelling in lives which are not mine. I confront them, I make one known to the other, I make them equally possible in an order of truth, I make myself responsible for all of them, and I create a universal life. Just as by the thick and living presence of my body, in one fell swoop I take up my dwelling in space. And like the functioning of the body, that of words or paintings remains obscure to me. The words, lines, and colors which express me come out of me as gestures. They are torn from me by what I want to say as my gestures are by what I want to do. In this sense, there is in all expression a spontaneity which will not tolerate any commands, not even those which I would like to give to myself. Words, even in the art of prose, carry the speaker and the hearer into a common universe by drawing both toward a new signification through their power to designate in excess of their accepted definition, through the muffled life they have led and continue to lead in us, and through what Ponge [30] appropriately called their "semantic thickness" and Sartre their "signifying soil." This spontaneity of language which unites us is not a command, and the history which it establishes is not an external idol: it is ourselves with our roots, our growth, and, as we say, the fruits of our toil.

Perception, history, expression—it is only by bringing together these three problems that we can put Malraux' analyses in their proper perspective. And, at the same time, we shall be able to see why it is legitimate to treat painting as a language. This way of dealing with the problem will emphasize a perceptual meaning which is captured in the visible configuration of the painting and yet capable of gathering up a series of antecedent expressions into an always-to-be-made-again eternity. The comparison is profitable not only for our analysis of painting but also for our analysis of language. For perhaps it is going to lead us to detect beneath spoken language an operant or speaking language whose words live a little-known life and unite with and separate from

30. Francis Ponge, contemporary French poet and essayist.—Trans.

one another as their lateral or indirect signification demands, even though these relations seem *evident* to us once the expression is accomplished. The transparency of spoken language, that fine clarity of word which is only sound and that meaning which is only meaning, the property which it apparently has of extracting the meaning of signs and isolating that meaning in its pure state (which is perhaps simply the anticipation of several different formulations in which it would really remain *the same*), and its would-be power of recapitulating and enclosing a whole process of expression in a single act—are these not simply the highest point of a tacit and implicit accumulation of the same sort as that of painting?

* * *

Like a painting, a novel expresses tacitly. Its subject, like that of a painting, can be related. But Julien Sorel's trip to Verrières and his attempt to kill Mme de Rênal after he has learned that she has betrayed him are not as important as that silence, that dream-like journey, that unthinking certitude, and that eternal resolution which follow the news. Now these things are nowhere said. There is no need of a "Julien thought" or a "Julien wished." In order to express them, Stendhal had only to insinuate himself into Julien and make objects, obstacles, means, and hazards appear before our eyes with the swiftness of the journey. He had only to decide to narrate in one page instead of five. That brevity, that unusual proportion of things omitted to things said, is not even the result of a *choice*. Consulting his own sensitivity to others, Stendhal suddenly found an imaginary body for Julien which was more agile than his own body. As if in a second life, he made the trip to Verrières according to a cadence of cold passion which itself decided what was visible and what was invisible, what was to be said and what was to remain unspoken. The desire to kill is thus not in the words at all. It is between them, in the hollows of space, time, and signification they mark out, as movement at the cinema is between the immobile images which follow one another.

The novelist speaks for his reader, and every man to every other, the language of the initiated—initiated into the world and into the universe of possibilities confined in a human body and a human life. What he has to say he supposes known. He takes up his dwelling in a character's behavior and gives the reader only a suggestion of it, its nervous and peremptory trace in the surroundings. If the author is a writer (that is, if he is capable of finding the elisions and caesuras which indicate the behavior), the reader responds to his appeal and joins him at the virtual center of the writing, *even if neither one of them is aware of it.* The novel as a report of events and an announcement of ideas, theses, or conclusions—as manifest or prosaic signification—and the novel as an expression of style—as oblique and latent signification—are in a simple relationship of homonymy. Marx clearly understood this when he adopted Balzac. We can be sure that there was no question here of some return to liberalism. Marx meant that a certain way of *making* the world of money and the conflicts of modern society *visible* was worth more than Balzac's theses—even political—and that this vision, once acquired, would have its consequences, with or without Balzac's consent.

It is certainly right to condemn formalism, but it is ordinarily forgotten that its error is not that it esteems form too much, but that it esteems it so little that it detaches it from meaning. In this respect formalism is no different than a literature of "subject," which also separates the meaning of the work from its configuration. The true contrary of formalism is a good theory of style, or of speech, which puts both above "technique" or "device." Speech is not a means in the service of an external end. It contains its own rule of usage, ethics, and view of the world, as a gesture sometimes bears the whole truth about a man. This living use of language, ignored both by formalism and the literature of "subjects," is literature itself as search and acquisition. A language which only sought to reproduce things themselves would exhaust its power to teach in factual statements. On the contrary, a language which gives our perspectives on things and cuts out relief in them opens up a discussion which does not end with the language and itself invites further investigation. What is irreplaceable in the work of art? What makes it far more a voice of the spirit, whose analogue is found in all productive philosophic or political thought, than a means to pleasure? The fact that it contains, better than ideas, *matrices of ideas*—the fact that it provides us with symbols whose meaning we never stop developing. Precisely because it dwells and makes us dwell in a world we do not have the key to, the work of art teaches us to see and ultimately gives us something to think about as no analytical work can; because when we analyze an object, we find only what we have put into it.

What is hazardous in literary communication, and ambiguous and irreducible to the theme in all the great works of art, is not a provisional weakness which we might hope to overcome. It is the price we must pay to have a literature, that is, a conquering language which introduces us to unfamiliar perspectives instead of confirming us in our own. We would not see anything if our eyes did not give us the means of catching, questioning, and giving form to an indefinite number of configurations of space and color. We would not do anything if our body did not enable us to leap over all the neural and muscular means of locomotion in order to move to the goal. Literary language fills the same kind of office. In the same imperious and brief way the writer transports us without transitions or preparations from the world of established meanings to something else. And as our body guides us among things only on condition that we stop analyzing it and make use of it, language is literary (that is, productive) only on condition that we stop asking justifications of it at each instant and follow it where it goes, letting the words and all the means of expression of the book be enveloped by that halo of signification that they owe to their singular arrangement, and the whole writing veer toward a second-order value where it almost rejoins the mute radiance of painting.

The meaning of a novel too is perceptible at first only as a *coherent deformation* imposed on the visible. And it will never be otherwise. Criticism may well compare one novelist's mode of expression with another's and incorporate one type of narrative in a family of other possible ones. This work is legitimate only if it is preceded by a perception of the novel in which the particularities of "technique" merge with those of the over-all project and meaning, and only if it is intended to explain what we have already perceived. As the description of a face does not allow us to imagine it, even if it specifies certain of its characteristics, the language of the critic who claims to possess the object of his criticism does not replace the language of the novelist who shows us what is true or makes it show through without touching it. It is essential to what is true to be presented first, last, and always in a movement which throws our image of the world out of focus, distends it, and draws it toward fuller meaning. It is thus that the auxiliary line introduced into a diagram opens the road to new relations. It is thus that the work of art operates and will always operate upon us—as long as there are works of art.

But these remarks are far from exhausting the question. There are still the exact forms of language—and philosophy—to be considered. We may wonder whether their ambition to recover the slippery hold on our experience that literature gives us and gain actual possession of what is said does not express the essence of language much better than literature does. This problem would involve logical analyses which cannot be considered here. Without dealing with it completely, we can at least situate it and show that in any case no language ever wholly frees itself from the precariousness of mute forms of expression, reabsorbs its own contingency, and wastes away to make the things themselves appear; that in this sense the privilege language enjoys over painting or the practices of life remains relative; and, finally, that expression is not one of the curiosities that the mind may propose to examine but is its existence in act.

Certainly the man who decides to write takes an attitude in respect to the past which is his alone. All culture prolongs the past. Today's parents see their childhood in their own children's and adopt toward them the behavior of their own parents. Or, through rancor, they go to the opposite extreme. If they have been subjected to an authoritarian upbringing, they practice a permissive one. And by this detour they often come back to the tradition, for in twenty-five years the dizzy heights of freedom will bring the child back to a system of security and make him an authoritarian father. The novelty of the arts of expression is that they make tacit culture come out of its mortal circle. From the outset the artist is unwilling to continue the past by veneration or revolt. He recommences his effort from top to bottom.

One reason why the painter takes up his brush is that in one sense the art of painting still remains to be created. But the arts of language go much farther toward true creation. Precisely because painting is always something to be created, the works which the new painter is going to produce will be added to already created works. The new do not make the old useless, nor do they expressly contain them. They rival them. Today's painting denies the past too deliberately to be able to really free itself from it. It can only forget it while it profits from it. The ransom of its novelty is that in making what came before it seem to be an unsuccessful effort, it foreshadows a different painting tomorrow which will make it seem in turn to be another unsuccessful effort. Thus painting as a whole presents itself as an abortive effort to say something which still remains to be said. Although the man who writes is not content to simply extend existing language, he is no more anxious to replace it by an idiom which, like a painting, is sufficient unto itself and closed in upon its intimate signification. If you wish, he destroys ordinary language, but by realizing it. The given language, which penetrates him through and through and from the beginning sketches a general diagram of his most secret thoughts, does not stand before him as an enemy. It is entirely *ready to* convert everything new he stands for as a writer into an acquisition. It is as if it had been made for him, and he for it; as if the task of speaking to which he had been devoted in learning the language were more deservedly he than his heart beat; and as if the established language called into existence, along with him, one of *his* possibilities.

Painting fulfills a vow of the past. It has the power to act in the name of the past, but it contains the past as a memory for us and not in its manifest state. Even if we know the history of painting too, the past which is present in a painting is not memory "for itself"—it does not pretend to sum up what has made it possible. Speech, not content to push beyond the past, claims to recapitulate, retrieve, and contain it in substance. And since without repeating it textually speech could not give us the past in its presence, it makes the past undergo a preparation which is the property of language—it offers us the *truth* of it. It is not content to push it aside in making a place for itself in the world. It wants to preserve it in its spirit or its meaning. Thus it twists back upon itself, takes itself up, and gets possession of itself once more.

There is a critical, philosophic, universal use of language which claims to retrieve things as they are—whereas painting transforms them into painting—to retrieve everything, both language itself and the use other doctrines have made of it. From the moment he seeks the truth, the philosopher does not think that it had to wait for him in order to be true; he seeks it as what has always been true for everyone. It is essential to truth to be integral, whereas no painting has ever pretended to be. The Spirit of Painting appears only in the Museum, because it is a Spirit external to itself. Speech, on the contrary, tries to gain possession of itself and conquer the secret of its own inventions. Man does not paint painting, but he speaks about speech, and the spirit of language wants to depend upon nothing but itself.

A painting makes its charm dwell from the start in a dreaming eternity where we easily rejoin it many centuries later, even without knowing the history of the dress, furnishings, utensils, and civilization whose stamp it bears. Writing, on the contrary, relinquishes its most enduring meaning to us only through a precise history which we must have some knowledge of. The *Provincial Letters* put the theological discussions of the seventeenth century back in the present; *The Red and the Black,* the gloom of the Restoration. But painting pays curiously for this immediate access to the enduring that it grants itself, for it is subject much more than writing to the passage of time. The pleasure of an anachronism is mixed with our contemplation of paintings, whereas Stendhal and Pascal are entirely in the present. To the exact extent that it renounces the hypocrite eternity of art and, boldly confronting its times, displays them instead of vaguely evoking them, literature surges forth victorious and gives significance to an age. Although the statues of Olympia play a great part in attaching us to Greece, they also foster (in the state in which they have come down to us—bleached, broken, detached from the work as a whole) a fraudulent myth about Greece. They cannot resist time as a manuscript, even incomplete, torn, and almost illegible, does. Heraclitus' writing casts light for us as no broken statues can, because its signification is deposited and concentrated in it in another way than theirs is in them, and because nothing equals the ductility of speech. In short, language speaks, and the voices of painting are the voices of silence.

The reason is that statements claim to unveil the thing itself; language goes beyond itself toward what it signifies. Yet try as each word may (as Saussure explains) to extract its meaning from all the others, the fact remains that at the moment it occurs the task of expressing is no longer differentiated and referred to other words—it is accomplished, and we understand something. Saussure may show that each act of expression becomes significant only as a modulation of a general system of expression and only insofar as it is differentiated from other linguistic gestures. The marvel is that before Saussure we did not know anything about this, and that we forget it again each time we speak—to begin with when we speak of Saussure's ideas. This proves that each partial act of expression, as an act common to the whole of the given language, is not limited to expending an expressive power accumulated in the language, but recreates both the power and the language by making us verify in the obviousness of given and received meaning the power that speaking subjects have of going beyond signs toward their meaning. Signs do not simply evoke other signs for us and so on without end, and language is not like a prison we are locked into or a guide we must blindly follow; for what these linguistic gestures mean and gain us such complete access to that we seem to have no further need of them to refer to it finally appears at the intersection of all of them. Thus when we compare language to mute forms of expression such as gestures or paintings, we must point out that unlike these forms language is not content to sketch out directions, vectors, a "coherent deformation," or a tacit meaning on the surface of the world, exhausing itself as animal "intelligence" does in kaleidoscopically producing a new landscape for action. Language is not just the replacement of one meaning by another, but the substitution of equivalent meanings. The new structure is given as already present in the old, the latter subsists in it, and the past is now understood.

There is no doubt that language is the presumption to a total accumulation; and present speech confronts the philosopher with the problem of this provisional self-possession, which is provisional yet no mean thing. The fact remains that language could deliver up the thing itself only if it ceased to be in time and in situation. Hegel is the only one who thinks that his system contains the truth of all the others, and the man who knew the others only through Hegel's synthesis would not know them at all. Even if Hegel were true from one end to the other, nothing would dispense with reading the "pre-Hegelians," for he can contain them only "in what they affirm." By what they deny they offer the reader another situation of thought which is not eminently contained in Hegel—which is not there at all—and in which Hegel is visible in a light which he is himself unaware of. Hegel is the only one to think that he has no existence "for others," and that he is in the eyes of others exactly what he knows himself to be. Even if it be admitted that there is progress from them to him, there has been room in such a movement for Descartes' *Meditations* or Plato's dialogues. And there has been room precisely because of the "naivetés" which still separated these thinkers from Hegelian "truth"—a contact with things and a spark of meaning that one will find in Hegel only on condition of having found them in Plato and Descartes, and that one must always return to, if only to understand Hegel.

Hegel is the Museum. He is if you wish all philosophies, but deprived of their finiteness and power of impact, embalmed, transformed, he believes, into themselves, but really transformed into Hegel. We only have to see how a truth wastes away when it is integrated into different ones (how the Cogito, for example, in going from Descartes to the Cartesians, becomes almost a listlessly repeated ritual) to agree that the synthesis does not effectively contain all past systems of thought, that it is not all that they have been, and finally that it is never a synthesis which is both "in and for itself"—that is, a synthesis which in the same movement is and knows, is what it knows, knows what it is, preserves and suppresses, realizes and destroys. If Hegel means that as the past becomes distant it changes into its meaning, and that we can trace an intelligible history of thought in retrospect, he is right; but on condition that in this synthesis each term remain the whole of the world at the date considered, and that in linking philosophies together we keep them all in their place like so many open significations and let an exchange of anticipations and metamorphoses subsist between them. The meaning of philosophy is the meaning of a genesis. Consequently, it could not possibly be summed up outside of time, and it is still expression.

It is all the more true of non-philosophical writing that the writer can have the feeling of attaining things themselves only by using language and not by going beyond language. Mallarmé himself was well aware that nothing would fall from his pen if he remained absolutely faithful to his vow to say everything without leaving anything unsaid, and that he was able to write minor books only by giving up the Book which would dispense with all the others. The signification without any sign, the thing itself—that height of clarity—would be the disappearance of all clarity. And whatever clarity we can have is not at the beginning of language, like a golden age, but at the end of its effort. Language and the system of truth do displace our life's center of gravity by suggesting that we cross-check and resume our operations in terms of one another, in such a way that each one shifts into all of them and they seem independent of the step-by-step formulations which we first gave them. They do thereby reduce the other expressive operations to the rank of "mute" and subordinate ones. Yet language and the system of truth are not lacking in reticence, and meaning is not so much designated by them as it is implied by their word structure.

We must therefore say the same thing about language in relation to meaning that Simone de Beauvoir says about the body in relation to mind: it is neither primary nor secondary. No one has ever made the body simply a means or an instrument, or maintained for example that one can love by principles. And since it is no more true that the body loves all by itself, we may say that it does everything and nothing, that it is and is not ourselves. Neither end nor means, always involved in matters which go beyond it, always jealous nevertheless of its autonomy, it is powerful enough to oppose itself to any end which is merely deliberate, but it has none to propose to us if we finally turn toward it and consult it. Sometimes—and then we have the feeling of being ourselves—it lets itself be animated and becomes responsible for a life which is not simply its own. Then it is happy or spontaneous, and we with it. Similarly, language is not meaning's servant, and yet it does not govern meaning. There is no subordination between them. Here no one commands and no one obeys. What we *mean* is not before us, outside all speech, as sheer signification. It is only the excess of what we live over what has already been said. With our apparatus of expression we set ourselves up in a situation the apparatus is sensitive to, we confront it with the situation, and our statements are only the final balance of these exchanges. Political thought itself is of this order. It is always the elucidation of an historical perception in which all our understandings, all our experiences, and all our values simultaneously come into play—and of which our theses are only the schematic formulation. All action and knowledge which do not go through this elaboration, and which seek to set up values which have not been embodied in our individual or collective history (*or*—what comes down to the same thing—which seek to choose means by a calculus and a wholly technical process), fall short of the problems they are trying to solve. Personal life, expression, understanding, and history advance obliquely and not straight towards ends or concepts. What one too deliberately seeks, he does not find; and he who on the contrary has in his meditative life known how to tap its spontaneous source never lacks for ideas and values.

2 / On the Phenomenology of Language[1]

[1] Husserl and the Problem of Language

In the philosophical tradition, the problem of language does not pertain to "first philosophy," and that is just why Husserl approaches it more freely than the problems of perception or knowledge. He moves it into a central position, and what little he says about it is both original and enigmatic. Consequently, this problem provides us with our best basis for questioning phenomenology and recommencing Husserl's efforts instead of simply repeating what he said. It allows us to resume, instead of his theses, the very movement of his thought.

The contrast between certain early and late texts is striking. In the fourth of the *Logische Untersuchungen,* Husserl sets forth the concept of an eidetic of language and a universal grammar which would establish the forms of signification indispensable to every language if it is to be a language, and which would allow us to think with complete clarity about empirical languages as "confused" realizations of the essential language. This project assumes that language is one of the objects supremely constituted by consciousness, and that actual languages are very special cases of a possible language which consciousness holds the key to—that they are systems of signs linked to *their* meaning by univocal relationships which, in their structure as in their function, are susceptible to a total explication. Posited in this way as an object before thought, language could not possibly play any other role in respect to thought than that of an accompaniment, substitute, memorandum, or secondary means of communication.

In more recent writings, on the other hand, language appears as an original way of intending certain objects, as thought's body (*Formale*

1. A paper presented at the first *Colloque international de phénoménologie,* Brussels, 1951.

und transzendentale Logik [2]), or even as the operation through which thoughts that without it would remain private phenomena acquire intersubjective value and, ultimately, ideal existence (*Ursprung der Geometrie* [3]). According to this conception, philosophical thinking which reflects upon language would be its beneficiary, enveloped and situated in it. Pos ("Phénoménologie et linguistique," *Revue Internationale de philosophie,* 1939) defines the phenomenology of language not as an attempt to fit existing languages into the framework of an eidetic of all possible languages (that is, to objectify them before a universal and timeless constituting consciousness), but as a return to the speaking subject, to my contact with the language I am speaking. The scientist and the observer see language in the past. They consider the long history of a language, with all the random factors and all the shifts of meaning that have finally made it what it is today. It becomes incomprehensible that a language which is the result of so many accidents can signify anything whatsoever unequivocally. Taking language as a *fait accompli*—as the residue of past acts of signification and the record of already acquired meanings—the scientist inevitably misses the peculiar clarity of speaking, the fecundity of expression. From the phenomenological point of view (that is, for the speaking subject who makes use of his language as a means of communicating with a living community), a language regains its unity. It is no longer the result of a chaotic past of independent linguistic facts but a system all of whose elements cooperate in a single attempt to express which is turned toward the present or the future and thus governed by a present logic.

Such being Husserl's points of departure and arrival as far as language is concerned, we would like to submit for discussion a few propositions concerning first the phenomenon of language and next

2. "Diese aber (sc.: die Meinung) liegt nicht äusserlich neben den Worten; sondern redend vollziehen wir fortlaufend ein inneres, sich mit den Worten verschmelzendes, sie gleichsam beseelendes Meinen. Der Erfolg dieser Beseelung ist dass die Worte und die ganzen Reden in sich eine Meinung gleichsam verleiblichen und verleiblicht in sich als Sinn tragen." (p. 20)

3. "Objektives Dasein 'in der Welt' das als solches zugänglich ist für jedermann kann aber die geistige Objektivität des Sinngebildes letzlich nur haben vermöge der doppelschichtigen Wiederholungen und vornehmlich der sinnlich verkörpernden. In der sinnlichen Verkörperung geschiet die 'Lokalisation' und 'Temporalisation' von Solchem das seinen Seinssinn nach nicht-lokal und nicht-temporal ist . . . Wir fragen nun: . . . Wie macht die sprachliche Verleiblichung aus dem bloss innersubjektiven Gebilde, dem Gedanke, das *objektive,* das etwa als geometrischer Begriff oder Satz in der Tat für jedermann und in aller Zukunft verständlich da ist? Auf das Problem des Ursprunges der Sprache in ihrer idealen und durch Ausserung und Dokumentierung begründeten Existenz in der realen Welt wollen wir hier nicht eingehen, obschon wir uns bewusst sind, dass eine radikale Aufklärung der Seinsart der 'idealen Sinngebilde' hier ihren tiefsten Problemgrund haben muss." (*Revue Internationale de philosophie,* 1939, p. 210).

the conception of intersubjectivity, rationality, and philosophy implied by this phenomenology.

[2] The Phenomenon of Language

1. *Language and speech*

Can we simply juxtapose the two perspectives on language we have just distinguished—language as object of thought and language as mine? This is what Saussure did, for example, when he made a distinction between a synchronic linguistics of speech and a diachronic linguistics of a language, which are irreducible to one another because a panchronic view would inevitably blot out the originality of the present. Pos similarly limits himself to describing the objective and the phenomenological attitude by turns without saying anything about their relationship. But then we might think that phenomenology is distinguished from linguistics only as psychology is distinguished from the science of language. Phenomenology would add our inner experience of a language to our linguistic knowledge of it as pedagogy adds to our knowledge of mathematical concepts the experience of what they become in the minds of those who learn them. Our experience of speech would then have nothing to teach us about the being of language; it would have no ontological bearing.

But this is impossible. As soon as we distinguish, alongside of the objective science of language, a phenomenology of speech, we set in motion a dialectic through which the two disciplines open communications.

At first the "subjective" point of view envelops the "objective" point of view; synchrony envelops diachrony. The past of language began by being present. The series of fortuitous linguistic facts brought out by the objective perspective has been incorporated in a language which was at every moment a system endowed with an inner logic. Thus if language is a system when it is considered according to a cross-section, it must be in its development too. No matter how strongly Saussure insisted upon the duality of the two perspectives, his successors have had to conceive of a mediating principle in the form of the *sublinguistic schema* (Gustave Guillaume).[4]

In another connection, diachrony envelops synchrony. If language allows random elements when it is considered according to a longitudinal section, the system of synchrony must at every moment allow fissures where brute events can insert themselves.

Thus a double task is imposed upon us:

4. Gustave Guillaume, contemporary French linguist.—Trans.

a) We have to find a meaning in the development of language, and conceive of language as a moving equilibrium. For example, certain forms of expression having become decadent by the sole fact that they have been used and have lost their "expressiveness," we shall show how the gaps or zones of weakness thus created elicit from speaking subjects who want to communicate a recovery and a utilization, in terms of a new principle, of linguistic débris left by the system in process of regression. It is in this way that a new means of expression is conceived of in a language, and a persistent logic runs through the effects of wear and tear upon the language and its volubility itself. It is in this way that the French system of expression, based upon the preposition, was substituted for the Latin system, which was based upon declension and inflectional changes.

b) But correlatively, we must understand that since synchrony is only a cross-section of diachrony, the system realized in it never exists wholly in act but always involves latent or incubating changes. It is never composed of absolutely univocal meanings which can be made completely explicit beneath the gaze of a transparent constituting consciousness. It will be a question not of a system of forms of signification clearly articulated in terms of one another—not of a structure of linguistic ideas built according to a strict plan—but of a cohesive whole of convergent linguistic gestures, each of which will be defined less by a signification than by a use value. Far from particular languages appearing as the "confused" realization of certain ideal and universal forms of signification, the possibility of such a synthesis becomes problematical. If universality is attained, it will not be through a universal language which would go back prior to the diversity of languages to provide us with the foundations of all possible languages. It will be through an oblique passage from a given language that I speak and that initiates me into the phenomenon of expression, to another given language that I learn to speak and that effects the act of expression according to a completely different style—the two languages (and ultimately all given languages) being contingently comparable only at the outcome of this passage and only as signifying wholes, without our being able to recognize in them the common elements of one single categorial structure.

Far from our being able to juxtapose a psychology of language and a science of language by reserving language in the present for the first and language in the past for the second, we must recognize that the present diffuses into the past to the extent that the past has been present. History is the history of successive synchronies, and the contingency of the linguistic past invades even the synchronic system. What the phenomenology of language teaches me is not just a psychological curiosity—the language observed by linguistics experienced in me and bearing my particular additions to it. It teaches me a new conception of the being of language, which is now logic in contingency—an oriented system which nevertheless always elaborates random factors, taking what was fortuitous up again into a meaningful whole—incarnate logic.

2. *The quasi-corporeality of the signifying*

BY COMING BACK to spoken or living language we shall find that its expressive value is not the sum of the expressive values which allegedly belong individually to each element of the "verbal chain." On the contrary, these elements form a system in synchrony in the sense that each of them signifies only its difference in respect to the others (as Saussure says, signs are essentially "diacritical"); and as this is true of them all, there are only differences of signification in a language. The reason why a language finally intends to say and does say [*veut dire et dit*] something is not that each sign is the vehicle for a signification which allegedly belongs to it, but that all the signs together allude to a signification which is always in abeyance when they are considered singly, and which I go beyond them toward without their ever containing it. Each of them expresses only by reference to a certain mental equipment, to a certain arrangement of our cultural implements, and as a whole they are like a blank form we have not yet filled out, or like the gestures of others, which intend and circumscribe an object of the world that I do not see.

The speaking power the child assimilates in learning his language is not the sum of morphological, syntactical, and lexical meanings. These attainments are neither necessary nor sufficient to acquire a language, and once the act of speaking is acquired it presupposes no comparison between what I want to express and the conceptual arrangement of the means of expression I make use of. The words and turns of phrase needed to bring my significative intention to expression recommend themselves to me, when I am speaking, only by what Humboldt called *innere Sprachform* (and our contemporaries call *Wortbegriff*), that is, only by a certain style of speaking from which they arise and according to which they are organized without my having to represent them to myself. There is a "languagely" ["*langagière*"] meaning of language which effects the mediation between my as yet unspeaking intention and words, and in such a way that my spoken words surprise me myself and teach me my thought. Organized signs have their immanent meaning, which does not arise from the "I think" but from the "I am able to."

This action at a distance by language, which brings significations together without touching them, and this eloquence which designates them in a peremptory fashion without ever changing them into words or breaking the silence of consciousness, are eminent cases of corporeal intentionality. I have a rigorous awareness of the bearing of my gestures or of the spatiality of my body which allows me to maintain relationships with the world without thematically representing to myself the objects I am going to grasp or the relationships of size between my body and the avenues offered to me by the world. On the condition that I do not reflect expressly upon it, my consciousness of my body immediately signifies a certain landscape about me, that of my fingers a certain fibrous or grainy style of the object. It is in the same fashion that the spoken word (the one I utter or the one I hear) is pregnant with a meaning which can be read in the very texture of the linguistic gesture (to the point that a hesitation, an alteration of the voice, or the choice of a certain syntax suffices to modify it), and yet is never contained in that gesture, every expression always appearing to me as a trace, no idea being given to me except in transparency, and every attempt to close our hand on the thought which dwells in the spoken word leaving only a bit of verbal material in our fingers.

3. *The relationship of the signifying and the signified. Sedimentation*

SPEECH IS COMPARABLE to a gesture because what it is charged with expressing will be in the same relation to it as the goal is to the gesture which intends it, and our remarks about the functioning of the signifying apparatus will already involve a certain theory of the significations expressed by speech. My corporeal intending of the objects of my surroundings is implicit and presupposes no thematization or "representation" of my body or milieu. Signification arouses speech as the world arouses my body—by a mute presence which awakens my intentions without deploying itself before them. In me as well as in the listener who finds it in hearing me, the significative intention (even if it is subsequently to fructify in "thoughts") is at the moment no more than a *determinate gap* to be filled by words—the excess of what I intend to say over what is being said or has already been said.

This means three things: (a) The significations of speech are already ideas in the Kantian sense, the poles of a certain number of convergent acts of expression which magnetize discourse without being in the strict sense given for their own account. Consequently, (b) expression is never total. As Saussure points out, we have the feeling that our language expresses totally. But it is not because it expresses totally that it is ours; it is because it is ours that we believe it expresses totally. For an Englishman, "the man I love" is just as complete an expression as "l'homme *que* j'aime" is for a Frenchman. And for a German who by declension can expressly indicate the function of the direct object, "j'aime cet homme" is a wholly allusive way of expressing oneself. Thus there are always things understood in expression; or rather the idea of things understood is to be rejected. It is meaningful only if we take as the model and absolute norm of expression a language (ordinarily our own) which, like all the others, can never in fact lead us "as if by the hand" to the signification, to the things themselves. So let us not say that every expression is imperfect because it leaves things understood. Let us say that every expression is perfect to the extent it is unequivocally understood, and admit as a fundamental fact of expression *a surpassing of the signifying by the signified which it is the very virtue of the signifying to make possible.* The fact that the significative intention is only a determinate gap means, finally, that (c) this act of expression—this joining through transcendence of the linguistic meaning of speech and the signification it intends—is not for us speaking subjects a second-order operation we supposedly have recourse to only in order to communicate our thoughts to others, but our own taking possession or acquisition of significations which otherwise are present to us only in a muffled way. The reason why the thematization of the signified does not precede speech is that it is the result of it. Let us stress this third consequence.

For the speaking subject, to express is to become aware of; he does not express just for others, but also to know himself what he intends. Speech does not seek to embody a significative intention which is only *a certain gap* simply in order to recreate the same lack or privation in others, but also to know *what* there is a lack or privation of. How does it succeed in doing so? The significative intention gives itself a body and knows itself by looking for an equivalent in the system of available significations represented by the language I speak and the whole of the writings and culture I inherit. For that speechless want, the significative intention, it is a matter of realizing a certain arrangement of already signifying instruments or already speaking significations (morphological, syntactical, and lexical instruments, literary *genres,* types of narrative, modes of presenting events, etc.) which arouses in the hearer the presentiment of a new and different signification, and which inversely (in the speaker or the writer) manages to anchor this original signification in the already available ones. But why, how, and in what sense are they available? They became such when, in their time, they were *established* as significations I can have recourse to—that I *have*—through the same sort of expressive operation. It is this operation which must be described if I want to comprehend the peculiar power of speech.

I understand or think I understand the words and forms of French; I have a certain experience of the literary and philosophical modes of expression offered me by the given culture. I express when, utilizing all these already speaking instruments, I make them say something they have never said. We begin reading a philosopher by giving the words he makes use of their "common" meaning; and little by little, through what is at first an imperceptible reversal, his speech comes to dominate his language, and it is his use of words which ends up assigning them a new and characteristic signification. At this moment he has made himself understood and his signification has come to dwell in me. We say that a thought is expressed when the converging words intending it are numerous and eloquent enough to designate it unequivocally for me, its author, or for others, and in such a manner that we all have the experience of its presence in the flesh in speech. Even though only *Abschattungen* of the signification are given thematically, the fact is that once a certain point in discourse has been passed the *Abschattungen,* caught up in the movement of discourse outside of which they are nothing, suddenly contract into a single signification. And then we feel that *something has been said*—just as we perceive a thing once a minimum of sensory messages has been exceeded, even though the explanation of the thing extends as a matter of principle to infinity; or, as beholders of a certain number of actions, we come to *perceive someone* even though in the eyes of reflection no one other than myself can really and in the same sense be an *ego*.

The consequences of speech, like those of perception (and particularly the perception of others), always exceed its premises. Even we who speak do not necessarily know better than those who listen to us what we are expressing. I say that I *know an idea* when the power to organize discourses which make coherent sense around it has been established in me; and this power itself does not depend upon my alleged possession and face-to-face contemplation of it, but upon my having acquired a certain style of thinking. I say that a signification is acquired and henceforth available when I have succeeded in making it dwell in a speech apparatus which was not originally destined for it. Of course the elements of this expressive apparatus did not really contain it—the French language did not, from the moment it was established, contain French literature; I had to throw them off center and recenter them in order to make them signify what I intended. It is just this "coherent deformation" (Malraux) of available significations which arranges them in a new sense and takes not only the hearers *but the speaking subject as well* through a decisive *step*.

For from this point on the preparatory stages of expression—the first pages of the book—are taken up again into the final meaning of the whole and are directly given as derivatives of that meaning, which is now installed in the culture. The way will be open for the speaking subject (and for others) to go straight to the whole. He will not need to reactivate the whole process; he will possess it eminently in its result. A personal and interpersonal tradition will have been founded. The *Nachvollzug*, freed from the cautious gropings of the *Vollzug*, contracts the steps of the process into a single view. Sedimentation occurs, and I shall be able to think farther. Speech, as distinguished from language, is that moment when the significative intention (still silent and wholly in act) proves itself capable of incorporating itself into my culture and the culture of others—of shaping me and others by transforming the meaning of cultural instruments. It becomes "available" in turn because in retrospect it gives us the illusion that it was contained in the already available significations, whereas by a sort of *ruse* it espoused them only in order to infuse them with a new life.

4. *Consequences for phenomenological philosophy*

WHAT PHILOSOPHICAL BEARING must we grant these descriptions? The relation of phenomenological analyses to philosophy proper is not clear. They are often considered *preparatory*, and Husserl himself always distinguished "phenomenological investigations" in the broad sense from the "philosophy" which was supposed to crown them. Yet it is hard to maintain that the philosophical problem remains untouched after the phenomenological exploration of the *Lebenswelt*. The reason why the return to the "life-world" is considered an absolutely indispensable first step in Husserl's last writings is undoubtedly that it is not without consequence for the work of universal constitution which should follow, that in some respects something of the first step remains in the second, that it is in some fashion preserved in it, that it is thus never gone beyond completely, and that phenomenology is already philosophy. If the philosophical subject were a transparent constituting consciousness before which the world and language were wholly explicit as its significations and its objects, any experience whatsoever—phenomenological or no—would suffice to motivate our passing to philosophy, and the systematic exploration of the *Lebenswelt* would not be necessary. The reason why the return to the *Lebenswelt* (and particularly the return from objectified language to speech) is considered absolutely necessary is that philosophy must reflect upon the object's mode of presence to the subject—upon the conception of the object and of the subject as they appear to the phenomenological revelation—instead of replacing them by the object's relationship to the subject as an idealistic philosophy of total reflection conceives of it. From this point on, phenomenology envelops philosophy, which cannot be purely and simply added on to it.

This is particularly clear in the case of the phenomenology of language. More clearly than any other, this problem requires us to make a decision concerning the relationships between phenomenology and philosophy or metaphysics. For more clearly than any other it takes the form of both a special problem and a problem which contains all the others, including the problem of philosophy. If speech is what we have said it is, how could there possibly be an ideation which allows us to dominate this *praxis*? How could the phenomenology of speech possibly help being a philosophy of speech as well? And how could there possibly be any place for a subsequent elucidation of a higher degree? It is absolutely necessary to underline the *philosophical* import of the return to speech.

The description we have given of the signifying power of speech, and in general of the body as mediator of our relation to the object, would provide no philosophical information at all if it could be considered a matter of mere psychological depiction. In this case we would admit that in effect the body, such as it is in our living experience of it, seems to us to involve the world, and speech a landscape of thought. But this would be only an appearance. In the light of serious thinking, my body would still be an object, my consciousness pure consciousness, and their coexistence the object of an *apperception* which (as pure consciousness) I would still be the subject of (in Husserl's early writings, things are set forth in more or less this way). Similarly, since the relationship according to which my speech or the speech I hear points beyond itself toward a signification could (like every other relationship) only be posited by me *qua* consciousness, thought's radical autonomy would be restored at the very moment it seemed to be in doubt.

Yet in neither case can I classify the phenomenon of incarnation simply as psychological appearance; and if I were tempted to do so, I would be blocked by my perception of others. For more clearly (*but not differently*) in my experience of others than in my experience of speech or the perceived world, I inevitably grasp my body as a *spontaneity which teaches me what I could not know in any other way except through it.* Positing another person as an other myself is not as a matter of fact possible if it is *consciousness* which must do it. To be conscious is to constitute, so that I cannot be conscious of another person, since that would involve constituting him as constituting, and as constituting in respect to the very act through which I constitute him. This difficulty of principle, posited as a limit at the beginning of the fifth *Cartesian Meditation,* is nowhere eliminated. Husserl *disregards* it: since I have the idea of others, it follows that in some way the difficulty mentioned *has in fact been overcome.* But I have been able to overcome it only because he within me who perceives others is capable of ignoring the radical contradiction which makes theoretical conception of others impossible. Or rather (since if he ignored it he would no longer be dealing with others), only because he is able to live that contradiction as the very definition of the presence of others.

This subject which experiences itself as constituted at the moment it functions as constituting is my body. We remember that Husserl ended up basing my perception of a way of behaving (*Gebaren*) which appears in the space surrounding me upon what he calls the "mating phenomenon" and "intentional transgression." It happens that my gaze stumbles against certain sights (those of other human and, by extension, animal bodies) and is thwarted by them. I am invested by them just when I thought I was investing them, and I see a form sketched out in space that arouses and convokes the possibilities of my own body as if it were a matter of my own gestures or behavior. Everything happens as if the functions of intentionality and the intentional object were paradoxically interchanged. The scene invites me to become its adequate viewer, as if a different mind than my own suddenly came to dwell in my body, or rather as if my mind were drawn out there and emigrated into the scene it was in the process of setting for itself. I am snapped up by a second myself outside me; I perceive an other.

Now speech is evidently an eminent case of these "ways of behaving" ["*conduites*"] which reverse my ordinary relationship to objects and give certain ones of them the value of subjects. And if objectification makes no sense in respect to the living body (mine or another's), the incarnation of what I call its thinking in its total speech must also be considered an ultimate phenomenon. If phenomenology did not really already involve our conception of being and our philosophy, when we arrived at the philosophical problem we would find ourselves confronted again with the very difficulties which gave rise to phenomenology to begin with.

In a sense, phenomenology is all or nothing. That order of instructive spontaneity—the body's "I am able to," the "intentional transgression" which gives us others, the "speech" which gives us the idea of an ideal or absolute signification—cannot be subsequently placed under the jurisdiction of an acosmic and a pancosmic consciousness without becoming meaningless again. It must teach me to comprehend what no constituting consciousness can know—my involvement in a "pre-constituted" world. But how, people will object, can the body and speech give me more than I have put into them? It is clearly not my body as organism which teaches me to see the emergence of *another myself* in a way of behaving [*conduite*] that I witness; as such it could at best only be reflected and recognize itself in *another organism.* In order for the alter ego and the thought of others to appear to me, I must be the *I* of *this* body of mine, *this* incarnate life's thought. The subject who effects the intentional transgression could not possibly do so except insofar as he is situated. The experience of others is possible to the exact degree that the situation is part of the Cogito.

But then we must take with equal strictness what phenomenology has taught us about the relationship between the signifying and the signified. If the central phenomenon of language is in fact *the common act of the signifying and the signified,* we would deprive it of its distinctive characteristic by realizing the result of expressive operations in advance in a heaven of ideas; we would lose sight of the *leap* these operations take from already available significations to those we are in the process of constructing and acquiring. And the intelligible substitute we would try to base them on would not exempt us from understanding how our knowing apparatus expands to the point of understanding what it does not contain. We would not husband our transcendence by prescribing it to a factual transcendent. In any case the place of truth would still be that anticipation (*Vorhabe*) through which each spoken word or acquired truth opens a field of understanding, and the symmetrical recovery (*Nachvollzug*) through which we bring this advent of understanding or this commerce with others to a conclusion and contract them into a new view.

Our present expressive operations, instead of driving the preceding ones away—simply succeeding and annulling them—salvage, preserve, and (insofar as they contain some truth) take them up again; and the same phenomenon is produced in respect to others' expressive operations, whether they be past or contemporary. Our present keeps the promises of our past; we keep others' promises. Each act of philosophical or literary expression contributes to fulfilling the vow to retrieve the world taken with the first appearance of a language, that is, with the first appearance of a finite system of signs which claimed to be capable in principle of winning by a sort of ruse any being which might present itself. Each act of expression realizes for its own part a portion of this project, and by opening a new field of truths, further extends the contract which has just expired. This is possible only through the same "intentional transgression" which gives us others; and like it the phenomenon of truth, which is theoretically impossible, is known only through the praxis which *creates* it.

To say there is a truth is to say that when my renewal meets the old or alien project, and successful expression frees what has always been held captive in being, an inner communication is established in the density of personal and interpersonal time through which our present becomes the *truth of* all the other knowing events. It is like a wedge we drive into the present, a milestone bearing witness that in this moment something has taken place which being was always waiting for or "intending to say" [*voulait dire*], and which will never stop if not being true at least signifying and stimulating our thinking apparatus, if need be by drawing from it truths more comprehensive than the present one. At this moment something has been founded in signification; an experience has been transformed into its meaning, has become truth. Truth is another name for sedimentation, which is itself the presence of all presents in our own. That is to say that even and especially for the ultimate philosophical subject, there is no objectivity which accounts for our super-objective relationship to all times, no light that shines more brightly than the living present's light.

In the late text we cited to begin with, Husserl writes that speech realizes a "localization" and "temporalization" of an ideal meaning which, "according to the meaning of its being," is neither local nor temporal. And later on he adds that speech also objectifies, as concept or proposition, what was heretofore only a formation internal to a single subject, thereby opening it up to the plurality of subjects. So there would seem to be a movement through which ideal existence descends into locality and temporality, and an inverse movement through which the act of speaking here and now establishes the ideality of what is true. These two movements would be contradictory if they took place between the same extreme terms; and it seems to us that their relationship must be conceived of in terms of a circuit of reflection. In a first approximation, reflection recognizes ideal existence as neither local nor temporal. It then becomes aware of a locality and temporality of speech that can neither be derived from those of the objective world nor suspended from a world of ideas. And finally, it makes the mode of being of ideal formations rest upon speech. Ideal existence is based upon the document. Not, undoubtedly, upon the document as a physical object, or even as the vehicle of one-to-one significations assigned to it by the language it is written in. But ideal existence is based upon the document insofar as (still through an "intentional transgression") the document solicits and brings together all knowing lives—and as such establishes and re-establishes a "Logos" of the cultural world.

Thus the proper function of a phenomenological philosophy seems to us to be to establish itself definitively in the order of instructive spontaneity that is inaccessible to psychologism and historicism no less than to dogmatic metaphysics. The phenomenology of speech is among all others best suited to reveal this order to us. When I speak or understand, I experience that presence of others in myself or of myself in others which is the stumbling-block of the theory of intersubjectivity, I experience that presence of what is represented which is the stumbling-block of the theory of time, and I finally understand what is meant by Husserl's enigmatic statement, "Transcendental subjectivity is intersubjectivity." To the extent that what I say has meaning, I am a different "other" for myself when I am speaking; and to the extent that I understand, I no longer know who is speaking and who is listening.

The ultimate philosophical step is to recognize what Kant calls the "transcendental affinity" of moments of time and temporalities. This is undoubtedly what Husserl is trying to do when he takes up the finalist vocabulary of various metaphysics again, speaking of "monads," "entelechies," and "teleology." But these words are often put in quotations in order to indicate that he does not intend to introduce along with them some agent who would then assure externally the connection of related terms. Finality in a dogmatic sense would be a compromise; it would leave the terms to be connected and their connecting principle unconnected. Now it is at the heart of my present that I find the meaning of those presents which preceded it, and that I find the means of understanding others' presence at the same world; and it is in the actual practice of speaking that I learn to understand. There is finality only in the sense in which Heidegger defined it when he said approximately that finality is the trembling of a unity exposed to contingency and tirelessly recreating itself. And it is to the same undeliberated and inexhaustible spontaneity that Sartre was alluding when he said that we are "condemned to freedom."

3 / The Philosopher and Sociology

PHILOSOPHY AND SOCIOLOGY have long lived under a segregated system which has succeeded in concealing their rivalry only by refusing them any meeting-ground, impeding their growth, making them incomprehensible to one another, and thus placing culture in a situation of permanent crisis. As always, the spirit of inquiry has gotten around these interdicts; and it seems to us that both philosophy and sociology have now progressed far enough to warrant a reexamination of their relationships.

We would also like to call attention to the thought Husserl gave to these problems. Husserl seems to us to be exemplary in that he may have realized better than anyone else that all forms of thought are in a certain sense interdependent. We need neither tear down the behavioral sciences to lay the foundations of philosophy, nor tear down philosophy to lay the foundations of the behavioral sciences. Every science secretes an ontology; every ontology anticipates a body of knowledge. It is up to us to come to terms with this situation and see to it that both philosophy and science are possible.

The segregation of philosophy and sociology has perhaps nowhere been described in the terms in which we are going to state it. Fortunately, the practices of philosophers and sociologists are often less exclusive than their principles. Yet this segregation nevertheless constitutes a part of a certain common sense of philosophers and sociologists which, by reducing philosophy and the behavioral sciences to what it believes is their ideal type, ultimately endangers scientific knowledge just as much as philosophical reflection.

Even though all the great philosophies are recognizable by their attempt to think about the mind *and its dependency*—ideas and their movement, understanding and sensibility—there is a myth about philosophy which presents it as an authoritarian affirmation of the mind's absolute autonomy. Philosophy so conceived is no longer an inquiry. It is a certain body of doctrines, made to assure an absolutely *unfettered* spirit full possession of itself and its ideas. In another connection, there is a myth about scientific knowledge which expects to attain from the mere recording of facts not only the science of the things of the world but also the science of that science—a sociology of knowledge (conceived of itself in an empiricist fashion) which should make the universe of facts self-contained by including even the ideas we invent to interpret the facts, and thus rid us, so to speak, of ourselves. These two myths sustain one another in their very antagonism. For even though the philosopher and the sociologist are opposed to one another, they at least agree upon a delimitation of boundaries which assures them of never meeting. But if the *cordon sanitaire* were removed, philosophy and sociology would destroy one another. Even now, they battle for our minds. Segregation is cold war.

In this atmosphere, any investigation which seeks to take both ideas and facts into account is immediately bifurcated. Facts, instead of being taken as the spur and warrant for a constructive effort to reach their inner dynamics, are worshipped as a sort of peremptory grace which reveals all truth. And ideas are exempted as a matter of principle from all confrontation with our experience of the world, others, and ourselves. The movement back and forth from facts to ideas and from ideas to facts is discredited as a bastard process—neither science nor philosophy—which denies scientists the final interpretation of the very facts that they have taken the pains to assemble, and which compromises philosophy with the always provisional results of scientific research.

We must be fully aware of the *obscurantist* consequences of this rigid segregation. If "mixed" investigations really have the inconveniences we have just mentioned, then we shall have to admit that a simultaneously philosophical and scientific view of experience is impossible, and that philosophy and sociology can attain certain knowledge only if they ignore one another. We shall have to hide from the scientist that "idealization" of brute fact which is nevertheless the essence of his work. He will have to ignore the deciphering of meanings which is his reason for being, the construction of intellectual models of reality without which there would no more be any sociology today than there would formerly have been Galilean physics. We shall have to put the blinders of Baconian or "Millian" induction back on the scientist, even though his own investigations obviously do not follow these canonical recipes. Consequently, he will pretend to approach social fact as if it were alien to him, as if his study owed nothing to the experience which, as social subject, he has of intersubjectivity.

Under the pretext that as a matter of fact sociology is not yet constructed with this lived experience but is instead an analysis, an explicit formulation and objectification of it which reverses our initial consciousness of social relationships (and ultimately shows that these experienced social relationships are very special variants of a dynamics we are originally unaware of and can learn about only in contact with other cultural formations), objectivism forgets another evident fact. We can expand our experience of social relationships and get a proper view of them only by analogy or contrast with those we have lived. We can do so, in short, only by subjecting the social relationships we have experienced to an *imaginary variation.* These lived relationships will no doubt take on a new meaning in comparison with this imaginary variation (as the fall of a body on an inclined plane is put in a new light by the ideal concept of free fall), but they will provide it with all the sociological meaning it can have.

Anthropology teaches us that in such and such cultures children treat certain cousins as their "kin," and facts of this sort allow us ultimately to draw up a diagram of the kinship structure in the civilization under consideration. But the correlations thus noted give only the silhouette or contour of kinship in that civilization, a cross-section of behavior patterns which are nominally defined as those of "kinship" at certain significant but still anonymous points X . . . , Y . . . , Z . . . . In short, these correlations do not yet have a sociological meaning. As long as we have not succeeded in installing ourselves in the institution which they delimit, in understanding the style of kinship which all these facts allude to and *the sense in which* certain subjects in that culture perceive other subjects of their generation as their "kin," and finally, in grasping the basic personal and interpersonal structure and the institutional relationships with nature and others which make the established correlations possible, the formulas which sum up these correlations could just as well represent a given physical or chemical process of the same form. Let us make it perfectly clear that the underlying dynamics of the social whole is certainly not *given* with our narrow experience of living among others, yet it is only by throwing this experience in and out of focus that we succeed in representing it to ourselves, just as the generalized number remains number for us only through the link which binds it to the whole number of elementary arithmetic.

On the basis of Freudian conceptions of pre-genital sexuality, we can make up a list of all the possible modes of accentuation of the orifices of the child's body, and the ones which are realized by our cultural system and have been described by the Freudians appear on the list as singular variants among a great number of possible ones which are perhaps current in civilizations as yet unknown to us. But this list tells us *nothing* about the relationships with others and with nature which define these cultural types, as long as we do not refer to the psychological meaning of the mouth, the anus, or the genital equipment in our own experience, so as to see in the different uses which are made of them by different cultures, different crystallizations of an initial polymorphism of the body as vehicle of being-in-the-world. The list we are shown is only an invitation to imagine, on the basis of our experience of the body, other techniques of the body. The technique which happens to be actualized in us can never be reduced to simply one among all possible techniques; for it is against the background of this privileged experience, where we learn to know the body as a "structuring" principle, that we glimpse the other "possibles," no matter how different from it they may be.

It is essential never to cut sociological inquiry off from our experience of social subjects (which of course includes not only what we have experienced ourselves but also the behavior we perceive through the gestures, tales, or writings of our fellow men). For the sociologist's equations begin to represent something social only at the moment when the correlations they express are connected to one another and enveloped in a certain unique *view* of the social and of nature which is characteristic of the society under consideration and has come to be institutionalized in it as the hidden principle of all its overt functioning—even though this view may be rather different than the official conceptions which are current in that society. If objectivism or scientism were ever to succeed in depriving sociology of all recourse to significations, it would save it from "philosophy" only by shutting it off from knowledge of its object. Then we might do mathematics in the social, but we would not have the mathematics *of* the society being considered. The sociologist philosophizes every time he is required to not only record but comprehend the facts. At the moment of interpretation, he is himself already a philosopher. This means that the professional philosopher is not disqualified to reinterpret facts he has not observed himself, if these facts say something more and different than what the scientist has seen in them. As Husserl says, eidetic analysis of the physical thing did not begin with phenomenology but with Galileo. And reciprocally, the philosopher has the right to read and interpret Galileo.

The segregation we are fighting against is no less harmful to philosophy than to the development of scientific knowledge. How could any philosopher aware of the philosophical tradition seriously propose to forbid philosophy to have anything to do with science? For after all the philosopher always thinks *about something:* about the square traced in the sand, about the ass, the horse, and the mule, about the cubic foot of size, about cinnabar, the Roman State, and the hand burying itself in the iron filings. The philosopher thinks about his experience and his world. Except by decree, how could he be given the right to forget what science says about this same experience and world? Under the collective noun "science" there is nothing other than a systematic handling and a methodical use—narrower and broader, more and less discerning—of this same experience which begins with our first perception. Science is a set of means of perceiving, imagining, and, in short, living which are oriented toward the same truth that our first experiences establish an urgent inner need for. Science may indeed purchase its exactness at the price of schematization. But the remedy in this case is to confront it with an integral experience, not to oppose it to philosophical knowledge come from who knows where.

Husserl's great merit is that from the time he reached philosophical maturity, and increasingly so as he pursued his efforts, he made use of his "intuition of essences," "morphological essences," and "phenomenological experience" to mark out a realm and an attitude of inquiry where philosophy and effective knowledge could meet. We know that he began by affirming, and continued to maintain, a rigorous distinction between the two. Nevertheless, it seems to us that his idea of a psycho-phenomenological parallelism (or as we may say in generalizing, his thesis of a parallelism between positive knowledge and philosophy such that there is for each affirmation of one a corresponding affirmation of the other) leads him in truth to the idea of *reciprocal envelopment.* As far as the social is concerned then, the problem is to know how it can be both a "thing" to be acquainted with without prejudices, and a "signification" which the societies we acquaint ourselves with only provide an occasion for—how, that is, the social can exist both in itself and in us. Having entered this labyrinth, let us follow the stages by which Husserl makes his way towards his last conceptions, in which, moreover, these stages will be as much retained as gone beyond.

At the outset, he asserts philosophy's rights in terms which seem to abolish those of actual knowledge. Speaking of that eminently social relation, language, he states as a principle [1] that we could not possibly understand the functioning of our own language, or break away from the pseudo-certainties which result from the fact that it is ours and gain a true acquaintance with other languages, unless we had first constituted a schema of the "ideal form" *of* language and of the modes of expression which must in strict necessity pertain to it if it is to be language. Only then will we be able to understand how German, Latin,

1. *Logische Untersuchungen,* II, 4te Unters., p. 339.

and Chinese participate (each in its own way) in this universal structure of essential meanings, and to define each of these languages as a mixture in original proportions of universal "forms of signification"—a "confused" and incomplete realization of the "general and rational grammar." The actually existing language was thus to be reconstructed by a synthetic operation which began with the essential structures of any possible language and enveloped it in their ideal clarity. Philosophical thought took on an air of absolute autonomy, it and only it being capable of attaining true understanding through recourse to essences which provided the key to things.

Generally speaking, this stage of Husserl's thought calls our whole historical experience of social relationships into question in the interest of determining essences. Historical experience does present us with many "social processes" and "cultural formations" such as forms of law, art, and religion. But as long as we stick to such empirical realizations, we do not even know the meaning of these headings we class them under. And, consequently, we know even less whether the historical changes in a given religion or a given form of law or art are really essential and provide a true standard of their value; or whether on the contrary this law, this art, this religion contain yet other possibilities. History, Husserl used to say at this point, cannot judge an idea; and when it does, this "evaluating" (*wertende*) history borrows surreptitiously from the "ideal sphere" the necessary connections which it pretends to bring forth from the facts.[2]

As for the "world-views" which submit to being no more than the balance of what the knowledge available at any given moment allows us to think, Husserl grants that the problem they raise is a real one, but he objects that it is raised in such a way as to block any serious solution. The real problem stems from the fact that philosophy would lose its meaning if it refused to judge the present. Just as a morality which was "as a matter of principle transfinite and endless" would no longer be a morality, a philosophy which as a matter of principle gave up taking any position in the present would no longer be a philosophy.[3] But the fact is that in wanting to face up to present problems, "to have their system, and in time enough to be able to live afterwards," [4] the *Weltanschauung* philosophers miss everything. They can bring no more rigor to the solution of these problems than other men, because like them they are within the *Weltanschauung* and have no *Weltwissenschaft*. And in devoting themselves entirely to thinking about the present, they rob true philosophy of the unconditional devotion she

2. *Philosophie als strenge Wissenschaft*, p. 325.
3. *Ibid.*, p. 332.
4. *Ibid.*, p. 338.

demands. Now once constituted, true philosophy would allow us to think about the present as well as the past and the eternal. To go straight to the present is thus to relinquish the solid for the illusory.

When in the second part of his career Husserl returns to the problems of history, and especially to the problem of language, we no longer find the idea of a philosopher-subject, master of all that is possible, who must first put *his own* language at a distance in order to find the ideal forms of a universal language this side of all actuality. Philosophy's first task in respect to language now appears to be to reveal to us anew our inherence in a certain system of speech of which we make fully efficacious use precisely because it is present to us just as immediately as our body. Philosophy of language is no longer contrasted to empirical linguistics as an attempt at total objectification of language to a science which is always threatened by the preconceptions of the native language. On the contrary, it has become the rediscovery of the subject in the act of speaking, as contrasted to a science of language which inevitably treats this subject as a thing. Pos [5] has shown quite clearly how the phenomenological attitude is contrasted to the scientific or observational attitude. The latter, since it is directed toward an already established language, takes that language in the past and breaks it down into a sum of linguistic facts in which its unity disappears. The former has become the attitude that permits direct access to the living language present in a linguistic community which uses it not only to preserve but to establish, and to envisage and define a future. So here a language is no longer broken down into elements which can be added up piece by piece; it is like an organ whose tissues all contribute to its unified functioning, irrespective of the diversity of their origins and the fortuitousness of their original insertion into the whole.

Now if it is really the peculiar office of phenomenology to approach language in this way, phenomenology is no longer the synthetic determination of all possible languages. Reflection is no longer the return to a pre-empirical subject which holds the keys to the world; it no longer circumambulates its present object and possesses its constitutive parts. Reflection must become aware of its object in a contact or frequenting which at the outset exceeds its power of comprehension. The philosopher is first and foremost the one who realizes that he is situated in language, that he *is speaking;* and phenomenological reflection can no longer be limited to a completely lucid enumeration of the "conditions without which" there would be no language. It must show why there is speech—that paradox of a subject turned toward the future who speaks

5. H. Pos, "Phénoménologie et Linguistique," *Revue Internationale de Philosophie* (January, 1939).

and understands—in spite of all we know about the accidents and shifts of meaning which have created the language. Present speech casts a light which is not found in any merely "possible" expression. It is an operation in our linguistic "field of presence" which, far from being a particular case of other possible systems of expression, serves as our model for conceiving of them. Reflection is no longer the passage to a different order which reabsorbs the order of present things; it is first and foremost a more acute awareness of the way in which we are rooted in them. From now on, the absolute condition of a valid philosophy is that it pass by way of the present.

To tell the truth, we do not have to wait until Husserl recognizes that the *Lebenswelt* is phenomenology's principal theme to note the repudiation of formal reflection in his thought. The reader of the *Ideen I* will have already noticed that eidetic intuition has always been a "confirmation," and phenomenology an "experience" (a phenomenology of seeing, Husserl said, should be constructed on the basis of a *Sichtigkeit* which we have actually experienced to begin with; and he generally rejected the possibility of a "mathematics of phenomena" or a "geometry of what is lived"). It is just that the ascending movement was not stressed. Thought barely supported itself on its actually existing structures in order to sift out its possible ones: a wholly imaginary variation extracted a treasure of eidetic assertions from the lowest-grade experience. When the recognition of the life-world, and thus too of language as we live it, becomes characteristic of phenomenology (as it does in the last writings), this is only a more resolute way of saying that philosophy does not possess the truth about language and the world from the start, but is rather the recuperation and first formulation of a Logos scattered out in our world and our life and bound to their concrete structures—that "Logos of the aesthetic world" already spoken of in the *Formal and Transcendental Logic*. Husserl will only be bringing the movement of all his previous thought to completion when he writes in a posthumous fragment that transitory inner phenomena are brought to ideal existences by becoming incarnate in language.[6] Ideal existence, which at the beginning of Husserl's thought was to have been the foundation for the possibility of language, is now the most characteristic possibility *of* language.

But if philosophy no longer consists in passing to the infinity of possibles or leaping into absolute objectivity, then it is understandable that certain linguistic investigations should anticipate Husserl's own, and that certain linguists should without knowing it tread upon the ground of phenomenology. Husserl does not say it, nor does Pos, but it

6. "Ursprung der Geometrie," *Revue Internationale de Philosophie* (January, 1939), p. 210.

is hard not to think of Saussure when Husserl insists that we return from language as object to the spoken word.

In reality, philosophy's whole relationship to history changes in the very movement of reflection which was trying to free philosophy from history. In proportion as he reflects further upon the relation between eternal and factual truths, Husserl finds it necessary to replace his initial delimitations with a far less simple relation. His meditations on transcendental reflection and its possibility, which he pursued for at least twenty years, show clearly enough that in his view this term did not designate some sort of distinct faculty which could be circumscribed, pointed out, and actually isolated side by side with other modalities of experience. In spite of all his trenchant formulations constantly reaffirming the radical distinction between the natural and the transcendental attitude, Husserl is well aware from the start that they do in fact encroach upon one another, and that every *fact of consciousness* bears the transcendental within it. As far as the relation of fact and essence is concerned, in any case, a text as old as *Philosophy as a Rigorous Science* (after having distinguished, as we have been recalling, the "ideal sphere" and historical facts) expressly foresaw the overlapping of the two orders. For it pointed out that the reason why historical criticism really shows that a given order of institutions has no substantial reality, and is actually only a common noun to designate a mass of facts with no internal relation, is that empirical history includes confused intuitions of essences, and criticism is always the reverse side or emergence of a positive assertion which is already there.

In the same article, Husserl was already admitting that history is precious to the philosopher *because it reveals the Gemeingeist to him*. It is not so hard to go from these first formulations to the later ones. To say that history teaches the philosopher what the *Gemeingeist* is, is to say that it gives him the problem of intersubjective communication to think about. It makes it necessary for him to understand how there are not only individual minds (each incumbent in a perspective on the world) which the philosopher can inspect by turns without being allowed (and even less required) to think of them *together*, but also a community of minds coexisting for one another and as a consequence invested individually with an exterior through which they become visible. As a result, the philosopher may no longer speak of mind in general, deal with each and every mind under a single name, or flatter himself that he constitutes them. Instead he must see himself within the dialogue of minds, situated as they all are, and grant them the dignity of self-constituting beings at the very moment that he claims that dignity for himself. We are on the verge of the enigmatic formulation Husserl will arrive at in the texts of the *Krisis der europäischen Wissenschaften,* when he writes that "transcendental subjectivity is intersubjectivity."

Now if the transcendental is intersubjectivity, how can the borders of the transcendental and the empirical help becoming indistinct? For along with the other person, all the other person sees of me—all my facticity—is reintegrated into subjectivity, or at least posited as an indispensable element of its definition. Thus the transcendental descends into history. Or as we might put it, the historical is no longer an external relation between two or more absolutely autonomous subjects but has an interior and is an inherent aspect of their very definition. They no longer know themselves to be subjects simply in relation to their individual selves, but in relation to one another as well.

In the unpublished manuscripts of the final period, the contrast between fact and essence will be explicitly mediated by the idea that the purest reflection discloses a "genesis of meaning" (*Sinngenesis*) immanent in its objects—the need for each manifestation of its objects to have a "before" and "after" and develop through a series of steps or stages in which each step anticipates and is taken up in a subsequent one that could not possibly exist "at the same time" as the preceding one yet presupposes it as its past horizon. Of course this intentional history is not simply the sum of all manifestations taken one by one. It takes them up again and puts them in order; in the actuality of a present, it reanimates and rectifies a genesis which could miscarry without it. But it can do so only in contact with what is given, by seeking its motives within it. It is no longer just through an unfortunate accident that the study of significations and the study of facts encroach upon one another. If it did not condense a certain development of *truth,* a signification would be empty.

It is to be hoped that we shall soon be able to read, in the complete works of Husserl,[7] the letter that he wrote to Lévy-Bruhl on March 11, 1935, after having read *La mythologie primitive.* Here he seems to admit that the philosopher could not possibly have immediate access to the universal by reflection alone—that he is in no position to do without anthropological experience or to construct what constitutes the meaning of other experiences and civilizations by a purely imaginary variation of his own experiences. "It is a possible and highly important task," he writes, "it is a great task to project ourselves into (*einzufühlen*) a human community enclosed in its living and tradi-

7. In the process of being published at The Hague by Martinus Nijhoff, under the direction of H. L. Van Breda. The editors have not granted us any rights to quote the few unpublished excerpts to be found here. Consequently we ask the reader not to expect any more than a foretaste of texts whose only authorized edition is being prepared by the Husserl Archives of Louvain.

tional sociality, and to understand it insofar as, in and on the basis of its total social life, that human community possesses the world, which is not for it a 'representation of the world' but the real world." Now our access to archaic worlds is barred by our own world. Lévy-Bruhl's primitives "have no history" (*geschichtlos*); for them "life is only a passing present" (*ein Leben, das nur stromende Gegenwart ist*). We on the contrary live in an historical world; a world, that is, which "has a partly realized future (the national 'past') and a partly to be realized future." No intentional analysis seeking to recover and reconstitute the structures of the archaic world could possibly limit itself to making those of our own explicit; for what gives meaning to these structures is the milieu or *Umwelt* of which they are the typical style, and thus we cannot understand them without understanding how time passes and being is constituted in these cultures. Husserl goes so far as to write that "on the path of that already largely developed intentional analysis, historical relativism is incontestably justified as an anthropological fact."

To bring things to a close, how does Husserl now conceive of philosophy? The last lines of the letter give us an idea: philosophy must accept all the acquisitions of science (which have the first word concerning knowledge), and thus historical relativism along with them. But as philosophy, it cannot be content to simply make note of the variety of anthropological facts. "Although anthropology, like every positive science and all these sciences as a whole, may have the first word concerning knowledge, it does not have the last." Judging by Husserl's later views, philosophy would gain autonomy after, not before, positive knowledge. This autonomy would not exempt the philosopher from gathering in everything anthropology has to offer us, which means, basically, testing our effective communication with other cultures. Nor could it withhold anything from the scientist's jurisdiction which was accessible to his methods of research. It would simply set itself up in a dimension where no scientific knowledge can dispute it. Let us try to show which one.

Suppose the philosopher no longer lays claim to the unconditional power to think his own thought through and through. He agrees that his "ideas" and his "certainties" are always to some extent naive, and that caught up as they are in the fabric of the culture he belongs to, they cannot be truly known by just being scrutinized and varied in thought, but must be confronted with other cultural formations and viewed against the background of other preconceptions. Then has he not from this moment on abdicated his office and handed his rights over to empirical investigation and the positive disciplines? No, he has not; that is just the point. The same dependence upon history which prohibits the philosopher from arrogating to himself an immediate access to the universal or the eternal prohibits the sociologist from taking the philosopher's place in this function and giving ontological value to the scientific objectification of the social. The concept of history in its most profound sense does not shut the thinking subject up in a point of space and time; he can seem to be thus contained only to a way of thinking which is itself capable of going outside all time and place in order to see him in his time and place.

Now it is precisely this presumption to absolute thought which is discredited by the historical sense. There can be no question of simply transferring to science the grand-mastery denied to systematic philosophy, as historicism does. "You believe you think for all times and all men," the sociologist says to the philosopher, "and by that very belief you only express the preconceptions or pretentions of your culture." That is true, but it is no less true of the dogmatic sociologist than it is of the philosopher. *Where does he speak from,* the sociologist who speaks in this way? The sociologist can only form this idea of an historical time which allegedly contains philosophers as a box contains an object by placing himself outside history in turn and claiming the privileged position of absolute spectator.

In reality, it is the very concept of the relationships of mind to its object that historical consciousness invites us to reshape. The point is that my thought's inherence in a certain historical situation of its own and, through that situation, in other historical situations which interest it—since it is the fundamental origin and original foundation of the objective relations which science speaks to us about—makes knowledge of the social self-knowledge, and calls forth and authorizes a *view of intersubjectivity as my own* which science forgets even as it utilizes it, and which is proper to philosophy. Since we are all hemmed in by history, it is up to us to understand that whatever truth we may have is to be gotten not in spite of but through our historical inherence. Superficially considered, our inherence destroys all truth; considered radically, it founds a new idea of truth. As long as I cling to the ideal of an absolute spectator, of knowledge with no point of view, I can see my situation as nothing but a source of error. But if I have once recognized that through it I am grafted onto every action and all knowledge which can have a meaning for me, and that step by step it contains everything which can *exist* for me, then my contact with the social in the finitude of my situation is revealed to me as the point of origin of all truth, including scientific truth. And since we have an idea of truth, since we are in truth and cannot escape it, the only thing left for me to do is to define a truth in the situation.

Knowledge will then be based upon the unimpeachable fact that we are not in a situation like an object in objective space. Our situation is for us the source of our curiosity, our investigations, and our interest in first other situations as variants of our own and then in our own life, illuminated by (and this time considered as a variant of) the lives of others. Ultimately, our situation is what links us to the whole of human experience, no less than what separates us from it. "Science" and "sociology" will designate the effort to construct ideal variables which objectify and schematize the functioning of this effective communication. We shall call "philosophy" the consciousness we must maintain—as our consciousness of the ultimate reality whose functioning our theoretical constructions retrace but could not possibly replace—of the open and successive community of *alter egos* living, speaking, and thinking in one another's presence and in relation to nature as we sense its presence behind, around, and before us at the limits of our historical field.

Thus philosophy is not defined by a peculiar domain of its own. Like sociology, it only speaks about the world, men, and mind. It is distinguished by a certain *mode* of consciousness we have of others, of nature, or of ourselves. It is nature and man in the present, not "flattened out" (Hegel) in a derivative objectivity but such as they are presented in our present cognitive and active commerce with them. Philosophy is nature in us, the others in us, and we in them. Accordingly, we must not simply say that philosophy is compatible with sociology, but that it is necessary to it as a constant reminder of its tasks; and that each time the sociologist returns to the living sources of his knowledge, to what operates within him as a means of understanding the forms of culture most remote from him, he practices philosophy spontaneously. Philosophy is not a particular body of knowledge; it is the vigilance which does not let us forget the source of all knowledge.

We are not claiming that Husserl would ever have agreed to some definition of this sort, since up until the end he always thought of the return to living history and the spoken word—the return to the *Lebenswelt*—as a preparatory step which should be followed by the properly philosophical task of universal constitution. Yet it is a fact that in his last published work, rationality is no longer more than one of two possible alternatives we face, the other being chaos. And it is precisely with an awareness of a sort of nameless adversity threatening rationality that Husserl searches for that which can stimulate knowledge and action. Reason as a summons and a task, the "latent reason" which must be changed into itself and brought to explicit consciousness, becomes the criterion of philosophy. "It is only in this way that it will be decided whether the end (*Telos*) innate in the European conception of man since the birth of Greek philosophy—his will to be human on the basis of philosophical reason (and his inability to be so in any other way), in an unending movement from latent to manifest reason, and in an unending attempt to govern himself through his own human truth and authenticity—whether all this is only the mere historical fact of an illusion, the accidental acquisition of one accidental human community among other wholly different human communities and histories. Or whether, on the contrary, there did not come to light for the first time in the Greek conception of man what is essentially inherent as entelechy in the quality of man as man. Taken in itself, the quality of man consists essentially in being human within human communities bound together generatively and socially. And if man is a rational being, he can be so only to the extent that the whole human community he belongs to is a rational community, either latently disposed to reason or openly disposed to an entelechy which has arrived at self-awareness or become evident to itself, and is thus consciously guiding human development according to its essential necessity. Philosophy and science would then be the historical movement of revelation of universal reason, 'innate' in the human community as such." [8] Thus the essence of man is not given, nor is his essential necessity unconditional. His essence will energize his actions only if the rationality first conceived for us by the Greeks does not remain accidental but proves to be essential by the knowledge and the action it makes possible, and gets itself recognized by irrational human communities. The Husserlian essence is now borne by an "entelechy."

Philosophy's role as consciousness of rationality in contingency is no insignificant residue. In the last analysis, only the philosophical consciousness of intersubjectivity enables us to understand scientific knowledge. Without this philosophical consciousness, scientific knowledge remains indefinitely in suspense, always deferred until the termination of discussions of causality which, having to do with man, are by their nature interminable. We wonder for example whether social relationships are (as psychoanalytic sociology would have it) only the amplification and generalization of the sexual-aggressive drama, or whether on the contrary this drama itself (in the form described by psychoanalysis) is only a particular case of the institutional relationships of Western societies. These discussions have the value of inducing the sociologists to make observations, of revealing facts, and of giving rise to analyses and insights. But they admit of no conclusion as long as we remain on the level of causal and "objective" thought, since we can neither reduce one of the causal chains to nothing nor think of them together as causal chains. We can hold that both these views are

8. "Die Krisis der Europäischen Wissenschaften und die transzendentale Phänomenologie," *Philosophia*, I (1936), p. 92.

true (as they are) only on the condition that we move to an a-causal mode of thought, which is philosophy. For there are two truths which must be grasped simultaneously. The individual drama takes place among *roles* which are already inscribed in the total institutional structure, so that from the beginning of his life the child proceeds—simply by perceiving the attentions paid to him and the utensils surrounding him—to a deciphering of meanings which from the outset generalizes his own drama into a drama of his culture. And yet it is the whole symbolic consciousness which in the last analysis elaborates what the child lives or does not live, suffers or does not suffer, feels or does not feel. Consequently, there is not a single detail of his most individual history which does not contribute something to that personal significance he will manifest when (having first thought and lived as he thought best, and perceived according to his culture's imagery) he finally comes to the point of reversing the relationship and slipping into the meanings of his speech and his behavior, converting even the most secret aspects of his experience into culture. From the causal point of view it is unthinkable that this centripetal movement and this centrifugal movement are compossible. These reversals, these "metamorphoses," this proximity and distance of the past and present (of the archaic and the "modern"), this way that cultural time and space roll up on themselves, and this perpetual overdetermination of human events which makes the social fact (no matter how singular the local or temporal conditions) always appear to us as a variant of a single life that ours is also part of, and makes every *other person another ourself* for us—all these things become conceivable or even visible to the philosophical attitude alone.

Philosophy is indeed, and always, a break with objectivism and a return from *constructa* to lived experience, from the world to ourselves. It is just that this indispensable and characteristic step no longer transports it into the rarified atmosphere of introspection or into a realm numerically distinct from that of science. It no longer makes philosophy the rival of scientific knowledge, now that we have recognized that the "interior" it brings us back to is not a "private life" but an intersubjectivity that gradually connects us ever closer to the whole of history. When I discover that the social is not simply an object but to begin with my situation, and when I awaken within myself the consciousness of this social-which-is-mine, then my whole synchrony becomes present to me, through that synchrony I become capable of really thinking about the whole past as the synchrony it has been in its time, and all the convergent and discordant action of the historical community is effectively given to me in my living present. Giving up systematic philosophy as an explanatory device does not reduce philosophy to the rank of an auxiliary or a propagandist in the service of objective knowledge; for philosophy has a dimension of its own, the dimension of coexistence—not as a *fait accompli* and an object of contemplation, but as the milieu and perpetual event of the universal *praxis*. Philosophy is irreplaceable because it reveals to us both the movement by which lives become truths, and the circularity of that singular being who in a certain sense already *is* everything he *happens to think*.

4 / From Mauss to Claude Lévi-Strauss

WHAT WE NOW CALL social anthropology (to use a term which is customary outside France and is spreading in France) is what sociology becomes when it admits that the social, like man himself, has two poles or facets: it is significant, capable of being understood from within, and at the same time personal intentions within it are generalized, toned down, and tend toward processes, being (as the famous expression has it) mediated by things. Now no one in France has anticipated this more supple sociology as Marcel Mauss has. In many respects, social anthropology consists of Mauss's works, which are still vital in our time.

After twenty-five years, the famous *Essai sur le Don, forme archaïque de l'Echange* has just been translated for Anglo-Saxon readers with a preface by Evans-Pritchard. "Few people," Claude Lévi-Strauss [1] writes, "have been able to read *Essai sur le Don* without having the still indefinable yet imperious certainty of being present at a decisive event in the development of science." A stage in the development of sociology which has made such impressions is worth reconsidering.

The new science had wanted, in Durkheim's well-known phrase, to treat social facts "as things," and no longer as "objectified systems of ideas." But as soon as it tried to be more precise, it only succeeded in defining the social as "pertaining to the psychical." Social facts, it was said, were "representations"; it was just that instead of being individual they were "collective." From this was derived the much discussed idea of "collective consciousness," conceived of as a distinct entity at the heart of history. The relation between it and the individual, like that between two things, remained external. What was given to sociological

1. Claude Lévi-Strauss, brilliant and unusual French authropologist, a friend and colleague of Merleau-Ponty at the Collège de France. His works on kinship structures have been the center of much scientific and philosophical debate in post-war France.—Trans.

explanation was taken away from psychological or physiological explanation, and vice versa.

In another connection, under the name of social morphology, Durkheim proposed an ideal genesis of societies through the combination of elementary societies and the composition of compounds among them. The simple was confused with the essential and the primitive. Lévy-Bruhl's idea of a "pre-logical mentality" went no further towards opening our eyes to all there can be in so-called primitive cultures which is irreducible to our own, since it congealed them in an insurmountable difference. In both ways the French School missed that access to another person which nonetheless defines sociology. How can we understand someone else without sacrificing him to our logic or it to him? Whether it assimilated reality too quickly to our own ideas, or on the contrary declared it impenetrable to them, sociology always spoke as if it could roam over the object of its investigations at will—the sociologist was an absolute observer. What was lacking was a patient penetration of its object, communication with it.

Marcel Mauss, on the contrary, met these lacks instinctively. Neither his teachings nor his works are a polemic against the principles of the French School. As Durkheim's nephew and collaborator, he had every reason to do him justice. It is in his particular way of making contact with the social that the difference between them bursts forth. In the study of magic, Mauss said, concomitant variations and external correlations leave a *residue* which must be described; for it is in this residue that the underlying reasons for belief are found. Consequently, we have to think our way into the phenomenon, reading or deciphering it. And this reading always consists in grasping the mode of exchange which is constituted between men through institutions, through the connections and equivalences they establish, and through the systematic way in which they govern the use of tools, manufactured or alimentary products, magical formulas, ornaments, chants, dances, and mythical elements, as a given language governs the use of phonemes, morphemes, vocabulary, and syntax. This social fact, which is no longer a massive reality but an efficacious system of symbols or a network of symbolic values, is going to be inserted into the depths of the individual. But the regulation which circumvents the individual does not eliminate him. It is no longer necessary to choose between the individual and the collective: "What is true," Mauss writes, "is not a prayer or law but the Melanesian on such and such an island, Rome, or Athens." Similarly, there are no longer just absolutes or mere summations, but everywhere totalities or articulated wholes of varying richness. Mauss notices contrasts in the supposed syncretism of primitive mentality which are just as important for him as the famous "participations." In conceiving of the social as a symbolism, he had provided himself with the means for respecting individual and social reality and cultural variety without making one impervious to the other. A more comprehensive way of thinking ought to be able to penetrate to the irrational in magic and the gift. "Above all," he said, "we must make up the largest possible list of categories; we must set out from all those we can know that men have made use of. Then we shall see that there are still many dead, or pale, or darkened moons in the firmament of reason."

But for Mauss this was more of an insight concerning the social than a theory about it. Perhaps that is why his conclusions fall short of his discovery. He looks for the principle of exchange in *mana*, as he had looked for that of magic in *hau*. These are enigmatic concepts which do not so much provide a theory about the facts as reproduce the society's own theory. In reality they only designate a sort of emotional cement between the multitudinous facts which he had to link together. But are these facts distinct to begin with, so that we must try to bring them together? Isn't the synthesis primary? Isn't *mana* precisely the obvious fact, for the individual, that there are certain relationships of equivalence between what he gives, receives, and gives back again? Isn't it his experience of a certain distance between himself and his institutional state of equilibrium with others, the primary fact of his behavior's double reference to himself and the other person, and the demands of an invisible totality which in his eyes both he and the other person are substitutable parts of? If so, the exchange would not be an effect of society but society itself in act. What there is of the numinous in *mana* would stem from the essence of symbolism and would become accessible to us through the paradoxes of speech and our relation to others. It would be analogous to that "zero phoneme" the linguists talk about which, without having any assignable value itself, is contrasted to the absence of phonemes; or to that "floating signifier" which articulates nothing yet opens a field of possible signification. But in speaking in this way we are following the movement of Mauss's thought beyond what he said and wrote. We are looking at him retrospectively in the perspective of social anthropology. We have already crossed the line which separates his thought from a different conception of and approach to the social, a conception which is brilliantly represented by Claude Lévi-Strauss.

* * *

In this new approach, the way in which exchange is organized in a sector of society or in society as a whole is called "structure." Social facts are neither things nor ideas; they are structures. Overused today, the term had a precise meaning to begin with. Psychologists used it to designate the configurations of the perceptual field, those wholes articulated by certain lines of force and giving every phenomenon its local value. In linguistics, too, structure is a concrete, incarnate system. When Saussure used to say that linguistic signs are diacritical—that they function only through their differences, through a certain spread between themselves and other signs and not, to begin with, by evoking a positive signification—he was making us see the unity which lies beneath a language's explicit signification, a systematization which is achieved in a language before its conceptual principle is known. For social anthropology, society is composed of systems of this type: systems of kinship and direct consanguinity (with the appropriate marriage regulations); systems of art, myth, and ritual. Social anthropology is itself the interacting totality of these systems. In saying that all these are structures, we distinguish them from the old social philosophy's "crystallized ideas." The subjects living in a society do not necessarily know about the principle of exchange which governs them, any more than the speaking subject needs to go through a linguistic analysis of his language in order to speak. They ordinarily make use of the structure as a matter of course. Rather than their having got it, it has, if we may put it this way, "got them." Suppose we compare it to language, either in the everyday or the poetic usage of speech, where words seem to speak by themselves and become entities.

Structure, like Janus, has two faces. On one side it organizes its constituent parts according to an internal principle; it is meaning. But this meaning it bears is, so to speak, a clumsy meaning. Thus when the scientist formulates and conceptually determines structures, and constructs models by means of which he intends to understand existing societies, there is no question for him of substituting the model for reality. As a matter of principle, structure is no Platonic idea. To imagine imperishable archetypes which dominate the life of all possible societies would be to make the mistake the old linguistics made when it supposed that there was a natural affinity for a given meaning in certain sonorous material. It would be to forget that the same traits of physiognomy can have a different meaning in different societies, according to the system they are caught up in. The reason why contemporary American society has rediscovered a path in its mythology which has already been taken in another time or place is not that a transcendent archetype has been embodied three times in Roman Saturnalia, Mexican katchinas, and the American Christmas. It is that this mythical structure offers a way of resolving some local, present tension, and is recreated in the dynamics of the present.

Structure does not deprive society of any of its weight or thickness. Society itself is a structure of structures: how could there be absolutely no relationship between the linguistic system, the economic system, and the kinship system it employs? But this relationship is subtle and variable. Sometimes it is a homology. At other times (as in the case of myth and ritual) one structure is the counterpart and antagonist of the other. Society as structure remains a many-faceted reality amenable to more than one interpretation. Up to what point can the comparison go? Will we end up finding, as sociology in the correct sense of the term would have it, universal invariants? That remains to be seen. Nothing limits structural research in this direction—but neither does anything require it to postulate the existence of such invariants at the outset. The primary concern of such research is to substitute relationships of complementarity for antimonies wherever it can.

Thus it is going to spread out in all directions, toward the universal and toward the monograph, each time going as far as possible to test just what may be lacking in each of the interpretations taken singly. The search for the elementary in kinship systems is going to be directed through the variety of customs toward a structural schema they can be considered variants of. From the moment that consanguinity excludes union—that the man gives up taking a wife in his biological family or his group and must go outside to form a union which requires, for reasons of equilibrium, an immediate or a mediate counterpart—a phenomenon of exchange begins which may be complicated indefinitely when direct reciprocity gives way to a general form of exchange. Thus models must be constructed which bring out the different possible constellations and the internal arrangement of different types of preferential marriage and different kinship systems. Our ordinary mental equipment is inadequate to reveal these extremely complex multidimensional structures; and perhaps we shall have recourse to a quasi-mathematical form of expression, which we shall be all the more able to make use of now that mathematics is no longer limited to quantitative relationships and what is measurable. One can even dream of a periodic table of kinship structures comparable to Mendeleev's periodic table of chemical elements. It is sound practice to envision at the limit the program of a universal code of structures, which would allow us to deduce them from one another by means of rules of transformation, and to construct possible systems different from existing ones—if it were only to direct empirical observation, as it has already been directed, toward certain existing institutions which would remain unnoticed without this theoretical anticipation.

There thus appears at the base of social systems a formal infrastructure (one is tempted to say an unconscious thought), an anticipation of the human mind, as if our science were already completed in events, and the human order of culture a second order of nature dominated by other invariants. But even if these invariants exist, even if social science were to find beneath structures a metastructure to which they conformed (as phonology does beneath phonemes), the universal we would thus arrive at could no more be substituted for the particular than general geometry annuls the local truth of Euclidean spatial relations. In sociology, too, there are considerations of scale, and the truth of general sociology in no way detracts from that of microsociology. The implications of a formal structure may well bring out the internal necessity of a given genetic sequence. But it is not these implications which make men, society, and history exist. A formal portrait of societies or even general articulations of every society do not constitute a metaphysics. The ideal models or diagrams traced out by a purely objective method are instruments of understanding. The elementary which social anthropology seeks is still elementary structures; that is, the connecting links of a thought network which leads us back from itself to the other face of the structure and to its own incarnation.

The surprising logical operations attested to by the formal structure of societies must certainly be effected in some way by the populations which live these kinship systems. Thus there ought to be a sort of lived equivalent of that structure, which the anthropologist must look for this time (through work which is no longer simply mental) at the price of his comfort and even his security. This process of joining objective analysis to lived experience is perhaps the most proper task of anthropology, the one which distinguishes it from other social science such as economics and demography. Value, yield, productivity, and maximum population are objects of a type of thinking which *encompasses* the social. We cannot require them to appear in the individual's experience in a pure state. The variables of anthropology, on the contrary, must be met with sooner or later on the level at which phenomena have an immediately human significance.

What disturbs us in this method of convergence is the old prejudice which opposes induction to deduction, as if the example of Galileo did not already show that actual thinking moves back and forth between experience and intellectual construction or reconstruction. Now experience in anthropology is our insertion as social subjects into a whole in which the synthesis our intelligence laboriously looks for has already been effected, since we live in the unity of one single life all the systems our culture is composed of. We can gain some knowledge from this synthesis which is ourselves. Furthermore, the equipment of our social being can be dismantled and reconstructed by the voyage, as we are able to learn to speak other languages. This provides a second way to the universal: no longer the overarching universal of a strictly objective method, but a sort of lateral universal which we acquire through ethnological experience and its incessant testing of the self through the other person and the other person through the self. It is a question of constructing a general system of reference in which the point of view of the native, the point of view of the civilized man, and the mistaken views each has of the other can all find a place—that is, of constituting a more comprehensive experience which becomes in principle accessible to men of a different time and country.

Ethnology is not a specialty defined by a particular object, "primitive societies." It is a way of thinking, the way which imposes itself when the object is "different," and requires us to transform ourselves. We also become the ethnologists of our own society if we set ourselves at a distance from it. For a few dozen years, since American society has become less sure of itself, it has given ethnologists access to governmental and military agencies. This is a remarkable method, which consists in learning to see what is ours as alien and what was alien as our own. And not even this expatriate eye of ours can be trusted; the will to go abroad itself has its personal motives, which may distort the evidence. Thus we shall have to say what these motives are too, precisely because we want to be true. Not because ethnology is literature, but because on the contrary its uncertainty ends only if the man who speaks of man does not wear a mask himself. At the point where two cultures cross, truth and error dwell together, either because our own training hides what there is to know from us, or on the contrary because it becomes, in our life in the field, a means of incorporating other people's differences. When Frazer used to say of field work, "God save me from it," he was depriving himself not only of facts but of a mode of understanding. Of course it is neither possible nor necessary for the same man to have experiential knowledge of all the societies he speaks about. He only has to have learned at some time and at sufficient length to let himself be taught by another culture. For from then on he has a new organ of understanding at his disposal—he has regained possession of that untamed region of himself, unincorporated in his own culture, through which he communicates with other cultures. Then even at his desk and from a distance he can cross-check the correlations of the most objective analysis with genuine perception.

Take, for example, knowledge of the structures of myth. We know how disappointing the attempts at general mythology have been. Perhaps they would have been less so if we had learned to listen to myths as we listen to an informant's account in the field, that is, to its tone, its style, its rhythm and its recurrent themes no less than to its manifest content. To want to understand myth as a proposition, in terms of what it says, is to apply our own grammar and vocabulary to a foreign language. Then the whole myth has to be decoded without our even being able to postulate, as cryptographers do, that the code we are looking for has the same structure as ours. Leaving aside what myth tells us at first sight, which would tend to divert us from its true meaning, let us study its inner articulation, taking its episodes only insofar as they have what Saussure calls a diacritical value and produce such and such a recurrent relation or contrast.

As an illustration of the method and not as a theory, let us say for example that the difficulty of walking straight reappears three times in the Oedipus myth, the murder of a chthonian creature twice. These elements would be confirmed by two other contrasting systems. We would be surprised to find comparable elements in North American mythology. And through cross-checkings which cannot be reproduced here, we would arrive at the hypothesis that the structure of the Oedipus myth expresses the conflict between belief in human autochthony and overvaluation of kinship relationships. From this point of view, we can classify the myth's known variants, derive one from another by rules of transformation, and see them as so many logical tools and modes of mediation serving to arbitrate a fundamental contradiction. We have listened in on myth, and we end up at a logical (or as we could say with equal justification, an ontological) diagram: such and such a myth of the Canadian Pacific coast presupposes, in the last analysis, that the existent appears to the native as the negation of the non-existent. What is common to these abstract formulations and the quasi-ethnological method we adopted at the outset is a guiding thread of structure, experienced first in its compulsive repetitions and finally grasped in its exact form.

Here anthropology comes into contact with psychology. The Freudian version of the Oedipus myth becomes a particular case of its structural version. Man's relationship to the earth is not present in it; but what produces the Oedipal crisis is certainly in Freud's view the duality of sires, the paradox of the human kinship order. The Freudian hermeneutics too, in its least disputable aspect, is certainly the deciphering of an oneiric and reticent language, the language of our conduct. Neurosis is an individual myth. And like it myth is clarified when we look at it as a series of stratifications or laminations or (to put it differently) as a spiral thinking which is always trying to hide its fundamental contradiction from itself.

But anthropology gives the acquisitions of psychoanalysis or psychology new depth by incorporating them in its own framework: Freud or today's psychologists are not absolute observers; they belong to the history of Western thought. Thus we must not think that Westerners' neuroses and complexes give us a clear view of the truth of myth, magic, or witchcraft. According to the ethnological method's rule of reciprocal criticism, we must be equally concerned with seeing psychoanalysis as myth and the psychoanalyst as a witch doctor or shaman. Our psychosomatic investigations enable us to understand how the shaman heals, how for example he helps in a difficult delivery. But the shaman also enables us to understand that psychoanalysis is our own witchcraft. Even in its most canonical and respectable forms, psychoanalysis reaches the truth about a life only through the rapport it establishes between two lives in the solemn atmosphere of transference, which is not a purely objective method (if such a method exists). When it is applied to so-called "normal" subjects themselves, with all the more reason it ceases completely to be a conception which can be discussed or justified by cases. It no longer heals; it persuades. Psychoanalysis itself fashions subjects who conform to its interpretation of man. It has its converts, and perhaps its defectors; it can no longer have its convinced adherents. For it is neither true nor false but a myth. When Freudianism has deteriorated to this degree it is no longer an interpretation of the Oedipus myth but one of its variants.

On a deeper level, anthropology's concern is neither to prove that the primitive is wrong nor to side with him against us, but to set itself up on a ground where we shall both be intelligible without any reduction or rash transposition. This is what we do when we take the symbolic function as the source of all reason and unreason. For the number and richness of significations man has at his disposal always exceed the circle of definite objects which warrant the name "signified," because the symbolic function must always be ahead of its object and finds reality only by anticipating it in imagination. Thus our task is to broaden our reasoning to make it capable of grasping what, in ourselves and in others, precedes and exceeds reason.

This attempt rejoins that of the other "semiological" sciences, and in general, of the other sciences. Niels Bohr wrote: "The traditional differences [between human cultures] . . . in many respects resemble the different and equivalent ways in which physical experience may be described." Today each traditional category calls for a complementary (that is, an incompatible and inseparable) view, and it is under these difficult conditions that we are looking for what makes up the framework of the world. Linguistic time is no longer that series of simultaneities familiar to classical thought, which Saussure was still thinking of when he set the perspectives of the simultaneous and the successive apart as two clearly distinct realms. In Troubetzkoy's linguistics, synchronics, like legendary or mythological time, encroaches upon succession and diachronics. If the symbolic function outstrips what is given, there is inevitably something confused in the whole order of the culture it sustains. The antithesis between nature and culture is no longer sharp and clear. Anthropology comes back to an important class of cultural facts which are not governed by the rule prohibiting incest. Indian endogamy and the Iranian or Egyptian or Arabian practice of consanguinous or collateral marriage attest to the fact that culture sometimes comes to terms with nature. Now the forms of culture involved here are just the ones which have made scientific knowledge and a cumulative and progressive social life possible. It would seem that in its most efficacious (if not its most beautiful) forms, culture is more of a transformation of nature—a series of mediations in which the structure never emerges at the outset as a pure universal. What except history can we call this milieu in which a form laden with contingency suddenly opens a cycle of future and commands it with the authority of an established institution? Of course this history is not the one which seeks to make up the whole human field from instantaneous decisions and events situated and dated in serial time, but that history which is well aware that myth and legendary time always haunt human enterprises in other forms, which looks on the near or far side of minutely divided events, and which is in fact called "structural history."

This notion of structure, whose present good fortune in all domains responds to an intellectual need, establishes a whole system of thought. For the philosopher, the presence of structure outside us in natural and social systems and within us as symbolic function points to a way beyond the subject-object correlation which has dominated philosophy from Descartes to Hegel. By showing us that man is eccentric to himself and that the social finds its center only in man, structure particularly enables us to understand how we are in a sort of circuit with the socio-historical world. But this is too much philosophizing, whose weight anthropology does not have to bear. What interests the philosopher in anthropology is just that it takes man as he is, in his actual situation of life and understanding. The philosopher it interests is not the one who wants to explain or construct the world, but the one who seeks to deepen our insertion in being. Thus his recommendation could not possibly endanger anthropology, since it is based upon what is most concrete in anthropological method.

The present works of Lévi-Strauss, and those in preparation, clearly proceed from the same inspiration; but at the same time his research is renewing itself, surging forward on the basis of its own acquisitions. He is in the field planning to gather documentation in Melanesia which would enable him to move on in theory to the complex kinship structures—that is, to those structures from which our matrimonial system in particular arises. Now it already seems to him that this will not be simply an extension of previous works, but will on the contrary give them an added significance. In his initial view, modern kinship systems—which leave the determination of husband and wife to demographic, economic, or psychological conditioning—had to be defined as "more complex" variants of exchange. But full knowledge of complex exchange has not left the meaning of the central phenomenon of exchange intact; it has required and made possible a decisive deepening of it. Claude Lévi-Strauss does not plan to compare the complex systems deductively and dogmatically with simple ones. On the contrary, he thinks that the historical approach (across the Middle Ages and Indo-European and Semitic institutions) is indispensable to our understanding of these complex systems, and that historical analysis will require a distinction between a culture which absolutely prohibits incest and is the simple, direct, or immediate negation of nature, and a different culture which is the source of contemporary kinship systems and tends to scheme with nature and sometimes get around the prohibition of incest. It is precisely this second type of culture which has shown itself capable of opening a "hand-to-hand struggle with nature" and creating science, man's technical domination, and what has been called cumulative history. Thus from the viewpoint of modern kinship systems and historical societies, exchange as direct or immediate negation of nature would seem to be the limiting case of a more general relationship of otherness.

It is only at this level that the final significance of Lévi-Strauss's first investigations and the underlying nature of exchange and the symbolic function will be definitively established. At the level of elementary structures, the laws of exchange (which completely envelop behavior) are susceptible to a static study; and man, without even always formulating them in an indigenous theory, obeys them almost as the atom follows the law of distribution which defines it. At the other end of the anthropological field, in certain complex systems, structures burst apart and (as far as the determination of husband and wife is concerned) become open to "historical" motivations. Here exchange, symbolic function, and society no longer act as a second nature which is as imperious as the other and effaces it. Each person is invited to define his own system of exchange. By this very process the frontiers between cultures are erased; for the first time, no doubt, a world civilization becomes the order of the day.

This complex human community's relationship to nature and life is neither simple nor clear. What animal psychology and ethnology unveil in animality is not, assuredly, the origin of humanity, but rough sketches, partial prefigurations, and something like anticipatory caricatures of it. Man and society are not exactly outside of nature and the biological; they distinguish themselves from them by bringing nature's "stakes" together and risking them all together. This upheaval means immense gains, wholly new possibilities, as it also means losses which we must be able to estimate, risks we are beginning to ascertain. Exchange and symbolic function lose their rigidity, but also their hieratic beauty. Mythology and ritual are replaced by reason and method, but also by a wholly profane practice of life, which is accompanied moreover by shallow little compensatory myths. It is in taking all this into consideration that social anthropology is wending its way toward a balanced account of the human spirit, and toward a view of what it is and can be.

Thus inquiry feeds on facts which seem foreign to it at first, acquires new dimensions as it progresses, and reinterprets its first results in the light of new investigations which they have themselves inspired. At the same time, the scope of the domain covered and the precision of factual knowledge are increased. These are the marks of a great intellectual endeavor.

5 / Everywhere and Nowhere[1]

[1] Philosophy and the "Outside"

Putting together an anthology about famous philosophers may seem to be an inoffensive undertaking. Yet one does not attempt it without reservations. It raises the question of what idea one should have of the history of philosophy, and even of philosophy itself.

For the reader is not going to find just anecdotes in this volume, but philosophers' visible lives—the rough sketch, drawn in a few pages by different authors, of what these philosophers have tried to say throughout volumes. Even if the life, the work, or preferably the work and the life together, had been perfectly discerned in every instance, we would have only a history of philosophers or philosophies, not a history of philosophy; and so this work about philosophers would be unfaithful to what they were greatly concerned with, a truth which rises above opinions.

How could an anthology possibly have a central perspective? In order to bring out relationships, progressions, and retrogressions, we have to ask all the philosophers the same question and mark out the development of the problem in reference to it. So we cannot have the genealogy of philosophers here, nor the evolution of truth; and philosophy in our work risks being no more than a catalogue of "points of view" or "theories." A series of intellectual portraits will leave the reader with the impression of a fruitless endeavor in which each philosopher presents the whims inspired by his temper and the accidents of his life as truth, taking questions up again at their beginning and leaving them entire to his successors without there being any possiblity of comparison from one mental universe to another. Since the same

1. Introduction to an anthology, *Les Philosophes célèbres*, published by Lucien Mazenod.

words—idea, freedom, knowledge—have different meanings for different philosophers, and since we lack the comprehensive witness who would reduce them to a common denominator, how could we possibly see one single philosophy developing through different philosophers?

In order to respect what they looked for and speak worthily of them, should we not on the contrary take their doctrines as aspects of one running doctrine, and preserve them in an Hegelian fashion by giving them a place in a unified system?

The system, it is true, is in its own way unconstrained: since it incorporates philosophers into an integral philosophy, it follows that it claims to lead the philosophical venture better and farther than they have led it. For a philosophy which wanted to express Being, to survive as an aspect of truth or a first draft of a final but different system is not to be preserved. When we "go beyond" a philosophy "from within," we cut the heart out of it. We insult it by retaining it without what we judge to be its "limitations"—that is, without its words and concepts—as if the meanderings of the *Parmenides* or the flow of the *Meditations* could be reduced without loss to a paragraph of the System.

In reality, the System assumes that they are known; and that is why it can go farther. Even if it brings them to a conclusion, it does not include them. We learn the full meaning of Hegelian philosophy, which wanted to "go beyond," by going to the school of other philosophers. The movement of contradictories which pass into one another, the positive which bursts into negation and the negative which establishes itself as positive, all this begins in Zeno, the *Sophist*, Descartes' doubt. The System begins in them. It is the focal point in which the rays from many mirrors are concentrated: if for one moment they stopped darting their fires toward it, it would fall into nothingness. The past transgresses upon and grows through the present; and Truth is that imaginary system, the contemporary of all philosophies, which would be able to retain their signifying power without loss. An existing philosophy is evidently no more than a crude sketch of such a system.

Hegel knows this too. "The history of philosophy," he says, "is all present history." Which means that Plato, Descartes, Kant are not true simply in what they saw, reservation made for what they did not see. The turnings which made straight the way for Hegelian philosophy are not completed; they are still permissible. More than that; they are necessary. They are the way, and Truth is only the memory of all that has been found along the way. Hegel walls history up again in the tomb of his system, but past philosophies keep on breathing and stirring within it—along with them he shut up uneasiness, movement, and the working of contingency. To say that the System is the truth of what preceded it is *also* to say that great philosophies are "indestructible." [2] Not because they saw in part what was to be fully unveiled in the System, but rather because they established landmarks—Plato's reminiscence and "ideas," Aristotle's φύσις, Descartes' *malin génie*—which posterity has not stopped recognizing.

Sartre once contrasted the Descartes who existed, lived that life, spoke those words, and wrote those works—an unshakable block and indestructible landmark—and Cartesianism, a "wandering philosophy" which necessarily escapes our grasp because it changes endlessly in the hands of its inheritors. He was right, except that no boundary marks the point where Descartes stops and his successors begin, and there would be no more sense in enumerating the thoughts which *are in Descartes* and those which *are in his successors* than there would be in making an inventory of a language. With this reservation, what counts certainly is that thinking life called Descartes, whose fortunately preserved wake is his works. The reason why Descartes is present is that—surrounded by circumstances which today are abolished, and haunted by the concerns and some of the illusions of his times—he responded to these hazards in a way which teaches us to respond to our own, even though they are different and our response is different too.

One does not enter the Pantheon of philosophers by having worked assiduously at having only eternal thoughts, and the ring of truth never resounds so long as it does when the author calls upon his life for it. Past philosophies do not survive in their spirit alone, as stages of a final system. Their access to the timeless is no museum entrance. They endure with their truths and follies as total undertakings, or they do not endure at all. Hegel himself, that mind which wanted to contain Being, lives today and gives us food for thought not only through his profundities but also through his manias and his tics. There is not *a* philosophy which contains all philosophies; philosophy as a whole is at certain moments in each philosophy. To take up the celebrated phrase again, philosophy's center is everywhere and its circumference nowhere.

Thus truth and the whole are there from the start—but as a task to be accomplished, and thus not yet there. This singular relationship between philosophy and its past generally clarifies its relationships with the outside and, for example, with personal and social history.

Like past doctrines, philosophy lives from everything which happens to the philosopher and his times. But it throws it out of focus or transports it into the order of symbols and of the truth it utters, so that there is no more sense in judging the works by the life than the life by the works.

We do not have to choose between those who think that the history

2. M. Gueroult.

of the individual or the society contains the truth of the philosopher's symbolic constructions, and those who think on the contrary that the philosophical consciousness has as a matter of principle the keys to personal and social history. The alternative is imaginary, and the proof is that those who defend one of these theses surreptitiously have recourse to the other.

One can think of replacing the internal study of philosophies with a socio-historical explanation only in reference to a history whose course and meaning one thinks he clearly knows. One assumes, for example, a certain idea of "the whole man," or a "natural" equilibrium between man and man and man and nature. Then, this historical τέλος being given, every philosophy can be presented as a diversion, an alienation, and a resistance in respect to that necessary future; or on the contrary as a step and an advance toward it. But where does the guiding principle come from, and what is it worth? The question *ought* not to be asked. To ask it is already to "resist" a dialectic which is in the course of things, to take sides against it. But how do you know it is there? By philosophy. It is just that it is a secret philosophy, disguised as Process. What is contrasted to the internal study of philosophies is never socio-historical explanation; it is always another philosophy concealed in it.

Marxists show us that Hegel conceived of alienation as he did *because* he had the alienation of capitalist society before his eyes and thought according to it. This "explanation" would account for the Hegelian idea of alienation and make it an episode of capitalism only if a society in which man objectifies himself without alienating himself could be shown. Such a society was only an idea for Marx; and even for us the least that can be said is that it is not a fact. What Marxism sets in opposition to Hegel is not a fact but an idea of the relationship between man and society as a whole. Under the name of objective explanation, it is still a way of thinking which challenges another way of thinking and denounces it as an illusion. If Marxists reply that the Marxist idea, as an historical hypothesis, clarifies the history of capitalism before and after Marx, they move to the realm of facts and historical probability. But in this realm it will be necessary to "try out" the Hegelian idea of alienation in the same way; and see, for example, whether it does not help us understand even the societies based upon the Marxist idea. It is just such an inquiry which is excluded when Marxists declare in a doctrinaire fashion that the Hegelian idea of alienation is a product of the society in which Hegel lived. Consequently, they do not stick to the realm of facts, and their historical "explanation" is a way of philosophizing without seeming to, of disguising ideas as things and thinking imprecisely. A conception of history explains philosophies only on the condition that it becomes philosophy itself, and implicit philosophy.

On their side, the philosophers who are the most smitten with interiority strangely fail to live up to their principles when they call régimes and cultures into their court and judge them from the outside, as if interiority stopped being important when it was not *their own.*

Thus the partisans of "pure" philosophy and those of socio-economic explanation exchange roles before our very eyes, and we do not have to enter their interminable debate. We do not have to choose between a false conception of the "interior" and a false conception of the "exterior." Philosophy is everywhere, even in the "facts," and it nowhere has a private realm which shelters it from life's contagion.

We need to do many things to eliminate the twin myths of pure philosophy and pure history and get back to their effective relationships. What we would need first of all would be a theory of concepts or significations which took each philosophical idea as it is: never unburdened of historical import and never reducible to its origins. As new forms of grammar and syntax arising from the rubble of an old linguistic system or from the accidents of general history are nevertheless organized according to an expressive intention which makes a new system of them, so each philosophical idea emerging in the ebb and flow of personal and social history is not simply a result and a thing but a beginning and an instrument as well. As the discriminant in a new type of thought and a new symbolism, it sets up for itself a field of application which is incommensurable with its origins and can be understood only from within. Its origin is no more a good work than it is a sin, and it is the developed whole which must be judged, according to the view and grasp of experience it gives us. Rather than "explaining" a philosophy, the historical approach serves to show how its significance exceeds its circumstances, and how as an historical fact it transmutes its original situation into a means of understanding it and other situations. The philosophical universal lies in that instant and point where a philosopher's limitations are invested in a different history which is not parallel to the history of psychological or social facts, but which sometimes crosses and sometimes withdraws from it—or rather which does not pertain to the same dimension.

In order to understand this relationship we would also have to change our idea of psychological or historical genesis. We would have to think through psychoanalysis and Marxism again as experiences in which principles and standards are always challenged by what is judged in the light of them. This is not a matter of classifying men and societies according to their approximation to the canon of the classless society or the man without conflicts; these negative entities cannot be used to think about existing men or societies. We would especially have to understand how their contradictions function, the type of equilibrium which they have somehow managed to reach, and whether it paralyzes them or lets them live. And we would have to understand these things in all respects, taking account of job and work as well as sexual life in psychoanalysis, and as far as Marxism is concerned, of relationships in living experience as well as variables of economic analysis, of human qualities of relationships as well as production, and of clandestine social roles as well as official regulations. Although comparisons of this sort can provide a basis for preference and choice, they do not give us an ideal genetic series; and the relationship of one historical formation to another, like that of one type of man to another, will never be simply the relationship of true to false. The "healthy" man is not so much the one who has eliminated his contradictions as the one who makes use of them and drags them into his vital labors. We would also have to relativize the Marxist idea of a pre-history which is going to give way to history—of an imminence of the complete, true Society in which man is reconciled with man and nature—for although this is indeed what our social criticism demands, there is no force in history which is destined to produce it. Human history is not from this moment on so constructed as to one day point, on all its dials at once, to the high noon of identity. The progress of socio-economic history, including its revolutions, is not so much a movement toward an homogenous or a classless society as the quest, through always atypical cultural devices, for a life which is not unlivable for the greatest number. The relationships between this history which always travels from positive to positive, never overcoming itself in *pure* negation, and the philosophical concept which never breaks its ties with the world are as close as one could wish. Not that a single unequivocal meaning dwells in the rational and in the real (as both Hegel and Marx in their own way thought), but because the "real" and the "rational" are both cut from the same cloth, which is the historical existence of men, and because the real is so to speak *engaged* to reason through their common inherence in historical existence.

Even if we consider only one philosopher, he swarms with inner differences, and it is through these discordancies that we must find his "total" meaning. If I have difficulty finding the "fundamental choice" of the absolute Descartes Sartre spoke of, the man who lived and wrote once and for all three centuries ago, it is perhaps because Descartes himself did not at any moment coincide with Descartes. What he is in our eyes according to the texts, he was only bit by bit through his reaction upon himself. And the idea of grasping him in his entirety at his source is perhaps an illusory one if Descartes—instead of being some "central intuition," an eternal character, and an absolute individual—is this discourse, hesitant at first, which is affirmed through experience and use, which is apprised of itself little by little, and which never wholly stops intending the very thing it has resolutely excluded. A philosophy is not chosen like an object. Choice does not suppress what is not chosen, but sustains it marginally. The same Descartes who distinguishes so well between what arises from pure understanding and what pertains to the practice of life happens to map out at the same time the program for a philosophy which was to take as its principal theme the cohesion of the very orders he distinguishes. Philosophical choice (and doubtless all other choice) is never simple. And it is through their ambiguity that philosophy and history touch.

Although these remarks do not provide an adequate definition of philosophy, they are sufficient to absolve a work like this one, a mixture of philosophy, history, and anecdote. This disorder is a part of philosophy, which finds in it the means of creating its unity through digression and return to the center. Its unity is that of a landscape or a discourse, where everything is indirectly linked by secret references to a center of interest or central perspective which no guideline marks out in advance. Like Europe or Africa, the history of philosophy is a whole, even though it has its gulfs, its capes, its relief, its deltas and its estuaries. And even though it is lodged in a wider world, the signs of everything that is happening can be read in it. Then how could any mode of approach possibly be forbidden and unworthy of philosophers? A series of portraits is not in itself a criminal attempt on philosophy's life.

And as for the plurality of perspectives and commentators, it would disrupt the unity of philosophy only if that unity were one of juxtaposition or accumulation. But since philosophies are so many languages not immediately translatable into one another or able to be superimposed word for word upon one another, since each is necessary to the others in its own singular way, the diversity of commentators scarcely increases that of philosophies. Furthermore, if each commentator is asked, as we have asked ours, more for his reaction to a philosopher than for an "objective" account, we may find at this height of subjectivity a sort of convergence, and a kinship between the questions each of these contemporaries puts to his famous philosopher, face to face.

These problems are not settled by a preface, and need not be. If philosophy is unified by the successive reduction of differences and separations, we must necessarily encounter the difficulty of thinking about it at each stage of this book. When we come to distinguishing philosophy from Oriental thought or Christianity, we shall have to ask ourselves whether the term philosophy applies only to doctrines which are expressed conceptually, or whether it can be extended to experiences, forms of wisdom, and disciplines which do not attain to this degree or kind of consciousness, in which case we shall meet the

situations, and what India tells about them does not have the inexhaustible significance of Greek myths or Christian parables. They are almost entities or philosophemes, and the Chinese flatter themselves with having the least religious and most philosophical civilization there is. In fact, it is no more philosophical than religious, since it lacks knowledge of the mind's work in contact with the immediate world. Thus Oriental thought is original; it yields its secrets to us only if we forget the terminal forms of our culture. But in our individual or collective past we have what it takes to understand it. It dwells in the unsettled region where there is *not yet* religion and *not yet* philosophy; it is the impasse of immediate mind which we have been able to avoid. It is in this way that Hegel goes beyond it by incorporating it into the true development of mind as aberrant or atypical thought.

These Hegelian views are everywhere. When the West is defined in terms of the intervention of science or capitalism, the definition is always of Hegelian inspiration. For capitalism and science can define a civilization only when they are understood as "this-worldly asceticism" or "the labor of the negative," and the reproach made to the Orient is always that it has ignored them.

So the problem is completely clear: Hegel and those who follow him grant philosophical dignity to Oriental thought only by treating it as a distant approximation of conceptual understanding. Our idea of knowledge is so demanding that it forces every other type of thought to the alternative of resigning itself to being a first sketch of the concept or disqualifying itself as irrational. Now the question is whether we can claim as Hegel did to have this absolute knowledge, this concrete universal that the Orient has shut itself off from. If we do not in fact have it, our entire evaluation of other cultures must be re-examined.

Even at the end of his career, and just when he is laying bare the *crisis of Western knowledge,* Husserl writes that "China . . . India . . . are empirical or anthropological specimens." [7] Thus he seems to be setting out again on Hegel's way. But even though he retains the privileged position of Western philosophy, he does so not by virtue of its right to it—as if its possession of the principles of all possible cultures were absolutely evident—but in the name of a fact, and in order to assign a task to it. Husserl admitted that all thought is part of an historical whole or a "life-world"; thus in principle all philosophies are "anthropological specimens," and none has any special rights. He also admits that so-called primitive cultures play an important role in the exploration of the "life-world," in that they offer us variations of

7. *Die Krisis der europäischen Wissenschaften und die transzendentale Phänomenologie;* French translation, *Les Etudes Philosophiques* (April–June, 1949), p. 140.

this world without which we would remain enmeshed in our preconceptions and would not even see the meaning of our own lives. Yet the fact remains that the West has invented an idea of truth which requires and authorizes it to understand other cultures, and thus to recover them as aspects of a total truth. There has in fact been this miraculous turning back upon itself of an historical formation, through which Western thought has emerged from its particularity and "locality." A presumption and an intention which are still awaiting their fulfillment. If Western thought is what it claims to be, it must prove it by understanding all "life-worlds." It must bear factual witness to its unique significance beyond "anthropological specimens." So the idea of philosophy as a "rigorous science"—or as absolute knowledge—does reappear here, but from this point on with a question mark. Husserl said in his last years: "Philosophy as a rigorous science? The dream is all dreamed out." [8] The philosopher can no longer honestly avail himself of an absolutely radical way of thinking or presumptuously claim for himself intellectual possession of the world and conceptual rigor. His task is still to test himself and all things, but he is never done with it; because from now on he must pursue it through the phenomenal field, which no formal *a priori* assures him mastery of in advance.

Husserl had understood: our philosophical problem is to open up the concept without destroying it.

There is something irreplaceable in Western thought. The attempt to conceive and the rigor of the concept remain exemplary, even if they never exhaust what exists. A culture is judged by its degree of transparency, by the consciousness it has of itself and others. In this respect the West (in the broad sense of the term) is still the system of reference. It is the West which has invented the theoretical and practical means of becoming self-conscious and has opened up the way of truth.

But this possession of self and truth, which only the West has taken as its theme, nevertheless flits through the dreams of other cultures, and in the West itself it is not fulfilled. What we have learned about the historical relations of Greece and the Orient, and inversely, all the "Western" characteristics we have discovered in Oriental thought (Sophistry, Skepticism, elements of dialectics and logic), forbid us to draw a geographical frontier between philosophy and non-philosophy. Pure or absolute philosophy, in the name of which Hegel excluded the Orient, also excludes a good part of the Western past. It may be that a strict application of the criterion would spare Hegel alone.

And above all, since as Husserl said, the West has to justify its value as "historical entelechy" by new creations; since it too is an

8. "Philosophie als strenge Wissenschaft,—der Traum ist ausgeträumt," Husserliana, VI, p. 508.

historical creation, only committed to the onerous task of understanding others; its very destiny is to re-examine everything, including its idea of truth and conceptual understanding and all institutions—sciences, capitalism, and, if you wish, the Oedipus complex—which are directly or indirectly related to its philosophy. Not necessarily in order to destroy them, but to face up to the crisis they are going through and to rediscover the source from which they derive and to which they owe their long prosperity. From this angle, civilizations lacking our philosophical or economic equipment take on an instructive value. It is not a matter of going in search of truth or salvation in what falls short of science or philosophical awareness, or of dragging chunks of mythology as such into our philosophy, but of acquiring—in the presence of these variants of humanity that we are so far from—a sense of the theoretical and practical problems our institutions are faced with, and of rediscovering the existential field that they were born in and that their long success has led us to forget. The Orient's "childishness" has something to teach us, if it were nothing more than the narrowness of our adult ideas. The relationship between Orient and Occident, like that between child and adult, is not that of ignorance to knowledge or non-philosophy to philosophy; it is much more subtle, making room on the part of the Orient for all anticipations and "prematurations." Simply rallying and subordinating "non-philosophy" to true philosophy will not create the unity of the human spirit. It already exists in each culture's lateral relationships to the others, in the echoes one awakes in the other.

We would have to apply to the problem of philosophical universality what travelers tell us of their relationships with foreign civilizations. Photographs of China give us the impression of an impenetrable universe if they stop with the picturesque—stop, that is, with precisely *our* clipping, *our* idea of China. If, on the other hand, a photograph just tries to grasp Chinese people in the act of living together, they begin paradoxically to live for us, and we understand them. If we were able to grasp in their historical and human context the very doctrines which seem to resist conceptual understanding, we would find in them a variant of man's relationships to being which would clarify our understanding of ourselves, and a sort of oblique universality. Indian and Chinese philosophies have tried not so much to dominate existence as to be the echo or the sounding board of our relationship to being. Western philosophy can learn from them to rediscover the relationship to being and initial option which gave it birth, and to estimate the possibilities we have shut ourselves off from in becoming "Westerners" and perhaps reopen them.

This is why we should let the Orient appear in the museum of famous philosophers, and why (not being able to give it as much space as a detailed study would require) we have preferred to offer in the place of generalities some rather precise samples in which the reader will perhaps discern the Orient's secret, muted contribution to philosophy.

[3] Christianity and Philosophy

One of the tests in which philosophy best reveals its essence is its confrontation with Christianity. Not that there is Christianity unanimous on one side and philosophy unanimous on the other. On the contrary, what was striking in the famous discussion of this subject which took place twenty-five years ago [9] was that behind disagreement about the idea of Christian philosophy or about the existence of Christian philosophies, one detected a more profound debate concerning the nature of philosophy, and that on this point neither Christians nor non-Christians were agreed.

Gilson and Maritain said that philosophy is not Christian in its *essence* but only according to its status, only through the intermingling of religious thought and life in the same age and ultimately in the same man. And in this sense they were not so far from Bréhier, who distinguished philosophy as a rigorous system of ideas from Christianity as the revelation of a supernatural history of man, and concluded, for his part, that no philosophy as philosophy can be Christian. When on the other hand Brunschvicg,[10] thinking of Pascal and Malebranche, reserved the possibility of a philosophy which confirms the discordancy between existence and idea (and thus its own insufficiency), and thereby serves as an introduction to Christianity as an interpretation of existing man and the world, he was not so far from Blondel, for whom philosophy *was* thought realizing that it cannot "close the gap," locating and palpating inside and outside of us a reality whose source is not philosophical awareness. Once a certain point of maturity, experience, or criticism has been passed, what separates men or brings them together is not so much the final letter or formulation of their convictions but rather the way in which, Christians or not, they deal with their own duality and organize within themselves relationships between idea and reality.

The real question underlying debate about Christian philosophy is that of the relation between essence and existence. Shall we assume

9. "La notion de philosophie chrétienne," *Bulletin de la Société française de Philosophie*, Séance du 21 mars, 1931.

10. Léon Brunschvicg, twentieth-century French philosopher and professor who influenced the young Merleau-Ponty.—Trans.

that there is an essence of philosophy or a purely philosophical knowledge which is jeopardized in human life (in this case, religious life) but nevertheless remains what it is, strictly and directly communicable, the eternal word which illuminates every man who comes into this world? Or shall we say on the contrary that philosophy is radical precisely because it digs down beneath what seems to be immediately communicable, beneath available thoughts and conceptual knowledge, and reveals a tie between men, as it does between men and the world, which precedes and founds ideality?

To prove that this alternative governs the question of Christian philosophy, we need only follow the twists and turns of the discussion which took place in 1931. Some of the discussants, having granted that in the order of principles, ideas, and possibilities, philosophy and religion are both autonomous, admit when they turn toward facts or history that religion has made a contribution to philosophy, whether it be the idea of creation, of infinite subjectivity, or of development and history. Thus in spite of essences there is an exchange between religion and reason which entirely recasts the question. For if matters of faith can in fact provide food for thought (unless faith is only the opportunity for an awareness which is equally possible without faith), we must admit that faith reveals certain aspects of being, that thought (which ignores them) does not "tie it all up," and that faith's "things not seen" and reason's evidence cannot be set apart as two *domains*. If on the contrary we follow Bréhier in going straight to history in order to show that there has been no philosophy which was Christian, we succeed only by rejecting as alien to philosophy the ideas of Christian origin which block our efforts, or be seeking their antecedents outside Christianity at no matter what cost—which proves clearly enough that we are referring to a history which has been prepared and doctored in accordance with the idea of philosophical immanence. Thus two alternatives were presented in the discussion. We may ask a factual question; but since Christian philosophy can be neither affirmed or denied on the level of "pure" history except in a wholly nominal way, the supposed factual judgment will be categorical only if it includes a conception of philosophy. Or we may openly ask the question in terms of essences, and then everything has to be begun again as soon as we pass to the order of mixtures and existing philosophies. In both cases, we miss the problem, which exists only for an historico-systematic thought capable of digging beneath essences, accomplishing the movement back and forth between them and facts, challenging essences with facts and "facts" with essences, and in particular putting its own immanence in question.

For this "open" thinking the question is in a sense settled as soon as it is asked. Since it does not take its "essences" as such for the measure of all things, since it does not believe so much in essences as in knots of significations which will be unraveled and tied up again in a different way in a new network of knowledge and experience, and which will only continue to exist as its past, we cannot see in the name of what this projecting thought would refuse the title of philosophy to indirect or imaginative modes of expression and reserve it for doctrines of the intemporal and immanent Word which are themselves placed above all history. Thus there is certainly a Christian philosophy, as there is a Romantic or a French philosophy, and a Christian philosophy which is incomparably more extensive, since in addition to the two philosophies we have mentioned it contains all that has been thought in the West for twenty centuries. How can we take ideas like those of history, subjectivity, incarnation, and positive finitude away from Christianity in order to attribute them to a "universal" reason with no birthplace?

What is not thereby settled—and what constitutes the real problem of Christian philosophy—is the relationship between this instituted Christianity, a mental horizon or matrix of culture, and the Christianity effectively lived and practiced in a positive faith. To find a meaning and an enormous historical value in Christianity and to assume it personally are two different things. To say yes to Christianity as a fact of culture or civilization is to say yes to St. Thomas, but also to St. Augustine and Occam and Nicholas of Cusa and Pascal and Malebranche, and this assent does not cost us an ounce of the pains each one of them had to take in order to be himself without default. Historical and philosophical consciousness transmutes the struggles they sustained, at times in solitude and to the death, into the benevolent universe of culture. But the philosopher or historian, precisely because he understands them all, is not one of them. Furthermore, the historian pays the same attention and infinite respect to a bit of broken pottery, formless reveries, and absurd rituals. He is only concerned with knowing what the world is made of and what man is capable of, not with getting himself burned at the stake for this proposition or having his throat cut for that truth. For the philosopher, the Christianity which fills our philosophy is the most striking sign of self-transcendence. For the Christian, Christianity is not a symbol; it is the truth. In a sense, the tension between the philosopher who understands everything as human questioning and the narrow, profound practice of the very religion he "understands" is greater than it was between a rationalism which claimed to explain the world and a faith which was only nonsense to it—because the distance between the two is shorter.

So once again philosophy and Christianity are in conflict, but the conflict is one we meet within the Christian world and within each

Christian in the form of the conflict between Christianity "understood" and Christianity lived, between universality and choice. Within philosophy too, when it collides with the Manichaeism of *engagement.* The complex relationship between philosophy and Christianity would be disclosed only if a Christianity and a philosophy worked upon internally by the same contradiction were compared to one another.

The "Thomist peace" and the "Cartesian peace," the innocent coexistence of philosophy and Christianity taken as two positive orders or two truths, still conceal from us the hidden conflict of each with itself and with the other, as well as the tormented relationships which result from it.

If philosophy is a self-sufficing activity which begins and ends with conceptual understanding, and faith is assent to things not seen which are given for belief through revealed texts, the difference between them is too great even for there to be conflict. There will be conflict when rational adequation claims to be exhaustive. But if only philosophy recognizes, beyond the possibilities it is judge of, an actual world order whose detail arises from experience, and if the revealed given is taken as a supernatural experience, there is no rivalry between faith and reason. The secret of their agreement lies in infinite thought, whether it is conceiving of possibilities or creating the actual world. We do not have access to all it thinks, and its decrees are known to us only by their effects. We are thus in no position to understand the unity of reason and faith. What is certain is that it is brought about in God.

Reason and faith are thus in a state of equilibrium of indifference. Some have been astonished to see that Descartes, after having defined natural light so carefully, accepts a *different light* without difficulty, as if as soon as there are two, at least one must become relatively obscure. But the difficulty is no greater—and no differently met—than that of admitting the distinction which the understanding makes between soul and body, and, in another context, their substantial unity. There is the understanding and its sovereign distinctions, and there is the existing man (the understanding aided by imagination and joined to a body) whom we know through the practice of life because we are that man; and the two orders are a single one because the same God is both the sustainer of essences and the foundation of our existence. Our duality is reflected and surmounted in Him as the duality of his understanding and his will. We are not required to understand how. God's absolute transparency assures us of the fact, and for our part we can and must respect the difference between the two orders and live in peace on both levels.

Yet this is an unstable concordat. If man is really grafted onto the two orders, their connection is also made in him, and he should know something about it. His philosophical and his religious relationships to God should be of the same type. Philosophy and religion must symbolize. In our view, this is the significance of Malebranche's philosophy. Man cannot be part "spiritual automaton," part religious subject who receives the supernatural light. The structures and discontinuities of religious life are met with again in his understanding. In the natural order understanding is a sort of contemplation; it is vision in God. Even in the order of knowledge, we are neither our own light to ourselves nor the source of our ideas. We are our soul, but we do not have the idea of it; we only have feeling's obcure contact with it. All there can be in us of light and of intentional being comes from our participation in God. We do not have the power to conceive; our whole initiative in understanding is to address—this is what is called "attention"—a "natural prayer" to the Word which has only obligated itself to grant it always. What is ours is this invocation and the passive experience of the knowledge-events which result from it—in Malebranche's terms, "perception" and "feeling." What is also ours is this present, livelier pressure of intelligible extension on our soul, which makes us believe we see the world. In fact we do not see the world in itself. This appearance *is* our ignorance of ourselves, of our souls, and of the genesis of its modalities; and all there is of truth in our experience of the world is the fundamental certainty of an actual world existing beyond what we see and depending on which God makes us see what we do see. The slightest sense perception is thus a "natural revelation." Natural knowledge is divided between idea and perception, as religious life is divided between the light of mystical life and the chiaroscuro of revealed texts. The only thing that allows us to say that it is natural is that it obeys laws, and that God, in other words, intervenes in it only through general acts of will.

And even so the criterion is not an absolute one. If natural knowledge is woven out of religious relationships, the supernatural in return imitates nature. It is possible to sketch out a sort of dynamics of grace and glimpse laws and an order according to which the incarnate Word usually exercises its mediation. For the longitudinal cleavage between philosophy (the realm of pure understanding) and the created and existing world (the realm of natural or supernatural experience), Malebranche substitutes a transversal cleavage, and distributes the same typical structures of light and feeling, of ideal and real, between reason and religion. Natural philosophy's concepts invade theology; religious concepts invade natural knowledge. We no longer limit ourselves to evoking the infinite, which is for us incomprehensible, and in which orders that are for us distinct are believed to be unified. The articulations of nature hold only through God's action; almost all the interventions of grace are subjected to rules. God as cause is required by each idea we think of, and God as light is manifest in almost all His acts of will. No one has ever been closer to the Augustinian program: "True religion is true philosophy; and true philosophy, in turn, is true religion."

Thus Malebranche tries to think about the relationship between religion and philosophy instead of accepting it as a fact about which there is nothing to say. But can this relationship be formulated in terms of identity? Taken as contradictory, reason and faith coexist without difficulty. Similarly, and inversely, as soon as they are made identical they become rivals. The community of categories underlines the discordancy between natural revelation and natural prayer, which are open to all, and supernatural revelation and supernatural prayer, which were taught at first only to some; between the eternal and the incarnate Word; between the God we see as soon as we open our eyes and the God of the Sacraments and the Church, who must be gained and merited through supernatural life; and between the Architect divined in His works and the God of love who is reached only in the blindness of sacrifice. It is this very discordancy that one would have to take as one's theme if one wanted to construct a Christian philosophy; it is in it that one would have to look for the articulation of faith and reason. In so doing one would draw away from Malebranche, but one would also be inspired by him. For although he communicates something of reason's light to religion (and at the limit makes them identical in a single universe of thought), and although he extends the positivity of understanding to religion, he also foreshadows the invasion of our rational being by religious reversals, introducing into it the paradoxical thought of a madness which is wisdom, a scandal which is peace, a gift which is gain.

What would the relationship between philosophy and religion be in this case? Maurice Blondel [11] wrote: "Within and before itself philosophy hollows out a void which is prepared not only for the discoveries which it subsequently makes on its own grounds but also for the illuminations and contributions which it does not itself and never can really originate." Philosophy reveals a lack, a being out of focus, the expectation of forward movement. Without necessitating or presupposing positive options, it paves the way for them. It is the negative of a certain positive; not just any sort of void but precisely the lack of what faith will bring; and not hidden faith but the universally confirmable

11. Maurice Blondel, twentieth-century French philosopher. For further judgments of his thought by Merleau-Ponty, see *In Praise of Philosophy*.—Trans.

premise of a faith which remains free. We do not go from one to the other either by prolongation or simply by adjunction, but by a reversal which philosophy motivates without accomplishing.

Is the problem solved? Or does it not arise again at the suture of negative philosophy and positive faith? If, as Blondel would have it, philosophy is universal and autonomous, how could it leave responsibility for its conclusions to an absolute decision? What it roughs out with the broken lines of conceptual terms in the peace of the universal receives its full meaning only in the irreparable partiality of a life. But how could it help wanting to be a witness to this very passage from universal to particular? How could it possibly dwell in the negative and abandon the positive to a "wholly other" solicitation? It must itself recognize in a certain fullness what it sketched out beforehand in the void, and in practice at least something of what it has seen in theory. Philosophy's relationship to Christianity cannot be simply the relationship of the negative to the positive, of questioning to affirmation. Philosophical questioning involves its own vital options, and in a sense it maintains itself within a religious affirmation. The negative has its positive side, the positive its negative, and it is precisely because each has its contrary within itself that they are capable of passing into one another, and perpetually play the role of warring brothers in history.

Will this always be the case? Will there ever be a real exchange between philosopher and Christian (whether it is a matter of two men or of those two men each Christian senses within himself)? In our view this would be possible only if the Christian (with the exception of the ultimate sources of his inspiration, which he alone can judge) were to accept without qualification the task of mediation which philosophy cannot abandon without eliminating itself. It goes without saying that these lines commit their signer alone, and not the Christian collaborators who have so kindly agreed to give him their assistance. It would be a poor recognition of their aid to create the slightest ambiguity between their feelings and his. Nor does he give these lines as an introduction to their thought. They are more in the nature of reflections and questions he is writing in the margin of their texts in order to submit them to them.

These texts themselves (and on this point we are no doubt in unanimous agreement) give us a lively sense of the diversity of Christian inquiries. They remind us that Christianity has nourished more than one philosophy, no matter what privilege one of them may have been granted, that as a matter of principle it involves no single and exhaustive philosophical expression, and that in this sense—no matter what its acquisitions may be—Christian philosophy is never *something settled.*

[4] MAJOR RATIONALISM

THE RATIONALISM professed or discussed in 1900, which was the scientific explanation of Being, should be called "minor rationalism." It presupposed an immense Science already inscribed in the nature of things that actually existing science would rejoin on the day it reached the end of its inquiries, and that would leave us nothing more to ask, every meaningful question having been answered. It is very difficult for us to recapture this frame of mind, even though it is very close to us. But it is a fact that men once dreamed of a time in which the mind, having enclosed "the whole of reality" in a network of relations, would thenceforth (as if in a replete state) remain at rest or have nothing more to do than draw out the consequences of a definitive body of knowledge and, by some application of the same principles, ward off the last convulsive movements of the unforeseeable.

This "rationalism" seems full of myths to us: the myth of *laws of nature* vaguely situated halfway between norms and facts, and *according to which*, it was thought, this nevertheless blind world has been constructed; the myth of *scientific explanation,* as if knowledge of relations, even extended to all observable phenomena, could one day transform the very existence of the world into an analytic and self-evident proposition. To these two myths we would have to add all those related ones which proliferated at the limits of science, for example around the ideas of life and death. It was the time when men wondered with enthusiasm or anguish whether man could create life in the laboratory; a time when rationalist orators readily spoke of "nothingness," that different and calmer milieu of life which they felt sure they would regain after this life as one regains a supersensible destiny.

But they did not think they were giving way to a mythology. They believed they were speaking in the name of reason. Reason was confused with knowledge of conditions or causes: wherever a conditioning factor was discovered, it was thought that every question had been silenced, the problem of essence resolved along with the problem of origin, and the fact brought under the jurisdiction of its cause. The issue between science and religion was only to know whether the world is a single great Process obeying a single "generative axiom," the repetition of whose mystic formula would be the only thing left to do at the end of time, or whether there are (at the point where life emerges, for example) gaps and discontinuities in which the antagonistic power of mind can be lodged. Each conquest made for determinism was a defeat for the metaphysical sense, whose victory necessarily involved the "failure of science."

The reason why this rationalism is hard for us to think of is that it was (in a disfigured, unrecognizable form) a heritage, and what we have been concerned with in our times is the tradition which had gradually produced it. It was the fossil of a major rationalism (that of the seventeenth century) rich with a living ontology, which had already died out by the eighteenth century,[12] and only a few external forms of which remained in the rationalism of 1900.

The seventeenth century is that privileged moment when natural science and metaphysics believed they had discovered a common foundation. It created the science of nature and yet did not make the object of science the rule of ontology. It assumes that a philosophy surveys science without being its rival. The object of science is an aspect or a degree of Being; it is justified in its place, perhaps it is even through it that we learn to know the power of reason. But this power is not exhausted in it. In different ways Descartes, Spinoza, Leibniz, and Malebranche recognize, beneath the chain of causal relations, another type of being which sustains that chain without breaking it. Being is not completely reduced to or flattened out upon the level of external Being. There is also the being of the subject or the soul, the being of its ideas, and the interrelations of these ideas, the inner relation of truth. And the latter universe is as extensive as the former, or rather it encompasses it. For no matter how strict the connection between external facts, it is not the external world which is the ultimate justification of the internal; they participate together in an "interior" which their connection manifests. All the problems that a scientistic ontology will omit by setting itself up uncritically in external being as universal milieu, seventeenth century philosophy on the contrary never stops setting for itself. How can we understand that mind acts upon body and body upon mind, and even body upon body or mind upon another mind or upon itself, since in the last analysis, no matter how rigorous the connection between particular things within and outside us, no one of these things is ever in all respects a sufficient cause of what emerges from it? Where does the cohesion of the whole come from? Each Cartesian conceives of it in a completely different way. But all of them agree that beings and external relations present themselves for an inspection of their underlying premises. Philosophy is neither stifled by them nor compelled to contest their solidity in order to make a place for itself.

This extraordinary harmony of external and internal is possible

12. The eighteenth century is the greatest example of a time which does not express itself well in its philosophy. Its merits lie elsewhere: in its ardor; in its passion for living, knowing, and judging; in its "spirit." As Hegel has shown so well, there is for example a second meaning of its "materialism" which makes it an epoch of the human spirit, even though, taken literally, it is a meager philosophy.

only through the mediation of a *positive infinite* or (since every restriction to a certain type of infinity would be a seed of negation) an infinite infinite. It is in this positive infinite that the effective existence of things *partes extra partes* and extension as we think of it (which on the contrary is continuous and infinite) communicate or are joined together. If at the center and so to speak the kernel of Being there is an infinite infinite, every partial being directly or indirectly presupposes it, and is in return really or eminently contained in it. All the relationships we can have to Being must be simultaneously founded upon it. First of all our idea of truth, which is precisely what has led us to the infinite and thus cannot be called into question again by it, then all the lively and confused ideas of existing things given us by the senses. No matter how different these two kinds of understanding may be, they must have but one source; and even the sensible world (as discontinuous, partial, and mutilated as it is) must ultimately be understood, beginning with the organization of our body, as a particular case of the internal relations intelligible space is made of.

Thus the idea of the positive infinite is major rationalism's secret, and it will last only as long as that idea remains in force. Descartes had glimpsed in a flash the possibility of negative thinking. He had described mind as a being which is *neither* subtle matter, *nor* a breath of spirit, nor any existing thing, but a being which itself dwells in the absence of all positive certainty. With his gaze he had measured this power to do or not to do which, he said, admits of no degree and is thus infinite in man as it is in God—and is an infinite power of negation, since in a freedom which is freedom not to do as well as to do, affirmation can never be anything but negation denied. It is in this respect that Descartes is more modern than the Cartesians, anticipating the philosophies of subjectivity and the negative. But for him this is no more than a beginning, and he definitively moves beyond negativity when he ultimately states that the idea of the infinite precedes that of the finite in him, and that all negative thought is a shadow in this light. Whatever their differences in other respects, Cartesians will be unanimous on this point. Malebranche will say a hundred times that nothingness "has no properties" or "is not visible," and that there is thus nothing to say about this nothing. Leibniz will wonder why there is "something rather than nothing," at a certain moment positing nothingness in respect to Being; but this retreat to the near side of Being, this evocation of a possible nothingness, is for him like a proof by absurdity. It is only the basis, the minimum of shadow necessary for making Being's sovereign self-production appear. Finally, Spinoza's determination which "is negation," although subsequently understood in the sense of a determining power of the negative, can only be for him a way of underlining the immanence of determinate things in a substance which is equal to itself and positive.

Subsequent thought will never again attain this harmony between philosophy and science, this ease of going beyond science without destroying it and limiting metaphysics without excluding it. Even those of our contemporaries who call themselves and are Cartesians give a completely different philosophical function to the negative, and that is why they could not possibly recover the seventeenth century's equilibrium. Descartes said that God is conceived of but not understood by us, and this *not* expressed a privation and a defect in us. The modern Cartesian [13] translates: the infinite is as much *absence* as *presence*, which brings the negative and man into the definition of God. Léon Brunschvicg accepted all of Spinoza except the descending order of the *Ethics*. The *first book*, he used to say, is no more primary than the *fifth*; the *Ethics* ought to be read in a circle, and God presupposes man as man presupposes God. This interpretation of Cartesianism perhaps, in fact surely, extracts "its truth"; but a truth it did not itself possess. There is an innocent way of thinking *on the basis* of the infinite which made major rationalism what it was, and which nothing will ever allow us to recapture.

These words should not be taken to express nostalgia—except perhaps an indolent nostalgia for a time when the mental universe was not torn apart and man could without concessions or artificiality devote himself to philosophy, science, and (if he wished) theology. But this peace and harmony could last only as long as men remained at the entrance to the three paths. What separates us from the seventeenth century is not a decline but a growth of consciousness and experience. The intervening centuries have taught that the harmony between our evident thoughts and the existing world is not so immediate, that it is never beyond question, that our evidence can never take credit for governing the whole subsequent development of knowledge, that consequences flow back upon "principles," that we must be prepared to recast even the ideas we may believe to be "primary," that truth is not obtained by composition in going from simple to complex and from essence to properties, and that we neither can nor will be able to set ourselves up at the center of physical or even mathematical entities, but must gropingly inspect them from without, approaching them by oblique processes and questioning them like persons. A time came when the very conviction of grasping with inner certainty the principles according to which an infinite understanding conceived or conceives the world (the conviction which had sustained the Cartesians' undertakings and had long seemed justified by the progress of Cartesian

13. F. Alquié, *La découverte métaphysique de l'homme chez Descartes.*

science) ceased to be a stimulant of knowledge and became the threat of a new Scholasticism. Then it was indeed necessary to return to principles; reduce them to the rank of "idealizations" which are justified to the extent they give life to inquiry and disqualified when they paralyze it; learn to measure our thought by that existence which, Kant was to say, is not a predicate; go back to the origins of Cartesianism in order to go beyond it; and relearn the lesson of that creative act which, with Cartesianism, had instituted a long period of fruitful thought, but which had exhausted its force in the pseudo-Cartesianism of subsequent thinkers and from that time forward needed to be begun over again itself. It has been necessary to learn intellectual history, that queer movement by which thought abandons and preserves its old formulas by integrating them as particular and privileged cases into a more comprehensive and general thought which cannot decree itself exhaustive. This air of improvisation and the provisory, this somewhat haggard aspect of contemporary investigations (whether they be in science or philosophy, in literature or the arts), is the price we must pay in order to acquire a more mature consciousness of our relationships to Being.

The seventeenth century believed in the immediate harmony of science and metaphysics, and in another connection, of science and religion. And in this respect it is remote from our times indeed. For the past fifty years metaphysical thought has sought its way outside the physico-mathematical coordination of the world, and its role in relation to science seems to be to awaken us to the "non-relational background" [14] that science thinks about and does not think about. The fact that the most vital aspect of religious thought has taken the same course makes it consonant but also competitive with "atheistic" metaphysics. Unlike the atheism of 1900, contemporary "atheism" does not claim to explain the world "without God." It claims that the world is inexplicable, and in its view the rationalism of 1900 is a secularized theology. If the Cartesians were to come back among us, they would have the triple surprise of finding a philosophy and even a theology whose favorite theme is the radical contingency of the world, and which are rivals in just this respect. Our philosophical situation is entirely different from that of major rationalism.

And yet major rationalism is still of major importance for us, and is even close to us in that it is the indispensable way toward the philosophies which reject it, for they reject it in the name of the same exigency which gave it life. At the very moment when it was creating natural science it showed by the same movement that it was not the measure of being and carried consciousness of the ontological problem to its high-

14. Jean Wahl.

est point. In this respect, it is not *past*. As it did, we seek not to restrict or discredit the initiatives of science but to situate science as an intentional system in the total field of our relationships to Being; and the only reason why passing to the infinite infinite does not seem to us to be the answer is that we are taking up again in a more radical way the task which that intrepid century had believed itself rid of forever.

[5] The Discovery of Subjectivity

What is common to those philosophies, spread out across three centuries, which we group together beneath the banner of "subjectivity"? There is the Self which Montaigne preferred above all and Pascal hated, the Self which we take account of day by day—noticing its audacities, flights, intermittencies, and returns—and try out or put to the test like an unknown. There is the thinking Ego of Descartes and Pascal too, the Ego which rejoins itself only an instant, but in that instant exists wholly in its appearance, being everything it thinks it is and nothing else, open to everything, never fixed, and without any other mystery than this transparency itself. There is the subjective series of the English philosophers, the ideas which know themselves through a mute contact and as if by a natural property. There is the self of Rousseau, an abyss of innocence and guilt which itself organizes the "plot" in which it is aware of being implicated, and yet in the face of this destiny insists with good reason upon its incorruptible goodness. There is the transcendental subject of the Kantians, as close and closer to the world than psychological intimacy, which contemplates them both after having constructed them, and yet knows that it too is an "inhabitant" of the world. There is the subject of Biran which not only *knows* that it is in the world but is there, and could not even be subject if it did not have a body to move. There is finally subjectivity in the Kierkegaardian sense, which is no longer a region of being but the only fundamental way of relating oneself to being, which makes us *be* something instead of skimming over all things in "objective" thinking, and which in the last analysis does not really think of anything. Why make these discordant "subjectivities" stages of a single discovery?

And why "discovery"? Are we to believe then that subjectivity existed before the philosophers, exactly as they were subsequently to understand it? Once reflection had occurred, once the "I think" had been pronounced, the thought of being became so much a part of our being that if we try to express what preceded it our entire effort only succeeds in proposing a *pre-reflexive cogito*. But what is this contact of self with self before the self is revealed? Is it anything but another example of retrospective illusion? Is our investigation of it really no more than a *return* to what already *knew itself* through our life? But strictly speaking I did not know myself. Then what is this feeling of self which is not in possession of itself and does not yet coincide with itself? It has been said that to take consciousness away from subjectivity was to withdraw being from it, that an unconscious love is nothing, because to love is to see someone—actions, gestures, a face, a body—as lovable. But the *cogito* prior to reflection and the feeling of self without understanding present the same difficulty. Thus consciousness is either unaware of its origins or, if it wants to reach them, it can only project itself into them. In neither case should we speak of "discovery." Reflection has not only unveiled the unreflected, it has changed it, if only into its truth. Subjectivity was not waiting for philosophers as an unknown America waited for its explorers in the ocean's mists. They constructed, created it, and in more than one way. And what they have done must perhaps be undone. Heidegger thinks they lost being from the day they based it upon consciousness of self.

Yet we shall not give up speaking about a "discovery" of "subjectivity." These difficulties simply require us to say how we shall use the terms.

In the first place, the kinship of philosophies of subjectivity is evident as soon as they are contrasted to the others. Whatever the discordancies between them, the moderns share the idea that the being of the soul or subject-being is not a lesser being but perhaps the absolute form of being, and this is what our title is intended to indicate. Many elements of a philosophy of the subject were present in Greek philosophy. It spoke of "man the measure of all things." It recognized the soul's singular power not to know what it knows in pretending to know what it does not know, an incomprehensible capacity for error linked to its capacity for truth, a relationship to non-being just as essential to it as its relationship to being. In another connection, it conceived of a thought which is only thought of itself (Aristotle puts it at the summit of the world), and a radical freedom beyond the highest stage of our power. Thus it knew subjectivity as darkness and light. Yet the fact remains that for the Greeks the being of the subject or the soul is never the canonical form of being, that never for them is the negative at the center of philosophy, or charged with making the positive appear, assuming it, and transforming it.

From Montaigne to Kant and beyond, on the contrary, it is the same subject-being which is at issue. The discordancy of philosophies stems from the fact that subjectivity is neither thing nor substance but the extremity of both particular and universal—from the fact that it is

Protean. All the philosophies of subjectivity follow its metamorphoses in one way or another, and it is this dialectic which is hidden beneath their differences. There are at bottom only two ideas of subjectivity—that of empty, unfettered, and universal subjectivity, and that of full subjectivity sucked down into the world—and it is the same idea, as can be clearly seen in Sartre's idea of nothingness which "comes to the world," drinks in the world, needs the world in order to be no matter what (even nothingness), and remains alien to the world in sacrificing itself to being.

Of course this is no discovery in the sense that America or even potassium was discovered. Yet it is still a discovery in the sense that once introduced into philosophy, "subjective" thinking no longer allows itself to be ignored. Even if philosophy finally eliminates it, it will never again be what it was before this kind of thinking. After it, that which is true—constructed though it may be (and America is also a construction, which has just become inevitable through an infinite number of witnesses)—becomes as solid as a fact, and subjective thinking is one of these solids that philosophy will have to digest. Or let us say that once "infected" by certain ways of thinking, philosophy can no longer annul them but must cure itself of them by inventing better ones. The same philosopher who now regrets Parmenides and would like to give us back our relationships to Being such as they were prior to self-consciousness owes his idea of and taste for primordial ontology to just this self-consciousness. There are some ideas which make it impossible for us to return to a time prior to their existence, even and especially if we have moved beyond them, and subjectivity is one of them.

[6] Existence and Dialectic

We know how uncomfortable a writer is when he is asked to do a history of his thoughts. We are scarcely less uncomfortable when we have to summarize our famous contemporaries. We cannot separate them from what we have learned in reading them, or from the "climates" which have received their books and made them famous. We would have to guess what counts now that the hue and cry has died down, and what will count tomorrow for new readers (if there are any), those strangers who are going to come, lay hold of the same books, and make something else out of them. Perhaps there is a sentence—written one day in the stillness of the 16th arrondissement, in the pious stillness of Aix, in the academic stillness of Freiburg, or in the din of the rue de Rennes, or in Naples or Vésinet—which its first readers roared through like a whistle-stop and tomorrow's readers (a new Bergson, Blondel, Husserl, Alain, or Croce we cannot imagine) are going to pull up short before. To imagine them would mean distributing our evidence and questions, our hits and misses, as they will be distributed among our descendants. It would mean making ourselves different selves, and all the "objectivity" in the world cannot do that. In designating the themes of existence and dialectic the essential ones of the past half-century, we are perhaps saying what one generation saw in its philosophy, not to be sure what the following one will see in it, and far less still what the philosophers in question were conscious of saying.

Yet it is *a fact, for us,* that they all labored to go beyond critical philosophy (even those who put the most stock in it), and to unveil, on the far side of relations, what Brunschvicg used to call the "uncoordinatable" and we call existence. When Bergson made perception the fundamental mode of our relation to being; when Blondel meant to develop the implications of a thought which always in fact precedes itself, is always beyond itself; when Alain described freedom upheld by the world's flux like a swimmer on the water which holds him up and is his force; when Croce put philosophy back into contact with history; and when Husserl took the carnal presence of things as the model of obvious fact; all of them were calling the narcissism of self-consciousness into question, all of them were seeking a way between the possible and the necessary toward the real, all were pointing out our own and the world's factual existence as a new dimension of inquiry. For existential philosophy is not, as a hurried reader who limited himself to Sartre's manifesto [15] would believe, simply the philosophy which puts freedom before essence in man. This is only a striking consequence; and behind the idea of sovereign choice there was even in Sartre's thinking (as can be seen in *Being and Nothingness*) the different and really antagonistic idea of a freedom which is freedom only embodied in the world as work done upon a factual situation. And from then on, even in Sartre's thinking, "to exist" is not merely an anthropological term. Facing freedom, existence unveils a wholly new face of the world—the world as a promise and threat to it; the world which sets traps for, seduces, or gives in to it; not the flat world of Kantian objects of science any more but a landscape full of routes and roadblocks; in short, the world we "exist" and not simply the theater of our understanding and free will.

Perhaps we shall have more trouble convincing the reader that in going toward existence the century was also going toward dialectic.

15. *Existentialism and Humanism.*

Blondel, Alain talked about it, and Croce of course. But Bergson, Husserl? It is pretty well known that they sought intuition, and that dialectic for them was the philosophy of argufiers, blind and garrulous philosophy, or as J. Beaufret says, "ventriloquous" philosophy. Reading over old manuscripts, Husserl would sometimes write in the margin, "*Das habe ich angeschaut.*" What do these philosophers, dedicated to what they see, positive, and systematically naive, have in common with the cunning philosopher who digs ever deeper beneath his intuition in order to find another intuition there, and who is referred back to himself by every spectacle?

To answer these questions it would be necessary to evoke the contemporary history of dialectic and the Hegelian revival. The dialectic our contemporaries are rediscovering is, as von Hartmann has already pointed out, a dialectic of the real. The Hegel they have rehabilitated is not the one the nineteenth century had turned away from, the possessor of a marvelous secret which enabled him to speak of all things without a thought by mechanically applying dialectical order and connection to them. It is the Hegel who had not wanted to choose between logic and anthropology, who made dialectic emerge from human experience but defined man as the empirical bearer of Logos, and who placed these two perspectives and the reversal which transforms them both at the center of philosophy. This dialectic and intuition are not simply compatible; there is a point at which they meet. Through Bergsonism as through Husserl's career we can follow the laborious process which gradually sets intuition in motion, changes the positive notation of "immediate data" into a dialectic of time and the intuition of essences into a "phenomenology of genesis," and links together in a living unity the contrasting dimensions of a time which is ultimately coextensive with being.

This being—which is glimpsed through time's stirrings and always intended by our temporality, perception, and our carnal being, but to which there can be no question of our being transported because to abolish its distance would be to take away its consistency of being—this being "of distances" as Heidegger will put it, which is always offered to our transcendence, is the dialectical idea of being as defined in the *Parmenides*—beyond the empirical multiplicity of existent things and as a matter of principle intended through them, because separated from them it would be only lightning flash or darkness. As for the subjective side of dialectic, modern thinkers rediscover it as soon as they want to grasp us in our *effective* relationship to the world. For then they encounter the first and most fundamental antithesis, the inaugural and never liquidated phase of dialectic, the birth of reflection which as a matter of principle separates and separates only in order to grasp the unreflected. As soon as it becomes sufficiently conscious, the search for the "immediate" or the "thing itself" is not the contrary of mediation. Mediation is only the resolute recognition of a paradox that intuition willy-nilly suffers: to possess ourselves we must begin by abandoning ourselves; to see the world itself, we must first withdraw from it.

If these remarks are just, only the logical positivism of the Anglo-Saxon and Scandinavian countries would be left outside this century's philosophy. All the philosophies we have just named speak a common language, and for logical positivism all their problems put together are meaningless. The fact can neither be hidden nor attenuated. We can only wonder if it will last. If all terms which offer no immediately assignable meaning are eliminated from philosophy, does not this purge, like all the others, reveal a crisis? Once we have set the field of apparently clear univocal meanings in order, will we not let ourselves be tempted anew by the problematic regions which lie all around it? Is it not just the contrast between a transparent mental universe and a lived universe which is less and less a contrast, is it not just this pressure of the meaningless on the meaningful, which will lead logical positivism to revise its criteria of clarity and obscurity through a development which Plato said is the development of philosophy itself? If this reversal of values were to occur, logical positivism would have to be appraised as the last and most energetic "resistance" to the concrete philosophy which, in one way or another, the beginning of this century has not stopped looking for.

A concrete philosophy is not a happy one. It must stick close to experience, and yet not limit itself to the empirical but restore to each experience the ontological cipher which marks it internally. As difficult as it is under these conditions to imagine the future of philosophy, two things seems certain: it will never regain the conviction of holding the keys to nature or history in its concepts, and it will not renounce its radicalism, that search for presuppositions and foundations which has produced the great philosophies.

It will renounce it all the less to the extent that while philosophical systems were being discredited, more advanced techniques were replacing old ones and giving new life to philosophy. At no time like the present has scientific knowledge overturned its own *a priori*. Literature has never been as "philosophical" as it has in the twentieth century; never has it reflected as much upon language, truth, and the significance of the act of writing. At no time like the present has political life shown its roots or its web and challenged its own certitudes, first those of conservatism and now those of revolution. Even if philosophers were to weaken, others would be there to call them back to philosophy. Unless this uneasiness consumes itself, and the world destroys itself in experiencing itself, much can be expected of an age which no longer believes in philosophy triumphant but is through its difficulties a permanent appeal to rigor, criticism, universality, and philosophy militant.

Perhaps it will be asked what is left of philosophy when it has lost its rights to the *a priori,* system, or construction, when it no longer dominates the whole of experience. Almost all of it is left. For system, explanation, and deduction have never been essential. These arrangements expressed—and concealed—a relation to being, other men, and the world. In spite of appearances, the system has never been more than a language (and in this respect it has been precious) for translating a Cartesian, Spinozist, or Leibnizian way of situating oneself in relation to being. And it suffices for the continuing existence of philosophy that this relationship remain problematic, that it not be taken as self-evident, that there continue to exist the *tête-à-tête* between being and the one who (in every sense of the word) comes forth from it, judges it, receives it, rejects it, transforms it, and finally departs from it. It is this same relationship we are at present trying to formulate expressly, and it is for this reason that philosophy feels at home wherever it takes place—that is, everywhere—as much in the testimony of an ignorant man who has loved and lived as he could, in the "tricks" science contrives without speculative shame to get around problems, in "barbarian" civilizations, and in the regions of our life which formerly had no official existence, as in literature, in the sophisticated life, or in discussions of substance and attribute. The established human community feels problematic, and the most immediate life has become "philosophical." We cannot conceive of a new Leibniz or Spinoza entering that life today with their fundamental confidence in its rationality. Tomorrow's philosophers will have no "anaclastic line," "monad," "conatus," "substance," "attributes," or "infinite mode." But they will continue to learn in Leibniz and Spinoza how happy centuries thought to tame the Sphinx, and in their own less figurative and more abrupt fashion, they will keep on giving answers to the many riddles she puts to them.

6 / The Philosopher and His Shadow

ESTABLISHING A TRADITION means forgetting its origins, the aging Husserl used to say. Precisely because we owe so much to tradition, we are in no position to see just what belongs to it. With regard to a philosopher whose venture has awakened so many echoes, and at such an apparent distance from the point where he himself stood, any commemoration is also a betrayal—whether we do him the highly superfluous homage of our thoughts, as if we sought to gain them a wholly unmerited warrant, or whether on the contrary, with a respect which is not lacking in distance, we reduce him too strictly to what he himself desired and said. But Husserl was well aware of these difficulties—which are problems of communication between "egos"—and he does not leave us to confront them without resources. I borrow myself from others; I create others from my own thoughts. This is no failure to perceive others; it is the perception of others. We would not overwhelm them with our importunate comments, we would not stingily reduce them to what is objectively certified of them, if they were not there for us to begin with. Not to be sure with the frontal evidence of a thing, but installed athwart our thought and, like different selves of our own, occupying a region which belongs to no one else but them. Between an "objective" history of philosophy (which would rob the great philosophers of what they have given others to think about) and a meditation disguised as a dialogue (in which we would ask the questions and give the answers) there must be a middle-ground on which the philosopher we are speaking about and the philosopher who is speaking are present together, although it is not possible even in principle to decide at any given moment just what belongs to each.

The reason why we think that interpretation is restricted to either inevitable distortion or literal reproduction is that we want the meaning of a man's works to be wholly positive and by rights susceptible to an inventory which sets forth what is and is not in those works. But this is to be deceived about works and thought. "When we are considering a man's thought," Heidegger says in effect, "the greater the work accomplished (and greatness is in no way equivalent to the extent and number of writings) the richer the unthought-of element in that work. That is, the richer is that which, through this work and through it alone, comes toward us as never yet thought of." [1] At the end of Husserl's life there is an unthought-of element in his works which is wholly his and yet opens out on something else. To think is not to possess the objects of thought; it is to use them to mark out a realm to think about which we therefore are not yet thinking about. Just as the perceived world endures only through the reflections, shadows, levels, and horizons between things (which are not things and are not nothing, but on the contrary mark out by themselves the fields of possible variation in the same thing and the same world), so the works and thought of a philosopher are also made of certain articulations between things said. There is no dilemma of objective interpretation or arbitrariness with respect to these articulations, since they are not *objects* of thought, since (like shadow and reflection) they would be destroyed by being subjected to analytic observation or taken out of context, and since we can be faithful to and find them only by thinking again.

We should like to try to evoke this unthought-of element in Husserl's thought in the margin of some old pages. This will seem foolhardy on the part of someone who has known neither Husserl's daily conversation nor his teaching. Yet this essay may have its place alongside other approaches. Because for those who have known the visible Husserl the difficulties of communicating with an author are added on to those of communicating with his works. For these men, certain memories helpfully supply an incident or a short-circuit in conversation. But other memories would tend to hide the "transcendental" Husserl, the one who is at present being solemnly installed in the history of philosophy—not because he is a fiction, but because he is Husserl disencumbered of his life, delivered up to conversation with his peers and to his omnitemporal audacity. Like all those near to us, Husserl present in person (and in addition with the genius' power to fascinate and to deceive) could not, I imagine, leave those surrounding him in peace. Their whole philosophical life must have lain for a time in that extraordinary and inhuman occupation of being present at the continuing birth of a way of thinking, and of helping it become objective or even

1. "Je grösser das Denkwerk eines Denkers ist, das sich keineswegs mit dem Umfang und der Anzahl seiner Schriften deckt, um so reicher ist das in diesem Denkwerk Ungedachte, d.h. jenes, was erst und allein durch dieses Denkwerk als das Noch-nicht-Gedachte heraufkommt." *Der Satz vom Grund,* pp. 123–24.

exist as communicable thought. Afterwards, when Husserl's death and their own growth had committed them to adult solitude, how could they easily recover the full meaning of their earlier meditations, which they certainly pursued freely whether they agreed or disagreed with Husserl, but in any case pursued on the basis of his thought? They rejoin him across their past. Is this way always shorter than the way through a man's works? As a result of having put the whole of philosophy in phenomenology to begin with, do they not now risk being too hard on it at the same time they are too hard on their youth? Do they not risk reducing given phenomenological motifs to what they were in their original contingency and their empirical humility, whereas for the outside observer, these motifs retain their full relief?

* * *

Take for example the theme of phenomenological reduction, which we know never ceased to be an enigmatic possibility for Husserl, and one he always came back to. To say that he never succeeded in ensuring the bases of phenomenology would be to be mistaken about what he was looking for. The problems of reduction are not for him a prior step or preface to phenomenology; they are the beginning of inquiry. In a sense, they are inquiry, since inquiry is, as he said, a continuous beginning. We must not imagine Husserl hamstrung here by vexatious obstacles; locating obstacles is the very meaning of his inquiry. One of its "results" is the realization that the movement of return to ourselves—of "re-entering ourselves," St. Augustine said—is as if rent by an inverse movement which *it elicits*. Husserl rediscovers that identity of "re-entering self" and "going-outside self" which, for Hegel, defined the absolute. To reflect (Husserl said in *Ideen I*) is to unveil an unreflected dimension which is at a distance because we are no longer it in a naive way, yet which we cannot doubt that reflection attains, since it is through reflection itself that we have an idea of it. So it is not the unreflected which challenges reflection; it is reflection which challenges itself. For by definition its attempt to revive, possess, internalize, or make immanent has meaning only with respect to an already given terminus which withdraws into its transcendence beneath the very gaze which has set out in search of it in this attempt.

So it is not through chance or naivete that Husserl assigns contradictory characteristics to reduction. He is saying what he means here, what is imposed by the factual situation. It is up to us not to forget half the truth. Thus on the one hand reduction goes beyond the natural attitude. It is not "natural" (*natural*).[2] This means that reduced thought

2. *Ideen II*, Husserliana, Bd. IV, p. 180.

no longer concerns the Nature of the natural sciences but in a sense the "opposite of Nature." [3] In other words, reduced thought concerns Nature as the "ideal meaning of the acts which constitute the natural attitude" [4]—Nature become once more the noema it has always been, Nature reintegrated to the consciousness which has always constituted it through and through. In the realm of "reduction" there is no longer anything but consciousness, its acts, and their intentional object. This is why Husserl can write that Nature is relative to mind, and that Nature is relative and mind absolute.[5]

But this is not the whole truth. The fact that there is *no* Nature *without* mind, or that Nature may be *done away with* in thought *without* doing away with mind, does not mean that Nature is produced by mind, or that any combination (even a subtle one) of these two concepts suffices to give the philosophical formula of our situation in being. Mind without Nature can be thought about and Nature without mind cannot. But perhaps we do not have to think about the world and ourselves in terms of the bifurcation of Nature and mind. The fact is that phenomenology's most famous descriptions go in a direction which is not that of "philosophy of mind." When Husserl says that reduction goes beyond the natural attitude, he immediately adds that this going beyond preserves "the whole world of the natural attitude." The very transcendence of this world must retain a meaning in the eyes of "reduced" consciousness, and transcendental immanence cannot be simply its antithesis.

From *Ideen II* on it seems clear that reflection does not install us in a closed, transparent milieu, and that it does not take us (at least not immediately) from "objective" to "subjective," but that its function is rather to unveil a third dimension in which this distinction becomes problematic. There is indeed an I which makes itself "indifferent," a pure "knower," in order to grasp all things without remainder—to spread all things out before itself—and to "objectify" and gain intellectual possession of them. This I is a purely "theoretical attitude" which seeks to "render visible the relationships which can provide knowledge of being as it comes to be." [6] But it is just this I which is not the philosopher, just this attitude which is not philosophy. It is the science of Nature, or in a deeper sense, a certain philosophy which gives birth to the natural sciences and which comes back to the pure I and to its correlative, "things simply as things" (*blosse Sachen*),

3. *Ibid.*, "Ein Widerspiel der Natur."

4. *Ibid.*, p. 174, "Als reiner Sinn der die natürliche Einstellung ausmachende Akte."

5. *Ibid.*, p. 297.

6. *Ibid.*, p. 26, "Zusammenhänge sichtbar zu machen, die das Wissen vom erscheinenden Sein fördern könnten."

stripped of every action-predicate and every value-predicate. From *Ideen II* on Husserl's reflections escape this tête-à-tête between pure subject and pure things. They look *deeper down* for the fundamental. Saying that Husserl's thought goes in another direction tells us little. His thought does not disregard the ideal correlation of subject and object; it very deliberately goes beyond it, since it presents it as relatively founded, true derivatively as a constitutive result it is committed to justifying in its proper time and place.

But what is the starting point for this new turn in Husserl's thought, and what is the deeper urgency behind it? What is false in the ontology of *blosse Sachen* is that it makes a purely theoretical or idealizing attitude absolute, neglecting or taking as understood a relation with being which founds the purely theoretical attitude and measures its value. Relative to this scientific *naturalism*, the *natural* attitude involves a higher truth that we must regain. For the natural attitude is nothing less than naturalistic. We do not live naturally in the universe of *blosse Sachen*. Prior to all reflection, in conversation and the practices of life, we maintain a "personalist attitude" that naturalism cannot account for, and here things are not nature in itself for us but "our surroundings." [7] Our most natural life as men intends an ontological milieu which is different from that of being in itself, and which consequently cannot be derived from it in the constitutive order.

Even when our knowledge of things is concerned, we know far more about them in the natural attitude than the theoretical attitude can tell us—and above all we know it in a different way. Reflection speaks of our natural relationship to the world as an "attitude," that is, as an organized totality of "acts." But this is a reflection which presupposes that it is in things and which sees no farther than itself. At the same time Husserl's reflection tries to grasp the universal essences of things, it notes that in the unreflected there are "syntheses which dwell this side of any thesis." [8] The natural attitude really becomes an attitude—a tissue of judicatory and propositional acts—only when it becomes a naturalist thesis. The natural attitude itself emerges unscathed from the complaints which can be made about naturalism, because it is "prior to any thesis," because it is the mystery of a *Weltthesis* prior to all theses. It is, Husserl says in another connection, the mystery of a primordial faith and a fundamental and original opinion (*Urglaube, Urdoxa*) which are thus not even in principle translatable in terms of clear and distinct knowledge, and which—more ancient than any "attitude" or "point of view"—give us not a representation of the world but the world itself.

7. *Ibid.*, p. 183, "Unsere Umgebung."
8. *Ibid.*, p. 22, "Synthesen, die vor aller Thesis liegen."

Reflection cannot "go beyond" this opening to the world, except by making use of the powers it owes to the opening itself. There is a clarity, an obviousness, proper to the zone of *Weltthesis* which is not derived from that of our theses, an unveiling of the world precisely through its dissimulation in the chiaroscuro of the doxa. When Husserl insistently says that phenomenological reflection begins in the natural attitude (in *Ideen II* he repeats it in order to relate the analysis he has just made of the corporeal and intersubjective implications of the *blosse Sachen* [9] to the realm of constituted phenomena), this is not just a way of saying that we must necessarily begin with and go by way of opinion before we can attain knowledge. The doxa of the natural attitude is an Urdoxa. To what is fundamental and original in theoretical consciousness it opposes what is fundamental and original in our existence. Its rights of priority are definitive, and reduced consciousness must take them into account.

The truth is that the relationships between the natural and the transcendental attitudes are not simple, are not side by side or sequential, like the false or the apparent and the true. There is a preparation for phenomenology in the natural attitude. It is the natural attitude which, by reiterating its own procedures, seesaws in phenomenology. It is the natural attitude itself which goes beyond itself in phenomenology—and so it does not go beyond itself. Reciprocally, the transcendental attitude is still and in spite of everything "natural" (*natürlich*).[10] There is a truth of the natural attitude—there is even a secondary, derivative truth of naturalism. "The soul's reality is based upon corporeal matter, not the latter upon the soul. More generally, within the total objective world, the material world is what we call Nature, a self-contained and particular world which does not require the support of any other reality. On the contrary the existence of mental realities and a real mental world is tied to the existence of a nature in the first sense of the term, to the existence of a material nature, and it is so linked not for contingent reasons but for reasons of principle. Whereas the *res extensa,* when we examine its essence, contains neither anything which arises from mind nor anything which mediately (*über sich hinaus*) requires connection with a real mind; we find on the contrary that a real mind, according to its essence, can only exist tied to materiality as the real mind of a body." [11] We quote these lines only to provide a counterpoise to those which affirmed the relativity of Nature and the non-relativity of mind, and demolished the sufficiency of Na-

9. *Ibid.*, p. 174.

10. *Ibid.*, p. 180, "Eine Einstellung . . . die in gewissen Sinn sehr natürlich . . . ist."

11. *Ideen III*, Husserliana, Bd. V, Beilage I, p. 117.

ture and the truth of the natural attitudes that are here reaffirmed. In the last analysis, phenomenology is neither a materialism nor a philosophy of mind. Its proper work is to unveil the pre-theoretical layer on which both of these idealizations find their relative justification and are gone beyond.

How will that infrastructure, that secret of secrets this side of our theses and our theory, be able in turn to rest upon the *acts* of absolute consciousness? Does the descent into the realm of our "archeology" leave our analytical tools intact? Does it make no changes at all in our conception of noesis, noema, and intentionality—in our ontology? After we have made this descent, are we still entitled to seek in an analytics of acts what upholds our own and the world's life without appeal? We know that Husserl never made himself too clear about these questions. A few words are there like indicators pointing to the problem—signaling unthought-of elements to think about. To begin with, the element of a "pre-theoretical constitution," [12] which is charged with accounting for "pre-givens," [13] those kernels of meaning about which man and the world gravitate. We may with equal truth say of these pre-givens (as Husserl says of the body) either that they are always "already constituted" for us or that they are "never completely constituted"—in short, that consciousness is always behind or ahead of them, never contemporaneous. Husserl was undoubtedly thinking of these singular beings when in another connection he evoked a constitution which would not proceed by grasping a content as an exemplification of a meaning or an essence (*Auffassungsinhalt-Auffassung als . . .*), an operating or latent intentionality like that which animates time, more ancient than the intentionality of human *acts*. There must be beings for us which are not yet kept in being by the centrifugal activity of consciousness: significations it does not spontaneously confer upon contents, and contents which participate obliquely in a meaning in the sense that they indicate a meaning which remains a distant meaning and which is not yet legible in them as the monogram or stamp of thetic consciousness. In such cases we do still have a grouping of intentional threads around certain knots which govern them, but the series of retro-references (*Rückdeutungen*) which lead us ever deeper could not possibly reach completion in the intellectual possession of a noema. There is an ordered sequence of steps, but it is without end as it is without beginning. Husserl's thought is as much attracted by the haecceity of Nature as by the vortex of absolute consciousness. In the absences of explicit theses about the relationship of one to the other, we can only examine the samples of "pre-theoretical

12. *Ideen II*, p. 5, "Vortheoretische Konstituierung."
13. *Ibid.*, "Vorgegebenheiten."

constitution" he offers us and formulate—at our own risk—the unthought-of elements we think we see there. There is undeniably something between transcendent Nature, naturalism's being in itself, and the immanence of mind, its acts, and its noema. It is into this interval that we must try to advance.

* * *

Ideen II brings to light a network of implications beneath the "objective material thing" in which we no longer sense the pulsation of constituting consciousness. The relation between my body's movements and the thing's "properties" which they reveal is that of the "I am able to" to the marvels it is within its power to give rise to. And yet my body must itself be meshed into the visible world; its power depends precisely on the fact that it has a place *from which* it sees. Thus it is a thing, but a thing I dwell in. It is, if you wish, on the side of the subject; but it is not a stranger to the locality of things. The relationship between my body and things is that of the absolute here to the there, of the source of distances to distance. My body is the field within which my perceptive powers are localized. But then what is the connection between my body and things if it is not one of objective co-variation? Suppose, Husserl says, that a consciousness were to experience satiety whenever a locomotive's boiler was full, and warmth each time its fire was lit; the locomotive would still not be its body.[14] Then what link is there between my body and me in addition to the regularities of occasional causality? There is a relation of my body to itself which makes it the *vinculum* of the self and things. When my right hand touches my left, I am aware of it as a "physical thing." But at the same moment, if I wish, an extraordinary event takes place: here is my left hand as well starting to perceive my right, *es wird Leib, es empfindet.*[15] The physical thing becomes animate. Or, more precisely, it remains what it was (the event does not enrich it), but an exploratory power comes to rest upon or dwell in it. Thus I touch myself touching; my body accomplishes "a sort of reflection." In it, through it, there is not just the unidirectional relationship of the one who perceives to what he perceives. The relationship is reversed, the touched hand becomes the touching hand, and I am obliged to say that the sense of touch here is diffused into the body—that the body is a "perceiving thing," a "subject-object."[16]

It is imperative that we recognize that this description also overturns our idea of the thing and the world, and that it results in an

14. *Ideen III*, Beilage I, p. 117.
15. *Ideen II*, p. 145.
16. *Ibid.*, p. 119, "Empfindendes Ding"; p. 124, "Das subjektive Objekt."

ontological rehabilitation of the sensible. For from now on we may literally say that space itself is known through my body. If the distinction between subject and object is blurred in my body (and no doubt the distinction between noesis and noema as well?), it is also blurred in the thing, which is the pole of my body's operations, the terminus its exploration ends up in,[17] and which is thus woven into the same intentional fabric as my body. When we say that the perceived thing is grasped "in person" or "in the flesh" (*leibhaft*), this is to be taken literally: the flesh of what is perceived, this compact particle which stops exploration, and this optimum which terminates it all reflect my own incarnation and are its counterpart. Here we have a type of being, a universe with its unparalleled "subject" and "object," the articulation of each in terms of the other, and the definitive definition of an "irrelative" of all the "relativities" of perceptual experience, which is the "legal basis" for all the constructions of understanding.[18]

All understanding and objective thought owe their life to the inaugural fact that with this color (or with whatever the sensible element in question may be) I have perceived, I have had, a singular existence which suddenly stopped my glance yet promised it an indefinite series of experiences, which was a concretion of possibles real here and now in the hidden sides of the thing, which was a lapse of duration given all at once. The intentionality that ties together the stages of my exploration, the aspects of the thing, and the two series to each other is neither the mental subject's connecting activity nor the ideal connections of the object. It is the transition that as carnal subject I effect from one phase of movement to another, a transition which as a matter of principle is always possible for me because I am that animal of perceptions and movements called a body.

Certainly there is a problem here. What will intentionality be then if it is no longer the mind's grasping of an aspect of sensible matter as the exemplification of an essence, no longer the recognition in things of what we have put there? Nor can intentionality be the functioning of a transcendent preordination or teleology we undergo, or of an "institution of nature" (in the Cartesian sense) which works in us without us. This would mean reintegrating the sensible order to the world of plans or objective projects at the moment we have just distinguished the two. It would mean forgetting that the sensible order is *being at a distance*—the fulgurating attestation here and now to an inexhaustible richness—and that things are only half-opened before us, unveiled and hidden. We give just as poor an account of all these

17. *Ibid.*, p. 60, "Die Erfahrungstendenz terminiert in ihr, erfüllt sich in ihr."
18. *Ibid.*, p. 76, "Rechtsgrund."

characteristics by making the world an *aim* as we do by making it an *idea*. The solution—if there is one—can only lie in examining this layer of sensible being or in becoming accustomed to its enigmas.

We are still far from Cartesian *blosse Sachen*. The thing for my body is the "solipsist" thing; it is not yet the thing itself. It is caught up in the context of my body, which itself pertains to the order of things only through its fringes or periphery. The world has not yet closed about my body. The things it perceives would really be being only if I learned that they are seen by others, that they are presumptively visible to every viewer who warrants the name. Thus being in itself will appear only after the constitution of others. But the constitutive steps which still separate us from being in itself are of the same type as the unveiling of my body; as we shall see they make use of a universal which my body has already made appear. My right hand was present at the advent of my left hand's active sense of touch. It is in no different fashion that the other's body becomes animate before me when I shake another man's hand or just look at him.[19] In learning that my body is a "perceiving thing," that it is able to be stimulated (*reizbar*)—it, and not just my "consciousness"—I prepared myself for understanding that there are other *animalia* and possibly other men.

It is imperative to recognize that we have here neither comparison, nor analogy, nor projection or "introjection." [20] The reason why I have evidence of the other man's being-there when I shake his hand is that his hand is substituted for my left hand, and my body annexes the body of another person in that "sort of reflection" it is paradoxically the seat of. My two hands "coexist" or are "compresent" because they are one single body's hands. The other person appears through an extension of that compresence; [21] he and I are like organs of one single intercorporeality. For Husserl the experience of others is first of all "esthesiological," and must be if the other person exists effectively and not as the ideal terminus or fourth term of a proportion which supposedly would come to complete my consciousness' relationships to my objective body and his. What I perceive to begin with is a different "sensibility" (*Empfindbarkeit*), and only subsequently a different man and a different thought. "That man over there sees and hears; on the basis of his perceptions he brings such and such judgments to bear, propounds such and such evaluations and volitions, according to all the different forms possible. That an 'I think' springs forth 'within' him, in that man over there, is a natural fact (*Naturfaktum*) based upon the body and

19. *Ideen II*, pp. 165–66.
20. *Ibid.*, p. 166, "ohne Introjektion."
21. *Ibid.*, "übertragene Kompräsenz."

corporeal events, and determined by the causal and substantial connection of Nature. . . ." [22]

It will perhaps be asked how I am able to extend the compresence of bodies to minds, and whether I do not do so through a turning back upon myself which restores projection or introjection. Is it not within myself that I learn that an "*Empfindbarkeit*" and sensorial fields presuppose a consciousness or a mind? But in the first place this objection assumes that another person can be mind for me in exactly the same sense as I am for myself, and after all nothing is less certain—others' thought is never *wholly* a thought for us. Furthermore, this objection would imply that the problem here is to constitute a different mind, whereas the one who is constituting is as yet only animate flesh himself; nothing prevents us from reserving for the stage when he will speak and listen the advent of another person who also speaks and listens.

But above all this objection would ignore the very thing that Husserl wanted to say; that is, *that there is no constituting of a mind for a mind, but of a man for a man.* By the effect of a singular eloquence of the visible body, *Einfühlung* goes from body to mind. When a different behavior or exploring body appears to me through a first "intentional encroachment," [23] it is the man as a whole who is given to me with all the possibilities (whatever they may be) that I have in my presence to myself in my incarnate being, the unimpeachable attestation. I shall never in all strictness be able to think the other person's thought. I can think *that* he thinks; I can construct, behind this mannequin, a presence to self modeled on my own; but it is still my self that I put in it, and it is then that there really is "introjection." On the other hand, I know unquestionably that that man over there *sees*, that my sensible world is also his, because *I am present at his seeing,* it *is visible* in his eyes' grasp of the scene. And when I say I see *that* he sees, there is no longer here (as there is in "I think that he thinks") the interlocking of two propositions but the mutual unfocusing of a "main" and a "subordinate" viewing. A form that resembles me was there, but busy at secret tasks, possessed by an unknown dream. Suddenly a gleam appeared a little bit below and out in front of its eyes; its glance is raised and comes to fasten on the very things that I am seeing. Everything which for my part is based upon the animal of perceptions and movements, all that I shall ever be able to build upon it—including my "thought," but as a modalization of my presence at the world—falls all at once

22. *Ibid.*, p. 181.

23. "Intentionale überschreiten." The expression is used in the *Cartesian Meditations.*

into the other person. I say that there is a man there and not a mannequin, as I see that the table is there and not a perspective or an appearance of the table.

It is true that I would *not* recognize him if I were *not* a man myself; and that if I did *not* have (or think I had along with myself) the absolute contact of thought, a different *cogito* would *not* spring forth before me. But these catalogues of absences do not translate what has just happened inclusively; they note down partial solidarities which stem from but do not constitute the advent of the other person. All introjection presupposes what is meant to be explained by it. If it were really my "thought" that had to be placed in the other person, I would never put it there. No appearance would ever have the power to convince me that there is a *cogito* over there, or be able to motivate the transference, since my own *cogito* owes its whole power of conviction to the fact that I am myself. If the other person is to exist for me, he must do so to begin with in an order beneath the order of thought. On this level, his existence for me is possible. For my perceptual opening to the world, which is more dispossession than possession, claims no monopoly of being and institutes no death struggle of consciousnesses. My perceived world and the half-disclosed things before me have in their thickness what it takes to supply more than one sensible subject with "states of consciousness"; they have the right to many other witnesses besides me. When a comportment is sketched out in this world which already goes beyond me, this is only one more dimension in primordial being, which comprises them all.

So from the "solipsist" layer on, the other person is not impossible, because the sensible thing is open. The other person becomes actual when a different comportment and a different gaze take possession of my things. And this articulation of a different corporeality in my world is itself effected without introjection; because my sensible existents—through their aspect, configuration, and carnal texture—were already bringing about the miracle of things which are things by the fact that they are offered to a body, and were already making my corporeality a proof of being. Man can create the alter ego which "thought" cannot create, because he is outside himself in the world and because one ek-stasis is compossible with other ek-stases. And that possibility is fulfilled in perception as *vinculum* of brute being and a body. The whole riddle of *Einfühlung* lies in its initial, "esthesiological" phase; and it is solved there because it is a perception. He who "posits" the other man is a perceiving subject, the other person's body is a perceived thing, and the other person himself is "posited" as "perceiving." It is never a matter of anything but co-perception. I see that this man over there sees, as I touch my left hand while it is touching my right.

Thus the problem of *Einfühlung*, like that of my incarnation, opens on the meditation of sensible being; or, if you prefer, it betakes itself there. The fact is that sensible being, which is announced to me in my most strictly private life, summons up within that life all other corporeality. It is the being which reaches me in my most secret parts, but which I also reach in its brute or untamed state, in an absolute of presence which holds the secret of the world, others, and what is true. There are "objects" in this absolute of presence "which are not only fundamentally and originally present to a subject but (since they are so present to one subject) can ideally be given in a fundamental and original presence to all the other subjects (as soon as they are constituted). The whole of the objects which may be fundamentally and originally present, and which constitute a common realm of fundamental and original presence for all communicating subjects, is Nature in its primary and fundamental and original sense." [24] Perhaps nowhere better than in these lines can we see the dual direction of Husserl's reflection, which is both an analytics of essences and an analytics of existences. For it is "ideally" (*idealiter*) that whatever is given to one subject is as a matter of principle given to all others, but it is from the "fundamental and original presence" of sensible being that the obviousness and universality which are conveyed by these relationships of essences come. Re-read, if you doubt it, the extraordinary pages [25] in which Husserl implies that even if we meant to posit absolute or true being as the correlative of an absolute mind, such an absolute being would not merit its name unless it had some relationship to what we men call being. We and absolute mind would have to recognize each other, as two men "can only through understanding each other recognize that the things one of them sees and those the other sees are *the same*." [26] Absolute mind would thus have to see things "through sensible appearances which can be exchanged between it and us in an act of reciprocal comprehension—or at least in a unidirectional communication—as our phenomena can be exchanged between us men." And finally, "it would also have to have a body, which would involve dependency with respect to sense organs."

There are certainly more things in the world and in us than what is perceptible in the narrow sense of the term. The other person's life itself is not given to me with his behavior. In order to have access to it, I would have to be the other person himself. Correlatively, no matter what my pretentions to grasp being itself in what I perceive, I am in the other person's eyes closed into my "representations"; I remain on this

24. *Ideen II*, p. 163.
25. *Ibid.*, p. 85.
26. *Ibid.*

side of his sensible world and thus transcend it. But things seem this way to us because we are making use of a mutilated idea of Nature and the sensible world. Kant said Nature is "the whole of sense-objects." [27] Husserl rediscovers sensible being as the universal form of brute being. Sensible being is not only things but also everything sketched out there, even virtually, everything which leaves its trace there, everything which figures there, even as divergence and a certain absence. "That which can be grasped through experience in the fundamental and original meaning of the term, the being which can be given in a fundamental and original presence (*das urpräsentierbare Sein*), is not the whole of being, and not even all being there is experience of. *Animalia* are realities which cannot be given in a fundamental and original presence to several subjects; they enclose subjectivities. They are the very special sorts of objects which are fundamentally and originally given in such a way that they presuppose fundamental and original presences without being able to be given in a fundamental and original presence themselves." [28] This is what *animalia* and men are: absolutely present beings who have a wake of the negative. A perceiving body that I see is also a certain absence that is hollowed out and tactfully dealt with behind that body by its behavior. But absence is itself rooted in presence; it is through his body that the other person's soul is soul in my eyes. "Negativities" also count in the sensible world, which is decidedly the universal one.

* * *

So what is the result of all this as far as constitution is concerned? By moving to the pre-theoretical, pre-thetic, or pre-objective order, Husserl has upset the relationships between the constituted and the constituting. Being in itself, being for an absolute mind, from now on draws its truth from a "layer" where there is neither absolute mind nor the immanence of intentional objects in that mind, but only incarnate minds which through their bodies "belong . . . to the same world," [29] Of course this does not mean that we have moved from philosophy to psychology or anthropology. The relationship between logical objec-

27. "Der Inbegriff der Gegenstände der Sinne." (*Krit. der Urteilskraft*)

28. *Ideen II*, p. 163.

29. *Ibid.*, p. 82: "Logical objectivity is also, *eo ipso*, objectivity in the sense of intersubjectivity. What one knower knows in logical objectivity . . . any knower can also know, to the extent he fulfills the conditions any knower of such objects must satisfy. That means in this context that he must have the experience of things and of the *same* things, so that in order to be capable of recognizing that identity itself, he must be in a relationship of *Einfühlung* with the other knowers and, to this end, have a corporeality and belong to the same world. . . ." ["zur selben Welt gehören"].

tivity and carnal intersubjectivity is one of those double-edged relationships of *Fundierung* Husserl spoke about in another connection. Intercorporeality culminates in (and is changed into) the advent of *blosse Sachen* without our being able to say that one of the two orders is primary in relation to the other. The pre-objective order is not primary, since it is established (and to tell the truth fully begins to exist) only by being fulfilled in the founding of logical objectivity. Yet logical objectivity is not self-sufficient; it is limited to consecrating the labors of the pre-objective layer, existing only as the outcome of the "Logos of the esthetic world" and having value only under its supervision. Between the "deeper" and the higher layers of constitution, we perceive the singular relationship of *Selbstvergessenheit* that Husserl already names in *Ideen II*,[30] and that he was to take up again later in the theory of sedimentation. Logical objectivity derives from carnal intersubjectivity on the condition that it has been forgotten as carnal intersubjectivity, and it is carnal intersubjectivity itself which produces this forgetfulness by wending its way toward logical objectivity. Thus the forces of the constitutive field do not move in one direction only; they turn back upon themselves. Intercorporeality goes beyond itself and ends up unconscious of itself as intercorporeality; it displaces and changes the situation it set out from, and the spring of constitution can no more be found in its beginning than in its terminus.

These relationships are found again at each stage of constitution. The perceived thing rests upon the body proper. This does not mean that the thing is made of kinestheses in the psychologists' sense of the term. We can just as well say that the entire functioning of the body proper hangs upon the perceived thing the circuit of behavior closes upon. The body is nothing less but nothing more than the things' condition of possibility. When we go from body to thing, we go neither from principle to consequence nor from means to end. We are present at a kind of propagation, encroachment, or enjambment which prefigures the passage from the *solus ipse* to the other person, from the "solipsist" thing to the intersubjective thing.

For the "solipsist" thing is not *primary* for Husserl, nor is the *solus ipse*. Solipsism is a "thought-experiment";[31] the *solus ipse* a "constructed subject."[32] This isolating method of thinking is intended more to reveal than to break the links of the intentional web. If we could break them in reality or simply in thought—if we could really cut the *solus ipse* off from others and from Nature (as Husserl, we must admit, sometimes does when he imagines that first mind, then Nature

30. *Ibid.*, p. 55.
31. *Ibid.*, p. 81, "Gedankenexperiment."
32. *Ibid.*, "Konstruiertes Subjekt."

is annihilated, and wonders what the consequences are for mind and Nature)—there would be fully preserved, in this fragment of the whole which alone was left, the references to the whole it is composed of. In short, we still would not have the *solus ipse*. " . . . In reality the *solus ipse* does not merit its name. Although the abstraction we have carried out is justified intuitively, it does not give us the isolated man or the isolated human person. Furthermore, an abstraction which did succeed in doing so would not consist in preparing a mass murder of the men and animals surrounding us, a murder in which the human subject I am would alone be spared. The subject who would be left alone in this case would still be a human subject, still the intersubjective object understanding itself and still positing itself as such." [33]

This remark goes a long way. To say that the ego "prior to" the other person is alone is already to situate it in relation to a phantom of the other person, or at least to conceive of an environment in which others could be. This is not the true and transcendental solitude. True, transcendental solitude takes place only if the other person is not even conceivable, and this requires that there be no self to claim solitude either. We are truly alone only on the condition that we do not know we are; it is this very ignorance which is our solitude. The "layer" or "sphere" which is called solipsist is without ego and without ipse. The solitude from which we emerge to intersubjective life is not that of the monad. It is only the haze of an anonymous life that separates us from being; and the barrier between us and others is impalpable. If there is a break, it is not between me and the other person; it is between a primordial generality we are intermingled in and the precise system, myself-the others. What "precedes" intersubjective life cannot be numerically distinguished from it, precisely because at this level there is neither individuation nor numerical distinction. The constitution of others does not come after that of the body; others and my body are born together from the original ecstasy. The corporeality to which the primordial thing belongs is more corporeality in general; as the child's egocentricity, the "solipsist layer" is both transitivity and confusion of self and other.

All this, it will undoubtedly be said, represents what the solipsist consciousness would think and say about itself if there could be thought and speech at this level. But whatever illusion of neutrality such a consciousness may be capable of, it is an illusion. The sensible realm is given as being for X . . . , but just the same it is I and no one else who live this color or this sound; pre-personal life itself is still one of my views of the world. The child who asks his mother to console *him* for the pains *she* is suffering is turned toward himself just the same.

33. *Ibid.*, p. 81.

At least this is the way we evaluate his conduct, we who have learned to distribute the pains and pleasures in the world among single lives. But the truth is not so simple: the child who anticipates devotion and love bears witness to the reality of that love, and to the fact that he understands it and, in his weak and passive way, plays his role in it. In the tête-à-tête of the *Füreinander* there is a linkage of egotism and love which wipes out their borders, an identification which goes beyond solipsism in the reigning as well as in the devoted one. Egotism and altruism exist against a background of belonging to the same world; and to want to construct this phenomenon beginning with a solipsist layer is to make it impossible once and for all—and perhaps to ignore the profoundest things Husserl is saying to us.

Every man reflecting upon his life does have the fundamental possibility of looking at it as a series of private states of consciousness, just as the white civilized adult does. But he can do so only if he forgets experiences which bestride this everyday and serial time, or reconstitutes them in a way which caricatures them. The fact that we die alone does not imply that we live alone; and if we consult nothing but suffering and death when we are defining subjectivity, subjective life with others and in the world will become logically impossible. On the other hand, we cannot legitimately consider ourselves instruments of a soul of the world, group, or couple. We must conceive of a primordial *We* [*On*] that has its own authenticity and furthermore never ceases but continues to uphold the greatest passions of our adult life and to be experienced anew in each of our perceptions. For as we have seen, communication at this level is no problem and becomes doubtful only if I forget the perceptual field in order to reduce myself to what reflection will make of me. Reduction to "egology" or the "sphere of belonging" is, like all reduction, only a test of primordial bonds, a way of following them into their final prolongations. The reason why I am able to understand the other person's body and existence "beginning with" the body proper, the reason why the compresence of my "consciousness" and my "body" is prolonged into the compresence of my self and the other person, is that the "I am able to" and the "the other person exists" belong here and now to the same world, that the body proper is a premonition of the other person, the *Einfühlung* an echo of my incarnation, and that a flash of meaning makes them substitutable in the absolute presence of origins.

Thus all of constitution is anticipated in the fulguration of *Urempfindung*. The absolute here of my body and the "there" of the perceptible thing, the near and the distant thing, the experience I have of what is perceptible to me and that which the other person should have of what is perceptible to him—all are in the relationship of the "fundamental and original" to the "modified." Not because the "there" is a lesser or attenuated "here," and the other person an ego projected outside; [34] but because (according to the marvel of carnal existence) along with the "here," the "near," and the "self," there is set forth over there the system of their "variants." Each "here," each nearby thing, each self—lived in absolute presence—bears witness beyond itself to all the other ones which are not for me compossible with it and yet, *somewhere else,* are at this same moment being lived in absolute presence. Since constitution is neither just the development of a future which is implied in its beginning, nor just the effect which an external ordering has in us, it escapes the alternative of continuous or discontinuous. It is discontinuous, since each layer is made from forgetting the preceding one. It is continuous from one end to the other because this forgetting is not simply absence (as if the beginning had not existed) but a forgetting what the beginning literally was to the profit of what it has subsequently become—internalization in the Hegelian sense, *Erinnerung.* From its position, each layer takes up the preceding ones again and encroaches upon those that follow; each is prior and posterior to the others, and thus to itself.

No doubt this is why Hesserl does not seem to be too astonished at the circularities he is led into in the course of his analysis. There is the circularity of the thing and the experience of other people. For the fully objective thing is based upon the experience of others, and the latter upon the experience of the body, which in a way is a thing itself.[35] There is another circularity between Nature and persons. For Nature in the sense of the natural sciences (but also in the sense of the *Urpräsentierbare,* which for Husserl is the truth of the first) is the whole of the world (*Weltall*) [36] to begin with, and as such it encompasses persons who, in another connection in which they are expressly made explicit, encompass Nature as the object they constitute in common.[37] No doubt this is also why Husserl, in a prophetic text in 1912,

34. And yet it is in this way that Eugen Fink (*Problèmes actuels de la Phénoménologie,* pp. 80–81) seems to understand the absolute priority of the perceived in Husserl's thought.

35. *Ideen II,* p. 80, "Verwickeln wir uns nicht in einen Zirkel, da doch die Menschenauffassung die Leibesauffassung, und somit die Dingauffassung, voraussetzt?"

36. *Ibid.,* p. 27.

37. *Ibid.,* p. 210, "Wir geraten hier, scheint es, in einen bösen Zirkel. Denn setzen wir zu Anfang die Natur schlechthin, in der Weise wie es jeder Naturforscher und jeder naturalistisch Eingestellte sonst tut, und fassten wir die Menschen als Realitäten, die über ihre physiche Leiblichkeit ein plus haben, so waren die Personen untergeordnete Naturobjekte, Bestandstücke der Natur. Gingen wir aber dem Wesen der Personalität nach, so stellte sich Natur als ein im intersubjektiven Verband der Personen sich Konstituierendes also ihn Voraussetzendes dar."

did not hesitate to speak of a reciprocal relation between Nature, body, and soul; and, as it has been well put, of their "simultaneity." [38]

These adventures of constitutive analysis—these encroachments, reboundings and circularities—do not, as we were saying, seem to disturb Husserl very much. After having shown in one place [39] that the world of Copernicus refers to the world of lived experience, and the universe of physics to that of life, he calmly says that this view will undoubtedly seem rather excessive, and even completely mad.[40] But he adds that its only function is to enable us to examine experience better [41] and follow its intentional implications more closely. Nothing can prevail against the clarities of constitutive analysis. Does this involve asserting the claim of essences contrary to factual truths? Is it, Husserl himself wonders, "philosophical hubris"? Is it one more instance of *consciousness* assuming the right to confine itself to its thoughts against all challenges? But sometimes it is *experience* that Husserl appeals to as the ultimate basis for law. So his position would seem to be that since we *are* at the junction of Nature, body, soul, and philosophical consciousness, since we live that juncture, no problem can be conceived of whose solution is not sketched out within us and in the world's spectacle—our existence should provide means of arranging in our thought what is all of a piece in our life. If Husserl holds fast to the clarities of constitution, this is no madness of consciousness, nor does it mean that consciousness has the right to substitute what is clear to it for established natural dependencies. It means that the transcendental field has ceased to be simply the field of our thought and has become the field of the whole of experience, and that Husserl trusts the truth which we are *in* from birth and which ought to be able to contain both the truths of consciousness and the truths of Nature. The reason why the "retro-references" of constitutive analysis do not have to win out over the principle of a philosophy of consciousness is that this philosophy has been sufficiently expanded or transformed to be the match for anything, even for what challenges it.

Although it was later on that Husserl spoke of the possibility that

38. Marly Biemel: *Husserliana,* Bd IV, Einleitung des Herausgebers. Here is Husserl's text: "Nature, the body, and also, interwoven with the body, the soul are constituted all together in a reciprocal relationship with one another." *Husserliana,* Bd V, p. 124: " . . . Ist ein wichtiges Ergebnis unserer Betrachtung, dass die 'Natur' und der Leib, in ihrer Verflechtung mit dieser wieder die Seele, sich in Wechselbezogenheit aufeinander, in eins miteinander, konstituieren."

39. *Umsturz der kopernikanischen Lehre in der gewöhnlichen weltanschaulichen Interpretation. Die Ur-Arche Erde bewegt sich richt,* 7–9 May, 1934.

40. *Ibid.,* "Aber nun wird man das arg finden, geradezu toll."

41. For example, *Ideen II,* pp. 179–80. There is the same development of thought at the end of *Umsturz.*

phenomenology is a question for itself, of the existence of a "phenomenology of phenomenology" upon which the ultimate meaning of all foreseeable analyses depends, and on the continuing problematic nature of integral, self-contained, or self-supporting phenomenology, these possibilities can already be seen in a reading of *Ideen II*. He does not hide the fact that intentional analytics leads us conjointly in two opposite directions. On the one hand it descends toward Nature, the sphere of the *Urpräsentierbare;* whereas it is drawn on the other hand toward the world of persons and minds. "This does not necessarily mean," he continues, "and should not mean, that the two worlds have nothing to do with one another, and that their meaning does not manifest relationships of essence between them. We know of other cardinal differences between 'worlds' which are nevertheless mediated by relationships of meaning and essence. The relationship between the world of ideas and the world of experience, for example, *or that between the 'world' of pure, phenomenologically reduced consciousness and the world of transcendent unities constituted within it.*" [42] Thus there are problems of mediation between the world of Nature and the world of persons—even more, between the world of constituting consciousness and the results of the labor of constitution—and the ultimate task of phenomenology as philosophy of consciousness is to understand its relationship to non-phenomenology. What resists phenomenology within us—natural being, the "barbarous" source Schelling spoke of—cannot remain outside phenomenology and should have its place within it. The philosopher must bear his shadow, which is not simply the factual absence of future light.

It is already "exceptionally" difficult, Husserl says, to not only "grasp" but "understand from within" the relationship between the "world of Nature" and the "World of mind." At least this difficulty is overcome practically in our life, since we drift constantly and without difficulty from the naturalist to the personalist attitude. It is only a question of making reflection equal to what we do with complete naturalness in going from one attitude to another—of describing alterations of intentional apprehensions, articulations of experience, and essential relationships between constituting multiplicities which give an account of differences of being among what is constituted. In this respect phenomenology can clear up what is confused and eliminate misunderstandings which are precisely the result of our going naturally and unknowingly from one attitude to the other. Yet there is no doubt that these misunderstandings and this "natural" transition exist because clearing up the connection between Nature and persons involves a fundamental difficulty. How much more difficulty will we have when

42. *Ideen II*, p. 211 (my italics).

we must *understand from within* the passage from the naturalist or personalist attitude to absolute consciousness, from powers which are natural to an "artificial" (*künstlich*) attitude [43]—which really should no longer be an attitude among others but the comprehension of all attitudes, being itself speaking within us? What is this "internality" which will be capable of the relationships between interior and exterior themselves? The fact that Husserl at least implicitly and *a fortiori* raises this question [44] means that he does not think that non-philosophy is included in philosophy from the outset, or that the transcendent is "constituted" in the immanence of constituting consciousness. It means that he at least glimpses, behind transcendental genesis, a world in which all is simultaneous, ὅμου ἦν πάντα.

Is this last problem so surprising? Had not Husserl warned from the outset that all transcendental reduction is inevitably eidetic? This meant that reflection does not coincide with what is constituted but grasps only the essence of it—that it does not take the place of intentional life in an act of pure production but only re-produces the outline of it. Husserl always presents the "return to absolute consciousness" as a title for a multitude of operations which are learned, gradually effected, and never completed. We are never wholly one with constitutive genesis; we barely manage to accompany it for short segments. What is it then which responds to our reconstitution from (if these words have a meaning) the other side of things? From our own side,

43. *Ibid.*, p. 180.

44. Here is the text we are commenting on: "We have in view here a new attitude which is in a certain sense completely natural (*natürlich*) but which is not natural (*natural*). 'Not natural' means that what we have experience of in this attitude is not Nature in the sense of the natural sciences, but so to speak a contrary of Nature. It goes without saying that what is exceptionally difficult is to not be satisfied with grasping the contrast between worlds but to comprehend it from within (*von innen her zu verstehen*). This difficulty does not lie in the adoption of attitudes itself. For—if we do not consider the attitude which bears on pure conciousness (*Einstellung auf das reine Bewusstsein*), this residue of different reductions which is, moreover, artificial—we slip constantly and with no trouble from one attitude to the other, from the naturalist to the personalist attitude and correlatively from the natural to the mental sciences. The difficulties begin with reflection, phenomenological comprehension of the change in intentional apprehensions and experiences, and correlates constituted through them. It is only within the framework of phenomenology and in relating the differences of being of objects which are being constituted to the essential relationships of the constituting multiplicities which correspond to them that these difficulties can be kept unembroiled (*unverwirrt*), in absolutely certain separation (*in absolut sicherer Sonderung*), freed from all the misunderstandings which arise from involuntary changes in attitude and which, in the absence of pure reflection, remain unperceived by us. It is only by returning to absolute consciousness, and to the totality of the relationships of essence we can follow in it, that we shall finally comprehend according to their meaning the relationships of dependency between objects which correspond to both attitudes, and their reciprocal relationships of essence."

there is nothing but convergent but discontinuous intentions, moments of clarity. We constitute constituting consciousness by dint of rare and difficult efforts. It is the presumptive or alleged subject of our attempts. The author, Valéry said, is the instantaneous thinker of works which were slow and laborious—and this thinker is nowhere. As the author is for Valéry the impostor of the writer, constituting consciousness is the philosopher's professional impostor. In any case, for Husserl it is the *artifact* the teleology of intentional life ends up at—and not the Spinozist attribute of Thought.

Originally a project to gain intellectual possession of the world, constitution becomes increasingly, as Husserl's thought matures, the means of unveiling a back side of things that we have not constituted. This senseless effort to submit everything to the proprieties of "consciousness" (to the limpid play of its attitudes, intentions, and impositions of meaning) was necessary—the picture of a well-behaved world left to us by classical philosophy had to be pushed to the limit—in order to reveal all that was left over: these beings beneath our idealizations and objectifications which secretly nourish them and in which we have difficulty recognizing noema. The Earth, for example, which is not in motion like objective bodies, but not at rest either, since we cannot see what it could be "tacked on" to. It is the "soil" or "stem" of our thought as it is of our life. We shall certainly be able to move it or carry it back when we inhabit other planets, but the reason we shall is that then we shall have enlarged our native soil. We cannot do away with it. As the Earth is by definition one, all soil we tread upon becoming simultaneously a province of it, the living beings with whom the sons of the Earth will be able to communicate will simultaneously become men—or if you prefer, terrestial men will become variants of a more general human community which will remain one. The Earth is the matrix of our time as it is of our space. Every constructed notion of time presupposes our proto-history as carnal beings compresent to a single world. Every evocation of possible worlds refers to a way of seeing our own world (*Weltanschauung*). Every possibility is a variant of our reality, an effective possibility of reality (*Möglichkeit an Wirklichkeit*). These late analyses of Husserl's [45] are neither scandalous nor even disturbing if we remember everything which foretold them from the start. They make explicit that "world's thesis" prior to every thesis and theory, this side of understanding's objectifications, which Husserl has always spoken of, and which has simply become in his eyes our sole recourse in the impasse into which these objectifications have led Western knowledge.

Willy-nilly, against his plans and according to his essential audac-

45. We are summarizing *Umsturz* . . . , cited above.

ity, Husserl awakens a wild-flowering world and mind. Things are no longer there simply according to their projective appearances and the requirements of the panorama, as in Renaissance perspective; but on the contrary upright, insistent, flaying our glance with their edges, each thing claiming an absolute presence which is not compossible with the absolute presence of the other things, and which they nevertheless have all together by virtue of a configurational meaning which is in no way indicated by its "theoretical meaning." Other persons are there too (they were already there along with the simultaneity of things). To begin with they are not there as minds, or even as "psychisms," but such for example as we face them in anger or love—faces, gestures, spoken words to which our own respond without thoughts intervening, to the point that we sometimes turn their words back upon them even before they have reached us, as surely as, more surely than, if we had understood—each one of us pregnant with the others and confirmed by them in his body. This baroque world is not a concession of mind to nature; for although meaning is everywhere figurative, it is meaning which is at issue everywhere. This renewal of the world is also mind's renewal, a rediscovery of that brute mind which, untamed by any culture, is asked to create culture anew. From then on the irrelative is not nature in itself, nor the system of absolute consciousness' apprehensions, nor man either, but that "teleology" Husserl speaks about which is written and thought about in parentheses—that jointing and framing of Being which is being realized through man.

7 / Bergson in the Making[1]

THERE IS MORE than one paradox in the fortunes of Bergsonism. This philosopher of freedom, Péguy said in 1913, had the radical party and the University against him; this enemy of Kant had the *action française* party against him; this friend of the spiritual life had the religious party against him. Thus not only his natural enemies but the enemies of his enemies were ranged against him. During those years when he seemed to have a predilection for unconventional men like Péguy and Georges Sorel, Bergson could almost be described as a *philosophe maudit*—if we were to forget that at the same time he had been followed by a unanimously favorable audience at the Collège de France for thirteen years, had been for twelve years a member of an academy, and was soon to become a member of the Academy.

The generation I belong to knew only the second Bergson, who was already retired from teaching and almost silent during his long preparation of the *Two Sources*, already considered an inspiration rather than a threat by Catholicism, already taught in classes by rationalist professors. Among our elders, whom he had shaped without there ever having been a Bergsonian school, he had immense standing. We have to wait for the recent period before we see a shadowy, exclusive post-Bergsonism appear, as if we would not do Bergson a greater honor by admitting that he belongs to everyone.

How has the man who had bowled over philosophy and letters managed to become this almost canonical author? Is it he who has changed? We shall see that he has scarcely changed at all. The truth is that there are two Bergsonisms. There is that audacious one, when Bergson's philosophy fought and, Péguy says, fought well. And there is

1. A paper read at the session in homage to Bergson which concluded the Congrès Bergson (May 17–20, 1959), and published by the *Bulletin de la Société Française de Philosophie*.

that one after the victory, persuaded in advance about what Bergson took a long time to find, and already provided with concepts while Bergson himself created his own. When Bergsonian insights are identified with the vague cause of spiritualism or some other entity, they lose their bite; they are generalized and minimized. What is left is only a retrospective or external Bergsonism. It found its formulation when Father Sertillanges [2] wrote that in this day the Church would no longer put Bergson on the Index; not that it is going back on its judgment in 1913, but because it now knows how Bergson's works turned out.

Bergson himself did not wait to know where his path was leading in order to take it, or rather to make it. He did not wait until he had written the *Two Sources* before he dared to write *Matter and Memory* and *Creative Evolution*. Even if the *Two Sources* really did rectify the condemned works, it would not have the meaning it has or be famous without them. You have to take or leave it. We cannot have truth without risks. If we begin our search for truth with an eye for conclusions, there is no more philosophy. The philosopher does not look for shortcuts; he goes all the way. Established Bergsonism distorts Bergson. Bergson disturbed; it reassures. Bergson was a conquest; Bergsonism defends and justifies Bergson. Bergson was a contact with things; Bergsonism is a collection of accepted opinions. Reconciliations and celebrations ought not to make us forget the path Bergson traced out alone and never renounced. They ought not to make us forget that direct, sober, immediate, unusual way of reconstructing philosophy, seeking the profound in appearances and the absolute beneath our eyes. Forget in short the spirit of discovery which, underneath the most extreme propriety, is Bergsonism's primary source.

He concluded his course of 1911 with these words picked up by the journal *les Etudes:* "If the scientist, the artist, and the philosopher devote themselves to the pursuit of fame, it is because they lack the absolute security of having created something viable. Give them that assurance, and immediately you will see them give little weight to the clamor which surrounds their name." In the last analysis, the only thing Bergson wished for was to have created books that live. Now we can bear witness to the vitality of his works only by saying how he is present in our own, showing the pages of his works in which, like his listeners in 1900, we with our own preferences and partialities think we perceive him "in contact with things."

He is first of all a philosopher in his way of regaining the whole of philosophy, as if he were unaware of what he was doing, by examining one of the principles of mechanics which Spencer used without rigor. It

2. Antonin-Dalmace Sertillanges, French Catholic author of (among *many* other works!) *Avec Henri Bergson.*—Trans.

is then that Bergson perceives that we do not draw near to time by squeezing it between the reference-points of measurement as if between pincers; but that in order to have an idea of it we must on the contrary let it develop freely, accompanying the continual birth which makes it always new and, precisely in this respect, always the same.

In this perception his philosopher's eye found something different and something more than he was looking for. For if this is what time is, it is nothing that I see from without. From without, I would only have the trail of time; I would not be present at its generative thrust. So time is myself; I am the duration I grasp, and time is duration grasped in me. And from now on we are at the absolute. A strange absolute knowledge, since we know neither all our memories nor even the whole thickness of our present, and since my contact with myself is "partial coincidence" (to use a term often used by Bergson which, to tell the truth, is a problematic one). In any case, when my self is at issue the contact is absolute *because* it is partial. I know my duration as no one else does because I am caught up in it; because it overflows me, I have an experience of it which could not be more narrowly or closely conceived of. Absolute knowledge is not detachment; it is inherence. In 1889 it was a great novelty—and one which had a future—to present as the basis of philosophy not an *I think* and its immanent thoughts but a Being-self whose self-cohesion is also a tearing away from self.

Since it is a non-coincidence I coincide with here, experience is susceptible to being extended beyond the particular being I am. My perception of my duration is an apprenticeship in a general way of *seeing.* It is the principle of a sort of Bergsonian "reduction" which reconsiders all things *sub specie durationis*—what is called subject, what is called object, and even what is called space—for in perceiving our own duration we already see an *inner space* or extension being sketched out which is the world Achilles walks in. There are beings or structures (Bergson calls them organizations) such as melody which are nothing but a certain way of enduring. Duration is not simply change, becoming, mobility; it is being in the vital, active sense of the term. Time is not put in place of being; it is understood as being coming to be, and now it is the whole of being which must be approached from the side of time.

This was evident when *Matter and Memory* appeared, or at least it should have been. But the book was a surprise, and seemed obscure; even today it is the least read of Bergson's great books. Yet it is in this book that the field of duration and the practice of intuition are enlarged in a decisive way. Forgetting, as he said, his preceding book, following a different line of facts for its own sake, making contact with the composite of soul and body, Bergson was led back to duration, but to a duration which had received new dimensions in this different approach. To reproach Bergson here for what is called a shift of meaning (but is really inquiry itself) would be to miss the law of a philosophy which does not aspire to system but to *complete* reflection, and which wants to make being speak. From this point forward duration is the milieu in which soul and body find their articulation because the present and the body, the past and the mind, although different in nature, nevertheless pass into one another. Intuition is definitely not simply coincidence or fusion any more. It is extended to "limits," such as pure perception and pure memory, and also to the region in between the two, to a being which Bergson says opens itself to the present and to space to the exact extent it aims at a future and disposes of a past. There is a life (a "hybridization," Maurice Blondel was to say) of intuitions, a "double expansion" toward matter and toward memory. It is by taking opposites in their extreme difference that intuition perceives their reunion.

We would for example greatly distort Bergson if we minimized the astonishing description of perceived being that is given in *Matter and Memory*. He does not say at all that things are images in the restrictive sense of the "psychical" or of souls. He says that their fullness beneath my gaze is such that it is as if my vision developed in them rather than in me, as if their being seen were only a degradation of their eminent being, as if their being "represented" (Bergson says appearing to the subject's "darkroom"), far from being their definition, were a result of their natural profusion. Never before had anyone established this circuit between being and myself which is such that being exists "for me," the spectator, but which is also such that the spectator exists "for being." Never had the brute being of the perceived world been so described. By unveiling it according to duration as it comes to be, Bergson regains at the heart of man a pre-Socratic and "prehuman" meaning of the world.

Durée et Simultanéité, which is, Bergson repeats, a philosophical book, will install itself yet more resolutely in the perceived world. Today as they did thirty-five years ago, physicists reproach Bergson for introducing the observer into relativity physics, which they say makes time relative only to measuring instruments or the system of reference. But what Bergson wants to show is precisely that there is no simultaneity between things in themselves, which no matter how closely they border on one another exist each one in itself. Perceived things alone can participate in the same line of present. And in return as soon as there is perception there is, without any measurement, simply perceived simultaneity, not only between two events in the same field but even between all perceptual fields, all observers, and all durations. If all observers were taken at once, and not as they are seen by one observer but as they are for themselves and in the absoluteness of their life, these solitary durations (which could no longer be applied to and measured against one another) would no longer present any displacement and would thus stop fragmenting the temporal universe. Now Bergson said that this restitution of all durations to a unified whole, which is not possible at their inner source because each of us coincides only with his own duration, is achieved when incarnate subjects mutually perceive one another—that is, when their perceptual fields cut across and envelop one another and they each see one another in the process of perceiving the same world. In its own order perception posits a universal duration; and the formulas which enable us to pass from one system of reference to another are, like physics as a whole, secondary objectifications which cannot make a determination about what is meaningful in our experience as incarnate subject, or about being as a whole. What Bergson was doing here was outlining a philosophy that would make the universal rest upon the mystery of perception and would propose as its task, as Bergson himself said, not sweeping over but penetrating into perception.

For Bergson perception is the whole of those "complementary powers of understanding" which alone are able to cope with being, and which in opening us to being "perceive themselves at work in nature's workings." If only we know how to perceive life, we shall see that its being is of the same type as those simple and undivided beings patterned for us by these things more ancient than all fabricated things, the things before our eyes; and life's working is going to appear to us as a sort of perception. When we observe that life by long preparations erects a visual apparatus along one line of evolution, and sometimes erects the same apparatus along divergent lines of evolution, we believe we see one single gesture—like my hand's gesture as I perceive it—behind convergent details; and the "march toward vision" in the species stems from the total act of vision as it was described in *Matter and Memory*. Bergson refers expressly to this total act. He says it is this act which descends in varying degrees into organisms. This does not mean that the world of life is a human representation, nor human perception a cosmic product. It means that the fundamental and original perception which we regain within ourselves and the perception which shows through in evolution as its inner principle intermingle with, transgress upon, or tie up with one another. Whether we find the opening to the world within us or grasp life from within, there is always the same tension between one duration and another duration which borders it from without.

Thus we can see rather clearly in the Bergson of 1907 the intuition of intuitions, the central intuition; and it is far from being, as it has incorrectly been called, an "I know not what," an inspired fact which is difficult to verify. Is there any reason why the source from which he draws and in which he takes the meaning of his philosophy should not simply be the articulation of his inner landscape; the way in which his glance encounters things or life; his lived relationship to himself, nature, and living beings; his contact with being within and outside of us? And is it not the visible and existing world itself, such as *Matter and Memory* described it, which provides the best "mediating image" for this inexhaustible intuition? Even when he goes on to transcendance from above, Bergson will think that he can have access to it only through a sort of "perception." Life in any case—life which, beneath us, always solves problems in a different way than we would have solved them—bears less resemblance to a human mind than it does to that imminent or eminent vision Bergson glimpsed in things. Perceived being is that spontaneous or natural being which Cartesians did not see because they were seeking being against a background of nothingness, and because, Bergson says, they lacked what is necessary to "conquer non-existence." Bergson himself describes a pre-constituted being that is always presupposed at the horizon of our reflections, and is always already there to lift the fuse out of the anguish and the vertigo that are about to explode within us.

It is hard to understand why Bergson did not think about history from within as he had thought about life from within. Why did he not also set about investigating in history the *simple and undivided acts* which arrange fragmentary facts for each period or event? In maintaining that each period is all it can be, a complete event existing wholly in act, and that pre-Romanticism for example is a post-Romantic illusion, Bergson seems to reject this depth-history once and for all. Yet Péguy had sought to describe the event's emergence, when some are beginning and others responding; and also historical fulfillment, one generation's response to what another had begun. He saw the essence of history in that junction of individuals and times which is difficult because act, work, and past in their simplicity are inaccessible to those who see them from without—because it takes years to make the history of that revolution which was made in one day, and an infinite commentary does not exhaust this page which was written in an hour. The chances of error, deviation, and failure are enormous. But the cruel law of those who write, act, or *live publicly* (that is, in the end, of all incarnate minds) is to expect from others or successors a different fulfillment than the one they are achieving. *A different and the same* fulfillment, Péguy profoundly says, because others or successors are also men; or more precisely, because by this substitution they make themselves fellow-men of the initiator. We have here a sort of scandal, Péguy said, but a "justified scandal" and consequently a "mystery." Meaning is remade at the risk of being unmade. It is a voluble meaning, closely conforming to the Bergsonian definition of meaning, which is "less a thing thought than a movement of thinking, less a movement than a direction." In this network of callings and responses, in which the beginning is transformed and fulfilled, there is a duration which belongs to no one and to everyone, a "public duration" or "rhythm and speed proper to the world's events" which Péguy said would be the theme of a true sociology. He had thus proven factually that a Bergsonian view of history is possible.

But even though Bergson said in 1915 that Péguy had known his "essential thought," he did not follow him on this point. For Bergson, the "historical inscription" has no value *peculiar* to it, nor do the calling and responding generations. There is only an heroic appeal from individual to individual, a mystique without a "mystical body." For him there is not one sole fabric in which good and evil hang together; there are natural societies perforated by irruptions of the mystical. During the long years he was preparing the *Two Sources,* he does not seem to have impregnated himself with history as he had with life; he did not find "complementary powers of understanding" on terms with our own duration, working in history as formerly he had found them working in life. He remains too optimistic about the individual and his power to regain sources, and too pessimistic in respect to social life, to accept a definition of history as a "justified scandal."

And perhaps this recoil of opposites harks back to his whole doctrine. The fact is that the relationships of implication which the *Introduction to Metaphysics* had established between philosophy and science, intuition and understanding, and mind and matter are rectified in the direction of a clear delimitation (although not without "transgressions") in the *Pensée et le Mouvant,* which was written at about the same time as the *Two Sources.* If there is definitely no mystery of history for Bergson, if he does not see men implicated in one another as Péguy does, if he is not sensitive to the attentive presence of symbols around us and the profound exchanges they are vehicles of (if he finds at the origins of democracy, for example, only its "evangelical essence" and the Christianity of Kant and Rousseau), then this way he has of drawing up short before certain possibilities and holding the ultimate meaning of his works in check must express a deep-seated preference. It is a part of his philosophy, and we must try to understand it.

What is opposed to all philosophy of mediation and history in Bergson is a very old theme of his thought, his conviction that there is a "semi-divine" state in which man does not know vertigo and anguish.

The mediation of history displaced this conviction without attenuating it. At the time of *Creative Evolution,* philosophical intuition of natural being sufficed to reduce the false problems of nothingness. In the *Two Sources*, "divine man" has become "inaccessible"; but Bergson still puts human history in perspective in terms of him. Natural contact with being, joy, serenity—quietism—remain essentials for Bergson; they are simply transferred from the philosopher's experience, which in principle is generalizable, to the mystic's exceptional experience, which opens upon a different nature and a second positivity, themselves unlimited. It is the doubling of nature into an irreconcilable *natura naturans* and *natura naturata* which in the *Two Sources* actualizes the distinction between God and his action upon the world that remained virtual in the previous works. It is true that Bergson does not say *Deus sive Natura*, but the reason why he does not is that God is *a different nature.* At the very moment he definitively disengages the "transcendent cause" from its "terrestial delegation," it is still the word nature which falls from his pen. From this point forward, all that was truly active and creative in the world is concentrated in God, and the world ends up as nothing but a "stopping point" or "created thing."

But man's relationship to this Super-nature is still the direct relationship the previous books found between intuition and natural being. There is the simple act which made the human species. There is God's simple and simplifying action in the realm of the mystical. There is no simple act which establishes the domain of history and evil, which is really only the in-between realm. Man is made of two simple principles rather than being dual. History, oscillating between *natura naturans* and *natura naturata,* has no substance of its own. Certainly, it is not accursed. The universe is still a "machine for fabricating gods"; and this after all is not impossible, since *natura naturans* is the source of *natura naturata.* But if the machine for fabricating gods one day succeeded where it had always failed, it would be as if arrested creation started up again. Nothing announces this Great Springtime. Nowhere, not even enigmatically, do we find any sign which reunites our two natures. Evil and failure have no meaning. Creation is not a drama going toward a future. It is instead a bogged-down effort, and human history an expedient to set the mass in motion once again.

This results in an extraordinary, extremely personal, and in some respects pre-Christian religious philosophy. Mystical experience is what remains of the primordial unity, which was sundered when the created thing appeared through a "simple stopping" of creative effort. How can we cross this wall behind us which is our origin, how can we find the trail of the *naturans* again? Intelligence will not do it; the creation cannot be re-created with what is created. Even the immediate experience of our duration cannot annul the fission which is its origin in order to rejoin *natura naturans* itself. That is why Bergson says that mystical experience need not wonder whether the source it puts us in contact with is God himself or his earthly delegation. It experiences the granted invasion of a being which "can do immensely more than it can." We must not even say an all-powerful being: Bergson says that the idea of the all is as empty as that of nothingness, and the possible for him remains the shadow of the real. Bergson's God is immense rather than infinite, or He is a qualitative infinite. He is the element of joy or love in the sense that water and fire are elements. Like sentient and human beings, He is a radiance, not an essence. Metaphysical attributes which seem to determine Him are, Bergson says, like all determinations, negations. Even if through some impossibility they became visible, no religious man would recognize the God he prays to in them. Bergson's God is, like the universe, a singular being, an immense *this;* and even in theology Bergson kept his promise of a philosophy fashioned for actual being and applying to it alone. If we indulge in imaginary computations we must admit, he says, that "the whole could have been much better than it is." No one can make someone's death a component of the best possible world. But not only are the solutions of classical theodicy false, the problems have no meaning in the order Bergson puts himself in—the order of radical contingency. Here it is not a question of the conceived world or a conceived God, but of the existing world and an existing God; and that within us which is acquainted with this order is beneath our opinions and our statements. No one will ever stop men from loving their life, no matter how miserable it may be. This vital judgment puts life and God this side of arraignment as well as of justification. And if we insisted upon understanding how *natura naturans* has been able to produce a *natura naturata* in which it is not really realized, why creative effort has been at least provisionally arrested, what obstacle it has encountered and how an obstacle could be insurmountable for it, Bergson would agree (with the exception of other planets, where life has perhaps been more successful) that his philosophy does not answer this type of question. But he would also say that the reason why it does not is that it does not have to ask such questions. For in the last analysis his philosophy is not a genesis of the world—not even, as it narrowly missed being, "integration and differentiation" of being—but the deliberately partial, discontinuous, almost empirical location of several foci of being.

* * *

All things considered, we must admit that Péguy is completely right when he says that this philosophy "for the first time . . . drew attention to what was peculiar to the very being and articulation of the present." Being coming to be, which no representation separates me from; which contains in advance the views (even the discordant, non-compossible ones) that we can take of it; which stands upright before us, younger and older than the possible and the necessary; and which, once brought to be, will never be able to stop having been and will continue to be in the depths of other presents—it is understandable that the books which at the beginning of the century rediscovered this forgotten being and its powers were experienced as a rebirth and deliverance of philosophy. And in this respect, their force is intact. It would have been nice if the same fundamental and original glance had then been turned toward events, techniques, law, language, and literature in order to find their own peculiar spirit by taking them as monuments and prophecies of an hieratic man, ciphers of a questioning mind. Bergson believed in confirmation and invention; he did not believe in interrogative thought. But within that very restriction of his field he is exemplary in his faithfulness to what he saw. In the religious conversations of his last years, when his philosophy was framed in the Thomist setting which he adopted as an experimental confrontation and a benevolent auxiliary—as if it were not evident that something essential is *lost* when we *add* something to Bergson's philosophy—what strikes me is the tranquillity with which Bergson sticks to his method in philosophy at the very moment he is giving Catholicism his personal assent and moral adherence. After having held strictly to his course during the storms, he kept to it during the final reconciliations. His effort and his works, which put philosophy back in the present and showed what can today be an approach to being, also teach us how a man of former times remained irreducible. They teach us that we must say nothing but what we can "show"; that we must know how to await and make things wait, displease and even please, be ourselves, be true—and that among men, moreover, this firmness is not even anathema, since there was also Bergsonism seeking what is true.

8 / Einstein and the Crisis of Reason

SCIENCE IN AUGUSTE COMTE'S DAY was getting ready to *dominate* existence, theoretically and practically. Whether it was a question of technical or political action, men thought they would soon have access to the laws according to which nature and society *are constructed,* and govern both according to their principles. Something entirely different, almost the inverse, has actually occurred. Far from light and efficaciousness having gone forward together in science, the applications which are changing the face of the world have sprung from a highly speculative science whose ultimate meaning men have difficulty agreeing upon. And far from science, including even political science, having submitted to these expectations, we have had instead a physics filled with philosophical, almost political debates.

Einstein himself was a classical thinker. As categorically as he claims the right to construct, with no respect whatsoever for the *a priori* notions which claim to be the mind's invariant framework,[1] he has never stopped thinking that this creation rejoins a truth set down in the world. "I believe in a world in itself, a world governed by laws I try to apprehend in a wildly speculative fashion." [2] But it is precisely this encounter between speculation and reality, between our image of the world and the world itself, which he sometimes calls "pre-established harmony," [3] that he does not dare to base categorically upon a divine infrastructure of the world, as Cartesian major rationalism did, or like idealism, upon the principle that reality for us cannot possibly be different from what we are able to think. Sometimes Einstein refers to Spinoza's God, but he more frequently describes ration-

1. Science "is a creation of the human mind by means of freely invented ideas and concepts." Einstein and Infeld, *The Evolution of Physics,* p. 286.

2. Letter to Max Born, November 7, 1944, quoted by T. Kahan, *La philosophie d'Einstein.*

3. Einstein, *The World As I See It,* p. 155.

ality as a mystery and the theme of a "cosmic religiosity." [4] The least comprehensible thing in the world, he said, is that the world is comprehensible.

If we call "classical" a way of thinking which assumes that the world is rational, the classical spirit reaches its extreme limit in Einstein. We know that he was never able to make up his mind to take as definitive the formulas of wave mechanics, which unlike the concepts of classical physics do not bear on the "properties" [5] of things or physical individuals, but describe the behavior and probabilities of certain collective phenomena within matter. He was never able to support this idea of a "reality" which is intrinsically and in the last analysis a tissue of probabilities. "Nevertheless," he added, "I am unable to invoke any logical argument to defend my convictions, unless it be my little finger, the sole and feeble witness to an opinion buried deep under my skin." [6] Humor was no evasion for Einstein; he made it an indispensable component of his conception of the world—almost a means of understanding. For him humor was the mode of risky certainties. His "little finger" was the creative physicist's paradoxical and irrepressible consciousness of having access to a reality through an invention which was nevertheless free. Einstein thinks that God must be either "sophisticated" or refined to hide himself so well. But it would not be possible for God to be malicious. Thus Einstein held on to both ends of the chain—classical physics' ideal of knowledge and his own "wildly speculative," revolutionary way. The physicists of the following generation have for the most part let the first end go.

As for the public, it does not hesitate to see a miracle in the encounter between speculation and reality which Einstein postulates as a limpid mystery. A science which confuses all the patent facts of common sense, and is at the same time capable of changing the world, inevitably arouses a sort of superstition even among the most cultivated witnesses. Einstein protests that he is not a god, that these immoderate praises are not addressed to him but "to my mythical homonym who makes my life singularly difficult." [7] No one believes him, or rather his simplicity further magnifies his legend. Since he is so astonished at his glory, and it means so little to him, it must be because his genius is not wholly of his own making. Einstein is more the consecrated place, the tabernacle of some supernatural operation. "This detachment is so complete that sometimes in his presence one must remember that one is really dealing with him. One thinks one is associating with a

4. *Ibid.*, p. 35.
5. Einstein and Infeld, p. 289.
6. Kahan, *ibid.*
7. Reply to Bernard Shaw, quoted by Antonina Vallentin, *Le Drame d'Albert Einstein*, p. 9.

double . . . I have even had the improbable suspicion that he thinks he is the same as other men."[8] Louis XIV said calmly, "We must admit that Racine is a pretty clever fellow"; and Vietà, Descartes, and Leibniz never passed for supermen in the eyes of their times. In times which believed in an eternal source of all our acts of expression, the great writer or scientist was only the man ingenious enough to capture a few of these words or laws inscribed in things. When there is no more universal Reason, they must be miracle-workers.

Yet today as in the past there is only one single marvel—a considerable one it is true—which is that man speaks or calculates. In other words, the marvel is that he has constituted for himself these prodigious organs of algorithm and language which do not wear out, but on the contrary grow through use, being capable of indefinite labor, of returning more than has been invested in them, and yet relating themselves unceasingly to things. But we have no rigorous theory of symbolism. So we prefer to evoke who knows what animal power which allegedly engenders the theory of relativity in Einstein as it produces respiration in us. Einstein may protest all he wants; he must be made differently than we are, have a different body and perceptions, and among these, by good luck, relativity. American doctors stretch him out on a bed, cover this noble forehead with detectors, and order, "Think about relativity," as one orders, "Say 'ah' " or "Count 'one, two' "—and as if relativity were the object of a sixth sense, a beatific vision, and it did not require as much neural energy, conducted by just as subtle circuits, to learn to speak when one is but a babe in arms as to think about relativity when one is Einstein. It is only a step from here to the extravagances of journalists who consult the genius about the questions which are most alien to his field. After all, since science is thaumaturgy, why should it not perform one more miracle? And since it was precisely Einstein who showed that at a great distance a present is contemporaneous with a future, why not ask him the questions which were asked of the Pythian oracle?

Such foolishness is not peculiar to Western journalism. At the other extreme of the world, Soviet judgments of Einstein's works (prior to the recent thaw) also smacked of occultism. To condemn as "idealistic" or "bourgeois" a physics which in another context is not found guilty of any lack of coherence or agreement with the facts is to presuppose a *malin génie*, wandering through the infrastructures of capitalism, whispering thoughts to Einstein which this time are suspect. In the name of an apparently rational social doctrine, reason is repudiated just where it shines most brightly.

8. Vallentin, *ibid.*

From one end of the world to the other, whether they are extolled or repressed, Einstein's "wildly speculative" works make unreason abound. Let us repeat that he did nothing to put his thought in this light; he remained a classic. But was this not just the good fortune of a well-born man, the strength of a good cultural tradition? And when this tradition is exhausted, will not the new science inevitably be just a lesson in irrationality for those who are not physicists?

On April 6, 1922, Einstein met Bergson at the Philosophical Society of Paris. Bergson had come "to listen." But as he was arriving, the discussion flagged. So he made up his mind to present some of the ideas he was in the process of defending in *Durée et simultanéité*—and in short offered Einstein a way of disarming the paradoxical appearance of his theory and reconciling it with men as men. Take, for example, the famous paradox of multiple times, each linked to the observer's standpoint. Bergson proposed to make a distinction here between physical truth and truth. If in the physicist's equations a certain variable, customarily called time (because it marks elapsed times), seems to vary according to the system of reference adopted, no one will deny the physicist the right to say that "time" expands or contracts according to whether it is considered here or there, and thus that there are several "times." But is he then speaking about what other men call time? Would this variable, this entity, this expression still designate time if we did not attribute to it the properties of a different time—the only one which is succession, becoming, duration; in short the only one which is really time—that we experience or perceive prior to all physics?

There are simultaneous events in our perceptual field. There we also see, in another connection, different observers whose field transgresses upon our own, and we imagine still more of them whose field encroaches upon that of the preceding ones. It is thus that we come to extend our idea of simultaneity to events which are as distant from each other as can be, and which do not depend upon the same observer. It is thus that there is one single time for everyone, one single universal time. This certainty is not undercut, it is even presupposed, by the physicist's calculations. When he says that Peter's time is expanded or contracted at the point where Paul is located, he is in no way expressing what is lived by Paul, who for his part perceives all things from his point of view and thus has no reason whatsoever to experience the time elapsing within and around him in a different way than Peter experiences his. The physicist wrongly attributes to Paul the image Peter forms of Paul's time. He absolutizes the views of Paul, with which he makes common cause. He assumes he is the whole world's spectator.

He does just what philosophers are so often criticized for doing. And he speaks of a time which is not anyone's time, of a myth. Here, Bergson says, we must be more Einsteinian than Einstein.

"I am a painter, and I have to represent two figures, John and Jack, one of whom is beside me and the other, two or three hundred meters away from me. I shall sketch in the first size naturally, and reduce the other to a dwarf's dimensions. One of my fellow-painters, who is near Jack and also wants to paint both John and Jack, will do the inverse of what I do; he will show John very small and Jack in his natural size. Yet we shall both be right. But do we have the right to conclude from the fact that both of us are right that John and Jack are neither of normal height nor of the height of a dwarf, or that they are of both heights simultaneously, or that they are of whatever height we choose? Evidently not. . . . The multiplicity of Times I obtain in this way does not impede the unity of real time; it rather presupposes it, just as the diminution of height with distance in a series of paintings in which I represent Jack as more or less distant would indicate that Jack keeps the same size." [9]

A profound idea: rationality and the universal are founded anew, and not upon the divine right of a dogmatic science, but upon the prescientific evidence that there is one single world, upon that reason prior to reason which is implicated in our existence, in our commerce with the perceived world and with others. In speaking in this way, Bergson made an advance on Einstein's classicism. Relativity could be reconciled with all men's reasoning if only we agreed to treat multiple times as mathematical expressions, and to recognize—this or the other side of the physico-mathematical image of the world—a philosophical view of the world which is at the same time the view of existing men. If only we were willing to regain the concrete world of our perception with its horizons, and to situate the constructions of physics in it, physics could freely develop its paradoxes without authorizing unreason.

What would Einstein's answer be? He had listened very closely, as his opening words show: "So the question before us is this: Is the philosopher's time the same as the physicist's?" But he would not give an affirmative answer. It is true that he admitted that the time we experience, perceived time, is the starting point for our ideas about time, and that it has led us to the idea of a time which is the same from one end of the world to the other. But this lived time, Einstein said, had no jurisdiction beyond what each of us sees, and did not authorize extending our intuitive idea of simultaneity to the whole world. "So there is no philosopher's time." It is to science alone we must go for the

9. Bergson, *Durée et simultanéité*, pp. 100–2.

truth about time and everything else. And the experience of the perceived world with its obvious facts is no more than a stutter which precedes the clear speech of science.

All right. But this refusal puts us face to face with the crisis of reason again. The scientist will not agree to recognize any reason but the physicist's, and it is this reason he relies upon as he does upon the time of classical science. Now this physicist's reason, invested in this way with a philosophical dignity, abounds in paradoxes and destroys itself, as it does for example when it teaches that my present is simultaneous with the future of a different observer sufficiently distant from me, and thereby destroys the very meaning of the future.

Precisely *because* he kept the classical scientific ideal and claimed for physics the value, not of a mathematical expression and a language, but of a direct notation of reality, Einstein was condemned as a philosopher to the paradox that he never sought as a physicist or a man. It is not by claiming a kind of metaphysical or absolute truth for science that we will protect the values of reason taught us by classical science. Not counting its neurotics, the world includes a good number of "rationalists" who are a danger for living reason. And reason's vigor is on the contrary bound to the rebirth of a philosophical sense which will of course justify scientific expression of the world, but in its proper order and place in the whole of the human world.

9 / Reading Montaigne[1]

"I commit myself with difficulty."
(*Essays*, III, x)

"We must live among the living."
(*Essays*, III, viii)

We think we have said all there is to say about him when we say he is a skeptic, that is, that he questions himself and does not answer, refusing even to admit that he knows nothing, and holding himself to the famous "What do I know?" None of this takes us very far. Skepticism has two sides. It means that nothing is true, but also that nothing is false. It rejects *all* opinions and *all* behavior as absurd, but it thereby deprives us of the means of rejecting any one as false. Destroying dogmatic, partial, or abstract truth, it insinuates the idea of a total truth with all the necessary facets and mediations. If it multiplies contrasts and contradictions, it is because truth demands it. Montaigne begins by teaching that all truth contradicts itself; perhaps he ends up recognizing that contradiction is truth. *I do indeed contradict myself at random; but truth, as Demades said, I do not contradict at all.* The first and most fundamental of contradictions is that by which the refusal of each truth uncovers a new kind of truth. Thus we shall find in Montaigne a doubt which rests upon itself and is endless, we shall find religion, and we shall find Stoicism. It would be useless to pretend that he excludes any of these "positions," or that he ever makes anyone of them *his own*. But perhaps in the end he finds in this ambiguous *self*—which is offered to everything, and which he never finished exploring—the place of all obscurities, the mystery of all mysteries, and something like an ultimate truth.

* * *

Self-consciousness is his constant, the measure of all doctrines for him. It could be said that he never got over a certain wonder at himself

1. All the quotations from Montaigne are taken from Book III of the *Essays*.

which constitutes the whole substance of his works and wisdom. He never tired of experiencing the paradox of a *conscious being.* At each instant, in love, in political life, in perception's silent life, we adhere to something, make it our own, and yet withdraw from it and hold it at a distance, without which we would know nothing about it. Descartes will overcome the paradox and make consciousness mind: "It is never the eye which sees itself . . . , but clearly the mind, which alone knows . . . the eye and itself." [2] Montaigne's consciousness is not mind from the outset; it is tied down at the same time it is free, and in one sole ambiguous act it opens to external objects and experiences itself as alien to them. Montaigne does not know that resting place, that self-possession, which Cartesian understanding is to be. The world is not for him a system of objects the idea of which he has in his possession; the self is not for him the purity of an intellectual consciousness. For Montaigne—as for Pascal later on—we are interested in a world we do not have the key to. We are equally incapable of dwelling in ourselves and in things, and are referred from them to ourselves and from ourselves to them.

The Delphic oracle must be corrected. It is well to make us return to ourselves. But we do not escape ourselves any more than we escape things. *"It is always vanity for you, within and without, but it is less vanity when it is less extensive. Except for you, O man,"* said that God [at Delphi], *each thing studies itself first, and according to its need, has limits to its labors and desires. There is not a single one as empty and necessitous as you, who embrace the universe; you are the scrutinizer without knowledge, the judge without jurisdiction, and, after all, the fool in the farce.* Confronted with the world of objects, or even the world of animals resting in their nature, consciousness is hollow and avid. It is consciousness of all things because it is nothing; it grasps at all things and holds to none. Involved in spite of everything in this flux they wish to be unaware of, our clear ideas risk being masks we hide our being beneath rather than the truth about ourselves.

Self-understanding for Montaigne is dialogue with self. It is a questioning addressed to the opaque being he is and awaits a response from. It is like "essaying" or "experimenting on" himself. He has in view a questioning without which reason's purity would be illusory and in the end impure. Some are amazed that he should want to speak about even the details of his mood and temperament. It is because for him every doctrine, when it is separated from what we do, threatens to be mendacious; and he imagined a book in which for once there would be expressed not only ideas but also the very life which they appear in and which modifies their meaning.

2. Léon Brunschvicg, *Descartes et Pascal lecteurs de Montaigne.*

So beneath clear ideas and thoughts he finds a spontaneity abounding in opinions, feelings, and unjustifiable acts. *Myson, one of the seven wise men . . . , questioned as to why he was laughing to himself, replied: "For the very reason that I am laughing to myself." How many stupid things I say and answer every day in my own eyes, and thus how much more frequently I am apt to do so in the eyes of others.* Consciousness has an essential foolishness, which is its power to become no matter what, to become itself. In order to laugh to ourselves we need no external cause; we need only think that we can laugh to ourselves and be company for ourselves. We need only be dual and consciousness. *What is taken to be rare about Perseus King of Macedonia—that his mind attached itself to no rank but went wandering through all kinds of life and representing customs to itself which were so vagabond and flighty that it was not known to himself or others what man this was—seems to me more or less to apply to everyone. We are always thinking somewhere else,* and it could not possibly be otherwise. To be conscious is, among other things, to be somewhere else.

The very powers found in animals and related to the body are in man transformed and distorted because they are caught up in the movement of a consciousness. We see dogs who bark while they dream; so they have images. But man does not have just a few images painted into his brain. He can live in the realm of the imaginary. The sight of actors *so deeply involved in a mourning role that they still weep about it in the dressing room* is a wondrous one, as is the sight of a man by himself who fashions a crowd around him, grimaces, is astonished, laughs, fights and is triumphant in this invisible world. Or this prince who has his well-beloved brother killed as a result of a bad dream, or that other one who kills himself because his dogs howled. If the body alone is considered, the penis ought to give only a precise pleasure, comparable to that of other bodily functions. But *throughout most of the world, this part of our body was deified. In the same province some skinned theirs in order to offer up and consecrate a chunk of it, while others offered up and consecrated their semen. In another province, young men pierced theirs publicly, opening them in various places between flesh and skin, and through these openings they passed skewers, the longest and biggest they could bear; and afterwards made a fire from these skewers as an offering to their gods, who were held to have little vigor and chastity if they happened to be astonished at the force of this cruel suffering.* Thus life is borne away outside itself; the extreme of pleasure resembles pain.[3] *Nature itself, I fear, attaches*

3. ". . . considering . . . this face inflamed with cruelty and passion at the tenderest effect of love, and then this solemn, harsh, ecstatic haughtiness in

some instinct for inhumanity to man. It is because our body and its peaceful functions are traversed by the power that we have to devote ourselves to something else and give ourselves absolutes. Besides, there is no desire which goes to the body alone and does not seek another desire or an assent beyond the body. *Thus these men say it is the will that they contract for, and they are right. . . . I am horrified at imagining that a body deprived of affection is mine.* Love is not just love of the body, since it intends someone; and it is not just love of the mind, since it intends him in his body. The word "strange" is the one that most often recurs when Montaigne speaks of man. Or "absurd." Or "monster." Or "miracle." *What a monstrous animal he is who horrifies himself, whose pleasures weigh upon him, who clings to misfortune!*

Descartes will briefly confirm the soul and body's union, and prefer to think them separate; for then they are clear to understanding. Montaigne's realm, on the contrary, is the "mixture" of the soul and body; he is interested only in our factual condition, and his book endlessly describes this paradoxical fact that we are. That is to say that he thinks of death, the counter-proof of our incarnation. When traveling he never stopped in a house without wondering if he might be sick there and die comfortably. *I feel death continually gripping at my throat or loins.* He spoke very well against meditation upon death. It deforms and misses its object; for it concerns distant death, and distant death, being everywhere in our future, is harder than present death, which advances before our eyes in the form of an event. It is not a question of corrupting life by thinking about death. What interests Montaigne is not death's pathos—its ugliness, the last sighs, the funereal trappings which form the customary motif of discourses on death and are images of death used by the living. *These men do not consider death itself at all; they make no judgment about it whatsoever: they do not bring their thought to rest on death but run toward, intend a new being.* Those who listen to the consolations of the priest, lift up their eyes and hands to heaven, and pray aloud, *these flee the struggle, turning their consideration away from death, as we amuse children while we intend to prick them with a lancet.* Montaigne wants us to measure non-being with an incisive glance and, knowing death in all is nakedness, know life laid wholly bare. Death is *the act of one person alone.* In the confused mass of being, death cuts out that particular zone which is ourselves. It puts in matchless evidence that inexhaustible source of opinions, dreams, and passions which secretly gave life to the spectacle of the world. And thus it teaches us better than any

---

such a foolish action . . . and that the greatest sensual delight can be as chilling and as doleful as pain . . ."

episode of life the fundamental accident which made us appear and will make us disappear.

When he writes: "*I study myself more than other subjects. It is my metaphysics and my physics,*" these words must be taken literally. He rejects in advance the explanations of man a physics or a metaphysics can give us, because it is still man who "proves" philosophies and sciences, and because they are explained by him rather than he by them. If for example we wanted to isolate mind and body by relating them to different principles, we would hide what is to be understood—"the monster," the "miracle," man. So there cannot in all good conscience be any question of solving the human problem; there can only be a question of describing man as problematic. Hence this idea of an inquiry without discovery, a hunt without a kill, which is not the vice of a dilettante but the only appropriate method for describing man. *The world is only a school for inquisitioners.* Hence too the attention he gives to thoughts' streaming and the spontaneity of dreams, which makes him anticipate at times Proust's tone,[4] as if for him already the only victory over time lay in expressing time.

* * *

Having set out in this way, attentive to all that is fortuitous and unfinished in man, he is at the opposite pole from religion, if religion is an explanation of and key to the world. Although he often puts it outside the range of his inquiries and beyond his reach, nothing he says is a preparation for belief.[5] *We are in the midst of the world's peat and dung,* tied to *the deadest, most stagnant part of the universe.* Animal instinct is more perfect than our reason. Our religion is a matter of custom: *we are Christians in the same way we are Perigordians or Germans.* Circumcision, fasting, Lent, the Cross, confession, the celibacy of priests, the use of a sacred language in worship, the Incarnation of God, Purgatory—all these elements of Christianity are found in pagan religions. In each village miracles are fabricated beneath our eyes through ignorance and hearsay. A Platonic legend has Socrates born of a virgin visited by Apollo. Men have looked for and found in Homer all the oracles and predictions that they needed. In short, revealed religion is not very different from the folly men cause to

4. "They befall me like dreams. In dreaming I commend them to my memory (for I readily dream that I dream); but the next day, although I easily represent their color to myself as it was, the more I strain to find out what else they were, the more I drown in forgetfulness. And also the only part of these fortuitous discourses which fall upon me in fantasy that remains in my memory is a shadowy image."

5. L. Brunschvicg collected a series of fragments which are very convincing in this respect (*Descartes et Pascal lecteurs de Montaigne,* pp. 56–78).

appear on earth. It remains to be seen whether we must conclude from this, as Montaigne does at times, that barbarian religions are already inspired—or that our own is still barbarous. How can there be any doubt as to his answer when he even reproaches Socrates for his *demonries* and *ecstasies*? In morals as in knowledge, Montaigne contrasts our terrestrial inherence to every supernatural relationship. We can repent an action, he says; we cannot repent being ourselves; and yet according to religion this is what we would have to do. There is no new birth. We cannot annul anything we have done: *I customarily do what I do completely, and proceed all of a piece.* He makes an exception in the case of a few men who already dwell in eternity, but casts suspicion upon them by adding: *just between us, supercelestial opinions and subterranean customs are things I have always judged to be in singular accord with one another.*

What he retains of Christianity is the vow of ignorance. Why assume hypocrisy in the places where he puts religion above criticism? Religion is valuable in that it saves a place for what is strange and knows our lot is enigmatic. All the solutions it gives to the enigma are incompatible with our monstrous condition. As a questioning, it is justified on the condition that it remain answerless. It is one of the modes of our folly, and our folly is essential to us. When we put not self-satisfied understanding but a consciousness astonished at itself at the core of human existence, we can neither obliterate the dream of an other side of things nor repress the wordless invocation of this beyond. What is certain is that if there is some universal Reason we are not in on its secrets, and are in any case required to guide our lives according to our own lights. *In ignorance and negligence I let myself be guided to the general way of the world. I will know it well enough when I perceive it.* Who would dare to reproach us for making use of this life and world which constitute our horizon?

* * *

But if we reject religious passion, must we not reject all other passions as well? Montaigne often speaks of the Stoics, and favorably. This man who wrote so well against reason, and showed that we can in no case get beyond opinion to see an idea face to face, has recourse to the *seed of universal reason embedded in every man who is not perverted.* As there is the invocation of an unknown god in Montaigne, there is the invocation of an impossible reason. Even though nothing is wholly "within our power," even though we are not capable of autonomy, must we not at least withdraw and carve a corner of indifference for ourselves from which we look upon our actions and our life as unimportant "roles"?

This view is found in Montaigne, among other things. *We must lend ourselves to others and give ourselves only to ourselves.* Marriage, for example, is an institution which has its laws and its conditions of equilibrium. It would be madness to mix passion with it. Love which *enslaves us to another* is acceptable only as a free and voluntary practice. At times Montaigne even speaks of it as of a bodily function which is a matter of hygiene, and treats the body as a mechanism we need not make common cause with. So much the more will he place the State among those external devices we find ourselves joined to by chance and ought to use according to their law without putting anything of ourselves into them. Imagination and prestige always reign in our relationships to others. And much more so still in public life, which associates us with those we have not chosen, and with many blockheads. Now *it is impossible to deal in good faith with a blockhead. At the hands of such an impetuous master, not only my judgment but my conscience as well is corrupted.* In public life I become mad with the madmen. Montaigne strongly feels that there is a witchcraft in social life: here everyone puts in the place of his thoughts their reflection in the eyes and idle chatter of others. There is no longer any truth; there is (Pascal will say) no longer any self-consent to oneself. Each is literally alienated. Let us withdraw from public life. *The common weal requires us to betray and lie and massacre; let us resign this commission to those more pliant and obedient.* It is true that we are not always able to abstain, that furthermore to do so is to let things slide and that after all there is certainly a need for men of state or a Prince. How can they help it? The Prince will have to lie, kill, and deceive. Let him do it, but let him know what he is doing and not disguise crime as virtue. *What remedy is there? There is no remedy. If he was really bothered between the two extremes, he had to do it; but if he did it with no regrets, if it did not weigh upon him to do it, this is a sign that his conscience is in a bad state.* And we who look on? All there is left for us to do is (as it will be said later) to obey despising what we obey. We must despise, since the State is against everything that matters in the world: against freedom, against conscience. But we must obey, since this folly is the law of life with others, and since it would be another folly not to deal with the State according to its laws. Yet Plato puts the philosopher in the government. He imagines a just city and sets out to construct it. *But is there any evil in a polis which is worth being fought against with such a mortal drug? . . . Plato . . . does not consent to violence being done to his country's peace in order to heal his country; he does not accept an improvement which costs the blood and ruin of its citizens, but establishes it as the office of a virtuous man to leave everything as it is in such a case. . . .* It is absurd to want to rule a history made of accidents by reason. . . . *In my time I have seen the wisest heads of this Kingdom assembled, with great ceremony and public expense, for treaties and agreements about which the true decision nevertheless depended in all sovereignty upon the desires of milady's chamber and the inclination of some silly little woman.* Foresight and laws will never be equal to the variety of cases; reason will never be able to judge public life. In a time when public life is split into a thousand particular conflicts, Montaigne does not even suspect that a meaning can be found for it. It is impossible to be reconciled with this chaos. To live in public affairs is *to live according to others.* Montaigne is clearly inclined to live according to himself.

And yet is this his final word? He sometimes spoke differently of love, friendship, and even politics. Not that he simply contradicted himself in doing so. It is because the Stoic separation of external and internal, necessity and freedom, is abstract, or destroys itself; and because we are indivisibly within and without. We cannot always obey if we despise, or despise always if we obey. There are occasions when to obey is to accept and to despise is to refuse, when a life which is in part a double life ceases to be possible, and there is no longer any distinction between exterior and interior. Then we must enter the world's folly, and we need a rule for such a moment. Montaigne knew it; he did not swerve from it. And how could he have? He had described consciousness, even in its solitude, as already mixed according to its very principle with the absurd and foolish. How could he have prescribed that consciousness dwell in itself, since he thinks it is wholly outside itself? Stoicism can only be a way-point. It teaches us to be and judge in opposition to the external world; it could not possibly rid us of it. What is most peculiar to Montaigne may be the little bit he has told us about the conditions and motives for this return to the world.

* * *

It is not a question of reaching a reassuring conclusion at no matter what cost, nor of forgetting at the end what has been found on the way. It is from doubt that certainty will come. So we must measure the extent of it. Let us repeat that all belief is passion and makes us beside ourselves, that we can believe only by ceasing to think, that wisdom is a *resolution to be irresolute,* that it condemns friendship, love, and public life. And so here we are back to ourselves again. And we find chaos still, with death, the emblem of all disorders, on the horizon. Cut off from others, cut off from the world, incapable of finding in himself (like the Stoic wise man) and in an inner relationship to God the means of justifying the world's comedy, Montaigne's wise man, it would seem, no longer has any conversation except with that life he perceives welling madly within him for a little while longer, any resource except the most general derision, any motive except despising himself and all things. In this disorder, why not give up? Why not take animals for a model—these neighing horses, these swans who sing as they die—why not join them in unconsciousness? The best thing would be to go back to the *puerile security, the ignorance* of beasts. Or to invent, against the feeling of death, some natural religion: *the extinction of a life is the way to a thousand other lives.*

This movement is to be found in Montaigne. But there is another one too, which appears just as often. For after all the doubts, there remains to be explained—precisely because we know that every attempt to know multiplies questions and obscures what it wants to clarify, and that for each head severed, the Hydra of ignorance grows three new ones—why there are opinions, why we believed to begin with that we held truths, and why doubt needs to be learned. *I know what it is to be human better than I know what it is to be animal, mortal, or rational.* Descartes will remember this saying. It means that the mind's movement and irresolution are only half of the truth. The other half is the marvel that our volubility has stopped, and at each moment stops again, in appearances which we may indeed show cannot withstand examination, but which at least had the air of truth and gave us the idea of it. Thought, when it questions itself, never stops prolonging and contradicting itself; but there is a thought in act which is no little thing, and which we have to take into account. The critique of human understanding destroys it only if we cling to the idea of a complete or absolute understanding. If on the contrary we rid ourselves of this idea, then thought in act, as the only possible thought, becomes the measure of all things and the equivalent of an absolute. The critique of passions does not deprive them of their value if it is carried to the point of showing that we are never in possession of ourselves and that passion is ourselves. At this moment, reasons for doubting become reasons for believing. The only effect of our whole critique is to make our passions and opinions more precious by making us see that they are our only recourse, and that we do not understand our own selves by dreaming of something different. Then we find the fixed point we need (if we want to bring our versatility to a stop) not in the bitter religion of nature (that somber divinity who multiplies his works for nothing), but in the fact that there is opinion, the appearance of the good and true. Then regaining nature, naivete, and ignorance means regaining the grace of our first certainties in the doubt which rings them round and makes them visible.

In fact, Montaigne did not simply doubt. Doubting is an action; thus doubt cannot demolish our action, our doing, which is in the right against it. The same author who wanted *to live according to himself* felt passionately that we are among other things what we are for others, and that their opinion reaches us at the core of our being. *I would gladly come back from the other world,* he says in sudden anger, *to give the lie to the man who would shape me differently than I was, even though it were to honor me.* His friendship with La Boétie was exactly the kind of tie which *enslaves us to another.* He did not think he knew himself better than La Boétie knew him. He lived beneath his eyes, and after his death he continued to do so. It is in order to know himself as La Boétie knew him that Montaigne questions and studies himself; *he alone possessed my true image and took it away with him. That is why I decipher myself so curiously.* We rarely see such a complete gift. Far from La Boétie's friendship having been accidental to his life, we would have to say that Montaigne and the author of the *Essays* were born of this friendship, and that for him, in sum, existing meant existing beneath his friend's gaze. The fact of the matter is that true skepticism is movement toward the truth, that the critique of passions is hatred of false passions, and finally, that in *some* circumstances Montaigne recognized outside himself men and things he never dreamed of refusing himself to, because they were like the emblem of his outward freedom, and because in loving them he was himself and regained himself in them as he regained them in himself.

Even in pleasure, which he sometimes speaks about as a doctor, Montaigne is not after all cynical. *It is madness to devote all one's thoughts to it and commit oneself to it with a furious and indiscreet affection. But on the other hand, to get mixed up in it without love and willing obligation, in the manner of actors—in order to play a common role of the age and its customs and put nothing of one's own into it except words—is in truth to provide for one's safety, but in a very cowardly way, like the man who would abandon his honor or advantage or his pleasure out of fear of danger. For it is certain that those who set up such a practice cannot hope to gain from it any fruit which would touch or satisfy a noble soul.* As an old man, Montaigne says that success in seduction depends upon choosing the right moment. But what does this late wisdom prove? When he was young and amorous, he never carried on his love affairs like battles and according to tactics. *I often had a lack of luck, but sometimes of enterprise as well; God save the man who can still joke about it! In this century it requires more temerity, which our young people excuse under pretext of ardor; but if they looked more closely, they would find that it comes more from scorn than ardor. I feared superstitiously to offend, and I gladly respect what I love. Not to mention that whoever takes away reverence for this commodity rubs away its luster. I like a man to be a bit of the child and fearful servitor in his love. If this is not enough, I have besides some aspects of the stupid shame Plutarch speaks about, and have been in the course of my life wounded and spotted by it in different ways. . . . I have as tender an eye for sustaining a refusal as I do for refusing; and it weighs upon me so much to weigh upon others that on those occasions when duty forces me to test someone's will in something which is doubtful and costs him dear, I do it sparingly and in spite of myself.* There is a very tender cynic. Fate did not have him love from love as he did from friendship, but he himself had nothing to do with it.

He entered the bewitched realm of public life; he did not withhold himself. *I do not want a man to shrink from attention, steps, speeches, and if need be sweat and blood in the responsibilities he assumes.* The people named him mayor several times. *I wish them all possible good; and certainly, if the occasion had arisen, I would have spared nothing to serve them. I was as disturbed for their sake as I am for my own.* How was he able to live a public life if he was *disgusted with mastery, both active and passive*? He obeys without liking obedience and commands without liking command. He would not even like to be a prince. The prince is alone. He is not a man, since he cannot be challenged. He does not live, he sleeps, since everything gives way before him. But the passion to obey is ugly too, and useless. How could a man who delivers himself up body and soul be esteemed? Capable of giving himself unconditionally to a master, he is also capable of changing masters. Yes, we must take sides, and follow the consequences to the very end; but *just opportunities* are less frequent than is believed, and we must not choose too readily, for then it is no longer the cause but the sect we love. *I am not subject to these penetrating, intimate mortgages and commitments. Wrath and hatred are beyond the call to be just, and are passions serving only those who do not hold strictly enough to their duty simply through reason. . . . We must not (as we do every day) give the name "duty" to an intestine bitterness and acerbity which is born of private interest and passions; nor "courage" to a treacherous, malicious behavior. They call their propensity to spitefulness and violence "zeal." They fan the flames of war, not because it is just but because it is war. When my will is given to a party, it is not with such a violent obligation that my understanding is infected by it.* A man can serve a party and be a harsh judge of what is going on there, find intelligence and honor in his enemy, in short, continue to exist in the social world. *I have been able to get mixed up in public responsibilities without swerving from myself by a hair's breadth, and to give myself to others without abandoning myself.*

Perhaps it will be said that these rules make snipers, not soldiers. That is true, and Montaigne knows it. He is able at times, and lucidly, to force himself to lie; he does not make a habit or a way of life of it. *Whoever wants to make use of me as I am, let him give me things to do requiring rigor and freedom, and conduct which is short and to the point yet still risky, and I shall be able to do something for him. If long, subtle, laborious, artificial, crooked conduct is required, he would do better to ask someone else.* Maybe there is some scorn here. But it is also possible that Montaigne means more than that. We always ask questions as if they were universal, as if in an instant we chose the good of all men in choosing our own. But what if this were a presumption? Being what he is, Montaigne will never be partisan. We do well only what we do willingly. He must not affect a lofty manner. He can serve better and more outside the ranks. Is it unimportant, this weight attached to his words because men knew he neither lied nor flattered? And did he not act all the more effectively because he did not care too much for action?

Passions seemed to be the death of the self, since they swept it away outside itself, and Montaigne felt threatened by them as by death. Now he tries to describe to us what have since been called *free passions*. Having experienced that what he loves is at stake, out there, he resolutely confirms the natural movement which was bearing him outward. He joins the human game. Upon contact with this freedom and courage, passions and death itself are transformed. No, it is not meditation upon death which overcomes death. The good arguments are *those which make a peasant and whole peoples die just as steadfastly as a philosopher*, and they all come back to a single one—we are living beings, it is here we have our tasks, and as long as we draw breath they are the same. Meditation upon death is hypocritical, since it is a morose way of living. In the movement which throws him at things, and precisely because he has shown what is arbitrary and perilous in it, Montaigne discovers the remedy for death. *It is my impression that it is indeed the end, yet not the aim of life; it is its end, its extremity, yet not its object. Life should have itself as its aim and design; its proper study is to govern, conduct, and undergo itself. Among the several other offices that this general and principal chapter comprehends is this article of knowing how to die; and if our fear did not give it weight, it would be among the lightest.* The remedy for death and passions is not to turn away from them, but on the contrary to go beyond them as everything bears us beyond them. Others threaten our freedom? But *we must live among the living.* We risk slavery there? But there is no true freedom without risk. Action and attachments disturb us? But *life is a material and corporeal movement, an action that by its own essence is imperfect and disordered; I occupy myself with serving it as it is.* There is no sense cursing our fate; both good and evil are found only in our life.

Montaigne tells that the doctors had advised him to lace himself tight with a napkin when he traveled on shipboard, in order to fight seasickness. *Which I did not even try,* he adds, *having accustomed myself to contend with my defects and master them by myself.* His whole morality rests upon a movement of pride through which he decides to take his risky life in hand, since nothing has meaning if it is not in his life. After this detour toward himself, all seems good to him again. He said he would rather die *on horseback than in his bed.* Not that he counted on the warrior's anger to help him, but because he found in things, along with a threat, a viaticum. He saw the ambiguous link that bound him to them. He saw that he was not required to choose between himself and things. The self is not *serious;* it does not like to be tied down. But *is there anything as certain, resolute, disdainful, contemplative, solemn, and serious as an ass*? It is unconditional freedom which makes us capable of absolute attachment. Montaigne says of himself: *I have been so sparing in promises that I think I have kept more than I have promised or owed.* He sought and maybe found the secret of being simultaneously ironic and solemn, faithful and free.

10 / A Note on Machiavelli[1]

HOW COULD HE HAVE BEEN UNDERSTOOD? He writes against good feelings in politics, but he is also against violence. Since he has the nerve to speak of *virtue* at the very moment he is sorely wounding ordinary morality, he disconcerts the believers in Law as he does those who believe that the State is the Law. For he describes that knot of collective life in which pure morality can be cruel and pure politics requires something like a morality. We would put up with a cynic who denies values or an innocent who sacrifices action. We do not like this difficult thinker without idols.

He was certainly tempted by cynicism: he had, he says, "much difficulty in shielding himself" from the opinion of those who believe the world is "ruled by chance." [2] Now if humanity is an accident, it is not immediately evident what would uphold collective life if it were not the sheer coercion of political power. Thus the entire role of a government is to hold its subjects in check.[3] The whole art of governing is reduced to the art of war,[4] and "good troops make good laws." [5] Between those in power and their subjects, between the self and the other person, there is no area where rivalry ceases. We must either undergo or exercise coercion. At each instant Machiavelli speaks of oppression and aggression. Collective life is hell.

But what is original about Machiavelli is that, having laid down the source of struggle, he goes beyond it without ever forgetting it. He finds something other than antagonism in struggle itself. "While men are

1. A paper sent to the Umanesimo e scienza politica Congress, Rome-Florence, September, 1949.
2. *The Prince*, Chap. XXV.
3. *Discourses*, II, 23, quoted by A. Renaudet, *Machiavel*, p. 305.
4. *The Prince*, Chap. XIV.
5. Chap. XVII.

trying not to be afraid, they begin to make themselves feared by others; and they transfer to others the aggression that they push back from themselves, as if it were absolutely necessary to offend or be offended." It is in the same moment that I am about to be afraid that I make others afraid; it is the same aggression that I repel and send back upon others; it is the same terror which threatens me that I spread abroad—I live my fear in the fear I inspire. But by a counter-shock, the suffering that I cause rends me along with my victim; and so cruelty is no solution but must always be begun again. There is a circuit between the self and others, a Communion of Black Saints. The evil that I do I do to myself, and in struggling against others I struggle equally against myself. After all, a face is only shadows, lights, and colors; yet suddenly the executioner, because this face has grimaced in a certain way, mysteriously experiences a slackening—*another anguish* has relayed his own. A sentence is never anything but a statement, a collection of significations which as a matter of principle could not possibly be equivalent to the unique savor that each person has for himself. And yet when the victim admits defeat, the cruel man perceives another life beating through those words; he finds himself before *another himself*. We are far from the relationships of sheer force that hold between objects. To use Machiavelli's words, we have gone from "beasts" to "man." [6]

More exactly, we have gone from one way of fighting to another, from "fighting with force" to "fighting with laws." [7] Human combat is different from animal combat, but it is a fight. Power is not naked force, but neither is it the honest delegation of individual wills, as if the latter were able to set aside their differences. Whether new or hereditary, power is always described in *The Prince* as questionable and threatened. One of the duties of the prince is to settle questions before they have *become insoluble* as a result of the subjects' emotion.[8] It would seem to be a matter of keeping the citizens from becoming aroused. There is no power which has an absolute basis. There is only a crystallization of opinion, which tolerates power, accepting it as acquired. The problem is to avoid the dissolution of this consensus, which can occur in no time at all, no matter what the means of coercion, once a certain point of crisis has been passed. Power is of the order of the tacit. Men let themselves live within the horizon of the State and the Law as long as injustice does not make them conscious of what is unjustifiable in the two. The power which is called legitimate is

6. Chap. XVIII.
7. *Ibid.*
8. Chap. III.

This does not mean that it is necessary or even preferable to deceive. It means that at the distance and the degree of generality at which political relations are established, a legendary character composed of a few words and gestures is sketched out; and that men honor or detest blindly. The prince is not an impostor. Machiavelli writes expressly: "A prince should try to fashion for himself a reputation for goodness, clemency, piety, loyalty, and justice; *furthermore, he should have all these good qualities. . . .*"[25] What he means is that even if the leader's qualities are true ones, they are always prey to legend, because they are not *touched* but *seen*—because they are not known in the movement of the life which bears them, but frozen into historical attitudes. So the prince must have a feeling for these echoes that his words and deeds arouse. He must keep in touch with these witnesses from whom all his power is derived. He must not govern as a visionary. He must remain free even in respect to his virtues. Machiavelli says the prince should have the qualities he seems to have but, he concludes, "remain sufficiently master of himself to show their contraries when it is expedient to do so."[26] A political precept, but one which could well be the rule for a true morality as well. For public judgment in terms of appearances, which converts the prince's goodness into weakness, is perhaps not so false. What is a goodness incapable of harshness? What is a goodness which wants to be goodness? A meek way of ignoring others and ultimately despising them.

Machiavelli does not ask that one govern through vices—lies, terror, trickery; he tries to define a political *virtue*, which for the prince is to speak to these mute spectators gathered around him and caught up in the dizziness of communal life. This is real spiritual strength, since it is a question of steering a way between the will to please and defiance, between self-satisfied goodness and cruelty, and conceiving of an historical undertaking all may adhere to. This virtue is not exposed to the reversals known to moralizing politics, because from the start it establishes a relationship to others which is unknown to the latter. It is this virtue and not success which Machiavelli takes as a sign of political worth, since he holds up Cesare Borgia (who did not succeed but had *virtù*) as an example and ranks Francesco Sforza (who succeeded, but by good fortune) far behind him.[27] As sometimes happens, tough politics loves men and freedom more truly than the professed humanist: it is Machiavelli who praises Brutus, and Dante who damns him. Through mastery of his relationships with others, the man in power clears away obstacles between man and man and puts a little daylight in our

25. Chap. XVII. My italics.
26. *Ibid.*
27. Chap. VII.

relationships—as if men could be close to one another only at a sort of distance.

The reason why Machiavelli is not understood is that he combines the most acute feeling for the contingency or irrationality in the world with a taste for the consciousness or freedom in man. Considering this history in which there are so many disorders, so many oppressions, so many unexpected things and turnings-back, he sees nothing which predestines it for a final harmony. He evokes the idea of a fundamental element of chance in history, an adversity which hides it from the grasp of the strongest and the most intelligent of men. And if he finally exorcises this evil spirit, it is through no transcendent principle but simply through recourse to the givens of our condition. With the same gesture he brushes aside hope and despair. If there is an adversity, it is nameless, unintentional. Nowhere can we find an obstacle we have not helped create through our errors or our faults. Nowhere can we set a limit to our power. No matter what surprises the event may bring, we can no more rid ourselves of expectations and of consciousness than we can of our body. "As we have a free will, it seems to me that we must recognize that chance rules half, or a little more than half, our actions, and that we govern the rest." [28] Even if we come to assume a hostile element in things, it is as nothing for us since we do not know its plans: "men ought never give way to despair; since they do not know their end and it comes through indirect and unknown ways, they always have reason to hope, and hoping, ought never give way to despair, no matter what bad luck and danger they are in." [29] Chance takes shape only when we give up understanding and willing. Fortune "exercises her power when no barriers are erected against her; she brings her efforts to bear upon the ill-defended points." [30] If there seems to be an inflexible course of events, it is only in past events. If fortune seems now favorable, now unfavorable, it is because man sometimes understands and sometimes misunderstands his age; and according to the case, his success or ruin is created by the same qualities—but not by chance.[31]

Machiavelli defines a virtue in our relationships with fortune which (like the virtue in our relationships with others) is equally remote from solitude and docility. He points out as our sole recourse that presence to others and our times which makes us find others at the moment we give up oppressing them—that is, find success at the moment we give up chance, escape destiny at the moment we under-

28. Chap. XXV.
29. *Discourses*, II, 29, quoted by A. Renaudet, *Machiavel*, p. 132.
30. *The Prince*, Chap. XXV.
31. *Ibid.*

stand our times. Even adversity takes on a human form for us: fortune is a woman. "I think it is better to be too bold than too circumspect, because fortune is a woman; she gives in only to violence and boldness; experience shows she gives herself to fierce men rather than to cold ones." [32] For a man it matters absolutely not who is wholly against humanity, for humanity is alone in its order. The idea of a fortuitous humanity which has no cause already won is what gives absolute value to our *virtue*. When we have understood what is humanly valuable within the possibilities of the moment, signs and portents never lack. "Must heaven speak? It has already manifested its will by striking signs. Men have seen the sea half open up its depths, a cloud mark out the path to follow, water spring forth from the rock, and manna fall from heaven. It is up to us to do the rest; since God, by doing everything without us, would strip us of the action of our free will, and at the same time of that portion of choice reserved for us." [33]

What humanism is more radical than this one? Machiavelli was not unaware of values. He saw them living, humming like a shipyard, bound to certain historical actions—barbarians to be booted out, an Italy to create. For the man who carries out such undertakings, his terrestrial religion finds the words of that other religion: "*Esurientes implevit bonis, et divites dimisit inanes.*" [34] As Renaudet puts it: "This student of Rome's prudent boldness never intended to deny the role played in universal history by inspiration, genius, and that action of some unknown daemon which Plato and Goethe discerned. . . . But in order for passion, aided by force, to have the property of renewing a world, it must be nourished just as much by dialectical certainty as by feeling. If Machiavelli does not set poetry and intuition apart from the practical realm, it is because this poetry is truth, this intuition is made of theory and calculation." [35]

* * *

What he is reproached for is the idea that history is a struggle and politics a relationship to men rather than principles. Yet is anything more certain? Has not history shown even more clearly after Machiavelli than before him that principles commit us to nothing, and that they may be adapted to any end? Let us leave contemporary history aside. The progressive abolition of slavery had been proposed by Abbé Gregory in 1789. It is passed by the Convention in 1794, at the moment

32. *Ibid.*
33. Chap. XXVI.
34. *Discourses*, I, 26, quoted by A. Renaudet, *Machiavel*, p. 231.
35. *Ibid.*, p. 301.

when, in the words of a colonist, "domestic servants, peasants, workers, and day-laborers are manifesting against the appointive aristocracy," [36] and the provincial bourgeoisie, which drew its revenues from San Domingo, is no longer in power. Liberals know the art of holding up principles on the slope of inopportune consequences.

Furthermore, principles applied in a suitable situation are instruments of oppression. Pitt discovers that fifty per cent of the slaves brought into the British Islands are being resold to French colonies. English Negroes are creating San Domingo's prosperity and giving France the European market. So he takes a stand against slavery. "He asked Wilberforce," James writes, "to join the campaign. Wilberforce represented the influential Yorkshire region. He was a man of great reputation. Expressions such as humanity, justice, national shame, etc. pealed from his mouth. . . . Clarkson came to Paris to stir the torpid energies [of the *Société des Amis des Noirs*], to subsidize them, and to inundate France with British propaganda." [37] There can be no illusions about the fate this propaganda had in store for the slaves of San Domingo. At war with France a few years later, Pitt signs an agreement with four French colonists which places the colony under English protection until peacetime, and re-establishes slavery and discrimination against mulattoes. Clearly, it is important to know not only *what principles* we are choosing but also what forces, which men, are going to apply them.

There is something still more clear: The same principles can be used by two adversaries. When Bonaparte sent troops against San Domingo who were to perish there, "many officers and all the men believed they were fighting for the Revolution; they saw in Toussaint a traitor sold to the priests, the émigrés, and the English . . . the men still thought they belonged to a revolutionary army. Yet certain nights they heard the Blacks within the fortress sing *La Marseillaise*, the *Ça ira*, and other revolutionary songs. Lacroix tells how the deluded soldiers, hearing these songs, raised up and looked at their officers as if to say: 'Could justice be on the side of our barbaric enemies? Are we no longer soldiers of republican France? Could it be that we have become vulgar political tools?' " [38] But how could this be? France was the fatherland of the Revolution. Bonaparte, who had consecrated a few of its acquisitions, was marching against Toussaint-L'Ouverture. So it was evident that Toussaint was a counter-revolutionary in the service of the enemy.

Here, as is often the case, everyone is fighting in the name of the same values—freedom and justice. What distinguishes them is the

36. James, *Les Jacobins noirs*, p. 127.
37. *Ibid.*, p. 49.
38. *Ibid.*, p. 295.

kind of men for whom liberty or justice is demanded, and with whom society is to be made—slaves or masters. Machiavelli was right: values are necessary but not sufficient; and it is even dangerous to stop with values, for as long as we have not chosen those whose mission it is to uphold these values in the historical struggle, we have done nothing. Now it is not just in the past we see republics refuse citizenship to their colonies, kill in the name of freedom, and take the offensive in the name of law. Of course Machiavelli's toughminded wisdom will not reproach them for it. History is a struggle, and if republics did not struggle they would disappear. We should at least realize that the means remain bloody, merciless, and sordid. The supreme deception of the Crusades is not to admit it. The circle should be broken.

It is evidently on these grounds that a criticism of Machiavelli is possible and necessary. He was not wrong to insist upon the problem of power. But he was satisfied with briefly evoking a power which would not be unjust; he did not seek very energetically to define it. What discourages him from doing so is that he believes men are immutable, and that régimes follow one another in cycles.[39] There will always be two kinds of men, those who live through history and those who make it. There are the miller, the baker, and the innkeeper with whom the exiled Machiavelli spends his day, chatters, and plays backgammon. ("Then," he says, "disputes, vexatious words, insults arise; they argue at the drop of a hat and utter cries that carry all the way to San Casciano. Closed up in this lousy hole, I drain the cup of my malignant destiny down to the lees.") And there are the great men whom he reads history with and questions in the evening, clothed in court dress, and who always *answer him.* ("And during four long hours," he says, "I no longer feel any boredom; I forget all misery; I no longer fear poverty; death no longer terrifies me. I pass completely into them.") [40] No doubt he never resigned himself to parting company with spontaneous men. He would not spend days contemplating them if they were not like a mystery for him. Is it true that these men *could* love and understand the same things he understands and loves? Seeing so much blindness on one side, and such a natural art of commanding on the other, he is tempted to think that there is not one mankind, but historic men and enduring men—and to range himself on the side of the former. It is then that, no longer having any reason to prefer one "armed prophet" to another, he no longer acts except at random. He bases rash hopes upon Lorenzo di Medici's son; and the Medici, following their own rules, compromise him without employing him. A republican, he repudiates in the preface to the *History of Florence* the judgment the

39. *Discourses,* I, quoted by A. Renaudet, *Machiavel,* p. 71.
40. Letter to Francesco Vettori, quoted by A. Renaudet, *Machiavel,* p. 72.

republicans had brought against the Medici; and the republicans, who do not forgive him for it, will not employ him either. Machiavelli's conduct accentuates what was lacking in his politics: a guideline allowing him to recognize among different powers the one from which something good could be hoped for, and to elevate *virtue* above opportunism in a decisive way.

To be just we must also add that the task was a difficult one. For Machiavelli's contemporaries the political problem was first of all one of knowing if Italians would long be prevented from farming and living by French and Spanish incursions, when they were not those of the Papacy. What could he reasonably hope for, if not for an Italian nation and soldiers to create it? It was necessary to begin by creating this bit of human life in order to create the human community. Where in the discordancy of a Europe unaware of itself, of a world which had not taken stock of itself and in which the eyes of scattered lands and men had not yet met, was the universal people which could be made the accomplice of an Italian city-state? How could the peoples of all lands have recognized, acted in concert with, and rejoined each other? There is no serious humanism except the one which looks for man's effective recognition by his fellow man throughout the world. Consequently, it could not possibly precede the moment when humanity gives itself its means of communication and communion.

Today these means exist, and the problem of a real humanism that Machiavelli set was taken up again by Marx a hundred years ago. Can we say the problem is solved? What Marx intended to do to create a human community was precisely to find a different base than the always equivocal one of principles. In the situation and vital movement of the most exploited, oppressed, and powerless of men he sought the basis for a revolutionary power, that is, a power capable of suppressing exploitation and oppression. But it became apparent that the whole problem was to constitute a power of the powerless. For those in power either had to follow the fluctuations of mass consciousness in order to remain a proletarian power, and then they would be brought down swiftly; or, if they wanted to avoid this consequence, they had to make themselves the judge of proletarian interests, and then they were setting themselves up in power in the traditional sense—they were the outline of a new ruling class. The solution could be found only in an absolutely new relationship between those in power and those subject to it. It was necessary to invent political forms capable of holding power in check without annulling it. It was necessary to have leaders capable of explaining the reasons for their politics to those subject to power, and to obtain from themselves, if necessary, the sacrifices power ordinarily imposes upon subjects.

These political forms were roughed out and these leaders appeared in the revolution of 1917; but from the time of the Commune of Kronstadt on, the revolutionary power lost contact with a fraction of the proletariat (which was nevertheless tried and true), and in order to conceal the conflict, it begins to lie. It proclaims that the insurgents' headquarters is in the hands of the White Guards, as Bonaparte's troops treat Toussaint-L'Ouverture as a foreign agent. Already difference of opinion is faked up as sabotage, opposition as espionage. We see reappearing within the revolution the very struggles it was supposed to move beyond. And as if to prove Machiavelli right, while the revolutionary government resorts to the classic tricks of power, the opposition does not even lack sympathizers among the enemies of the Revolution. Does all power tend to "autonomize" itself, and is this tendency an inevitable destiny in all human society? Or is it a matter of a contingent development which was tied to the particular conditions of the Russian Revolution (the clandestine nature of the revolutionary movement prior to 1917, the weakness of the Russian proletariat) and which would not have occurred in a Western revolution? This is clearly the essential problem. In any case, now that the expedient of Kronstadt has become a system and the revolutionary power has definitely been substituted for the proletariat as the ruling class, with the attributes of power of an unchecked élite, we can conclude that, one hundred years after Marx, the problem of a real humanism remains intact—and so we can show indulgence toward Machiavelli, who could only glimpse the problem.

If by humanism we mean a philosophy of the inner man which finds no difficulty in principle in his relationships with others, no opacity whatsoever in the functioning of society, and which replaces political cultivation by moral exhortation, Machiavelli is not a humanist. But if by humanism we mean a philosophy which confronts the relationship of man to man and the constitution of a common situation and a common history between men as a problem, then we have to say that Machiavelli formulated some of the conditions of any serious humanism. And in this perspective the repudiation of Machiavelli which is so common today takes on a disturbing significance: it is the decision not to know the tasks of a true humanism. There is a way of repudiating Machiavelli which is Machiavellian; it is the pious dodge of those who turn their eyes and ours toward the heaven of principles in order to turn them away from what they are doing. And there is a way of praising Machiavelli which is just the opposite of Machiavellianism, since it honors in his works a contribution to political clarity.

11 / Man and Adversity[1]

It is clearly impossible to tick off in one hour the advances made in the philosophical investigation of man during the past fifty years. Even if we could assume that this infinite ability existed in one single brain, we would be brought up short before the discordancy among the authors who must be taken into account. The impossibility of ever progressing in any other than an oblique fashion operates like a cultural law, each new idea becoming, after the one which instituted it, different than it was for this instituting idea. A man cannot receive a heritage of ideas without transforming it by the very fact that he comes to know it, without injecting his own and always different way of being into it. In proportion as ideas arise, a tireless volubility sets them stirring; just as a never satisfied "need for expressiveness," the linguists say, transforms languages at the very moment one would think that, having succeeded in ensuring an apparently unequivocal communication among speaking subjects, they were reaching their goal. How would we dare enumerate *acquired ideas*, since even when they have gotten themselves almost universally accepted, they have always done so by also becoming different from themselves?

Furthermore, a catalogue of acquired knowledge would not suffice. Even if we were to lay the "truths" of this half century end-to-end, in order to restore their hidden affinity, we would still have to revive the personal and interpersonal experience they are a *response* to, and the logic of situations in reference to which they were defined. The great or valuable work is never an effect of life, but it is always a *response* to life's very particular events or most general structures. Although the writer is free to say yes or no to such circumstances, and to justify and limit his refusal or assent in different ways, he never can arrange

1. Lecture given on September 10, 1951, at the *Rencontres Internationales* in Geneva.

things so that he does not have to choose his life in a certain historical landscape or state of problems which excludes certain solutions even if it imposes none, and which gives Gide, Proust, and Valéry (no matter how different they may be) the undeniable quality of contemporaries. The movement of ideas comes to discover truths only by responding to some pulsation of interpersonal life, and every change in our understanding of man is related to a new way he has of carrying on his existence. If man is the being who is not content to coincide with himself like a thing but represents himself to himself, sees himself, imagines himself, and gives himself rigorous or fanciful symbols of himself, it is quite clear that in return every change in our representation of man translates a change in man himself. Thus it is the whole history of this half century, with its projects, disappointments, wars, revolutions, audacities, panics, inventions, and failures, that we would have to evoke here. We can only refuse this unlimited task.

Yet this transformation of our understanding of man, which we cannot hope to determine by a rigorous method on the basis of works, ideas, and history, is sedimented in us. It is our substance; we have a lively, total feeling for it when we look back to the writings or the facts of the beginning of the century. What we can try to do is to mark within ourselves, according to two or three selected relationships, modifications in the human situation. We would have to present infinite explanations and commentaries, clear up a thousand misunderstandings, and translate quite different systems of concepts into one another in order to establish an objective relationship between, for example, Husserl's philosophy and Faulkner's works. And yet within us readers they are connected. The very men who (like Ingres and Delacroix) think themselves adversaries are reconciled in the eyes of a third person who witnesses them, because they are responding to a single cultural situation. We men who have lived as our problem the development of communism and the War, and who have read Gide and Valéry and Proust and Husserl and Heidegger and Freud are the same. Whatever our responses have been, there should be a way to circumscribe perceptible zones of our experience and formulate, if not ideas about man that we hold in common, at least a new experience of our condition.

With these reservations, we propose to acknowledge that our century is distinguished by a completely new association of "materialism" and "idealism," of pessimism and optimism, or rather by the fact that it has gone beyond these antitheses. Our contemporaries have no difficulty thinking both that human life is the demand for an original order and that this order could not possibly endure or even truly exist except under certain very precise and very concrete conditions which can fail to materialize, no natural arrangement of things and the world predestining them to make a human life possible.

It is true that there were philosophers and scientists in 1900 who set certain biological and material conditions for human existence. But they were ordinarily "materialists" in the sense the term had at the end of the last century. They made humanity an episode of evolution, civilizations a particular case of adaptation, and even resolved life into its physical and chemical components. For them the properly human perspective on the world was a superfluous phenomenon; and those who saw the contingency of humanity ordinarily treated values, institutions, works of art, and words as a system of signs referring in the last analysis to the elementary needs and desires of all organisms.

It is true, on the other hand, that there were "idealist" authors who assumed other motive forces than these in humanity; but when they did not derive them from some supernatural source, they related them to a human nature which guaranteed their unconditional efficacy. *Human nature* had truth and justice for attributes, as other species have fins or wings. The epoch was full of these absolutes and these divided notions. There was the absolute of the State pervading all events; and a State which did not reimburse its lenders was considered dishonest, even if it was in the midst of a revolution. The value of money was an absolute, and men scarcely dreamed of treating it as simply an aid to economic and social functioning. There was also a moral gold-standard: family and marriage were the good, even if they secreted hatred and rebellion. "Things of the spirit" were intrinsically noble, even if books (like so many works in 1900) translated only morose reveries. There were values and, on the other hand, realities; there was mind and, on the other hand, body; there was the interior and, on the other hand, the exterior. But what if it were precisely the case that the order of facts invaded that of values, if it were recognized that dichotomies are tenable only this side of a certain point of misery and danger? Even those among us today who are taking up the word "humanism" again no longer maintain the *shameless humanism* of our elders. What is perhaps proper to our time is to disassociate humanism from the idea of a humanity fully guaranteed by natural law, and not only reconcile consciousness of human values and consciousness of the infrastructures which keep them in existence, but insist upon their inseparability.

* * *

Our century has wiped out the dividing line between "body" and "mind," and sees human life as through and through mental and corporeal, always based upon the body and always (even in its most carnal modes) interested in relationships between persons. For many thinkers at the close of the nineteenth century, the body was a bit of matter, a network of mechanisms. The twentieth century has restored and deepened the notion of flesh, that is, of animate body.

In psychoanalysis for example it would be interesting to follow the development from a conception of the body which for Freud was initially that of nineteenth-century doctors to the modern notion of the experienced body. Did not psychoanalysis originally take up the tradition of mechanistic philosophies of the body—and is it not still frequently understood in this same way today? Does not the Freudian system explain the most complex and elaborate behavior of adults in terms of instinct and especially sexual instincts, that is to say physiologically, in terms of a composition of forces beyond the grasp of our consciousness or even realized once and for all in childhood prior to the age of rational control and properly human relationships to culture and to others? Perhaps things seemed this way in Freud's first works, and for a hurried reader; but as his own and his successors' psychoanalysis rectifies these initial ideas in contact with clinical experience, we see the emergence of a new idea of the body which was called for by the initial ideas.

It is not false to say that Freud wanted to base the whole of human development upon the development of instincts; but we would get farther if we said that from the start his works overturn the concept of instinct and break down the criteria by which men had previously thought they could circumscribe it. If the term instinct means anything, it means a mechanism within the organism which with a minimum of use ensures certain responses adapted to certain characteristic situations of the species. Now what is proper to Freudianism is surely to show that in this sense man has no sexual instincts, that the "polymorphous perverse" child establishes a so-called normal sexual activity (when he does so) only at the end of a difficult individual history. Unsure about its instruments as it is about its goals, the power to love wends its way through a series of investments which approach the canonical form of love, anticipates and regresses, and repeats and goes beyond itself without our ever being able to claim that what is called normal sexual love is nothing but that. The child's attachment to his parents, so powerful at the beginning as to retard that history, is not itself of the instinctual order. For Freud it is a mental attachment. It is not because the child has the same blood as his parents that he loves them; it is because he knows he is their issue or because he sees them turned toward him, and thus identifies himself with them, conceives of himself in their image, and conceives of them in his image. For Freud the ultimate psychological reality is the system of attractions and tensions which attaches the child to parental images, and then through these to all the other persons, a system within which he tries out different *positions* in turn, the last of which will be his adult attitude.

It is not simply the love-object which escapes every definition in terms of instinct, but the very way of loving itself. As we know, adult love, sustained by a trusting tenderness which does not constantly insist upon new proofs of absolute attachment but takes the other person as he is, at his distance and in his autonomy, is for psychoanalysis won from an infantile "erotic attachment" ["*aimance*"] which demands everything at all times and is responsible for whatever devouring, impossible aspects may remain in any love. And though development to the genital stage is a necessary condition of this transformation to adult love, it is never sufficient to guarantee it. Freud himself described an infantile relationship to others which is established through the intermediary of those regions and functions of the child's body which are least capable of discrimination and articulated action: the mouth, which does not know whether to suck or bite—the sphincteral apparatus, which can only hold in or let go. Now these primordial modes of relationship to others may remain predominant even in the genital life of the adult. In this case the relation to others remains trapped in the impasses of absolute immediacy, oscillating between an inhuman demand, an absolute egotism, and a voracious devotion which destroys the subject himself. Thus sexuality and, more generally, corporeality, which Freud considers the basis of our existence, is a power of investment which is absolute and universal to begin with. This power is *sexual* only in the sense that it reacts immediately to the visible differences of the body and the maternal and paternal roles. Instinct and the physiological are enveloped in a central demand for absolute possession which could not possibly be the act of a bit of matter but is of the order of what is ordinarily called consciousness.

And yet it is a mistake to speak of consciousness here, since to do so is to reintroduce the dichotomy of soul and body at the moment Freudianism is in the process of contesting it, and thus to change our idea of the body as well as our idea of the mind. "Psychical facts have a meaning," Freud wrote in one of his earliest works. This meant that no human behavior is simply the result of some bodily mechanism, that in behavior there is not a mental center and a periphery of automatism, and that all our gestures in their fashion participate in that single activity of making explicit and signifying which is ourselves. At least as much as he tries to reduce superstructures to instinctive infrastructures, Freud tries to show that in human life there is no "inferior" or "lower part." Thus we could not be further from an explanation "in terms of the lower part." At least as much as he explains adult behavior by a fate inherited from childhood, Freud shows a *premature* adult life in childhood, and in the child's sphincteral behavior, for example, a first choice of his relationships of generosity or avarice to others. At least as much as he explains the psychological by the body, he shows the psychological meaning of the body, its hidden or latent logic. Thus we can no longer speak of the sexual organ taken as a localizable mechanism, or of the body taken as a mass of matter, as an ultimate cause. Neither cause nor simply instrument or means, it is the vehicle, the fulcrum, and the steadying factor of our life. None of the notions philosophy had elaborated upon—cause, effect, means, end, matter, form—suffices for thinking about the body's relationships to life as a whole, about the way it meshes into personal life or the way personal life meshes into it. The body is enigmatic: a part of the world certainly, but offered in a bizarre way, as its dwelling, to an absolute desire to draw near the other person and meet him in his body too, animated and animating, the natural face of mind. With psychoanalysis mind passes into body as, inversely, body passes into mind.

Along with our idea of the body, these investigations cannot fail to disrupt the idea we form of its partner, the mind. It must be admitted that in this respect much remains to be done to draw from psychoanalytic experience all that it contains, and that psychoanalysts, beginning with Freud himself, have been satisfied with a structure of hardly satisfactory ideas. In order to account for that osmosis between the body's anonymous life and the person's official life which is Freud's great discovery, it was necessary to introduce something *between* the organism and our selves considered as a sequence of deliberate acts and express understandings. This was Freud's *unconscious.* We have only to follow the transformations of this Protean idea in Freud's works, the diverse ways in which it is used, and the contradictions it involves to be convinced that it is not a fully developed idea, and that (as Freud himself implies in his *Essais de Psychanalyse,* we still have to find the right formulation for what he intended by this provisional designation. At first glance "the unconscious" evokes the realm of a dynamics of impulses whose results alone would presumably be given to us. And yet the unconscious cannot be a process "in third person"; since it is the unconscious which chooses what aspect of us will be admitted to official existence, which avoids the thoughts or situation we are resisting, and which is therefore not *un-knowing* but rather an un-recognized and unformulated knowing that we do not want to assume. In an approximative language, Freud is on the point of discovering what other thinkers have more appropriately named *ambiguous perception.* It is by working in this direction that we shall find a civil status for this consciousness which brushes its objects (eluding them at the moment it is going to designate them, and taking account of them as the blind man takes account of obstacles rather than recognizing them), which does not want to know about them (which does not know about them to the extent that it knows about them, and knows about them to the extent that it does not know about them), and which subtends our express acts and understandings.

Whatever their philosophical formulations may be, there is no denying that Freud had an increasingly clear view of the body's mental function and the mind's incarnation. In his mature works he speaks of the "sexual-aggressive" relationship to others as the fundamental datum of our life. As aggression does not aim at a thing but a person, the intertwining of the sexual and the aggressive signifies that sexuality has, so to speak, an interior (that it is lined throughout with a person-to-person relationship), and that the sexual is our way (since we are flesh, our carnal way) of living our relationships with others. Since sexuality is relationship to other persons, and not just to another body, it is going to weave the circular system of projections and introjections between other persons and myself, illuminating the unlimited series of reflecting reflections and reflected reflections which are the reasons why I am the other person and he is myself.

Such is this idea of the individual incarnate and (through incarnation) given to himself but also to others—incomparable yet stripped of his congenital secret and faced with his *fellows*—that Freudianism ends up offering us. At the very moment Freud was forming it, and without there being ordinarily any *influence,* writers were expressing the same experience in their own way.

It is in this way, to begin with, that the *eroticism* of writers during this half century must be understood. When in this respect we compare Proust's or Gide's works with the particular works of the preceding literary generation, the contrast is striking. Passing over the generation of writers of the 1900's, Proust and Gide pick up from the start the Sadian and Stendhalian tradition of a direct expression of the body. With Proust, with Gide, an unwearying report on the body begins. It is confirmed, consulted, listened to like a person. The intermittencies of its desire and (as they put it) its fervor are spied on. With Proust it becomes the keeper of the past; and it is the body which, in spite of the deteriorations which render it almost unrecognizable itself, maintains from one time to another a substantial relationship between us and our past. In the two inverse cases of death and awakening, Proust describes the meeting-point of mind and body, showing how, in the dispersion of the sleeping body, our gestures at awakening renew a meaning from beyond the grave; and how on the contrary meaning is undone in the tics of the death agony. He analyzes Elstir's paintings and the milk-seller glimpsed in a country station with the same emotion; because in both instances there is the same queer experience, the experience of *expression,* the moment when color and flesh begin to speak to eyes or body. Gide, enumerating a few months before his death what he had loved in his life, calmly named pleasure and the Bible side by side.

As an inevitable consequence, obsession with other persons appears in their works too. When man takes an oath to exist universally, concern for himself and concern for others become indistinguishable for him; he is a person among persons, and the others are other himselves. But if on the contrary he recognizes what is unique in incarnation lived from within, the other person necessarily appears to him in the form of torment, envy, or at least uneasiness. Cited by his incarnation to appear beneath an alien gaze and justify himself before it, yet riveted to his own situation by the same incarnation; capable of feeling the lack of and need for others, but incapable of finding his resting place in others; he is enmeshed in the to-and-fro of being for self and being for others that produces the tragic element of love in Proust's works and what is perhaps the most striking element in Gide's *Journal.*

We find admirable formulations of the same paradoxes in the writer who is perhaps least capable of being satisfied with the approximations of Freudian expression, that is, in Valéry. The reason is that for him the taste for rigor and the keen awareness of the fortuitous are two sides of the same coin. Otherwise he would not have spoken so well of the body as a double-edged being, responsible for many absurdities but also for our most certain accomplishments. "The artist brings along his body, withdraws, puts down and takes away something, behaves with his whole being as his eye and completely becomes an organ which makes itself at home, changes its shape, and seeks the point, the sole point, which belongs virtually to the profoundly sought *oeuvre*—which is not always the one we are seeking." [2] And for Valéry too consciousness of the body is inevitably obsession with others. "No one could think freely if his eyes could not take leave of different eyes which followed them. As soon as glances meet, we are no longer wholly two, and it is hard to remain alone. This exchange (the term is exact) realizes in a very short time a transposition or metathesis—a chiasma of two 'destinies,' two points of view. Thereby a sort of simultaneous reciprocal limitation occurs. You capture my image, my appearance; I capture yours. You are not *me,* since you see me and I do not see

2. *Mauvaises Pensées,* p. 200.

myself. What I lack is this me that you see. And what you lack is the you I see. And no matter how far we advance in our mutual understanding, as much as we reflect, so much will we be different. . . ." [3]

As we approach mid-century, it becomes increasingly evident that incarnation and the other person are the labyrinth of reflection and feeling—of a sort of feeling reflection—in contemporary works. Including this famous passage in which a character in *Man's Fate* in turn poses the question: if it is true that I am welded to myself, and that for me there is still an absolute difference between other persons (whom I hear with my ears) and myself, the "incomparable monster" (who hears me with my throat), then which one of us will ever be able to be accepted by others as he accepts himself, beyond things said or done, praise or blame, even beyond crimes. But Malraux, like Sartre, has read Freud; and whatever they may think of him in the last analysis, it is with his help that they have learned to know themselves. And that is why, seeking as we are to establish certain traits of our times, it has seemed more significant to us to disclose an earlier experience of the body which is their starting point because their elders had prepared it for them.

* * *

Another characteristic of this half century's investigations is the recognition of a strange relationship between consciousness and its language, as between consciousness and its body. Ordinary language thinks that it can establish, as the correlate of each word or sign, a thing or signification which can exist and be conceived of without any sign. But literature has long taken exception to ordinary language. As different as the ventures of Rimbaud and Mallarmé may well have been, they had this much in common: they freed language from the control of "obvious facts" and trusted it to invent and win new relationships of meaning. Thus language ceased to be (if it ever has been) simply a tool or means the writer uses to communicate intentions given independently of language. In our day, language is of a piece with the writer; it is the writer himself. It is no longer the servant of significations but the act of signifying itself, and the writer or man speaking no longer has to control it voluntarily any more than living man has to premeditate the means or details of his gestures. From now on there is no other way to comprehend language than to dwell in it and use it. As a professional of language, the writer is a professional of insecurity. His expressive operation is renewed from *oeuvre* to *oeuvre*. Each work, as it has been said of the painter, is a step constructed by

3. *Tel Quel*, I, p. 42.

the writer himself upon which he installs himself in order to construct (with the same risk) another step and what is called the *oeuvre*—the sequence of these attempts—which is always broken off, whether it be by the end of life or through the exhaustion of his speaking power. The writer endlessly attempts to cope with language which he is not the master of, and which is nevertheless incapable of anything without him, a language that has its own caprices and its graces, but always won through the writer's labor. Distinctions of figure and ground, sound and meaning, conception and execution are now blurred, as the limits of body and mind were previously. In going from "signifying" language to pure language, literature freed itself at the same time painting did from resemblance to things, and from the idea of a *finished* work of art. As Baudelaire already said, there are finished works which we cannot say have ever been *completed,* and unfinished works which say what they meant. What is proper to expression is to never be more than approximate.

In our century this *pathos of language* is common to writers who mutually detest one another but whose kinship is from this moment on confirmed by it. In its first stages, surrealism certainly had the air of an insurrection against language, against all meaning, and against literature itself. The fact is that Breton, after a few hesitant formulations which he quickly corrected, proposed not to destroy language to the profit of non-sense but to restore a certain profound and radical usage of speech which he realized all the writings called "automatic" were far from giving an adequate example of.[4] As Maurice Blanchot recalls, Breton already replies to the celebrated investigation, *Pourquoi Ecrivez-vous?'* by describing a task or vocation of speech which has always been expressed in the writer and which bids him enunciate and endow with a name what has never been named. To write in this sense, Breton concludes [5]—that is, in the sense of revealing or making manifest—has never been a vain or frivolous occupation. The polemic against the critical faculties or conscious controls was not carried on in order to deliver speech up to chance or chaos; it sought to recall language and literature to the whole extent of their task by freeing them from the literary world's petty formulas and fabrications of talent. It was necessary to go back to that point of innocence, youth, and unity at which speaking man is not yet man of letters, political man, or moral man—to that "sublime point" Breton speaks about elsewhere, at which literature, life, morality, and politics are equivalent and substituted for one another, because in fact each of us is the same man who loves or hates, who reads or writes, who accepts or refuses political destiny. Now that

4. Cf. *Le Langage automatique,* in *Point du Jour.*
5. *Légitime Défense.*

surrealism, in slipping into the past, has rid itself of its narrownesses—at the same time it has rid itself of its fine virulence—we can no longer define it in terms of what it originally rejected. For us it is one of those recalls to *spontaneous speech* which from decade to decade our century issues.

At the same time, surrealism has intermingled with these other recalls in our memory, and with them constitutes one of the constants of our time. Valéry, who was at first greatly admired and subsequently rejected by the surrealists, remains beneath his academic image very close to their experience of language. For it has not been sufficiently noticed that what he contrasts to *signifying* literature is not, as might be thought at a hasty reading, simply a literature of exercises based upon linguistic and prosodic conventions which are more efficacious to the extent they are more complicated and, in short, more absurd. What constitutes the essence of poetic language for him (he sometimes goes so far as to say the essence of all literary language) is that it does not die out in the face of what it communicates to us. It is that in poetic language meaning calls again for the very words which have served to communicate it, and no others. It is that a work cannot be summed up but must be re-read to be regained. It is that in poetic language the idea is not produced by the words as a result of the lexical significations assigned to them in the common language but as a result of more carnal relationships of meaning, the halos of signification words owe to their history and uses—as a result, in short, of the life that words lead within us, a life which from time to time ends up in those meaning-laden accidents, the great books. In his own way, Valéry calls again for the same adequation of language to its total meaning that motivates the surrealistic uses of language.

Both Valéry and the surrealists have in view what Francis Ponge was to call the "semantic thickness" and Sartre the "signifying humus" of language, that is the characteristic power that language as gesture, accent, voice, and modulation of existence has to signify in excess of what it signifies part by part according to existing conventions. It is not very far from here to what Claudel calls the word's "intelligible mouthful." And the same feeling for language is found even in contemporary definitions of prose. For Malraux too, to learn to write is "to learn to speak with one's own voice." [6] And in the works of Stendhal, who believed he was writing "like the civil laws," Jean Prévost detects a *style* in the strong sense of the term. That is, a new and very personal ordering of the words, forms, and elements of the narrative; a new order of correspondence between signs; an imperceptible yet character-

6. *Psychologie de l'Art.*

istically Stendhalian warping of the whole language system—a system which has been constituted by years of usage and of life, which (having become Stendhal himself) finally allows him to improvise, and which should not be called a system of thought (since Stendhal was so little aware of it) but rather a system of speaking.

Thus language is that singular apparatus which, like our body, gives us more than we have put into it, either because we apprise ourselves of our thought in speaking, or because we listen to others. For when I read or listen, words do not always come touch significations already present in me. They have the extraordinary power to draw me out of my thoughts; they cut out fissures in my private universe through which *other thoughts* irrupt. "At least in that moment, I have been you," Jean Paulhan rightly says. As my body (which nevertheless is only a bit of matter) is gathered up into gestures which aim beyond it, so the words of language (which considered singly are only inert signs that only a vague or banal idea corresponds to) suddenly swell with a meaning which overflows into the other person when the act of speaking binds them up into a single whole. Mind is no longer set apart but springs up beside gestures and words as if by spontaneous generation.

* * *

These changes in our conception of man would not echo so deeply within us if they did not converge in a remarkable way with an experience which all of us, scientists or non-scientists, have been participating in, and which has therefore contributed more than any other to shaping us: I mean the experience of political relationships and history.

It seems to us that for at least thirty years our contemporaries have in this respect been living through an adventure that is much more dangerous than, but analogous to, that which we have thought to meet in the mild order of our relationships to literature or to our body. The same ambiguity that, upon analysis, leads the idea of mind into the idea of body or language has visibly invaded our political life. And in both cases it is more and more difficult to distinguish what is violence and what is idea, what is power and what is value, with the aggravating circumstance that in political life the mixture risks ending up in convulsion and chaos.

We grew up in a time when, *officially*, world politics were juridical. What definitively discredited juridical politics was seeing the victors of 1918 concede (and then some) to a Germany which had become powerful again what they had previously refused Weimar Germany. But six months later this new Germany took Prague as well. Thus the demonstration was complete: the victors' juridical politics was the mask for their preponderance, the vanquished's claim to "equality of rights" was the mask for a coming German preponderance. We were still faced with power relationships and death struggles; each concession was a weakness and each gain a step toward further gains. But what is important is that the decline of juridical politics has in no way involved a pure and simple return among our contemporaries to a power politics or politics of efficiency. It is a remarkable fact that political cynicism and even political hypocrisy are discredited too, that public opinion remains astonishingly sensitive about this point, that until these last months governments took care not to collide with it, and that even now there is not one of them which openly declares that it is relying on naked force, or which is effectively doing so.

The truth is that during the period immediately following the War it could almost be said that there was no world politics. Forces did not confront one another. Many questions had been left open, but just for that reason there were "no man's lands," neutral zones, provisional or transitional régimes. Europe, totally disarmed, lived through years without invasion. We know that for some years now the aspect of things has changed. From one end of the world to the other, zones which were neutral for the two rival powers no longer are; armies have appeared in a "no man's land"; economic aid has turned into military aid. Yet to us it seems remarkable that this return to power politics is nowhere lacking in reticence. Perhaps it will be said that it has always been easy to hide violence with declarations of peace, and that this is propaganda. But seeing the powers' behavior, we have come to wonder if it is only a matter of pretexts. It is possible that all the governments believe their propaganda; that in the confusion of our present they no longer know themselves what is true and what is false, because in a sense everything they say conjointly is true. It is possible that each policy is really and simultaneously peaceful and warlike.

There would be room here to analyze a whole series of curious practices which clearly seem to be becoming general in contemporary politics. For example, the twin practices of *purging* and crypto-politics, or the politics of fifth columns. Machiavelli has pointed out the recipe for it, but in passing; and it is today that these practices are tending on all sides to become institutional. Now if we really think about it, this presupposes that a government always expects to find accomplices on the side of its adversary and traitors in its own house. It is thus an admission that all causes are ambiguous. It seems to us that today's policies are distinguished from former ones by this doubt which is extended even to their own cause, coupled with expeditious measures to suppress the doubt.

The same fundamental uncertainty is expressed in the ease with which the heads of state turn aside or turn back from their policies, without of course ever recognizing that these oscillations are oscillations. After all, history has seldom seen a head of state discharge an illustrious and long-unchallenged commander-in-chief, and grant his successor more or less what he refused him a few months earlier. We have seldom seen a great power refuse to intervene in order to restrain one of its satellites in the process of invading a neighbor—and after one year of war, propose a return to the status quo.

These oscillations are understandable only if, in a world whose peoples are against war, governments cannot look it in the face and yet do not dare to make peace, which would mean admitting their weakness. Sheer power relationships are altered at each instant; governments *also* want opinion to be in their favor. Each troop movement becomes a political operation *as well.* Governments act less to obtain a certain factual result than to put their adversary in a certain moral predicament. Thus we have the strange idea of a *peace offensive;* to propose peace is to disarm the adversary, to win over opinion, and thus almost to win the war. But at the same time governments are well aware that they must not lose face, that by speaking too much of peace they would encourage their adversary. This is so true that on all sides governments alternate or, better yet, associate peaceful speeches and forceful measures, verbal threats and actual concessions. Peace overtures are made in a discouraging tone and are accompanied by new preparations for war. No one wants to reach an agreement and no one wants to break off negotiations. So we have actual armistices that are observed by everyone for weeks or months on end and that no one wants to legalize, as among irritated people who put up with one another but no longer speak. We ask a former ally to sign a treaty he disapproves of with a former enemy. But we fully expect him to refuse. If he accepts, it is a felony. This is how we have a peace that is not a peace. And also a war that—except for the combatants and the inhabitants—is not completely a war. We let our friends fight because by providing them with arms which would decide the battle we would really risk war. We withdraw before the enemy and seek to suck him into the trap of an offensive that would put him in the wrong. In addition to its manifest meaning, each political act bears a contrary and latent meaning.

It seems to us that governments get lost in these double meanings and, in the extraordinary subtlety of means-ends relationships, are no longer able to know themselves what they are actually doing. The dialectic invades our newspapers, but a fear-crazed dialectic which turns on itself and solves no problems. In all this we see less duplicity than confusion, and less wickedness than perplexity.

We are not saying that this situation itself is without risk: it is possible that we could go to war obliquely, and it could suddenly loom up before us at one of the detours of some main political highway which seemed no more likely than another to set it going. We are only saying that these characteristics of our politics prove (all things considered) that there is no profound basis for war today. Even if it comes out of all this, no one will be entitled to say that it was ineluctable. For the contemporary world's true problems are due less to the antagonism of two ideologies than to their common disarray before certain major facts that neither one controls. If war comes, it will come as a diversion or as bad luck.

The two great powers in their rivalry have accused and are accusing one another concerning Asia. Now it is not the Satanism of one government or another which has caused countries like India and China (where for centuries men have died of hunger) to come to refuse famine, debility, disorder, or corruption. It is the development of radio, a minimum of instruction, newspapers, communications with the outside, and the population increase which have suddenly made an age-old situation intolerable. It would be shameful to allow our obsessions as Europeans to hide the real problem posed there, the drama of countries to be equipped that no humanism can ignore. With the awakening of these countries, the world is closing on itself. Perhaps for the first time, the developed countries are being faced with their responsibilities toward a human community which cannot be reduced to two continents.

This fact in itself is not a mournful one. If we were not so obsessed by our own concerns, we would not find it without grandeur. But what is serious is that *all* Western doctrines are too narrow to face up to the problem of developing Asia. The classical means of the liberal economy or even those of American capitalism are not, it seems, up to operating even India's equipment. As for Marxism, it has been conceived of to assure the passage of a developed economic apparatus from the hands of a bourgeoisie which has become parasitical to those of an old and highly conscious and cultivated proletariat. It is a wholly different matter to bring an underdeveloped country up to modern forms of production, and the problem posed for Russia is posed in a far more extreme way for Asia. It is not surprising that Marxism, confronted with this task, has been profoundly modified, that it has in fact abandoned its conception of a revolution rooted in the history of the working class, substituting transferals of property managed from the top for revolutionary contagion, and putting the theory of the withering away of the State and that of the proletariat as the universal class in cold storage. But this also means that the Chinese revolution (which the U.S.S.R. has not especially encouraged) to a large extent escapes the previsions of Marxist politics.

So just when Asia is intervening as an active factor in world politics, none of the conceptions Europe has invented enables us to think about its problems. Here political thought is mired down in historical and local circumstances; it gets lost in these voluminous societies. This is undoubtedly what makes the antagonists circumspect; it is our chance for peace. It is also possible that they will be tempted to go to war, which will not solve any problems but which would allow them to put them off. So it is at the same time our risk of war. World politics is confused because the ideas it appeals to are too narrow to cover its field of action.

* * *

If we were asked in concluding to give our remarks a philosophical formulation, we would say that our times have experienced and are experiencing, more perhaps than any other, contingency. The contingency of evil to begin with: there is not a force at the beginning of human life which guides it towards its ruin or towards chaos. On the contrary, each gesture of our body or our language, each act of political life, as we have seen, spontaneously takes account of the other person and goes beyond itself in its singular aspects toward a universal meaning. When our initiatives get bogged down in the paste of the body, of language, or of that world beyond measure which is given to us to finish, it is not that a *malin génie* sets his will against us; it is only a matter of a sort of inertia, a passive resistance, a dying fall of meaning—an anonymous *adversity*. But good is contingent too. We do not guide the body by repressing it, nor language by putting it in thought, nor history by dint of value judgments; we must always espouse each one of these situations, and when they go beyond themselves they do so spontaneously. Progress is not necessary with a metaphysical necessity; we can only say that experience will very likely end up by eliminating false solutions and working its way out of impasses. But at what price, by how many detours? We cannot even exclude in principle the possibility that humanity, like a sentence which does not succeed in drawing to a close, will suffer shipwreck on its way.

It is true that the totality of beings known by the name of men and defined by the commonly known physical characteristics also have in common a natural light or opening to being which makes cultural acquisitions communicable to all men and to them alone. But this lightning flash we find in every glance called human is just as visible in the most cruel forms of sadism as it is in Italian painting. It is precisely this flash which makes everything possible on man's part, and right up to the end. Man is absolutely distinct from animal species, but precisely in the respect that he has no original equipment and is the place of contingency, which sometimes takes the form of a kind of miracle (in the sense in which men have spoken of the *miracle of Greece*), and sometimes the form of an unintentional adversity. Our age is as far from explaining man by the lower as it is by the higher, and for the same reasons. To explain the *Mona Lisa* by the sexual history of Leonardo da Vinci or to explain it by some divine motion Leonardo da Vinci was the instrument of or by some human nature capable of beauty still involves giving way to the retrospective illusion, realizing the valuable in advance—misunderstanding the human moment *par excellence* in which a life woven out of chance events turns back upon, regrasps, and expresses itself.

If there is a humanism today, it rids itself of the illusion Valéry designated so well in speaking of "that little man within man whom we always presuppose." Philosophers have at times thought to account for our vision by the image or reflection things form upon our retina. This was because they presupposed a second man behind the retinal image who had different eyes and a different retinal image responsible for seeing the first. But with this man within man the problem remains untouched, and we must still come to understand how a body becomes animate and how these blind organs end up bearing a perception. The "little man within man" is only the phantom of our successful expressive operations; and the admirable man is not this phantom but the man who—installed in his fragile body, in a language which has already done so much speaking, and in a reeling history—gathers himself together and begins to see, to understand, and to signify. There is no longer anything decorous or decorative about today's humanism. It no longer loves man in opposition to his body, mind in opposition to its language, values in opposition to facts. It no longer speaks of man and mind except in a sober way, with modesty: mind and man never *are;* they show through in the movement by which the body becomes gesture, language an *oeuvre,* and coexistence truth.

Between this humanism and classical doctrines there is almost an homonymous relationship. In one way or another the latter affirmed a man of divine right (for the humanism of necessary progress is a secularized theology). When the great rationalist philosophies joined battle with revealed religion, what they put in competition with divine creation was some metaphysical mechanism which evaded the idea of a fortuitous world just as much as it had. Today a humanism does not oppose religion with an explanation of the world. It begins by becoming aware of contingency. It is the continued confirmation of an astonishing junction between fact and meaning, between my body and my self, my self and others, my thought and my speech, violence and truth. It is the methodical refusal of explanations, because they destroy the mixture we are made of and make us incomprehensible to ourselves. Valéry profoundly says: "One does not see what a god could think about"—a god and, moreover (he explains in another connection), a demon as well. The Mephistopheles of *Mon Faust* quite rightly says: "I am the fleshless being who neither sleeps nor thinks. As soon as these poor fools draw away from instinct, I lose my way in caprice, in the uselessness or depth of these irritations of their brains they call 'ideas.' . . . I lose myself in this Faust who seems to me sometimes to understand me in a wholly different fashion than he should, as if there were another world than the other world! . . . It is here that he shuts himself in and amuses himself with what there is in the brain, and brews and ruminates that mixture of what he knows and does not know, which they call Thought. . . . I do not know how to think and I have no soul. . . ."[7] Thinking is man's business, if thinking always means coming back to ourselves and inserting between two distractions the thin empty space by which we see something.

A stern and (if you will excuse the word) almost vertiginous idea. We have to conceive of a labyrinth of spontaneous steps which revive one another, sometimes cut across one another, and sometimes confirm one another—but across how many detours and what tides of disorder!—and conceive of the whole undertaking as resting upon itself. It is understandable that our contemporaries, faced with this idea (which they glimpse as well as we do), retreat and turn aside toward some idol. With all reservations made concerning other modes of approaching the problem, fascism is a society's retreat in the face of a situation in which the contingency of moral and social structures is clear. It is the fear of the new which galvanizes and reaffirms precisely the very ideas that historical experience had worn out. A phenomenon which our times are far from having gone beyond. The favor an *occult* literature meets with in France today is somewhat analogous. Under the pretext that our economic, moral, or political ideas are in a state of crisis, occult thought would like to establish institutions, customs, and types of civilizations which answer our problems much less well, but which are supposed to contain a *secret* we hope to *decipher* by dreaming around the documents left for us. Whereas it is the role of art, literature, and perhaps even philosophy to create sacred things, oc-

7. *Mon Faust*, p. 157.

cultism seeks them readymade (in sun cults or the religion of American Indians, for example), forgetting that ethnology shows us better each day what terrors, what dilapidation, what impotence archaic paradise is often made of.

In short, fear of contingency is everywhere, even in the doctrines which helped reveal it. Whereas Marxism is based entirely upon going beyond nature through human *praxis*, today's Marxists veil the risk such a transformation of the world implies. Whereas Catholicism, particularly in France, is being crossed by a vigorous movement of inquiry next to which the Modernism of the beginning of the century seems sentimental and vague, the hierarchy reaffirms the most worn-out forms of theological explanation with the Syllabus. Its position is understandable: it is indeed true that a man cannot seriously think about the contingency of existence and hold to the Syllabus. It is even true that religion is bound up with a minimum of explanatory thought. In a recent article François Mauriac implied that atheism could receive an honorable meaning if it took issue only with the God of philosophers and scientists, God in idea. But without God in idea, without the infinite thought which created the world, Christ is a man and his birth and Passion cease to be acts of God and become symbols of the human condition. It would not be reasonable to expect a religion to conceive of humanity, according to Giraudoux's beautiful phrase, as the "caryatid of the void." But the return to an explanatory theology and the compulsive reaffirmation of the *Ens realissimum* drag back all the consequences of a massive transcendence that religious reflection was trying to escape. Once again the Church, its sacred depository, its unverifiable secret beyond the visible, separates itself from actual society. Once more the Heaven of principles and the earth of existence are sundered. Once more philosophic doubt is only a formality. Once more adversity is called Satan and the war against it is already won. Occult thought scores a point.

Once again, between Christians and non-Christians, as between Marxists and non-Marxists, conversation is becoming difficult. How could there possibly be any real exchange between the man who knows and the man who does not know? What can a man say if he sees no relationship, not even a dialectical one, between state communism and the withering away of the state, when another man says that he does? If a man sees no relationship between the Gospels and the clergy's role in Spain, when another says they are not irreconcilable? Sometimes one starts to dream about what culture, literary life, and teaching could be if all those who participate, having for once rejected idols, would give themselves up to the happiness of reflecting together. But this dream is not reasonable. The discussions of our time are so convulsive only because it is resisting a truth which is right at hand, and because in recognizing—without any intervening veil—the menace of adversity, it is closer perhaps than any other to recognizing the metamorphoses of Fortune.

PART III

1 / Paranoid Politics

THE *New York Times* of February 14, 1948, published an article by its special correspondent C. L. Sulzberger that we would all profit from reading. The title was: "Europe's Anti-Red Trend Inspiring Strange Tie-Ups." The subtitle: "New Coalitions Courting Leftist Support to Bring Workers Into Pale." Here is the essential part of the text:

> The gradual development of anti-Communist fronts in Europe is making for some curious ideological combinations and odd political bedfellows. Almost every important coalition in countries hoping to receive Marshall Plan aid is doing its utmost to appeal to the Left and appear somewhat leftist itself to gain workers' support and avoid accusations of being reactionary. . . .
>
> In France, both the "Third Force" Government coalition and the de Gaullist movement, to its right, are appealing continually for labor support. In this connection André Malraux, famous author and former Leftist in Spain and China, who is now one of Charles de Gaulle's chief advisers, showed this reporter a copy of a letter sent to him by Victor Serge shortly before the latter's death last year in Mexico. The letter said:
>
> "I want to tell you that I consider the political position you have adopted courageous and probably reasonable. Had I been in France I would myself have been among the Socialists collaborating with the movement you are in.
>
> "I consider the electoral victory of your movement a great step toward the immediate salvation of France. * * * Real salvation at a more distant date will depend on how you and so many others will accomplish what I call your double duty: To fight the enemies of Europe's regeneration and to master the dangers that we all bear within ourselves."
>
> Malraux always says that, had Leon Trotsky won his party battle with Joseph Stalin, he himself would today be a Trotskyist Communist. Therefore it is not surprising that Mr. Serge felt the same way. Victor Serge

Chibaltchish, who was 52 when he died, was a grandson of the famous Chibaltchish who was a member of the Russian 'People's Will,' which attempted to assassinate Czar Alexander II. In Mexico he was a great friend of Mr. Trotsky until the latter was assassinated. . . .

. . . One of the great difficulties of forming a really free European labor movement opposing left-wing dictatorship from Moscow is at the same time to avoid compromised elements from the right-wing extremist corner.

Another problem is to insure cooperation between Socialists and non-Socialists. Many Socialist leaders would like to capture the new free labor federations. However, American advisers particularly are stressing the necessity of keeping any and all kinds of politics out of these developments—even including western Socialism.

* * *

The *New York Times* for March 9, 1948,[1] published a short reply by Natalia Sedova-Trotsky. In fact, her letter had been cut by the editors. Here is the complete text of it:

TO THE EDITOR OF THE NEW YORK TIMES:

My attention has been drawn to a dispatch from your foreign correspondent, Cyrus L. Sulzberger, in *The Times* of Feb. 14. The implications in the statements attributed to André Malraux are so palpably false that, unavoidably late as is this rejoinder, I urgently request that you publish it.

It is with profound indignation that one finds Malraux, after all the years of consort with Stalinism, casting himself in the role of sympathizer with Leon Trotsky at a time when Malraux allies himself with the center of French reaction. Malraux was at no time a Trotskyist sympathizer. On the contrary, he was always an enemy, one who lent himself to diverting public attention from the real issues in the Moscow trials by speaking of them as merely a personal quarrel between Trotsky and Stalin. The act of Malraux as de Gaulle's Minister of Information in a coalition with the Stalinists, in supressing the French Trotskyist press, is itself the fitting commentary on Malraux' statement. Once more one sees the miserable attempt to form an amalgam between Trotskyism and fascism. Malraux, who has apparently broken with Stalinism, is only aping his former masters in trying to establish a connection between Trotskyism and reaction.

The name of Victor Serge is used to lend credence to the supposed Trotskyist support of de Gaulle's movement. The break between Serge and Trotsky was complete and can be attested by numerous quotations from published literature. Here is what Trotsky wrote in number 73 of the bulletin of the Russian Opposition (January, 1939): "Our friends are asking us what Victor Serge's position is in respect to the Fourth International.

1. March 10—Trans.

We are obliged to answer that he has the attitude of a member of the opposition. . . . The Russian Section, like the Fourth International as a whole, refuses all responsibility in respect to Victor Serge's politics." In number 79 of the same bulletin, Leon Trotsky also wrote: "And Victor Serge? He has no definite point of view at all. . . . His moralizing attitude, like that of several others, is the bridge leading from revolution to reaction. . . ." Mr. Sulzberger implies that relations between Serge and Trotsky in Mexico were friendly. He evidently does not know that Serge reached Mexico in September, 1941, thirteen months after the death of L. T. Serge's letter to Malraux can only confirm Serge's lack of a point of view which Trotsky spoke of.

Try as Malraux and others will, they cannot succeed in besmirching Trotsky and the movement he founded.

Sincerely,
Natalia Sedova-Trotsky

Coyoacan, Mexico, Feb. 16, 1948 [2]

The American friend to whom one of us owes this text adds the following comment to Malraux' declaration that he was in principle sympathetic to Trotsky's position as long as he had some chance of carrying the day against Stalin:

This confession of Malraux' is particularly surprising for two reasons. In the first place, he seems to be confirming the well-known Stalinist argument that Trotskyists are really Fascists working with the Gestapo—and correlatively, that Gaullists are Fascists. It is very strange that Malraux should lay himself open to such grounds for complaint at this time. In other respects Malraux, in spite of his admiration for Trotsky, has never in twenty years of political activity proved in practice that he preferred Trotsky to Stalin. On the contrary, on the sole occasion he was cited by Trotsky to testify in his favor during the Moscow trial about a subject concerning the life and honor of the revolutionaries, Malraux refused to speak. During the second trial, in February, 1937, a Russian journalist, Vladimir Romm, stated in his deposition that he had met Trotsky secretly in the Bois de Boulogne in July, 1933, and had received instructions from him concerning sabotage in Russia. Trotsky immediately replied through the *New York Times* that he had arrived in France in July, 1933, late in the month; that he had spent the following weeks at Royan, confined to his home by illness; and that Malraux was among those who had visited him during the last week of July. And he asked Malraux, who had just arrived in New York, to confirm or deny this. Malraux refused to testify. From then on Trotsky denounced Malraux as a Stalinist agent and as one of those responsible for the defeat of the working class in China in 1926 (dispatch of the *Universal Press* of Mexico, March 8, 1937). Malraux, in a letter addressed to the *New York Times* (March 17), "reserved the right to reply later concerning the basis

2. Feb. 26—Trans.

for the debate, which went far beyond Trotsky's personality and [his own]." This reply has yet to see the light of day, and we still do not know when and why Malraux broke with the Stalinist régime he had for so many years actively defended.

* * *

Everyone—except C. L. Sulzberger—knows that Victor Serge had not been a Trotskyist for years. In January, 1939, Burnham and Schachtman, who were at this time members of Trotsky's Socialist Workers Party, published an article in *The New International* against "intellectuals in retreat" and the "league of abandoned hopes"; and the editors of Trotsky's last book rank Victor Serge—along with Hook, Eastman, Souvarine, and others—in this "brotherhood of renegades." There is nothing common to Trotsky's Trotskyism, such as it is known to us through his posthumous work, *In Defense of Marxism* (Pioneer Publishers, December, 1942), and the band of "intellectuals in retreat" who have not gained the right to compromise Trotskyism in their avatars just because they drew near to and traveled along with it, or even militated in its ranks.

The reporter is not just ignorant. There is something two-faced about him. We imagine C. L. Sulzberger listening to Malraux with that minimum of agreement without which there is no conversation. Malraux is explaining that he gives his present action the meaning he would have given to a Trotskyist action if it had proven efficacious. Back home again, Sulzberger pins Malraux into his collection of impostors. His personal motivations (we shall speak about their soundness or lack of it later) are forgotten, and all that is left is complicity in the swindle of world anti-communism.[3]

But there is no reporter without articles, and the article reveals his duplicity. We catch him in the act of speaking to his public. Writing in the *New York Times*, Sulzberger is unrestrained; he speaks openly of American advisers who want to keep new unions away from the politics and even the ideology of "western socialism." So the Socialist framework is still too dangerous for our advisers? So the whole attempt of our coalitions to dress themselves in red is wasted effort beforehand? And the first ones to be duped by the maneuver are those who are carrying it out here? And all this is openly written in a great American newspaper? So all this is unquestionably true for its readers? Here is something to think about.

3. We are not for a minute assuming that Malraux is aware of the deceit. But then he can only be duped by it. According to Benjamin Peret (*Combat*, June 3, 1948), the authenticity of Victor Serge's letter is being challenged in court by his son.

As for Malraux' "Trotskyism," we get a glimpse at what has happened through the allusions of our texts. Malraux had a high regard for Trotsky and would have followed him if he had succeeded in changing the course of events in the U. S. S. R. and the world. But he no longer believed he would succeed. In another connection he believed in the revolutionary significance of the régime in the U.S.S.R. Whatever he had to say against the Trials, he did not want to say it, or did not want to at the time, since in the last analysis he supported Communist policies. In short, he takes the attitude expressed in *Man's Fate* and above all in *Man's Hope*. When Trotsky, having put Malraux to the test and met with a refusal, denounces him as a Stalinist—since Malraux, no matter how many reservations we may make (reservations which only make his support more pestiferous) really did refuse to do anything which could have impeded Communist action—there is nothing to say. A man cannot be held in high regard by everyone; he is what he chooses to do or approve of, even tacitly.

Or on the contrary we enter the realm of paranoid politics, when our American correspondent wants to find the Communist's eternal essence in today's Malraux, or when Malraux wants to find in the Gaullist movement a substitute for Trotskyism. Here is how Sulzberger reasons. Malraux *is* an amalgam of pseudo-Marxism and the reactionary spirit. So he is the *realization* of the Marxist compromise with reaction which is the Stalinist definition of Trotskyism. In this way he serves Stalinist propaganda. *Objectively*, he is a Stalinist. We are left to conclude that perhaps he remains a Stalinist subjectively as well. After all, he has nowhere given an explanation of his break with Stalinism. Is it not possible that his confession of his Trotskyist leaning could, like Rubashov's confession, be the last service he can render the Stalinists?

Here is an example of what we could call ultra-objective political thought. For our correspondent, Malraux is not of course what he thinks he is; but neither is he even what he is in the dynamics of observable history, that is, an anti-Stalinist. In depth history—which is the world's fear in the face of proletarian revolution—he is on the contrary a Stalinist; because the anti-Stalinism of a man who adheres to the R.P.F. gives the régime in the U.S.S.R. the deceptive appearance of a revolutionary régime and unmistakably serves its propaganda. By this reasoning Truman and, to the extent it is polarized by the rivalry between the U.S.S.R. and the United States, the whole political world are also Stalinist. The words no longer mean anything here. Exactly as "saboteur" and "spy" no longer had any assignable meaning at the Moscow Trials, being only striking ways of saying "opponent." Judged summarily in the name of proletarian goals of history, the whole present world, being nowhere proletarian, is leveled and confused in all its parts. The thought which meant to be the most historical and objective, being in the end unaware of the differences felt and lived by the actors in the drama, is delivered up to fantasms; it is the height of subjectivity.

For his part, Malraux is giving way to the ultra-subjective in politics when he says that his Gaullism of today does not differ essentially from his quasi-Trotskyism of yesterday, or that (*Carrefour*, March 31, 1948: *Dialogue Malraux-Burnham*) French anti-communism is "something which resembles the First Republic." He is evidently closing his eyes to the personnel of the R.P.F., who do not remind one of the members of the National Convention. He says what he would like to be true; he lends an arbitrary meaning to his action. The ambiguity, moreover, is not simply between his political will and the apparatus it is put to use in; it is in that will itself. He declares for freedom [speech of March 5 at the Salle Pleyel]. ". . . this conquest," he says [he is speaking of art], "is efficacious only through free inquiry. It is not because I believe in the superiority of non-censorship (although I do) that I say this. It is because everything opposed to this indomitable will to discovery means . . . the paralysis of the artist's most fruitful faculties. So we proclaim the need to maintain this freedom of inquiry against everything which intends to fix its direction in advance." And a few moments later: "For us the guarantee of political and spiritual liberty does not lie in political liberalism, which is condemned to death as soon as it is confronted by the Stalinists; the guarantee of freedom is the force of the State in the service of all its citizens." This ambiguity of intentions which oscillate between creative freedom and the force of the State corresponds to that of a movement which brings together a handful of ex-Communists (in its headquarters) and militants who, as the elections show, are for the most part conservatives. Giving way to the passion for *doing* something at any cost, Malraux consents to see his movement only through his own past; he implies that he remains the same, that his Gaullism of today is his Trotskyism of yesterday. (Only one question here: in case Trotsky had won out over Stalin, would General de Gaulle have been a Trotskyist too?) We are right in the middle of an individual fog. But at just this moment, and just to the extent he gives way to the vertigo of self, Malraux stops being a political cause and lets himself be sucked in by the wave Sulzberger speaks about. Through complacency towards himself, he becomes a thing and a tool.

The ultra-objective and the ultra-subjective attitudes are two aspects of a single crisis of political thought and the political world. (It is in this sense only that we can speak of Malraux' Stalinism; we could just as well speak of a Stalinist fideism and, in general, of an eclipse of vigilance.) There is so little conformity between political wills and the organizations they adhere to that neither Malraux nor the Stalinists can assume what their parties do with open eyes. There is such a distance between political thought and actual history that Trotskyists do not succeed in thinking about the world we are in. They find no recourse except in oneirism, faith, or delirious interpretation. Political action will become sane again only by means of an attentive examination of this situation—at a distance from these parties—and, since things for the moment do not allow of being grasped by thought, only on the basis of a circumscribed program.

* * *

It might be thought excessive to call a sickness of the contemporary world into question on the basis of a *New York Times* interview, if the conjugate functioning of communism and anti-communism were not at the same time attested to by the publication in *France-Dimanche* (March 21, 1948) of an alleged "will of Trotsky" which, as this weekly profoundly puts it, "will not fail to be used by both Communists and anti-Communists." If we could establish that in 1940 Trotsky abandoned the idea of proletarian revolution outside Russia and set down as an unconditional objective the destruction of the Stalinist apparatus, we would obtain, to the advantage of Stalinism, proof that Trotsky had practically speaking reached a compromise with all the enemies of the U.S.S.R. But at the same time all the anti-Communist movements would acquire the means of claiming a great revolutionary for themselves. The central part of this alleged will is marvelously suited for this double office.

> The working class of the Soviet Union ought to take advantage of this war to open fierce hostilities against Stalin's Bonapartist bureaucracy. We ought to put into this struggle the same furious energy that Lenin evidenced in opposing Kerensky at the time of the First World War.
>
> We know that our success would necessarily involve the defeat of fascism, even if our action were to help it win temporary military successes. I will go farther. I say that our victory over the bureaucratic-Bonapartist clique of Cain-Stalin within the Soviet Union is the condition *sine qua non* of the triumph of the proletariat on a world scale in the progressive capitalist countries. As a matter of fact, the existence of a pseudo-socialistic Stalinist State distorts the perspectives of the world revolution because it leads the working class in the progressive capitalist States into error.

For a long time I believed that a revolution in these countries would necessarily involve the downfall of Stalin's clique and the regeneration of Soviet democracy.

I deem it essential to declare openly to the workers of the world that I am no longer of this opinion [This sentence underlined in the original text].

The Stalinist bureaucracy, which began as simply an excrescence grafted onto the body of the workers' State, has become its sovereign master, a master animated by class interests of sinister historical significance. The victory of this bureaucracy over the forces of the workers' democracy will open the door to the most somber period of History humanity has ever known. This will be the era of the evolution of a new class of born exploiters from Stalin's Bonapartist bureaucracy.

It will then be necessary to recognize that this bureaucratic degeneration of the Soviet Union brings proof of the proletariat's congenital incapacity to become a ruling class, and that the Soviet Union has become the precursor and the embryonic form of a new and terrible régime of exploitation on a national scale [Underlined in the text].

If the proletariat of the Soviet Union were to fail in its duty to use this war to destroy Stalinist exploitation, we would enter a period of decadence of human society beneath the empire of a totalitarian bureaucracy.

The text, according to its introductory note, was supposed to have been stolen by a Soviet agent "at the end of July 1940," and sent to Moscow. Three copies were supposed to have stayed "in the hands of a personal friend of Trotsky, Chibaltchish [a writer known in France under the name of Victor Serge]." A friend of Victor Serge is supposed to have brought it back to Europe.

A mimeographed communiqué from the International Secretariat of the IVth International proves demonstratively that this document is false. How could the Kremlin have failed to make use of a document which practically established Trotskyism's complicity with nazism, either at the time Vishinsky was questioned about this point by the American press, or when Stalinist-inspired works like Sayers and Kahn's *The Great Conspiracy against the U.S.S.R.* (1946) appeared, or finally when Trotsky's widow asked at the Nuremberg Trials to examine the archives of the German government concerning alleged Hitlero-Trotskyist dealings? How could the introductory note originate in Trotskyist circles when it dates as July 20, 1940, an assassination which took place on August 20? How could Victor Serge have been made trustee of the "will" when he had broken politically with Trotsky in 1936 and was in France at the time of Trotsky's death? As for the "will's" content, it is incompatible with the theses Trotsky upheld until his death.

"[Trotsky's] whole argument," the Fourth International says, "turned around the fact that the Stalinist dictatorship *did not represent* that of a new social class. In his many writings, stretching from 1935 to 1940, Trotsky relentlessly defended this same idea. A violent discussion of the Russian question broke out among American Trotskyites at the end of 1939. This discussion was prolonged until May–June, 1940. In this discussion, Trotsky intervened through articles and letters which were published in a book entitled *In Defense of Marxism.* Throughout the two hundred pages of this book, which were written just before this alleged secret will, Trotsky fights violently against the idea that the bureaucracy could possibly constitute a new class. He also fights against this idea in the *Manifeste de la Conférence extraordinaire,* which was written at the very time this alleged will is supposed to have been written."

Here is a fragment of that text:

> But nationalized industry and the collectivized Soviet economy are fortunately among the conquests surviving the October Revolution. On this basis workers' Soviets can build a new and better society. We can on no condition abandon this base to the world bourgeoisie. The duty of revolutionaries is to defend tooth and nail each position won by the working class, whether it is a matter of democratic rights, wage scales, or such a great conquest of humanity as nationalization of the means of production and a planned economy. Those who are incapable of defending already acquired conquests can never struggle for new ones. We shall defend the U.S.S.R. against the imperialist enemy with all our strength. But the conquests of the October Revolution will serve the people only if they show themselves capable of treating the Stalinist bureaucracy as they once treated the Czarist bureaucracy and the bourgeoisie. [*Fourth International,* October, 1940].

The Fourth International continues:

> At the end of June, 1940 [one month after publication of the alleged "will"], Trotsky wrote an article entitled "We are not changing our line," in which, having learned lessons from imperialist France's defeat by German imperialism, he proclaims his confidence in the revolutionary future of the proletariat of Europe. He writes: "In the conquered countries, the situation of the masses will immediately be aggravated to the extreme. To social oppression is added national oppression, the principal burden of which is also borne by the workers. Of all forms of dictatorship, the totalitarian dictatorship of a foreign conqueror is the most intolerable. . . . It is impossible to put an armed soldier behind each Polish, Norwegian, Danish, Dutch, Belgian, or French worker or peasant. . . . We can foresee with certainty a rapid transformation of all the conquered countries into a powder keg. . . . It is true that Hitler has boasted and promised to establish the domination of the German people at the expense of all Europe and even the whole world, "for a thousand

years." But it is evident that this splendor will not last, not even ten years. [*Fourth International,* October, 1940].

The Fourth International's communiqué goes on to show that the alleged will falsifies an authentic text. In an article entitled *The U.S.S.R. in War* (September 25, 1939), Trotsky had written:

> If, however, it is conceded that the present war will provoke not revolution but a decline of the proletariat, then there remains another alternative: the further decay of monopoly capitalism, its further fusion with the State and the replacement of democracy wherever it still remained by a totalitarian régime. The inability of the proletariat to take into its hands the leadership of society could actually lead under these conditions to the growth of a new exploiting class from the Bonapartist Fascist bureaucracy. This would be, according to all indications, a régime of decline, signalizing the eclipse of civilization.
>
> An analogous result might occur in the event that the proletariat of advanced capitalist countries, having conquered power, should prove incapable of holding it and surrender it, as in the U.S.S.R., to a privileged bureaucracy. Then we would be compelled to acknowledge that the reason for the bureaucratic relapse is rooted not in the backwardness of the country and not in the imperialist environment but the congenital incapacity of the proletariat to become a ruling class. Then it would be necessary in retrospect to establish that in its fundamental traits the present U.S.S.R. was the precursor of a new exploiting régime on an international scale. [*In Defense of Marxism,* p. 9]

It is only a matter of an hypothesis (proposed, moreover, by minority elements of the S.W.P., whose tendencies Trotsky is analyzing here)—and the hypothesis is expressly that the proletariat of advanced countries has failed in its revolutionary task. The "will" transforms the hypothesis into an assertion and entrusts the revolutionary task to the Russian proletariat alone. It is in this way that a Marxist policy is made up as an anti-Communist adventure.

The weekly is not afraid to assume its own responsibility in comparing the text of the will and the declarations made by Trotsky's assassin to *France-Dimanche's* special correspondent and published in 1946 in the columns of that newspaper. Jacques Mornard had mentioned "frequent visits to Trotsky by the German consul" and declared that Trotsky wanted to send him first to China and then to Russia in order to "educate [his] teams of saboteurs." "Trotsky's will," *France-Dimanche* concludes, "illustrates in a singular light the declarations of his assassin." All those who have read Trotsky and know his past role and continuing theses will think as we do that although the weekly *France-Dimanche* could have been deceived by a false document, it is dishonoring itself by giving credence through this commentary to the detective fiction of Trotsky the saboteur and spy.

A letter of May 7 announces that Trotsky's widow is bringing suit against *France-Dimanche.*

* * *

So it is *certain* that Trotsky's theses have nothing in common with the false will—no more than they do with the politics of French anti-communism. But even though in 1940 Trotsky remained resolutely faithful to his positions, he lucidly explained their difficulties. He even envisaged the case in which they *would become* untenable, indicating in a word what *would have to be* done in this case, any compromise with reactionary anti-communism being of course excluded. Concretely, the difficulty is as follows: how can both the thesis of the workers' democracy and that of the unconditional defense of the U.S.S.R. be applied, for example, at the moment the U.S.S.R. invades Poland (1939)? Trotsky defined his line in the following terms:

> Let us for a moment conceive that in accordance with the treaty with Hitler, the Moscow government leaves untouched the rights of private property in the occupied areas and limits itself to "control" after the Fascist pattern. Such a concession would have a deep-going principled character and might become a starting point for a new chapter in the history of the Soviet régime; and consequently a starting point for a new appraisal on our part of the nature of the Soviet state.
>
> It is more likely, however, that in the territories scheduled to become a part of the U.S.S.R., the Moscow government will carry through the expropriation of the large land-owners and statification of the means of production. This variant is most probable not because the bureaucracy remains true to the socialist program but because it is neither desirous nor capable of sharing the power, and the privileges the latter entails, with the old ruling classes in the occupied territories. Here an analogy literally offers itself. The first Bonaparte halted the revolution by means of a military dictatorship. However, when the French troops invaded Poland, Napoleon signed a decree: "Serfdom is abolished." This measure was dictated not by Napoleon's sympathies for the peasants, nor by democratic principles, but rather by the fact that the Bonapartist dictatorship based itself not on feudal, but on bourgeois property relations. Inasmuch as Stalin's Bonapartist dictatorship bases itself not on private but on state property, the invasion of Poland by the Red Army should . . . result in the abolition of private capitalist property, so as thus to bring the régime of the occupied territories into accord with the régime of the U.S.S.R. . . .
>
> We do not entrust the Kremlin with any historic mission. We were

> and remain against seizures of new territories by the Kremlin. We are for the independence of Soviet Ukraine, and if the Byelo Russians themselves wish—of Soviet Byelo Russia. At the same time in the sections of Poland occupied by the Red Army, partisans of the Fourth International must play the most decisive part in expropriating the landlords and capitalists, in dividing the land among the peasants, in creating soviets and workers' committees, etc. While so doing, they must preserve their political independence, they must fight during elections to the soviets and factory committees for the complete independence of the latter from the bureaucracy, and they must conduct revolutionary propaganda in the spirit of distrust toward the Kremlin and its local agencies.
>
> But let us suppose that Hitler turns his weapons against the east and invades territories occupied by the Red Army. Under these conditions, partisans of the Fourth International, without changing in any way their attitude toward the Kremlin oligarchy, will advance to the forefront, as the most urgent task of the hour, the military resistance against Hitler. The workers will say: "We cannot cede to Hitler the overthrowing of Stalin; that is *our own task.*" During the military struggle against Hitler, the revolutionary workers will strive to enter into the closest possible comradely relations with the rank-and-file fighters of the Red Army. While arms in hand they deal blows to Hitler, the Bolshevik-Leninists will at the same time conduct revolutionary propaganda against Stalin preparing his overthrow at the next and perhaps very near stage.[4]

Clearly, this is the very language of 1917—as faithful to class and historical consciousness as it is to action. Clearly too, the Polish militants who might have followed—who did follow—this line could not have followed it long. Confronted with an expanding U.S.S.R., can one enter into public discussion with the Stalinist apparatus without being eliminated politically? Can one work for planned, collective production without being for the Stalinist apparatus as well? Can one separate in action Stalinism and the gains of the October Revolution? Can one, through analysis, separate the bases of the Octobrist régime and its bureaucratic apparatus? Is bureaucracy only a caste, a parasite, or is it henceforth tied so closely to the régime that it has become an indispensable part of its functioning? Trotsky said that the notion of "caste" (which he applied to the Soviet bureaucracy) has no scientific value.[5] It is an historical analogy which may be used provisorily to conduct a sociology of the present, insofar as the corresponding reality is still ambiguous. So he recognized that his theses could call for a reexamination if it turned out that, in the functioning of the U.S.S.R., the bases of the régime could no longer be disassociated theoretically or practically from its apparatus. It would then be the Marxist perspective

4. *In Defense of Marxism,* "The U.S.S.R. in War" (September 25, 1939), p. 20.
5. *Ibid.,* p. 6.

itself which would be in question; since the facts would then bring to light in the margin of the Marxist alternative—capitalism or socialism —a type of society which cannot be defined by either of the two concepts. Concerning this possibility there is a text which is a sequel to the one spoken about in the previously mentioned Trotskyist communiqué:

> The historic alternative, carried to the end, is as follows: either the Stalin régime is an abhorrent relapse in the process of transforming bourgeois society into a socialist society, or the Stalin régime is the first stage of a new exploiting society. If the second prognosis proves to be correct, then, of course, the bureaucracy will become a new exploiting class. However onerous the second perspective may be, if the world proletariat should actually prove incapable of fulfilling the mission placed upon it by the course of development, nothing else would remain except only to recognize that the socialist program, based on the internal contradictions of capitalist society, ended as a Utopia. It is self-evident that a new "minimum" program would be required—for the defense of the interests of the slaves of the totalitarian bureaucratic society.[6]

This, we repeat, was only an hypothesis; and Trotsky withheld judgment of the facts until the end of the period in course:

> Yet it is absolutely self-evident that if the international proletariat, as a result of the experience of our entire epoch and the current new war, proves incapable of becoming the master of society, this would signify the foundering of all hope for a socialist revolution, for it is impossible to expect any other more favorable conditions for it; in any case no one foresees them now, or is able to characterize them. Marxists do not have the slightest right (if disillusionment and fatigue are not considered "rights") to draw the conclusion that the proletariat has forfeited its revolutionary possibilities and must renounce all aspirations to hegemony in an era immediately ahead. Twenty-five years in the scales of history, when it is a question of profoundest changes in economic and cultural systems, weigh less than an hour in the life of man. What good is the individual who, because of empirical failures in the course of an hour or a day, renounces a goal that he set for himself on the basis of the experience and analysis of his entire previous lifetime? In the years of darkest Russian reaction (1907 to 1917) we took as our starting point those revolutionary possibilities which were revealed by the Russian proletariat in 1905. In the years of world reaction we must proceed from those possibilities which the Russian proletariat revealed in 1917. The Fourth International did not by accident call itself the world party of the socialist revolution. Our road is not to be changed. We steer our course toward the world revolution and by virtue of this very fact toward the regeneration of the U.S.S.R. as a workers' state.[7]

6. *Ibid.*, p. 9.
7. *Ibid.*, p. 15.

In this remarkable passage, Trotsky does not (like so many of Marxism's sacristans) evade the question of principle in the name of a dogmatic philosophy of history, which would presuppose some revelation of World Mind. He only defers it in contrasting to the experience of failure the experience of victory and the years of his life when history responded without ambiguity to reason. But this means that for those of us who have not lived 1917, another perspective is possible. To the extent we are better informed about the relative importance of slave and free labor in the U.S.S.R., the volume of the concentration-camp system, and the quasi-autonomy of the police system, it becomes increasingly difficult to see the U.S.S.R. as a *transition towards* socialism or even a degenerate workers' State, in a word, to put it in perspective according to 1917. More than that, as exploitative relationships are established on the bases of collective production in the U.S.S.R. itself, and as proletariats in the world at large seem less conscious of their historical mission than thirty years ago, we come to ask ourselves whether 1917 really marked the first flush of a logic of history which would sooner or later bring the problems and solutions of Marxism, or whether on the contrary 1917 was not a lucky break, a privileged case, which was exceptionally favorable to the Marxist view of history.

Supposing that this is so, neither the R.P.F. nor Americanism can expect any benefit from it. The reason why we have it in for Malraux, Koestler, Thierry Maulnier, Burnham, the "league of abandoned hopes" and the "intellectuals in retreat" is precisely that, having lived or at least understood Marxism, and encountering the question we are raising, they have fallen short. They have not tried to map out in spite of everything a path leading to a humanism for all men, but have, each in his own way, acquiesced to chaos and taken leave of the question. They have shirked the task of mapping out the *minimum program* Trotsky spoke of. Trotsky and his party raised the question in the form of an hypothesis—and withheld the answer till later. This discussion centering about the false will must not conclude with a pure and simple exposition of classical Trotskyism. Trotsky's tomb, if we may believe the newspaper photographs, bears a hammer and sickle, with nothing to distinguish this emblem from that of the U.S.S.R. Thus he continues to affirm his solidarity with the conquests of the October Revolution. But this is Trotsky's destiny; it is Trotsky bringing his life to a close. The Trotsky who still lives in his writings suggests a question that his tombstone does not answer. It is the business of all of us to answer it.

(July, 1948)

2 / Marxism and Superstition

Marxism has always agreed that cultural values, like everything else, are integrally related to social history; but it has never maintained that there is a one-to-one parallel between the two developments, or that, consequently, literature and criticism are simply aids to political action, varieties of propaganda. Engels said the curve of ideologies is much more complicated than that of political and social evolution. Marx speaks in a famous passage of the "eternal charm" of Greek art. So he recognized a register of art (and no doubt of literature) where "eternal" anticipations or even acquisitions were possible. This was optimistic communism, which has confidence in the spontaneity of the writer or the artist, and in the intrinsic development of their culture, and which, being convinced that there can never be a conflict between cultural needs and revolutionary action but on the contrary only convergence and communion, gives the writer and the artist no other command than to be a writer or an artist as profoundly as possible. Today's communism, on the contrary, behaves as if there were no longer any intrinsic criteria in cultural matters, as if literature and science were means, among others, to immediate political action, which is itself understood simply as the defense of the U.S.S.R.

In 1946, Lukacs [1] defended his conception of autocriticism in terms of culture. It consisted in the right, always resorted to by writers, philosophers, and scientists, to go beyond what they had previously said or written, to understand and judge their own past, to mature and grow without fearing apparent contradictions, without that concern with remaining formally in agreement with oneself which is in reality

1. George Lukacs, foremost Marxist literary historian and critic whose work on class-consciousness has had a great influence in French philosophical circles and who is now being translated into English. He was rewarded for going even farther than Merleau-Ponty indicates in the direction of Stalinism and self-betrayal by being imprisoned during the Hungarian uprising.—Trans.

a decadent pretension—a pretension to summing up a work before it has begun—a posthumous view of a life which has not yet been lived. In a word, we are not sure that this theory of autocriticism can justify the autocriticisms Lukacs made from 1946 on. We have difficulty believing that there has been maturation and growth from the Hegelianism of his *Geschichte und Klassenbewusstsein* to the realist theory of knowledge of his recent works. But anyhow this theory was at least sound. It was in fact the recognition of the writer's right to be mistaken, the energetic reaffirmation of the difficulties and even the ambiguities of expression and culture. And the apparent liberalism of those who defended Lukacs' first works against him was perhaps, on the contrary, only a tricky way of shutting him up in his pre-Marxist past.

Today it is no longer a question for Lukacs of seeking to determine, in the field of literary history, the moment when the novel reached its greatest power of expression, or whether there is not an "eternal charm" to Tolstoy and Goethe which makes them models. The models are all discovered: since there has been a revolution in Russia, it is in Russia that the literature of the future is being sketched out. The defense of Russia is as tight in the field of the novel as it is in diplomacy; it is not one of the revolutionary duties, but the only one. The rest is Westernism. Lukacs' autocriticism as defined in 1946 was a fact of culture. In today's sense, it is the negation of it.

In 1937 Bukharin, reconsidering his attitude of past years in the perspective of the world situation, declared himself a criminal for having been of the opposition, but refused to confess himself a spy or saboteur. In 1949 Rajk, contrary to all that is known about him, presents himself as an American agent. In 1946 Lukacs claimed for the writer the right to go beyond his past; in 1949 he must disqualify his works as a critic and an aesthetician, as if the high esteem in which he held Tolstoy and Goethe had been only thoughtlessness and precipitancy. Thus communism goes from historical responsibility to naked discipline, from autocriticism to repudiation, from Marxism to superstition.

(December, 1949)

3 / The U.S.S.R. and the Camps

So IT IS ESTABLISHED that Soviet citizens may be deported during an investigation, without judgment or time limit. The *Code de travail correctif de la R.F.S.S.R.*[1] lays down the principle of administrative decision only for collective labor without suppression of freedom.[2] But it very clearly mentions it in connection with deprivation of freedom and deportation in article 44.[3] So it is impossible to maintain, as Pierre Daix does,[4] that administrative decision is in force only for the harmless case of corrective labor without deprivation of freedom.

It is further established that the repressive apparatus tends to

1. "Recueil chronologique des lois et décrets du Présidium du Soviet suprême et Ordonnances du gouvernement de la RFSSR au 1er mars," 1940. Vol. 9, *O.G.I.* (Union des maisons d'édition d'Etat Gospolitzdat, 1941).

2. Section I du *Code,* article 8.

3. Article 44, Section II (*Privation de la liberté*). "The following persons may be sent to the places of deprivation of freedom indicated in article 28 of the present code:

a) Persons condemned for a period not exceeding three years;

b) *Persons whose case is under investigation or being tried by order of competent authorities* [my italics];

c) Persons condemned for periods exceeding three years . . ."

Specifically, the places of deprivation of freedom mentioned in article 28 are: "a) solitary confinement . . . ; b) deportation stations; c) corrective labor colonies, industrial colonies, agricultural colonies of mass labor, penal colonies" [article 28], to which the same article adds sanitary institutions and institutions for minors deprived of freedom.

Only persons whose case is under investigation may be kept in solitary confinement [art. 29]. But they are not necessarily kept there. We see them appearing again in article 31, which concerns deportation stations: "Persons deprived of freedom, or whose case is under investigation, are separated from condemned persons at the deportation stations." Solitary confinement is not necessarily followed by appearance before a court: "Persons are kept in solitary confinement only until the enforcement of the court's sentence or *of the decree of other competent authorities*" [my italics, article 29].

4. *Pourquoi D. Rousset a-t-il inventé les camps sovietiques?*, p. 6.

constitute a distinct power in the U.S.S.R. An ordinance of October 27, 1934,[5] transfers to the N.K.V.D. the management and administration of corrective labor which heretofore had derived from the People's Commissariat for Justice. The system has its own revenues, furnished by the prisoners' labor, which serve specifically to keep up the administrative apparatus.[6] Production is regulated by industrial and financial plans which are set up by the Directory of the corrective labor institutions and only ratified by the People's Commissariat for Justice.

In the third place, it is established that the proper functioning of corrective labor is assured by delegating power to common-law prisoners [7]—according to a tried and true method.

Finally, since official publications note one hundred and twenty-seven thousand prisoners freed by governmental decision after the completion of the canal from the Baltic to the White Sea and the Moscow-Volga Canal, it is *probable*, taking account of the volume of these workyards in the whole of the apparatus, that the total number of prisoners amounts to millions: some say ten million; others fifteen.

Unless we are specially inspired, we have to admit that these facts throw the meaning of the Russian system wholly open to question again. We are not applying to the U.S.S.R. here Péguy's principle that every city harboring a single individual suffering is an accursed city: by this standard they all are, and there can be no distinctions made among them. What we are saying is that there is no socialism when one out of every twenty citizens is in a camp. It is no good answering here that every revolution has its traitors, or that insurrection does not bring an end to class struggle, or that the U.S.S.R. could not defend itself against the enemy without by sparing the enemy within, or that Russia could not begin industrializing without violence. These answers are not valid if a twentieth of the population—a tenth of the male population—is involved after a third of a century. If there is one saboteur, spy, or shiftless person for every twenty inhabitants in the U.S.S.R., when more than one purge has already "purified" the country; if it is necessary today to "re-educate" millions of Soviet citizens when the babes of October 1917 have lived for thirty-two years, it is because the system itself unceasingly recreates *its* opposition. If there is permanent repression; and if, far from being reabsorbed, the repressive apparatus on the contrary becomes autonomous; it is because the régime is installed in a disequilibrium, because the forces of production are stifled by the modes of production. If common-law prisoners are

5. Same *Recueil*, addendum to article 129 of the *Code de travail correctif*.

6. *Ibid.*, article 139a.

7. *Ibid.*, article 87: "The most trusted prisoners—the workers—the persons condemned in first instance for ordinary offenses are placed in charge of overseeing the others."

more trustworthy men for the régime than political prisoners, it is because it is more pleased with the "*Lumpenproletariat*" than with the "conscious proletarians."

So if we are serious, all we can do is look squarely at this permanent crisis of the Russian régime. Is it a consequence of the very principle of collective production, or of State ownership and the type of planning practiced in Russia? Does it stem from the political structure of the U.S.S.R. and, on this hypothesis, concern only the Stalinist phase? Or was it pre-formed in the Bolshevist organization of the Party; and if so, what other political form can be conceived of, what guarantees invented, against this decadence? These questions and others cannot be evaded. Two years ago one of us wrote here that Soviet society is ambiguous, and that both signs of progress and symptoms of regression are found in it. If there are ten million concentration camp inmates—while at the other end of the Soviet hierarchy salaries and standard of living are fifteen to twenty times higher than those of free workers—then quantity changes into quality. The whole system swerves and changes meaning; and in spite of nationalization of the means of production, and even though private exploitation of man by man and unemployment are impossible in the U.S.S.R., we wonder what reasons we still have to speak of socialism in relation to it.

Such are the questions the French and European far Left should devote itself to, instead of wasting its time in short-lived speeches in defense of the régime—André Wurmser [8] saying, a few months ago, that there are no camps in Russia; Pierre Daix,[9] a few weeks ago, that the camps are "one of the Soviet régime's finest titles to glory." [10]

* * *

Yes, the question is becoming ever more imperious: how has October 1917 been able to end up in the cruelly hierarchical society whose features are gradually becoming clear before our eyes? In Lenin, Trotsky, and *a fortiori* Marx, there is not a word which is not sane, which does not still speak today to men of all lands, which does not help us understand what is going on in our own. And after so much lucidity, intelligence, and sacrifice—the ten million deported Soviet citizens, the stupidity of censorship, the panic of justifications.

If our Communists do not want to be aware of the question, their

8. André Wurmser, French novelist and literary critic for *Les Lettres Françaises*, as well as an editorialist for the French Communist newspaper, *L'Humanité*. —Trans.

9. Pierre Daix, French editor and critic.—Trans.

10. Pierre Daix, *Pourquoi David Rousset a-t-il inventé les camps soviétiques?*, p. 12.

adversaries have no more intention of raising it, and nothing in their writings gives us even the beginning of an answer. To speak of neurosis is no answer: in reading the testimony of former prisoners we do not find in Soviet camps the sadism, the religion of death, the nihilism which—paradoxically joined to precise special interests and at times agreeing, at times struggling with them—ended up producing the Nazi extermination camps. Nor is it any more of an answer to our question to implicate bureaucracy and its own special interests: we see very few men who let themselves be led by interest alone; they always provide themselves with convictions. Furthermore, interest, like sadism, is better hidden. It has not been sufficiently noticed that the *Code de travail correctif*, presesented by the British delegate to the United Nations and by Rousset in the *Figaro Littéraire* as a revelation, has been available since 1936 in its English version at Smith and Maxwell, publishers, Chancery Lane, London, for about three shillings, sixpence. The release of one hundred and twenty-seven thousand prisoners has been officially announced in Moscow.[11] It seems probable that the evolution which leads from October, 1917, to millions of slaves, and which beneath the permanence of forms or words gradually changes the system's meaning, happened little by little without deliberate intention, from crisis to crisis and expedient to expedient, and that its social significance escapes its own creators. Faced with the alternative, each time more imperious, of aggravating it or disappearing politically, they go on without understanding that the undertaking is changing beneath their hands. For lack of a background to see it against, the best are no doubt astonished by these cries of hatred which come to them from the capitalist world.

Let us look more closely at the situation. The formulas of the *Code de travail correctif* are those of an Edenic socialism itself: there is no longer any question of punishing, but of re-educating; criminals are blind men, we need only enlighten them; in a society where exploitation is forbidden, laziness and rebellion are misunderstandings; the asocial person must be sheltered from the righteous anger of the united populace at the same time the populace is sheltered from the undertakings of this retarded person; the best thing to do is to put him back to work, explaining to him with great indulgence the greatness of the new society. After which, soothed and saved, he will take his place again in the common undertaking. Nineteenth-century thoughts, which are still touching, and perhaps more profound than we think; since

11. An anti-Nazi German, who had deserted the German Army in order to join the Russians and was employed by them in forced labor, told us that the existence of the camps and the very heavy annual losses were known to the populace in the Leningrad region.

after all we have never succeeded so far in endowing men with truly comparable opportunities to begin with—since we have never tempted them with good.

And now these youthful thoughts suddenly begin to grimace like old men. These innocent ideas become the height of cant and trickery when one out of every twenty citizens is imprisoned in their name; when they adorn the camps where men are dying of work and hunger; when they conceal the repression of a harshly unequal society; when, under color of re-educating those who have strayed, it is a matter of breaking the opposition; when, under the pretext of autocriticism, it is a matter of repudiation. Then and all at once their virtue is changed into poison. But this is not so clearly perceived. Alongside the cynics and the perverse, who are found everywhere, no doubt a good number of young Soviet heroes who have never lived in a country without camps take the side of decency without the slightest scruple. Have we never seen anything similar? Many civil servants who were favorably endowed and who began well—as Kravchenko must have been in his first period—who never knew discussion and the critical spirit in the sense of 1917, continue to think the prisoners are hotheads, asocial persons, men of bad will, up to the day when the pleasure of living in New York gives them the chance to reconsider it all.

As for the survivors of 1917, they are not the best minds of Marxist humanism. They have always preferred empiricism to analysis of situations; they have always believed much more in the apparatus than in mass movements; they have always succeeded better as organizers than as popular orators; they have always trusted the Party maneuver rather than an understanding of the situation. They have always by preference been interested in the second term of Lenin's equation, the Soviets plus electrification. Well then, since the U.S.S.R. is electrifying without falling back into the system of individual profit, it must seem to them that the essential part of the October Revolution is saved. We must not ask them to revive Marx, to notice that in Marx's view the infrastructure is the forces of production, in other words, not simply the technology and riches produced but *men at work,* still men. They never went into these subtleties, and their materialism has always been scarcely dialectical at all.

And then, all that is so far away; it has been a long, long time since they have had to pull in their horns about the spontaneity of the masses. Koestler, they think, has explained this very well: we do not take feeling into consideration; if we give it an inch, it takes an ell; consequently, we must leave nothing to it. Think no more of it. The White Sea canal will be dug. The bases of collective production will be affirmed. And Communists throughout the world expect that, by a sort of magical emanation, so many canals, factories, and riches shall one day produce whole men, even if in order to produce them it is necessary to reduce ten million Russians to slavery, reduce their families to despair, be it even twenty or thirty million Russians, train another part of the population in the art of policing and denunciation, and the civil servants in servility or armed egotism. It is undoubtedly in this way that the best Communists are deaf to ten million prisoners.

* * *

By looking toward the origin of the system of concentration camps, we can measure the illusion of today's Communists. But it is also this illusion which forbids confusing communism and fascism. If our Communists accept the camps and oppression, it is because they expect the classless society to emerge from them through the miracle of infrastructures. They are mistaken, but this is what they think. They are making the mistake of believing in obscurity, but this is what they believe. The Nazi camps also bore the famous devices of re-education through labor; but from the moment gas chambers were established, no one could believe that, even in intention, it was a matter of re-educating. Before the gas chambers, the German camps were patterned after the Russian camps, and their penal devices after socialist ideology, exactly as the Party in the Fascist sense was patterned after the Party in the Bolshevik sense, and as fascism borrowed the idea of propaganda from bolshevism. Fascism is an anguish in the face of bolshevism, whose external form it takes in order to more surely destroy its content—the internationalist and proletarian *Stimmung.* If we conclude from this that communism is fascism, we fully gratify, after the event, the wish of fascism, which has always been to hide the crisis of capitalism and the humane inspiration of Marxism. No Nazi was ever burdened with ideas such as the recognition of man by man, internationalism, classless society. It is true that these ideas find only an unfaithful bearer in today's communism, and that they act more as its décor than its motive force. The fact remains that they are still part of it. They are what a young Russian or French Communist is taught. Whereas Nazi propaganda taught its listeners the pride of the German people, the pride of Aryans and the *Führerprinzip.*

This means we have nothing in common with a Nazi and the same values as a Communist. A Communist, it will be said, has no values. There are only loyalties. We answer that he does all he can to succeed in having none, but that no one, thank God, can live without breathing. He has values *in spite of himself*. We may think he compromises them by embodying them in today's communism. The fact remains that they are ours, and that on the contrary we have nothing in common with a good number of communism's adversaries. Now this is not a question of feeling. We mean that to the extent we draw away geographically and politically from the U.S.S.R., we find Communists who are increasingly men like us, and a Communist movement which is sound. If fate led us to meet one of the future Kravchenkos who must abound in Russia, there would undoubtedly be very little fraternity: the degradation of Marxist values is inevitable in Russia itself, the camps dissolve the humanist illusion, the experienced facts drive out imagined values as bad money drives out the good. But when one of us speaks to a Martiniquan Communist about Martiniquan affairs, he finds himself in constant agreement with him. A *Monde* reader wrote recently to that newspaper that all the declarations concerning the Soviet labor camps might well be true, but that still he was a worker without funds or lodging and he always found more support among the Communists than the others. And the *Monde* immediately started a fund so that it would not be said it was insensitive to suffering. The bad thing is that this letter was needed to call forth that philanthropy.

Let us move to the collective level. It is very possible that Chinese communism will in the long run follow the line of Russian communism and in the end realize an hierarchical society with a new type of exploitation. The fact still remains that, in the short run, this line seems to be the only one capable of bringing China out of the chaos and picturesque misery foreign capitalism has left it in. Whatever the nature of the present Soviet society may be, the U.S.S.R. is on the whole situated, in the balance of powers, on the side of those who are struggling against the forms of exploitation known to us. The decadence of Russian communism does not make the class struggle a myth, "free enterprise" possible or desirable, or the Marxist criticism in general null and void. From which we do not draw the conclusion that indulgence must be shown toward communism, but that one can in no case make a pact with one's adversaries. The only sound criticism is thus the one which bears on exploitation and oppression, inside and outside the U.S.S.R.; and every political position which *is defined* in opposition to Russia and localizes criticism within it is an absolution given to the capitalist world.

That is why we have always refused to associate ourselves with it in this journal. How many times American friends, after having asked us what we thought of communism, went on: "But then why aren't you with us?" It would be necessary to know whom or what they are for. For along with Stalinism and Trotskyism, they have jettisoned every kind of Marxist criticism, every kind of radical temper. The facts of exploitation throughout the world present them with only scattered problems which must be examined and solved one by one. They no longer have any political ideas. As for the United States, they say with a straight face, "We do not have class struggle here," forgetting fifty years and more of American history. "Participate in American prosperity," such were at last the words of one of them. Seated, as if on the world's axis, on American prosperity, which has felt many shocks and, judging by the decline of Marshall Plan policies and plans for world re-equilibrium, is in the process of feeling new ones, they ask us to make an absolute of it. And when we explain to them that they are in the process of sacrificing all political evaluation to this uncertain fact, and that all things considered the recognition of man by man and the classless society are less vague as principles of a world politics than American prosperity, that the historical mission of the proletariat is in the last analysis a more precise idea than the historical mission of the United States, we are told, as Sidney Hook put it in *Partisan Review,* that it is urgent to send a few masters of thought of his caliber to France. "Since you agree about oppression in the U.S.S.R. and the risk of a military expansion of communism, would you be willing to say," another one proposed, "that the U.S.S.R. is *the enemy number one*?" No indeed, we are not willing; for this formula has a corollary—for the moment, there is no other enemy than Russia—and thus means that we must give up discussing the non-Soviet world.

When the question of Soviet camps was brought up before the U. N., the Soviet delegation answered by asking that the liabilities of capitalism be investigated too: unemployment, working conditions in the colonies, the condition of Negroes in America. The delegate from the United Kingdom complained about what he called a diversion. A society is responsible for everything it produces, and Marx was right to reproach liberal thought, as for an accountable fraud, for the artifices by which it puts unemployment, colonial labor, and racial inequality beyond accountability by imputing them to nature or to chance. Among citizens and on the level of strictly political rights—not counting colonials, unemployed, and underpaid wage-earners—we have full freedom. The Communists have been sufficiently reproached for wiping ten million inmates of concentration camps off their balance-sheet for the same procedure not to be employed when it is a question of judging capitalism. Furthermore, the delegate from the United Kingdom gave himself away, as Freud's subjects confess as they deny. Speaking of the Russian labor camps he forgot himself and said, "It is the colonial system of the U.S.S.R." But then he would have to agree (with the necessary nuances) that the colonies are the democracies' labor camps.

There is one and only one response to what we are saying here (it is strange no one has made it to us)—criticism of all oppression weakens democracies, since it bears upon them and not upon the Urals. If this is what is thought, it is imperative to see the consequence: social criticism must be silent until the Soviet system disappears, and when the camps are finally opened in Siberia, here in the West we shall have a generation without political training, hallucinated by Western patriotism and years of anti-Communist propaganda. For our part, we trust governments and headquarters to do this job. Everything indicates that they will not lack auxiliaries. It is more urgent to maintain at least a few islets where men love and practice liberty in some other way than in opposition to the Communists.

* * *

We need not have it out at length now with David Rousset's [12] undertaking, which was the occasion for these pages. It was necessary to publish the Soviet *Code du travail forcé.* We are so convinced of it that we were getting ready to print it when Rousset, who had the document from other sources, used it in the way we are familiar with. We disapprove absolutely of the use he put it to, and we think that dating from this campaign Rousset abandoned the political line he had been following and initiated a propaganda which we do not in any case intend to be implicated in by the memory men may have retained of our collaboration with him, which is now definitively over.

". . . in order to struggle with some chance of effectiveness against the exploitation of man, we must concentrate our attack upon the system which is the most unrelenting, carries its attacks farthest, and closes every avenue to liberation most rigorously. We are not speaking of injustice in general, but of the specific injustice of concentration camps." [13] Rousset consequently refuses any investigation which would be addressed simultaneously to Russia, Spain, and Greece.[14] With all the more reason he could not possibly implicate diffuse or concealed forms of slavery in his protest—forced labor in colonies, colonial wars, the condition of American Negroes. But if there is no question of arousing each people against the oppressions it bears witness to as well as against oppression in Russia—if the only oppressors in question are those in Siberia or the Urals (where even without the Iron Curtain the *Figaro Littéraire* would have, we think, only a

12. David Rousset, French writer who engaged in a continuing struggle against the concentration camp system upon his return from German camps, an experience he analyzed in his *Les Jours de Notre Mort,* which Merleau-Ponty alludes to at the close of this essay.—Trans.

13. *Figaro Littéraire,* November 12, 1949.

14. *Ibid.,* November 19, 1949.

faint effulgence)—then this procedure can only *shift and concentrate upon the Russian system all the possibilities of rebellion in the world, and bring about on all sides the union of classes against it.* How could the struggle possibly be "more effective" because the injustices which are not those of the Soviet system are excluded? Undoubtedly because it will attract an audience who would steal away if the Spanish or Greek governments, the French or English colonial administrations were called into question. Who are these so delicate supporters then? Are we to believe that they are the masses, and in particular the French masses? Are the French masses so much in favor of colonial wars and the Franco régime? In short, who is Rousset writing for? Is it, as is said, for the former Communist deportees? But by declaring that he has it in for the U.S.S.R. alone he gives them exactly the only excuse they can find for withdrawing support. So it can only be a matter of rallying a public which is not tormented by camps or prisons as long as they are not Soviet camps or prisons. Here the sacred union against the Russian system solicits all those who detest it for bad reasons as well as good ones; through the concentration camp system it will aim at and hit all parties of socialist inspiration.

In short, Rousset takes sides with the principle of "the enemy number one" which we have previously discussed: first we'll fight against the Russian system, and then, in a régime which does not close off the future as it does, we'll see. But the immediate order of the day either means nothing or it means that the enemy number two is not, for the moment, an enemy. The choice of an immediate order is a choice of a public, an ally, and in the last analysis a pact with all that is not Soviet. This public and this ally are no longer the masses. Then has Rousset stopped being a Marxist, even though he still (in a very discreet way, it is true) pays homage to Marxism in his articles? Lenin said that the true revolutionary is known precisely by the fact that he denounces exploitation and oppression in his own country. A short time ago Rousset explained that Marxism had to be re-examined, and he was right. Yet when we undertake a revision of Marxism, we have to know what part of it we are taking and what part we are giving up. Otherwise we end up, like so many American intellectuals, who have gone beyond everything, at political nothingness, and the nothingness is governmental. Does or does not Rousset still believe that the only political force we should seek the support of is that which by its condition is independent of national, financial, and economic interests such as the speculations of headquarters—that is, the masses? And does he still believe this force loses its class consciousness and solidarity if it is made to accept compromises with colonial and social oppression? Considering his recent campaign, we must answer no. But he should say so then. He ought to formulate his new position. It cannot help being inadmissible. It would at least stop being equivocal.[15]

It is easy to answer that one does not need so many principles to denounce an injustice, and that it was sufficient for Rousset to consult his conscience or his memories as a deported person to know what he had to do. It will be said that concentration camp experience, the absolute of horror, makes it the duty of the person who has lived it to look first of all at the country which prolongs it. But we are not the ones who are asking that deported persons be forgotten; Rousset is. By "concentrating his attack" upon the Soviet system, he holds Spanish prisoners and Greek deported persons cheaply. That concentration camp experience, when it has been lived through, permanently forbids us to support a system which maintains camps is well and good. It forbids us no less to make pacts with the system's adversaries, if they have camps. The truth is that even the experience of an absolute like the horror of concentration camps does not determine a policy. The days of life are not the days of death. When we return to life, well or badly, we start to reason again, we choose our loyalties; and in the eyes of those we leave we seem cold, we seem to forget. We always forget death when we live. Daix forgets the inmates of Russian concentration camps. Rousset is forgetting the deported Greeks who are dying right now in the islands, provisioned when it so pleases the sea and the government. So let us not have these men invoking their loyalty to former deported persons in order to justify forgetful policies. They can be loyal to themselves only by seeking a policy which does not require them to choose *their* deported persons.

(January, 1950)

15. Rousset is bringing suit for damages against *Les Lettres Françaises* before the Court of Justice. Yet he well knows from the example provided by the Kravchenko trial that such debates weld the two blocs together again. Is that what he is after?

4 / The Yalta Papers

MARXISM DOES NOT MINIMIZE the action of men. History's infrastructure, production, is still a network of human actions, and Marxism teaches that men make their history. It only adds that they do not make just any history; they operate in situations that they have not chosen and that leave only a limited number of solutions to their choice. For an observer situated at the world's end, the possible choices would even be classifiable into two series, one of which would go toward proletarian revolution, the other toward chaos. History is made of human actions and interactions transformed into an anonymous drama by the logic of situations. These, Marx said, are "relations between persons mediated by things," embodied in mechanisms in which the agent's intention is often unrecognizable. Men make their history even though they often do not know the history they are making. This conception leaves room for all causal agents, particularly that of diplomacy.

If we referred not only to Marx and Engels' formulas but to Marx's work itself, we would see that he set no limit to the immanent study of diplomacy, nor to the effectiveness of diplomatic action. He spent long days at the British Museum digging through diplomatic manuscripts concerning the Anglo-Russian collaboration of Peter the Great up to the end of the eighteenth century, and devoting a detailed study [1] to them in which economic and social history play only an unobtrusive role.

How could it be otherwise? Marxism did not want to be one of those "points of view," those "conceptions of the world," those "philosophies of history" which order reality about an arbitrarily chosen principle,

1. The *Revelations of 18th-Century Diplomatic History,* which has never been translated into Russian and only recently into French under the title of *La Russie et l'Europe.*

but the expression of reality—the formulation of a movement of history which animates ideas, literature, morality, philosophy, and politics at the same time as relationships of production. How could it limit its investigation to one sector of reality? How could it help being pluralistic? How could it help finding the same truth everywhere? There is nothing in principle which prevents us from having access to history through several entrances: they all lead to the same road junction.

So the "personal conceptions" of Roosevelt, Churchill, and Stalin at Yalta are not a stumbling-block for the Marxist philosophy of history. Certainly they bring improvisation, approximation, prejudices, and reveries out into the broad light of day. But if we take account of words suited to the occasion, crude tricks, and the feigned frivolity of table talk, these whims have something Shakespearian about them when we think that they inhabit such illustrious brains:

"Marshal Stalin remarked that he did not believe that the Labor Party could ever succeed in forming a government in England."

"Roosevelt declared that China would need three generations of education and training before it became a serious military factor."

"The English seemed to believe that the Americans ought to reestablish order in France, then turn political control over to the English."

"Marshal Stalin said he did not understand why [the Communists and the Kuomintang] did not get along, since they had to form a united front against Japan. He was of the opinion that Chiang-Kai-Shek should ensure control of it. In this connection he recalled that several years earlier the united front had existed. He did not understand why it had not been maintained."

If we assume—generously—that these remarks are Machiavellian, there must at least have been some vagueness in the mind of the interlocutor who took them seriously. But why should this invasion of psychology bother a Marxist historian? Confused ideas and fantasms are not an empire within history's empire; they are part of social dynamics, and it is still social dynamics which is in play through them. There is no fantasm, for a Marxist, which does not have a meaning, even though it is not a manifest meaning.

* * *

A philosophical, rigorous, and coherent Marxism admits the plurality of causes in history, deciphers the same dialectic in all of them, and integrates "personal conceptions" instead of excluding them. But to the extent it does so, it is transformed into another philosophy which is quite different than vulgar Marxism, and which Marx undoubtedly would not have wished to recognize as his own.

Suppose that "conceptions" and "ideologies" also have their inner logic which incorporates them into the general logic of history. The fact that Stalin, Roosevelt, and Churchill face-to-face thought, spoke, and decided as they did at Yalta—and that such and such samples of their ideologies were produced, confronted, and combined in that compromise—is an event which, as comprehensible as it may be *after it happened* in the dynamics of general history, is not deducible from that dynamics. For it is this event which makes the probable become the real. If men do not know the history they are making, they are not making true history. If everything counts in history, development is not really inevitable since it is borne by the contingencies of a "psychism" as well as by social dynamics.

It can only be said, as Max Weber said, that if a contributing circumstance happened to be lacking, the same outcome would have been brought about by other ways that the logic of the situation would have opened up—in other words, that the outcome had a high degree of probability. There are indeed cases in history in which the "imminent" event seems to create the conditions required to bring it about. But how can we affirm that this is always so and that history as a whole is a process of this type, which regulates itself according to a norm and corrects its aim like a radar-controlled gun?

If everything counts in history we can no longer say as Marxists do that *in the last analysis* historical logic always finds its ways, that it alone has a *decisive* role, and that it is the *truth* of history. The Bolsheviks practically admitted that opportunity knocks only once. Trotsky writes: "Lately again one could hear the opinion expressed that if we had not seized power in October, we would have taken possession of it two or three months later. A gross error! If we had not seized power in October, we never would have seized it." [2] Good. But then we must not say that the revolution is "ineluctable." We must choose between the revolution as action and as truth. The true Marxist drama is there, rather than between "superstructures" and "infrastructures," or between men and things.

In its classical period, bolshevism tried to surmount this drama and rescue action from pragmatism and chance by sticking to Lenin's rule that the correct line should be explainable to the proletarians of all lands and understood by them.

You should see (in *My Life*) how painstakingly Trotsky and Lenin, on the eve of Brest-Litovsk, weigh the inconveniences there might be for the Revolution in signing a peace treaty with German imperialism if the Western proletariats did not understand—how rigorously Trotsky, having proclaimed the principle of democratic peace without

2. Trotsky, *Lenin*, pp. 77–78.

annexations, and the peoples' right to self-determination, refuses to disguise the annexations imposed upon him by the Germans.

The motive of worldwide proletarian opinion seemed serious enough to Lenin that he agreed to support Trotsky's solution, which was to sign only under the compulsion of a German offensive, and which in the end cost the new Soviet State several provinces. During the negotiations, when the French and English offered their military aid against Germany to the Soviet government, Lenin got the Central Committee to accept the offer with the formula, "Accept the aid of the brigands of French imperialism against the German brigands." [3] So they were struggling against equivocation.

Stalin does not take so many precautions. "Marshal Stalin said he was prepared, in concert with the United States and Great Britain, to protect the rights of the smaller powers, but that he would never agree to submit any act whatsoever of no matter which of the great powers to the judgment of the smaller powers." The style has changed, and Stalin does not seem to have great difficulty adopting the tone of his interlocutors. It is this free and easy manner which is new. The difficulty existed before Stalin. It was even more evident, because the revolutionary idea was living. It is the cross of revolutionary politics.

(April, 1955)

3. Trotsky, *Ma Vie*, Rosmer, ed., p. 398.

5 / The Future of the Revolution

Everyone senses that something is happening in the history of communism. Is it only a question, on a grand scale, of one of those periods of relaxation which have always alternated with periods of hard-line policy? It is also possible that we have reached the moment when revolution and counter-revolution are going to stop being alternatives, as they have been since 1917, the moment when politics will no longer be reduced, as in the past ten years, to choosing between the U.S.S.R. and the rest of the world. Marxism has never excluded the mere fact of coexistence. But when it becomes a principle it cannot leave the two régimes intact. Their contradiction must cease to be an antagonism; each must admit the existence of the other and, to that extent, a sort of pluralism. It goes without saying that those on the bourgeois side are pluralists. Simone de Beauvoir writes energetically: "Truth is one, error is multiple, so it is understandable that the bourgeoisie is pluralistic." [1] So if communism becomes pluralistic it will be because it no longer conceives of itself as the single, total, and final truth. Have we reached this point?

Just what does the accession to power of Malenkov and then of Bulganin and Zhukov signify in the history of the Soviet Union? Malenkov said (a little too soon, but his successors have revived the theme) that the atomic bomb threatened socialist civilization as well as the other. Is the revolution henceforth subordinated to that prior condition of existence of not risking atomic war? Do atomic techniques, by introducing into the course of events a massive factor of destruction—and tomorrow, perhaps, of production—which is incommensurable with those the Marxist analysis took into account, make the antagonisms Marx described obsolete and lead Marxists for the first time to a pacificism *of principle*? We know nothing exact about it. But these

1. "La pensée de droite aujourd'hui," I, *Les Temps Modernes*, May, 1955.

questions are not so decisive. Whatever the weight of the disappearance of Stalin; the rise to power of another generation and different social forces; and finally, the development of atomic techniques in the U.S.S.R. and elsewhere; the new men of this new time could have continued to say, as they did for a few months, that socialism is invulnerable to atomic war. Since they are no longer saying it and are determined to come to terms with this danger, they must have learned in some way to confront revolution with external adversities. It is not just in a few sensational facts but in the régime's contacts with the outside and in its evolution that the origin of the new Soviet policy must be sought.

Now we are not totally lacking in information concerning this matter. Academic circumstances have made known to me a remarkable, as yet unpublished work by Benno Sarel on the history of East Germany since 1945.[2] Through the fissure of East Berlin we enter the internal life of the system. Of course the events in East Germany do not explain the new policy; they followed it and, in the short run, checked rather than unleashed it. But they constitute a privileged documentation of the Soviet régime's encounter with a land of long-standing political and workers' culture. They clarify the problem of relationships with the outside that the new policy is trying to face up to, and so perhaps give that policy's significance in the history of the Russian revolution.

[I]

Before we consider the facts, let us ask ourselves how we can recognize where a Marxist revolution stands. The essence of revolutionary policy lies in the relationship between the proletariat and the Party. The proletariat is the negation and the living criticism of capitalism. But the historical working of revolution cannot be the simple, direct, *immediate* expression of the proletariat's thoughts or will. The proletariat becomes an historical factor capable of revolutionizing existing society and giving life to a new one only if the Party corrects its "spontaneous" struggle, clarifies it, and develops it into political struggle, carrying it to the level of the social whole it must measure itself against. The proletariat is ready for a universal role because it

2. *Classe ouvrière et nouveaux rapports de production dans les entreprises propriétés du peuple de la République démocratique allemande (d'après les sources officielles).* The author has kindly allowed me to take account of his analyses and the facts he has assembled—keeping, of course, the over-all interpretation he intends to give of them.

has no possessions, no interests, and almost no positive traits: it is as it were natural to it not to be a sect or band, and to take up the creation of society again from its foundations. It is *in itself* revolution. But it does not know it to begin with, and knows neither the means, the way, the episodes, nor the institutions through which what Marx called "the secret of its existence" will be expressed. It is the Party which transforms its rebellion into positive, long-term action. In philosophical terms, the Party goes beyond the proletariat's rebellion, realizing it by destroying it as immediate rebellion. It is the negation of that negation or, in other words, the mediation of it—it makes the class which denies become a class which founds and, in the end, a classless society. This philosophical language is far from being superfluous. It is like the algebraic formula of revolution; it gives the abstract contour of it in rigorous form, and is translated into practice in the most precise way. There will be revolution if the Party educates the proletariat while the proletariat gives life to the Party. An authoritarian apparatus unresponsive to the vital surging of the proletariat and a Party submissive to its every eddy are equally excluded.

Revolutionary action is based upon the two principles that in the last instance *the Party is always right*, and that in the last analysis *one is never right in opposition to the proletariat*. In order to observe these two principles *simultaneously*, revolutionary action must be a relationship of exchange between the Party and the proletariat. There must be a Party which accepts the proletarians' criticism as long as it does not set itself up as a second power, clique, or group; and there must be a proletariat which criticizes the Party, but loyally and fraternally as its own political expression, not as another person and a rival. In a word, there must be a criticism which is criticism of itself or autocriticism. We can understand the state a revolution is in, what point in its history it has reached, and where it is going by examining how things stand in terms of the *mediation* whose formula we just recalled. It is here that the facts brought together by Sarel are precious. They show beyond doubt that East German society is far from being homogeneous, and its relationships of production harmonious. Even in enterprises which are "the property of the people," differences of productive status suffice to create a compartmentation, tensions, alliances, and overturning of alliances. Herein lies a whole unofficial history of the régime, in respect to which the Party seems rather like an instance of external control. These confirmations are new only for those who develop a wholly theoretical idea of revolution and popular democracy. But due to a lack of sufficient information we are almost all in this situation, and the principle merit of a work like Sarel's is to raise the questions as they are raised on the spot.

1. *The managers*

To begin with, industrial managers are relatively autonomous. At the same time the principle of workers' co-management was laid down, it was specified that the new administration, "insofar as it represents the people . . . has the task of establishing plans." [3] The workers' initiative could consist only in finding the best means of seconding the management's projects. "Let's finally get used to the idea," the *Neues Deutschland* of March 11, 1950 writes impatiently, "that the responsibility for norms of production rests with management. . . . The unions' task is to equip workers with a new consciousness and good professional qualifications." Now only a small proportion of the new managers are former workers. According to the figures given by Ulbricht in 1947,[4] we count among them for the whole zone 21.7% workers, 30.7% employees, 17.8% engineers, 23.6% merchants, and 6.2% former managers. Beginning in 1951–52 the accession of workers to business management was further slowed down.

Managers are Party members. It nevertheless happens that "management falsifies balances, hides its profits, insists upon more raw materials than it needs. . . . It has its own investment plan" [5]—so much so that an order of July, 1949, will establish in enterprises which are the people's property a chief accountant who supervises the enterprise's management, and after June, 1953, the Party business committee's preponderance over management will be written into the laws of the Party.

The relative autonomy of managers sometimes works to the advantage of the workers against the Party. At the meeting of the nationalized Brandenburg works held on August 12, 1949, the managers opposed the raising of norms proposed by the activists. At other times the line of cleavage is drawn between workers and management.

"In the industrial sector one always finds 'gentlemen' from business management, ward management, or some other place who discuss among themselves; those who are not used to speaking cannot participate in the discussion. . . . Sometimes managerial comrades are considered by their own comrades as a sort of superior authority which cannot be safely and openly frequented. They think of the proverb: Don't go unless you're called." [6]

The social distance is underlined by the difference in salary, which for a big manager can reach fifteen thousand marks per month.

3. *Neuaufbau der deutschen Wirtschaft* (Berlin, 1946), p. 10.
4. Protocols of the 2nd *Parteitages* (Berlin, 1947), p. 321.
5. Benno Sarel, in the work cited, pp. 66 and 67, refers to *Volksbetrieb*, January, 1949, July, 1950; *Tägliche Rundschau*, March 31, 1949, February 25, 1950; etc.
6. *Neues Deutschland*, August 13, 1949.

2. *The technicians*

THE ANTAGONISM between workers and technicians becomes worse beginning with the years 1951–52, that is, at the beginning of planning. At this time it is joined to the antagonism between workers and management; the *old technicians*, reticent to begin with, often being rallied to the régime by planning. On April 25, 1951, the Central Committee prescribes the establishment of individual contracts for the technical *intelligenzia* and declares war upon egalitarianism.[7] In December, 1951, the Confederal Secretariat demands *proper* restaurants and clubs for the *intelligenzia*.[8] It is at about this time that the term *intelligenzler* is extended to all the factory managers. Workers say, "We're heading toward training a class of *intelligenzler* and activists." [9] A worker in a factory at Stralsund speaks of a *dictatorship of the intelligenzia*.[10] At Christmas, 1951, four Party members who are workers in the naval yards at Warnemünde sabotage the celebration reserved for the *intelligenzler* of their firm by cutting the electric cable which serviced the ballroom.[11] A worker in an industrial union meeting says, "They want us to establish friendly relationships with the intelligenzia. Then why segregate us at mealtimes?" [12] We are not presenting these remarks and minor incidents as *the truth about* East Germany. But the fact that they have appeared in the official press suffices to show that they are not unthinkable.

3. *The workers' élite*

FROM 1949 on an activist sometimes earns a thousand marks per month in the mines or in metallurgy, that is, six times more than the lowest paid of his comrades. The significant participation of women and young workers in the activist movement,[13] and the adult workers' *stubborn* opposition [14]—in railroads, for example—to the hiring of women, clearly seem to show that in the beginning activism succeeds only among the least mature elements of the working class. The Party journal, *Neuer Weg*, of December, 1950, describes a Thuringian spinning-mill where there are only twenty-two women among

7. *Dokumente des S.E.D.*, T. III, p. 479.
8. *Neues Deutschland*, December 22, 1951.
9. *Ibid.*, June 4, 1952.
10. *Ibid.*, July 31, 1952.
11. *Ibid.*, May 4, 1952.
12. *Ibid.*
13. *Informationsmaterial für Gewerkschaftsfunktionäre*, August, 1949. Berlin F.D.G.B.
14. *Neues Deutschland*, January 20, 1950.

one hundred and eighty Party members, but where, on the other hand, the female workers constitute the majority of activists.[15]

Even if the advantages given to Stakhanovites are not taken into account, the wage differential has been accentuated since the beginning of planning.[16] "In 1950, the hourly wages of workers are scaled from the maximum of 1.95 marks in coal mines to the minimum of 0.59 marks in the toy industry." [17]

In the same branch, the difference between categories I and VIII is stabilized at about 100%.

This salary scale, set by administrative channels, means that planning is tied to a workers' élite and recruits, so to speak, *its* proletariat. This is also the meaning of the competitive movement which develops at the same time. Alexander Stark writes in August 1949: "Competitions were ordered from above. . . . The significance of competition has been little discussed in the enterprises themselves. Among our responsible officials there are many who were afraid to discuss with the workers. It was more convenient for them, the union management of enterprise, to reach an agreement with another union management about a pretended competition instead of mobilizing their colleagues and thus developing a truly competitive movement." [18]

In March 1950, H. Warnke says: ". . . We ought to overcome the undeniable stagnation of the competitive movement. . . . Competitions between enterprises can do nothing but crown our efforts when, at the base, in the shops, there is a really serious mass movement for competition within the enterprise itself [Cries: That's right!]." [19]

At the 1950 union meeting, the rector of the main union school, Duncker, a seventy-eight-year-old man, "made an interruption which recalled the seriousness and ideological richness of the old German labor movement: '. . . It is important for us,' he said, 'that it be a matter above all of a new competition, distinct from the "competition" of an outmoded era—which unfortunately is not outmoded. . . . It seems that from a shortsighted spirit of competition, an individualistic spirit of competition, there may develop an egotism which subsequently, as business egotism, leads to keeping . . . methods of production a business secret.' " [20] This interruption was not followed by any reply.

15. B. Sarel, *op. cit.*, p. 80.

16. The salary spread decreases after 1953.

17. B. Sarel, p. 109. Unequal wages in different branches of industry is a means of steering manual workers toward the essential sectors of the economy.

18. *Berliner Beschlüsse*.

19. *Ibid.*, p. 8.

20. *Ibid.*, p. 75.

It is in relation to the establishment of norms that workers' resistance to planning from above and to the role of tailor-made proletariat played by activists clearly appears. At the same time that a *movement for the self-establishment of norms* develops, and the activists decide to raise their norms themselves each time it is possible (which often earns them the titles of *norm-breakers, wage-spoilers,* and *scabs*), a *center for technically-based norms* is created which is designed to train timekeepers. The self-establishment of norms led to abuses, the workers setting them too low and thus giving themselves bonus increases for a mediocre production—a procedure known as *Normenschaukelei.* Now timekeepers had operated in Germany under Hitler; often the same men were seen to reappear in the shop, and rationalization was carried out according to the same principles, which have even been abandoned by Taylorism itself: "Measurement of 'basic times' of each gesture in a cycle of movements, which makes labor stereotyped and destroys the living, individual relationship which ought to be established between man and machine." [21]

It is true that until 1951 the "technical," "objective," or "scientific" determination of norms was presented only as an argument, by the same title as the activists' example. Workers were invited to approve the norms in a union meeting. But the meeting "was presided over by the representative of a higher committee. . . . The workers who were not used to public speaking interrupted only from their seats. . . . At voting time, the president first asked those opposed to raise their hands." [22] Establishing norms became an *ideological* [23] or political affair. In 1951, authoritarian raising of norms by timekeeping takes precedence over self-establishment of norms. In 1952, there is a return to voluntary raising of norms. We know that the June, 1953, uprising came about when the authorities wanted to apply new norms to Stalinallee building-trades workers in an authoritarian way. Whether we appeal to the "subjective" argument of political loyalty or to the "objective" constraint of timekeeping, in both cases we are not guided by the demands of workers' labor, and in both cases it is evident that the proletariat refuses.

4. *The proletariat and its organizations*

GIVEN THIS SOCIAL CLEAVAGE and these tensions, we may presume that the proletariat is not the moving force of the political and union apparatus, which is rather the scene of a social struggle. As a

21. B. Sarel, pp. 121–22.
22. *Ibid.*, p. 124.
23. *Neues Deutschland,* June 8, 1949.

matter of fact, Sarel shows how the union representatives of the rank and file (sometimes even those of the Party) hold back the campaign for raising norms. There are "Party enterprise groups who job-contract norms as low as possible." [24] A certain union representative declares: "I am against Stakhanovism. We workers know that capitalism also gave us the possibility of increasing the productivity of labor, but then it stuck us with higher norms." [25]

By changing labor teams into brigades, the authorities try to tie the working class more closely to production and planning. But the brigade leader in turn (appointed by management with his comrades' approval) transmits at least as much union pressure on management as "pressure from above" on workers. In 1951 the *collective agreements of industry* are submitted for discussion to the brigades and unions. The discussions are interminable: "On October 14," Sarel writes, "the main newspaper of the Party publishes a two-page article of autocriticism on the question of industrial agreements. The article names those immediately responsible for the tension reigning in the factories—the union leaders. After having imposed the agreements in a dictatorial way, the author of the article confirms, these leaders are now afraid to appear before the workers. When they do appear, they 'cringe like timid orphans taking care not to break anything.' " [26]

Will the unions be the scapegoat, and the crisis come to an end at their expense? No. In a second episode, it is the unions which criticize the Party. "The united union Counsel in turn publishes (10/26/1951) a communiqué in which it assumes its share of responsibility, but counter-attacks by proving that in a whole series of factories the Party leaders also behaved in an authoritarian or deviationist manner in supporting resistance to the agreements—indeed, directing it." [27] "In the Leuna factory, the Zeitz, the Karl Marx Babelsberg and elsewhere . . . there were Party members who, during the discussion, collected signatures against the agreement and for the withdrawal of union management of industry. In the Mannesman factory at Leipzig the Party secretary protests against the branch collective agreement. And unfortunately it is not a matter of isolated cases. . . . Many members of union industrial committees elected the preceding year were no longer at their duties (at the time the agreements were made). They had been dismissed from their duties by the management of the industrial Party group . . . and replaced by other comrades without any election having been held. . . . These non-elected members of

24. *Neuer Weg*, July–September, 1949.
25. *Täglische Rundschau*, June 3, 1949.
26. *Neues Deutschland*, October 14, 1951.
27. B. Sarel, p. 158.

union industrial managements showed themselves totally incapable of convincing the workers. . . . They are afraid to appear before the personnel, who could ask them where they come from. It is particularly these union industrial managements who spent their time imposing the agreements by bureaucratic means. . . ." [28]

The polemic closes with a communiqué from the political bureau which reprimands the unions without announcing a purge. A part of the permanent union officials in the higher echelons are simply sent, still as permanent officials, to the shop committees. These mutual accusations, which implicate everyone, exonerate each a little. Yet there is no need to suppose that they are the result of a deliberate plan, and we must not think that we have only the parody of a polemic here. No. In a society which is simultaneously authoritarian and of the people, tensions are not factitious but adopt—and spontaneously too—the "responsible" language of autocriticism or brotherly correction. Opposed entreaties are united in error and innocence, since both had to get the movement coming from above accepted by the masses and did not succeed.

[2]

THESE FEW FACTS allow us to get a glimpse of the nature of the régime and the present state of the revolution. From the verified existence of tensions and contradictions in a society like East Germany's, the anti-Communist polemicists—and certain Marxists as well—conclude that the system is a new exploitation of the proletariat. As we see it—and Sarel seems to be of the same opinion—neither in intention and "subjectively" nor in its foreseeable results and "objectively" can the system *be defined* as a levy on the labor of all for the profit of a few. Levies exist; but if they result in a development of production, that accrued production will be distributed, if not in an egalitarian fashion at least to the benefit of the proletariat, since there is no possibility of accumulation by a private social power. With the suppression of private ownership of means of production, the democratic principle of the régime remains: it is still the proletariat the Party appeals to. It is an exception for it to use sheer coercion. Even when it intervenes arbitrarily in opposition to union entreaties, it is elections it has to come back to in order to finish the job. Everything it does to circumvent the proletariat turns into means for the proletariat to put pressure on it. All the information Sarel brings together is

28. *Neues Deutschland,* October 26, 1951.

taken from the official press and publications. As he profoundly says, the régime entails *a liberalism "sui generis."* [29] At the very moment the activist movement, the competitive movement, and piece-work labor separate this proletariat that the régime creates in its own image from the masses, there is concern for those without a party. In 1949 the percentage of workers admitted to vacation centers had been only 29%. It is 51% in 1951. One hundred thousand persons in 1948, three hundred and seventy-five thousand in 1951, and five hundred thousand in 1952 spend their vacation in vacation centers.[30] *The tendency to put the mass of those without party under guardianship* is expressly fought against.[31] So this means that this tendency exists. But it also means that it cannot exist officially.

The system is torn between its two principles (the Party is always right and no one can be right in opposition to the proletariat) because the exchange between Party and proletariat, and the revolutionary mediation, have not functioned. It is the social form which appears when the revolution does not "catch on." The more imperiously the Party insists that it is identical with the proletariat, the more the proletariat refuses to recognize it. We could almost say its power and privileges are the form proletarian revolution takes when it is challenged by the proletariat. Even then, they are thus never guaranteed by divine right. The régime has no single essence; it exists wholly in its oscillation between its two principles. At times it envisions imposing discipline by all possible means; at times it comes back to consultation and discussion. The régime would fall apart if it followed one of the two tendencies all the way through. Zigzag or spiral movement is its law. It has no other means of enduring.

It does not suffice to say that its policies are contradictory; in truth there is not even a contradiction between the phases of relaxation and tension. When mouths open, when the régime moves to autocriticism, this "liberalization" once again cements the unity of the proletariat and the Party—it reintegrates the proletariat, shapes it up, and readies it for a new period of "hard-line" policies. Inversely, purging is rarely sheer repression: it sets aside the representatives of certain resistances, but the resistances they represent are taken into account—and their policies are frequently even adopted. This is an essential ambiguity in which liberty profits from authority, repression authenticates the resistances it represses, criticism is a winning over, and condemnation a justification. All is expressed, but every expression is indirect, reversed, and tacit. Truth itself takes on an air of falseness because there is

29. B. Sarel, p. 71.
30. *Ibid.*, p. 155.
31. *Neues Deutschland*, March 25, 1950.

always an awareness of the imminent *other truth* behind it, and lies themselves evoke what the régime ought to have said and would like to be.

In 1950 and 1951, the *Neues Deutschland* writes: "What the Party says is true," then, "the Party is always right," and finally, "Only what the Party says is true." [32] On June 21, 1953, right after the rebellion, the Central Committee of the Party adopts a resolution which states: "When the working masses do not understand the Party, it is not they who are guilty but the Party." [33] And a little later Grotewohl declares before the workers of the Karl Liebknecht factory: "The Party no longer enjoys the love and total attachment of the great masses of laborers. It is we ourselves who are guilty of this. . . . The Party has the duty to put an end to its errors—to these tendencies to command the masses . . . and consider them subordinates—in a radical fashion." [34] The worker Bremse, of Siemens-Plania, declares to Rudolf Herrnstadt, member of the Central Committee and editor-in-chief of the *Neues Deutschland:* "I am proud of June 17. On June 17 the workers showed that they are a force, that they have a will." [35] But this is not all: on July 24 Herrnstadt is expelled from the Central Committee and Grotewohl asks that the *"spirit of penitence"* in the Party be brought to an end. As *No Exit* says, they "go on."

What can the Party be reproached with? What would they have it do? All tendencies are represented in it; all difficulties expressed. ". . . Between Party and class," Ulbricht says, "there is almost no difference, almost no line. All the arguments current among workers or laborers may be heard in the meetings of Party members or those responsible to the Party. . . . The Party is experiencing the same hesitations as the working class or the laborers." [36] It discusses honestly and decides the best it can. What are the workers waiting for in order to recognize themselves in it? They are waiting for signs: an increase in production which is not obtained by Taylorism, competition, and increased affliction; a manifestation of *peoples' property* in the modes of labor. It is easier after all for the Party to believe it is the proletariat than for the proletariat to hypostasize itself into the Party.

Certainly the régime is irrefutable: it can always be said that the antagonisms and the secession of adult workers are temporary, and that a new generation (trained by the régime) will recognize itself in the system. Above all it can be said if one lives in the future like the

32. *Ibid.*, March 17, 1950; B. Sarel, pp. 143–44.

33. *Ibid.*, June 23, 1953.

34. East Berlin Radio, June 23, 1953. B. Sarel points out (p. 182) that the press published only excerpts from Grotewohl's speech.

35. *Neues Deutschland*, June 26, 1953.

36. *Ibid.*, August 22, 1948.

leaders. If one has only one's present, like the rest, one can always answer that a proletariat in the image of the régime will be a minority; since by definition it is distinguished from the majority by the *special privileges* granted it, and making women and youngsters work is a classic expedient of exploitative societies. The régime is irrefutable only because it is also indemonstrable. The mediation of the proletariat and the Party is accomplished only in the thought of the leaders, the faith of the young, and the opportunism of the élite. An industrial manager cries out: "Colleagues, the spinning-mill is now the property of the people. . . . It should be an honor for you to serve the German fatherland by your labor!" The author adds: "Laughter ran around the hall. Truly patriotic speeches were alien to the majority of workers, and above all to the men." [37] That is because they are not shown their needs and wills translated into visible institutions. It is because they are asked to believe that the enterprise belongs to them by nominal definition, since it no longer belongs to anyone—that no trace of rivalry remains in competition, or of Taylorism in *technically based norms*. Instead of mediation, they are offered transubstantiation.

So it is no more correct to speak of a "proletarian" régime than of an "exploitative" régime. Those who are creating the régime and projecting a future through it may in good faith think of socialism. Those who tolerate it without creating it, and thus do not have the same motives for giving it an absolute and abstract adherence, do not see (unless it be ideologically) a proletarian civilization appearing. Sauvy [38] has repeatedly written that there can be no economic appraisal of communism and its returns; because wherever it "catches on" it banks on unlimited self-sacrifice, increased affliction, and progress in production even without technical progress (the East German press has defended this thesis), and that consequently progress in production cannot be credited to the relationships of production established by communism—it arises from heroism. Strictly speaking, the system cannot be judged; people want it or they do not; in its best respects it is the will to bring into being by force a mediation which has not taken place. In this respect it is certainly a novelty, but not the revolution whose theory was constructed by Marxism—production freed of its antagonisms by the suppression of capitalistic relationships of production. There is no doubt that the system assures a rapid development of new countries. The returns decrease when, as in Germany, it encounters an old proletariat which makes comparisons, asks for proofs, and does not identify itself with the venture from the start, because it has

37. *Helden der Arbeit* (Berlin, Kultur und Fortschritt, 1951), p. 63.

38. Alfred Sauvy, French political economist and demographer, holder of the Chair of Social Demography at the Collège de France.—Trans.

seen others. Sarel borrows from *The Times Review of Industry* a table of industrial production in Czechoslovakia, Poland, and East Germany based upon official data. It is clearly evident from it that the system is more suitable to underdeveloped countries.[39] Is it not possible that the experience of the U.S.S.R. beyond its borders has taught it that it must know when to stop and take account of the devil?

[3]

THE EASING OF TENSIONS now being effected by the U.S.S.R. is not one of these equivocal episodes which set the stage for taking things in hand again. An easing of tensions which admits that Tito is right could hardly bring the Yugoslav Party back to discipline. It is a new and quite important fact that Malenkov, although repudiated on the question of atomic war, has not been eliminated. So one can have outstripped the Party on the way toward truth without being a threat to the régime? So one can be different without being an enemy? Something is no longer working in the combination of repression and autocriticism we have described. Certainly, the decompression is progressive; it too has its pauses, its jolts, its ambiguities, but this time it seems irreversible. In addition, the tactical easings of tension concerned Socialist or Christian workers. There has never been a question up to now of an easing of tension toward capitalism. For the first time the revolutionary system is admitting that it does not cover all history. Perhaps the reason is that in going beyond its borders, and especially in Germany, it has learned to take account of something else. Such in any case is the meaning the new politics takes on in the light of the German episode.

What would the outlook be in this case? Sarel very soberly points out a path for the future, and he does so in the Marxist fashion. The proletariat is there, learning and growing through all its experiences. Turning back against those in power the attempts they are making to capture it, the proletariat, in spite of appearances, is getting closer to managing the economy. Through disappointments and frustrations, it is being trained to really play the role of managerial class, either by means of a new revolutionary push or even perhaps through the work-

39. Here is the table (in thousands of dollars based on 1938 prices):

	1938	1947	1948	1949
Poland	711	739	946	1180
Czechoslovakia	875	761	893	964
East Germany	2162	1020	1280	1500

ings of the inner dynamics of the system. Sarel still thinks that once private property is suppressed the proletarian future is the order of the day. It is hidden by privileges and contradictions, but it is present in the social struggle that the proletariat is waging.

This means leaving unexplained—or explaining by extremely general and vague causes—the existence of the contradictions so well described by the same author. If the proletarian revolution in Russia has been able to move to planning and to organize production only by making a place for a "managerial layer," perhaps it is also because planning from below, "dictatorship propelled from below," in short the proletarian society in which proletariat and Party are one, are fantasms—because there can be no mediation by dictatorship, no mediating dictatorship, no authoritarian historical creation. After having described so well what distinguishes a peoples' democracy from a proletarian revolution, how can Sarel avoid asking himself why proletarian revolution ends up in peoples' democracies? How can he put the proletarian revolution in their future when it is in their past? It is more probable that the peoples' democracies, and the U.S.S.R. itself, are seeking to harmonize their relationships of production not by a new revolutionary effort but precisely by easing tensions, by satisfying consumer needs, and by some new and prudent modality of "formal democracy"—by some appeal to the mystifications of ideology.

What can be more responsibly evaluated is the incidence which the easing of tension has had upon the non-Communist countries. For the moment the policy of the Western parties (which is, moreover, benumbed) seems dominated by the exigencies of the international easing of tensions. In France there is verbal opposition to the established government; but the Moroccan Party is going to propose a plan of pacification to the French Resident, and the C.G.T. is uniting its efforts with those of the government in order to reestablish calm at Saint-Nazaire. Under penalty of internal crisis, the Western parties will not long be able to sacrifice everything to the international easing of tensions. They will undoubtedly be led to define a policy of their own, even if the U.S.S.R. does not satisfy their desires by solemnly granting them their independence. The Vlahovitch study which appeared at Belgrade, proposing the definitive dissolution of the Cominform and the creation of a new International without disciplinary ties, can hardly be ascribed to the Soviets. It compromises them at least a little after the Soviet ministers' visit to Belgrade.

If this is something other than a reverie, the new Soviet policy would not be a chapter in the history of the proletarian revolution but the decision to limit the "dictatorship of the proletariat" to its existing geographic climate, the recognition of other forms of social struggle for the rest of the world, and the invitation to define or invent them without taking the peoples' democracies as models. Then it would be seen that the Left is not a hollow term, as revolutionary and counter-revolutionary thinkers say with one voice. What embraces the life of revolutionary countries is not the civilizing force of a class but the clenched will of an "élite." In order to change the proletarians' needs, suffering, and exploitation into a civilization, we should not count on a dictatorship established in their name but on their claims rendered in their immediate virulence, and on what they will demand from the new techniques men are about to seize upon.

(August, 1955)

6 / On De-Stalinization

"The big word in fashion is de-Stalinization."
Marcel Servin
(*L'Humanité,* 12/11/56)

Even had it been up to us, we ought not to have responded to the Hungarian intellectuals' appeal with war. But we owe them much more than a "yes," a signature, and a momentary compassion. Intellectuals are not here to unite; they are here, if they can, to cast light. The homage we owe to the Hungarians is to understand their sacrifice and explain it for all to hear, so that it may not have been in vain.

Thus disciplined Communists—disciplined to the point of the most painful autocriticisms and the worst invective (I am thinking, for example, of Lukacs)—put their trust in Nagy who, agreeing to side with the anti-Communists, was to seize upon the "bourgeois" tribunal of the U. N., consent to free elections, and denounce the Warsaw pact. Those who followed Nagy solemnly repudiated the principle that there must never be an appeal made to outsiders in struggles between Communists. This means that there is no longer any proletarian solidarity and literally no more communism when a "Communist" power has its whole proletariat against it and crushes it by military means. Appealing to the U. N. is the right and proper response to military intervention: both mark a crisis of communism which goes to the heart of the system. These Hungarian Communists did not risk their political honor and their lives on a misunderstanding or in a trap. They were not scatterbrained or unlucky men. We do not have the moral right to hail them if we pass over in silence their decision, which ratified the end of the Communist pact, destroyed by military intervention.

Now in all the recently published "leftist" protests (the only ones I am considering here), Soviet "socialism" is tacitly exonerated. There is talk of the "errors" of Khrushchev, who launched de-Stalinization in too conspicuous a fashion, and of the "mistake" of Geroe, who called for the Russians. Others, presenting the events in Hungary as a regrettable incidence of "inequality of development," would have it that the satellites are insisting upon consumer goods they cannot yet produce, while the Russian people, who have created their heavy industry and could produce them, are not asking for them. The Budapest repression becomes a trifle in the majestic history of the "socialist" economy. It is understood or said that *better* tactics and *better* planning would have avoided all this and will avoid it in the future.

As if the problem were not total, just as the uprising was. These learned puerilities result in hiding a crisis in which everything is in question; they presuppose the very ideology which is being challenged by the event. In sum, the insurgents of Budapest died in a doubtful cause; we who are not dead can, thank God, take the blunders, errors, and mistakes of unequal development into consideration, and keep our confidence in Soviet "socialism" more or less unshaken.

The Hungarian Communists' insurrection means that Stalinism has reached the socialist essence of the régime, and that de-Stalinization is not a minor alteration or tactical change in the system but a radical transformation in which it is risking its life yet which it must bring about if it is to become honorable again. Going back to de-Stalinization and showing its complete meaning without holding anything back is the only homage from the Left which is acceptable to the insurgents. We know that it is too soon to say as historians *what it is*. It cannot be demonstrated as a theorem that the repression of Budapest is the senile disorder of communism. But it can be proved that no one of its principles comes out of it unscathed, that the crisis spares no one, and that de-Stalinization is nothing if it is not the radical reform of a "system"—the word was used by Togliatti and is taken up again by Gomulka and by Tito—and its challenge to itself. As a matter of fact, these observations need no proof; all that was required to establish their truth was a close enough look at the facts of these last few months. We just want to emphasize a few of them, which are already strangely forgotten.

It is not Khrushchev who is frivolous, it is our intellectuals who do not read the texts, or who stick to those in the daily press. If they consulted the documents published by the French Communist Party [1] —or at least the remarkable analysis Claude Lefort [2] gives of them [3]—

1. *Les Cahiers du Communisme*, March, 1956, and the collection they published under the title, *XXe Congrès du parti communiste de l'U.S.*

2. Friend of Merleau-Ponty who has written an account of Merleau-Ponty's later philosophy in the memorial edition of *Les Temps Modernes*, nos. 184–85 (1961).—Trans.

3. *Socialisme ou barbarie*, July–September, 1956, no. 19, especially pp. 43–72. The quotations which follow are taken from Lefort.

they would see that we may speak today of a veritable criticism of the régime. Not only in Khrushchev's speech but in those of Bulganin, Suslov, and Malenkov, the description of the U.S.S.R.'s economic and political life is such that it challenges the system's two fundamental principles: that of the dictatorship of the proletariat and that of authoritarian planning, which is the modern form of the first.

It was believed that authoritarian planning had the merit of organizing what is elsewhere left to destiny, that is to special interests; and that wages, for example, were established in a planned economy according to needs, imperatives of production, and quantity of consumer goods. Here is what Khrushchev thinks about it:

"It must be said . . . that much disorder and confusion is evident in the wage-price system. . . . It is frequently the case that wages are made uniform. But it is also the case that the same work in different enterprises and even within the framework of a single one is paid for at a different rate. . . . Thus we are faced with an important political and economic task: regulation of remuneration for labor." [4]

It was believed that in a planned economy the quantity and rhythm of labor were set according to the necessities of a production which was estimated in advance, thought about, and carefully supervised. Bulganin explains that the official norms are on the contrary a means of getting around these necessities and somehow acceding to the wage-earners' needs:

"Setting lowered norms, and as a consequence exceeding them considerably, is the source of a deceptive appearance of prosperity in enterprise, and makes workers, technicians, and engineers less attentive to a real increase in the productivity of labor. At bottom, norms are presently defined not by the level of technics and organization of labor but by the desire to adapt them to a particular level of wages." [5] Thus the real cost of production has no relationship to the estimated cost and productivity is not managed. All this should certainly come out somewhere in the end: a moment arrives when the gap between will and results is flagrant. Then the pressure of facts is so strong that the system gives up keeping accounts: "If we examine," Khrushchev says, "how such and such a region, district, kolkhose, or sovkhose fulfills its socialist commitments, we shall see that words do not correspond to deeds. Furthermore, do we generally examine these commitments? No; we usually do not. No one is responsible, morally or materially, for the failure to carry out commitments." [6]

As approximate as it is, authoritarian planning is creative when it

4. *Les Cahiers du Communisme*, p. 318.
5. *XXe Congrès*, p. 164.
6. *Les Cahiers du Communisme*, p. 347.

works upon docile manpower in an underdeveloped country; and we know well enough what a power the U.S.S.R. has become. The question does not lie in planning. It lies in the fact that with the XXth Congress, the Soviet rulers no longer hide from a more advanced populace the fact that authoritarian planning does not suffice to manage the economy. After having by heroic means founded its own industry without appealing to capital, the régime feels the need to go from "planning" to the balance-sheet, from sheer authority to understanding, from heroism to reason. The XXth Congress is an appeal to truth and to an awareness born of the necessities of the Russian economy, and not a daring improvisation suggested by the difficulties of the satellites.

When the Congress moves to political criticism, the same separation of the official from the real appears, and this time at the heart of the régime. The dictatorship should be animated by the proletariat, or—since the proletariat cannot act in history without an apparatus which reinterprets its mission at each moment—the proletariat should at least recognize itself in its Party. According to the XXth Congress, the Party exists on the fringe of real life and society, the understanding it tries to gain of them through information and statistics is useless, and its action insignificant. Khrushchev declares: "The qualified workers in the Party apparatus are less concerned with organizing than with collecting all sorts of information and statistics, which, moreover, are in most cases useless. That is why all too often the Party apparatus turns in the void." [7] Here is how Suslov describes the activity of a kolkhose organizational secretary: "His desk and all his shelves are littered with dossiers and notebooks. He keeps books in which he enters the work of Party groups, the work among women, the work with young Communists, the aid given to the organization of the Komsomol, the requests and complaints, the missions entrusted to Communists, and the educational work of the Party and the art lovers' circle. There are dossiers bearing the inscription, 'Mural Newspapers,' 'Bulletins,' 'Emulation in Stock-breeding,' 'Emulation in Agriculture,' and 'Friends of Tree-planting.' The work of propagandists is entered in three notebooks: 'Register of Propagandists' Work,' 'Mass Political Work,' and 'Daily Missions Entrusted to Propagandists.' Imagine how much time is required to fill out all these official forms which inevitably cut into vital organizational work. It is to be remarked at the same time that in the kolkhose no educational work among the milkmaids and shepherds is provided. The farms are not mechanized; there is no schedule and there are no rations set up for the stock. The productivity of stock-farming is extremely low. The average milk per cow provided annually is 484 liters. As for the secretary's dossiers, they have not provided any

7. *Ibid.*, p. 345.

milk. In this respect they have shown themselves to be absolutely sterile."[8] The Congress laughs and applauds, the record indicates at this point. The incomparable pleasure of hearing what has long been known without being said finally stated in public.

Khrushchev extends these remarks to all political cadres: "At first sight," he says, "they seem very active; and they do in fact work very much, but all their activity is absolutely sterile. They sit in meetings till dawn, they gallop in kolkhoses, lecture the laggards, hold conferences and give speeches full of commonplaces and (as a general rule) drawn up beforehand, which call upon men to 'show themselves equal to,' 'overcome all difficulties,' 'effect a turning-point,' 'be worthy of confidence,' etc. But a manager of this sort may be as zealous as he likes; at year's end there is no improvement. As they say, 'he did his best,' which did not keep him from staying stuck like a log."[9]

In a word, the managers are "busy do-nothings." And it is not a question of human failings. The inefficiency is ideological: "Our ideological work," Suslov says, "is in good part useless; for it is limited to taking up the same well-known formulas and theses again, and at times it educates commentators and dogmatists cut off from life."[10] The degeneration of ideology is observable on all levels. The economists, Khrushchev says, ". . . *do not participate in the study of essential questions of industrial and agricultural development during the conferences held by the C.C. of the C.P.S.U. This means that our economic institutes and their collaborators have been fundamentally detached from the practice of Communistic edification.*"[11] (There is perhaps some injustice here: is it not the political apparatus which has confined the economists to technical tasks? And if it is only today discovering the size of the economy, is that the economists' fault?) Mikoyan is even harder on the philosophers: "*A few words ought to have been addressed to our philosophers. Even so, they ought to understand themselves that their situation is scarcely more brilliant, and that they are even more in arrears in the eyes of the Party than the historians and the economists.*"[12]

In sum, it is a question of knowing whether the "planned" economy can become a planned economy, and the dictatorship of the proletariat make itself understood to the proletariat instead of humming uselessly in its ears—whether appearance, which has fallen away from reality, can rejoin it. The XXth Congress is the denunciation of a fictitious, verbal life, the criticism of nominalism and fetishism, an appeal to the

8. *XX*ᵉ *Congrès*, pp. 237–38.
9. *Les Cahiers du Communisme*, p. 346.
10. *XX*ᵉ *Congrès*, p. 239.
11. *Les Cahiers du Communisme*, p. 346.
12. *Ibid.*, p. 253.

concrete. The apparatus and the legal society are seeking contact with the real society, men at work and things. Liberalization is not a vague concession or a tactic. Sheer authority, voluntarism, and dictatorship miss their mark by creating fraud, defrauders' complicity, passivity, and mythology, and by destroying that conjunction of the economy and human thought called planning, and that conjunction of the real society and those in power called dictatorship of the proletariat. We are face to face with a régime which is trying to rediscover its meaning, which is escaping it.

In this context the anti-Stalin polemic takes its exact place; it is the criticism of a superstructure or consequence. Dictatorship has created psychological mechanisms, customs, a mode of behavior, a style. A régime which wants to *do* and does not want to *know anything* treats failure as sabotage and discussion as treason. It does not want to know itself as it *is;* that would already be to fall into the relative. So it arranges its secret knowledge of itself with such care that it can succeed in not knowing about itself in good faith. It can think about itself only as Virtue, the negation of its adversary's vices, and perceives what is outside it only as an aid or obstacle. Its great rule is to judge without being judged—to judge without understanding in order not to be judged. It is all this that the XXth Congress is reproaching under the name of Stalin. Already it is risking a glance at the outside: it realizes that capitalism is not completely a shadow, that its survival is continuing, that it may last a long time, that all this is not negative, that there is technical—perhaps social—progress, and that the basis for the transition toward socialism is perhaps being laid there without going by way of insurrection, or even dictatorship. In short, the capitalist world is different than the U.S.S.R., but it is no longer Evil, the absolute Other. It exists, with its defects and relative qualities. And the U.S.S.R. itself is agreeing to exist in some other than an imaginary way, renouncing its oneiric life, and deciding to understand itself.

Only, if this conversion to understanding were complete, the dictatorship would fall to pieces. The XXth Congress concedes nothing concerning the Party's monopoly. So it is still the Party it addresses itself to in order to reform the Party's activity. This harassed and "do-nothing" apparatus is required to rejoin the production and the real society it is cut off from by redoubling its efforts. In short, it is asked to do the impossible: it has been shown to be in every case a *double* or an *understudy,* and it is asked to become a real historical factor again by multiplying its importunate interventions.[13] So the appeal to truth and reality could not be unreserved and consequential if the dictatorship is to remain a dictatorship. The break between pro-

13. Lefort, p. 55.

ductivity and planning, between the proletariat and the dictatorship, could not be openly denounced without questioning the essence and philosophy of the régime. And yet, since the productivity and life of the system are at stake, a blow had to be struck.

The solution was to present the criticism of the régime in the form of a repudiation of Stalin. The sacrilege was sufficient and the countersign clear enough to provoke a shock. And at the same time, by focusing on one person and the worship which had been afforded him, the criticism left the system and its principles untouched. The system was challenged by being reinforced, and reinforced by being challenged. This is perhaps the masterpiece of communism: an increased awareness without the subject's being aware of it, an imperceptible revolution, the advantages of rectification without the inconveniences of confession. Like all masterpieces, this one is difficult. Accumulating advantages, de-Stalinization accumulated dangers as well: there was also the risk that some would not want to take the hint being given them—and that others would understand it too well and translate it into clear language. This is what has happened so far. It is understandable that the XXth Congress' frankness has startled the West's Parties. When Suslov speaks ironically about dossiers which produce no milk, the militants are all delighted to see the official rejoin the real, and the régime immediately gains by it. To savor this higher form of humor, Western militants lack a sense of the relative which is acquired only through Communist life. They must stop their ears or, if they do listen, the sarcasms of the XXth Congress reawaken questions, memories, rebellions overcome—and immediately they go too far.

That is what happened to Togliatti. In a sense, the XXth Congress' theses were ahead of his thoughts and wishes. But precisely because they justified some of his old doubts, he could not be grateful to the Russian leaders for accepting responsibility for them again today after having repressed them before. Yet Togliatti was not the only one with grudges, temper, and violence—it is in this respect that he is so superior to the French leaders. He knows how to draw a little Marxist light from all this. In the last analysis, he says, it is not a question of knowing whether Stalin was good or bad: "We are limiting ourselves in substance to denouncing Stalin's personal defects as the cause of all ills. We are staying in the realm of the cult of personality. To begin with, all good was a result of the superhuman positive qualities of one man. Now all ills are a result of the exceptional and even stupefying defects of this same man. In one case as in the other we are beside the criterion of judgment proper to Marxism. The true problems are escaping us . . . those problems touching on the means and reasons which brought Soviet society to depart at certain points from the democratic and legal way it had traced out for itself, and even brought it to certain forms of degeneration."

Here the dialectic reappears: the anti-Stalin polemic goes beyond itself; the criticism of the "cult of personality" cannot consist in changing the signs and making a scapegoat of the great man. That is a Stalinist way of criticizing Stalin. The only criticism which really goes beyond Stalin, and is thus a real criticism, is the one which hits at the system. As is always the case in good dialectic, this goal cannot be reached by just any means. The criticism of the system was begun from "above"—and it could not have begun anywhere else, since it was precisely the system which had "restricted democratic life." It is at least necessary that, having come from above, it be developed to the base: "To learn a normal democratic life again—according to the model Lenin established in the first years of the Revolution—that is, to relearn initiative in the realm of ideas and practice, the quest for passionate debate, to relearn that degree of tolerance toward errors which is indispensable for discovering truth, to relearn full independence of judgment and character . . . reeducating the cadres of a Party, several hundred thousands of men and women, and through them the whole Party and an immense country where the conditions of civil life are still very different from region to region, is an enormous task which cannot be accomplished by three years' work or by a Congress."

Togliatti comes back three times to the point: the ill has been general and the remedy must be. There are "general errors" here, a "central problem common to the movement as a whole." If the criticism goes this far, if there is nothing in the régime which is not open to criticism, is it not questioning the essence and principles of the régime? It would be a mistake to think so, Togliatti says, *but we can make a mistake in good faith: "I do not exclude the possibility . . . and I intend to say so frankly, that there are people who in all good faith . . . come to wonder if, given the criticisms made of Stalin, and given the fact that Stalin was the main representative of Communist policy during a very long period, it is not necessary now to question the justice of all phases of that policy . . . going back . . . ultimately—why not?—to the decisive acts of the October Revolution. . . ."* He had understood too well; he was going to make the so delicate operation of half-awareness fail.

The French Party could be counted on to put things in order again, and the Russians yielded to its views. The brakes are put on, and Togliatti's Marxist question is repressed by the June 30 Resolution of the Central Committee of the C.P.S.U. Yet here too, how many difficulties there are. The job was almost impracticable. "We cannot agree," the Resolution says, "with the question put by Comrade Togliatti of knowing whether Soviet society has not ended up *in certain forms of degeneration.* There is no reason whatsoever to ask this question." [14] Yet Togliatti had given a good one: how would such ravages have been possible in a healthy revolutionary society? They understand, or pretend to understand, that he is attributing to Stalin the unlimited power to corrupt a society: "To think that a personality, be he as influential as Stalin, was able to change our social and political régime is to contradict the facts, Marxism and reality—it is to fall into idealism. That would mean attributing to a personality such incredible supernatural forces as the capacity to change the social régime and, far more, the social régime in which the millions of workers constitute a decisive force." [15]

Are the Resolution's publishers mocking the militants, or are they confused themselves? This is the question presented by the whole XXth Congress: To what extent do the reformers see what they are doing? It is not impossible that they had not understood Togliatti's question. Perhaps they no longer even imagine what an examination of the U.S.S.R. as an *object to be understood,* a Marxist study of its inner dynamics, could be? Perhaps they think of society as an agglomeration of things and men, of juridical institutions (forms of property, the famous "bases of socialism") and arbitrary wills, so that the analysis of Stalinism, since it has not touched the "bases," is reduced to Stalin's psychology? The Resolution's publishers translate Togliatti's very question into Stalinist language. The fact remains that the June Resolution stops the avalanche. The French Party breathes a sigh of relief. They are staying in the superstructures, and since after all Stalin was Russian, there is nothing of importance to be changed here.

It is then that questions of planning and dictatorship emerge anew, and in a striking way, in Gomulka's report. Here again we learn that planning has changed into its opposite. From 1949 to 1955 coal extraction went from 74 to 94.5 million tons. But during the same period labor output went from 1,320 kilos per miner to 1,163 kilos. Of the 20 million tons gained, 14 million were extracted outside normal working hours in overtime. There is no increase in productivity. Planning does not plan. The régime pays overtime so that extraction will be increased. It supervises gross results, not net results. "*We ought to know before anything else,*" Gomulka says, "*what the real costs of production are.*" "*This was what the realization of the Six-Year Plan consisted in in practice: the maximum means of investment were concentrated in particular areas without taking account of the needs of other areas of*

14. *L'Humanité,* July 3, 1956.
15. *Ibid.*

economic life. And yet the national economy constitutes a unified whole." This is what must be recalled after ten years of Polish planning, and twenty-five years of Russian planning. The very principle of planning remains a dead letter, because the concept does not cover the concrete whole of the Polish economy, and because the producers reject it. The plan is unreal because it is a voluntaristic project, and not an attempt to understand the exigencies of productivity and orient it.

We did not take it upon ourselves to say what de-Stalinization is. But whatever develops, we already see what it is not and cannot be—a limited reform. It diffuses from itself into the whole régime; it introduces throughout a dangerous and useful ferment, a risk and a hope. There are two ways of destroying this hope. One is to shield fetishistic principles from de-Stalinization, as if they were not at issue. The other is that of logicians and geometers, who are often the bellicose ones as well. Because they have found a contradiction in the régime, they act as if the U.S.S.R., not being a concept, were nothing. They have always said so: "dictatorship of the proletariat" and "planning" are terms like "squared circle"—and de-Stalinization is only a ruse for saving these formulas. They have refuted the U.S.S.R. and China as one refutes an opinion. We need only wipe the slate clean and begin over again. This is symbolic suppression in expectation of physical suppression. What will you put in its place then? It is quite remarkable that no one in Hungary or Poland is proposing that the old régime of property be re-established. So there must be a good way to manage the nationalized economy. Why not let Gomulka look for it?

De-Stalinization brings out the régime's fundamental contradiction. But there are many contradictory historical realities which endure in contradiction. Beginning with the economic reality of capitalism, which swarms with contradictions and is not about to disappear. De-Stalinization challenges the essence of dictatorship: as long as it lasts —and it must last; as Togliatti said, it is not a matter of three years and one Congress—it will endanger the régime; thus it is promised in advance to relapses and convulsions. But why should a régime not live with a wound in its side? This is the case in all those where there is freedom. "*The key to the solution for the difficulties which have piled up,*" Gomulka says, "*lies in the hands of the working class.*" This is a call for confidence, and it is coupled with only very timid reforms. Now Gomulka has the confidence he is asking for. But for how long, if he does not invent solutions and institutions? The dictatorship is asked to challenge itself without letting itself be eliminated, and the proletariat to liberate itself without rejecting the dictatorship's check on it. This is difficult, almost impossible. The world has a choice only between this way and chaos. It is in the social forms to be created that a solution must be sought.

Thus the only correct attitude is to see communism relatively as a fact without any special privilege, as an undertaking, preyed upon by its own contradiction, which has caught a glimpse of that contradiction and should go beyond it. Communism is not a solution, since we see it going back on its principles. It is not exactly a reality, since we are told that planning is still to be accomplished and that the Party's life is imaginary. The dictatorship is an attempt that failed, failed precisely because it did not wish to be an attempt but the end of history. As a universal model, as the future of mankind, it has proved abortive. But the French Revolution did too. In 1793 there were people who justifiably hated Robespierre. That does not prevent the French Revolution from being a phase of our history; it does not mean that after it history began again as before. What has happened since 1917 is not a parenthesis, but in every sense of the word the *testing,* still more bloody and painful than the first, of revolutionary voluntarism. We can speak equitably of the U.S.S.R., but only if it agrees to re-enter the ranks of history, and only if we *do not believe in it,* either as Good or Evil—only if we give up fetishes. To conclude, we would like to underline certain ambiguities which threaten de-Stalinization and peace.

In a sense the XXth Congress' decisions only formulate Stalinist practice. The Korean armistice, Communists in government after 1944; this was already the politics of coexistence. The de-Stalinizers, if we look at things closely, frankly go no further. Khrushchev says that the revolution does not necessarily require insurrection or civil war—not necessarily violence. *"The parliamentary way"* can *"also be used to move to socialism"* and *"conquer a solid majority in Parliament."* But a few lines further on: *"For all forms of moving to socialism, political direction by the working class, with its advance-guard leading it, is the express, decisive condition."* Now the advance-guard, as we know, is the Party; and if parliamentary action is—as it always was for Lenin—only one of the Party's means of action, which is "also" used, what Khrushchev is proposing here is only one of those National Front policies Stalin set up after the War.

Mikoyan is still more clear. He says the difference between Marxism and reform remains unchanged. For Marxists, *"the direction of the State in society must be assumed by the working class, so . . . that . . . having obtained a majority, it may take power in hand. . . . We must remember that revolution, peaceful or not, will always be revolution."* The only novelty in these texts is, in short, detouring by way of a parliamentary majority. Once a majority is won, the working class *"will take power in hand."* It is not stated whether this power will be checked by the very majority which has created it, and even less what will happen to the minority in that disturbing *second stage*.

Of course it is significant that they are trying to create ambiguities, and that Mikoyan denies being a reformer. Beneath words and concepts we sense that the dictatorship is relaxing, and that the Other is being taken into consideration. When Suslov, instead of speaking of socialism or communism, speaks of a *"new, advanced social régime,"* this is not the tone of Marx and Lenin, and it would be very difficult to distinguish concession from ruse. But nothing in the proposed formulas guarantees absolutely that there is anything new. And without changing them one whit they can fall back upon violence and the Cold War. The de-Stalinizers are still Stalinists. Stalinism's double nature contains everything, including de-Stalinization. As the best observers have noted, communism's political life in the Stalinist régime allowed struggles which were all the wilder because there were not several policies confronting one another and opposition could not be manifest. There was no doctrinal divergence from the Stalinist policy of compromise and coexistence, and only the "hard-liners" were given the satisfaction of surrounding compromises with threatening manifestations. What is proper to Stalinism or left-wing opportunism, Hervé [16] says, is to practice a policy of collaboration while keeping an intransigent ideology. The blustering compromise, the vociferous peace, the mixture of political concession and verbal violence are Stalinism itself. If there are a few de-Stalinizers at the head of the French Party today, they have not for that reason stopped being Stalinists. As Togliatti said, that will take many years.

All this cannot be forgotten when it is a question for example of evaluating the break Hervé himself made with Stalinism. The example is all the more significant because, having cropped up prior to the XXth Congress and independently of any ultimatum of events, it is the mature fruit of an experience—the fact of a man lucid enough to anticipate the evolution of communism, courageous enough to speak in the general silence, master of his criticism as he was formerly of his adherence, in a word faithful to himself. But it is precisely this very rare dignity which keeps his policy ambiguous. In many respects it is only a more conscious form of Stalinist policy. "As for the view according to which I am not supposed to have had 'a line opposed' to that of the F.C.P.," he himself says, "it is equally comprehensible. Owing to the

16. Pierre Hervé, member of the French Resistance, Communist journalist, and professor. The work Merleau-Ponty is alluding to, *La Révolution et les fétiches*, has been published together with his *Lettre à Sartre*.—Trans.

force of circumstances, and somehow or other, the leadership of the F.C.P. carries out in practice a policy its speeches give the lie to." He is bent on presenting conscious and active coexistence as a Marxist and even Leninist policy. We will pass over Marx and Engels, from whom more than one political philosophy can be drawn. Of course Lenin and Trotsky can serve to criticize Stalinism, but they do not deviate from it in the same direction as the de-Stalinizers. Even when he proposed the N.E.P., Lenin never set forth coexistence and emulation of capitalism and socialism as a principle. Furthermore, the N.E.P. precedes planning; an N.E.P. after twenty-five years of planning has a wholly different meaning. Is the policy of active coexistence a Bolshevist policy? Politically, what Gomulka is suggesting is a compromise with parliamentary democracy, a Diet which "evaluates" and "supervises the work of government," a Party which "guides" and does not govern, a State apparatus which regains its autonomy in respect to the Party—in short a sort of "constitutional communism" in the sense we speak of constitutional monarchy. All this has nothing in common with Trotsky's "workers' democracy," no more than it does with the theses of *State and Revolution*. De-Stalinization does not return to what existed before Stalin. It goes beyond Stalin toward a different future. The horizon of a de-Stalinized communism is not Lenin's horizon.

Hervé wonders, at the beginning of his *Révolution et les fétiches*, whether the revolution is indefinitely postponed by coexistence. He concludes at the end: it is not postponed, or suppressed; it is changing its character. For revolution is not necessarily insurrection, or even violence, or the "Prague coup." [17] He asks for a "reconsideration of the idea of reform," and of those of planning, nationalization, and State capitalism.[18] He speaks with a question mark about a "factual reformism," and finally envisages "reforms which would be provisionally inapplicable in the political situation, but which could, by reason of their power to attract the masses, advance the struggle and create the conditions for their being put into practice." [19] Here is something which is not far from the classical conception of reforms as a means of agitation and a primer for the seizure of power. But what is the good then of reconsidering reforms and the rest? These learned investigations will be swiftly surpassed by the logic of the struggle. "It seems, if we believe Khrushchev, that the form of the dictatorship of the proletariat may not be necessary." We would like to hear something more positive about such a subject. We would have to know whether it is a

17. *La Révolution et les fétiches*, p. 138.
18. *Ibid.*, p. 129.
19. *Lettre à Sartre*, p. 82.

matter only of initiating in a different manner the voluntarism of the dictatorship of the proletariat and authoritarian planning—and of a more intelligent and open form of Stalinism.

But a more conscious Stalinism is no longer Stalinism. It is a wholly different matter, as is apparent in Hervé's criticism of fetishes and the Communist attitude. "It is necessary," he says, "to take a position concerning the major problems of national life, propose solutions, and commit ourselves. If not, how can you expect the democrats and socialists to have confidence in us? They ought to take the responsibilities? We ought to set forth the claims? A convenient, but scarcely persuasive attitude." How could the militants and the Party, if they believe in the revolution as the solution, possibly be interested in knowing whether a reform is possible, instead of "advancing the struggle" by proposing inapplicable reforms? Is it a question of making the Republic live or passing through it on the way to dictatorship? It will not do to leave the matter undecided in order to reconcile the Communists and the others in action.

"It seems to me," Hervé also says, "that the Party exercises the right to express its opinion about all external or internal questions of other organizations. How could it possibly forbid the converse? On what principle would it base its action? On the principle that it is not 'a party like the others'? If it really wants to contract more extensive alliances instead of being satisfied with second-class supporters or honorary Party members, how could it possibly impose this principle upon other parties? How would an agreement be possible if the Communist Party upheld its principle that it has rights others do not have?" [20] But if the proletariat has an historical mission, and the Party is the interpreter of that mission, it has special rights; it is not a party like the others. Communism can make use of reciprocity with others only if it agrees to see itself through their eyes as well, that is, to relativize itself.

So we see what we should think of the countersign of Popular Front renewed by Hervé and, recently, by Sartre as well. It is not one of those which contribute to political clarity. For after all, what Popular Front are they talking about? There is the social movement of 1936, the strikes with occupations of factories, which made working-class seizure of the means of production the order of the day. It is undoubtedly not this Popular Front they are thinking of as a means of uniting the Left. Is it the Popular Front according to Thorez, which puts an end to strikes but fulfills the Party's responsibility by force of verbal violence? Or are they thinking of the postwar tripartism in which Communist ministers voted against a government they continued to be a part of? This is just the contrary of that "constitutional politics," that involve-

20. *Ibid.*, p. 111.

ment in the problems of the day, that serious action in common with non-Communists that Hervé, along with Togliatti, desires. Are they thinking, finally, of the Popular Front according to Blum—a Janus which is presented to the working class as the beginning of socialism and to the leaders of industry as their last chance, which is in the end neither one nor the other, and which fails on the level of reform and of revolution? A Popular Front can be spoken about seriously only by taking up anew the very problem Blum ran up against—only by defining an action which will effectively go beyond capitalist anarchy without being the beginning of the dictatorship of the proletariat. This is called reform.

The truth is that reform is not outmoded; it alone is the order of the day. Gomulka realizes that there must be national accounting, that there is no plan without a balance-sheet, that after the means of production have been transferred to the State the problem of man's effective management of the economy remains untouched, and that the dictatorial economy only stands at the threshhold of this problem. This means that rival forms of property are to be evaluated according to whether they allow for a solution to it or not, and that neither one nor the other is in itself a solution. To estimate real costs of production, needs, and possibilities of consumption, the market economy is a worn-out tool adapted in a muddling way to unforeseen practices. It is the only one available so far. If we want a better one, we have to invent it. Analogous problems stand on the horizon of dictatorship and capitalism. For dictatorship it is a question of moving to a planning which is not imperious; and inversely, for capitalism, of subjecting the mechanisms of the market economy to management in the public interest. On both sides it is a question of creating "artificial mechanisms" or servo-mechanisms which solicit and organize the economy without dictatorship. Confronted with this emerging new problem which revolution has not solved, we are no longer faced with the alternative, "reform or revolution."

In the immediate situation, a reformist farmer-labor party would involve the invasion of political life by a mass of electors which is presently set apart from it to the advantage of the Right. It would also mean the end of the Socialists' double game. It would be still more difficult to make Socialist militants accept the policy we all know about if their point of honor and permanent consolation and justification, the "Socialist program," were found to be wanting. The demand for a real, manifest, verifiable policy would transform the Socialist Party no less than the Communist Party. And only one single operation is involved here: Socialism has been able to degenerate to the point it has only because Communist policy made its reformist task impossible and unfailingly provided it with all the useful pretexts and diversions. A criterion for the Left is being sought on different sides; it is not so hard to find. A Leftist is a man who desires the success of de-Stalinization—a de-Stalinization which is unchecked, consequential, and extended beyond the frontiers of communism to the whole Left that communism has "frozen."

(November, 1956)

7 / On Eroticism

Is eroticism a form of intellectual courage and freedom? But what would become of Valmont without Cécile's innocence, without the president's chastity? He would have nothing to do. What would become of evil feelings without the good ones? The pleasure of profaning presupposes innocence and prejudice. Perhaps it even presupposes them in the profaner; and one suspects at the end of the book that Mme de Merteuil has perhaps accepted the competition in wickedness she and Valmont have established between themselves only because Valmont mattered to her. There are flowers of evil only if there is an Evil and a Good, and the solicitations of the Devil only if there are God's solicitations. A certain eroticism presupposes all the traditional ties, and has neither the courage to accept them nor the courage to break them. Here "libertine" is a diminutive term.

Surrealist eroticism would be worth a special study. It is quite a different thing than the pleasure of profaning. It is the return to primordial unity, to immediacy, to indistinction of love and desire, as automatic writing was the summoning of an uncontrolled speech undistinguished from its meaning. But it was precisely the Surrealists who soon understood that not all involuntary writing has this power: the Sibyl's words wear out; those that will endure are not all ready in our throats, they are readied by our attempt to live and speak. There was a Surrealism which sought for miracles in a crude state in every disorganization of the constituted world. At the limit, this is the art of farces and hoaxes. The Surrealism which endured was not satisfied to tear the customary world apart; it composed a different one. *L'Amour fou* is to be created, beyond self-love, the pleasure of dominating, and the pleasure of sinning.

The eroticism of profanation is too attached to what it denies to be a form of freedom. It is not always a sign of strength of soul. I knew a writer who spoke only of blood and destruction, and who, when he was asked what he felt after he had killed, answered that after all he had not killed anyone, but that if he had he certainly would have had the feeling of having "fallen into a hole." Our sadists are often innocent. There are letters by Sade which show him fretful and timid when confronted with public opinion. Neither Laclos nor Sade played the role of Lucifer during the French Revolution. And on the other hand, what is known of the personal life of Lenin and Trotsky shows that they were classical men. The candor and optimism of Marxist theses concerning sexuality do not have much relationship to libertinage. The adventure of a revolution is played upon a stage more open to the air than Sade's, and Lenin resembles Richelieu more than he does de Sade.

Consider the fact that our great erotics always have pen in hand: the religion of eroticism could well be a literary fact. What is proper to literature is to make the reader believe that he would find in the man and his life, in a concentrated state, the rare substance his works give him a hint of. This is not true: everything is there in the book, or at least the best. The public prefers to believe that the writer, as a being of unknown species, must have certain sensations which contain everything and are like Black Masses. The erotic writer banks on this legend (and makes it all the more credible to the extent that sex for many men is the only way to the extraordinary). But there is a trick with mirrors here between what is written and what is lived. A good part of eroticism is on paper. The writer who is not erotic, but more frank and courageous, does not evade any part of his task, which is to change the life of signs, unaided and all by himself.

As for philosophers, there are very great ones, like Kant, who pass for having been as little erotic as possible. In principle, how could they possibly remain in the labyrinth of Sade and Masoch, since they are trying to understand all this? In fact, they are there—as all of us are—but with the idea of getting out. Like Theseus, they carry a thread along with them. Since they are writers too, their freedom to observe is not gauged by the violence of what they experience, and it happens that a *piece of wax* teaches them a lot about the carnal world. Human life is not played upon a single scale. There are echoes and exchanges between one scale and another; but a given man who has never confronted passions faces up to history, another who thinks in an ordinary way is free with *mores*, and another one who lives to all appearances like everybody else has thoughts which uproot all things.

(October, 1954)

8 / On News Items

THERE IS PERHAPS no news item which cannot give rise to deep thoughts. I recall having seen a man in Fascist Italy throw himself onto the tracks from the top of an embankment in the railroad station in Genoa. The crowd came rushing up. Before they even thought of helping the wounded man, the "railway police" harshly pushed them back. This blood disturbed order; it had to be quickly wiped away, and the world restored to its reassuring aspect of an August evening in Genoa. All dizziness is akin. By seeing an unknown person die, these men could have learned to judge their life. They were defended against someone who had just disposed of his own. The taste for news items is the desire to see, and to see is to make out a whole world similar to our own in the wrinkle of a face.

But to see is also to learn that the pleasures and unlimited pains which flood our being are only a scant grimace for the unacquainted spectator. One can see everything and live after having seen everything. Seeing is that strange way of rendering ourselves present while keeping our distance and, without participating, transforming others into visible things. He who sees believes himself invisible: for him his acts remain in the flattering entourage of his intentions, and he deprives others of this alibi, reducing them to a few words, a few gestures. The voyeur is sadistic. Stendhal, who passionately loved to look but who surveyed himself, understood very well that even indignation is at times suspect: "What are the anecdotes about well-paid magistrates that I have not encountered on my way from Bordeaux to Bayonne, Pau, Narbonne, Montpellier and Marseille! When I am older and more weathered these things which are so sad will appear in the *Histoire de mon temps*. But great God, how ugly they are! Has the world always been so venal, low, so shamelessly hypocritical? Am I meaner than the next man? Am I envious? Where do I get this inordinate urge to rain blows upon this magistrate from . . . , for example?"

* * *

Thus there is a good and a bad use of news items, perhaps even two kinds of news items, according to the type of revelation they bring. What is hidden is first of all blood, the body, linen, the interiors of houses and lives; the canvas underneath the flaking painting, materials beneath what once had form; contingency; and finally, death. The street accident (seen through a window), a glove on the sidewalk, a razor next to the eye, the pins and needles of desire and its paralysis—Bunuel's *Le chien andalou* described all these encounters with the pre-human. And we can always obtain the same dreamlike lucidity, the same stupefying emotion, each time we cut ourselves off from ourselves and make ourselves a stranger to ourselves. That air of derisory intelligence, those nuances in the absurd of a man talking on the telephone are, if I do not hear what he is saying, a fascinating spectacle—but after all they teach us only our bias of looking without understanding.

Stendhal's true little incidents must be set aside from or above these. His reveal not just the underside, the dust, dirt, and residues of a life, but rather what is incontestable in a man—what he is in limiting cases, when he is simplified by circumstance, when he is not thinking of creating himself, in good fortune or bad. At Toulouse one rainy day Stendhal is saved from boredom by two images: "A soldier who was fleeing and despised himself for it stops a horse, recharges his pistols, rides this horse up from the path behind the hedge, kills one of the enemy, wounds another, and by so doing checks a rout." "After such a magnificent celebrity," Stendhal continues, "how would I dare say that I have ennobled my day and thereby rid it of boredom by going aboard the steamboat? . . . I was amused by a sailor's gallantry with a girl from the well-to-do class—and I must say a very pretty girl—who along with one of her companions had been driven out by the heat from her cabin below. The sailor covered her with a wrap to protect her and her child a bit, but the violent wind swept under the wrap and disturbed it. The sailor tickled and uncovered the pretty traveler while he pretended to cover her up. There was much gaiety, naturalness, and even grace in this action, which lasted for an hour. The girl friend who was not being courted directed her attention to me and said, 'That gentleman is getting wet.' I should have talked with her—she was a pretty creature—but the sight of the others' grace pleased me more."

* * *

The true little incident need not be heroic or gracious. It may be a life suffocated and lost in the social order: the instigator Korthis who gets a ball in the belly from a soldier and blackmails the Minister of the Interior who employs him—but only a little, because he knows he can be poisoned at the hospital, because he is a veteran like Leuwen, because he is used to affliction and guesses that one need not pay dearly for the silence of a poor wretch like himself. Today the same unending struggle with misfortune and the same exhausting game with laws, regulations, and necessities bring worn-out, crazy women into clinics: living four in a room, getting oneself and the children up at five to have room to get lunch ready, taking the children to the concièrge who keeps them till class-time, riding an hour and a half on the bus and subway to go work in Paris, coming back at eight in the evening to go shopping and fix dinner, beginning all over again the next day and, after a few years, not being able to go on—here are revelations newspapers could easily offer their youngest readers. True little incidents are not life's débris but signs, emblems, and appeals.

It is only with them that the novel can be compared. It makes use of them. Like them it expresses. And even when it invents, it still invents fictitious "little incidents": the half of Mathilde's hair thrown out the window to Julien, the workhouse boss who makes some prisoners shut up because their songs were spoiling his dinner. Yet there is more and less in the novel than there is in true little incidents. It foreshadows momentary speech and gesture, and comments on them. The author lends himself to the character, makes us enter his inner monologue. The novel gives the context. The news item on the contrary strikes us because it is a life's invasion of those who were unaware of it. The news item calls things by their name; the novel names them only through what the characters perceive. Stendhal does not tell Octave's secret: "It will take many centuries," he wrote to Mérimée, "before we can paint in black and white." Octave's malady then becomes the malady of the impossible—more irremediable and less bitter than his true malady. The novel is truer, because it gives a totality, and because a lie can be created from details which are all true. The news item is truer because it wounds us and is not pretty to look at. They meet only in the greatest, who find, as has been said, the "poetry of truth."

(December, 1954)

9 / On Claudel

If the genius is the man whose words have more meaning than he was able to impart to them himself—the man who in describing the contours of his private universe awakens in the men who differ from him most a sort of rememoration of what he is in the process of saying, as the labor of our eyes ingenuously constructs a spectacle before us which is the world of other men as well—Claudel was at times a genius. Knowing whether he was so as often as Shakespeare or Dostoevski (two of his masters), or whether on the contrary the Claudelian buzz (as Adrienne Monnier put it)—a certain way of organizing the deflagration of words—does not often come to replace Claudel's speech, is a different and relatively unimportant question. In any case there is no genius who is continually one; the genius is not a species or race of man.

Whether one calls Claudel a genius to honor him by placing him among the supermen, or on the contrary to get at his works by ricocheting off some selected anecdotes, to speak of genius is to postulate that a man can be cut from the same cloth as what he wrote, and that he produced his writings as an apple tree produces apples. At the moment of death, when the living man and the writer are more than ever linked, since they have just ended together and for the first time the silence of that voice is heard, it is natural that we should be tempted to raise the question of genius. But whether we do it piously or spitefully, we are still making the same cruel mistake about the writer's condition. Love and hate agree in having made it an honor, but also a duty, for him to have been infallible. If we want to find the proper attitude toward him, we must give up this fetishism. When we are concerned with any man as a whole, there is never any good ground for discerning or refusing the stamp of genius.

The contingent aspects of Claudel's existence are well known: they have been stressed often enough. He was not successful in public events. Formerly, and then again recently, he spoke of "*poilus*" in a tone combatants scarcely put up with. He paid homage, in almost *the same words*, to statesmen he ought to have chosen between. He produced dangerously warlike estimates of the world situation in *Le Figaro*. In these extreme circumstances he was scarcely more perspicacious or intransigent than an ordinary civil servant at the Quai d'Orsay. That intolerance of titles and administrative counsels which is the point of honor of professional writers must not be demanded of him. But this is not our subject: his genius, if he had genius, did not lie here.

Here is what is more important: he disappointed almost all those who tried to shift the burden of being themselves to him. To Jacques Rivière, who describes the odds and ends of his personal life to him (and who parenthetically and mischievously put some stupid things into his letters to see if the great man would notice them), Claudel replies that he needs to "pass through the confessional fire." He enjoins Gide to renounce Sodom or suffer the loss of his friendship. To a cultured lady who came to ask him about our efforts to establish purely human values, he replies—and this goes the strictest insistence upon integrity one better—"moral values are commandments of God and the Church. Outside these, there is no moral or spiritual value. What our writers discover seems derisory to me." But their tragedy, the lady says, their loyalty. . . . "That makes absolutely no difference to me," Claudel says, "Let them get along the best they can." Such is this sectarian. Such are, Gide said, this "willful [and instinctive] intelligence, and this bias of denying what one cannot annex." [1]

And yet it is to an atheist, Philippe Berthelot, that he was attached, as he himself says, "by the bonds of an affection and a gratitude stronger than any I have ever felt for any human being." [2] Now here there is nothing to annex: "Each appeal I addressed to him met only his silence and an evasive glance." [3] Berthelot, stricken by pectoral angina at his desk at the Quai d'Orsay, calls one of his collaborators and says to him: "I shall be dead in ten minutes. . . . I want you to know that there is nothing after death, and that I am sure of it." Claudel comments: "It is the honest and courageous confirmation of a fact and of a personal lack of power to see farther beyond." [4] On April 6, 1925, Claudel learns aboard ship of Jacques Rivière's death. And this

1. *Journal*, November 2, 1930.
2. *Accompagnements*, p. 182.
3. *Ibid.*, p. 205.
4. *Ibid.*, p. 193.

man who refused so flatly to enter the labyrinths of Rivière now speaks up for him and writes for the *Feuilles de Saints:*

"But how, without participating in it, can we go about understanding all this thought being born as from water?

"All this noise becoming speech may be of interest after all. Who will be there to understand if I make off?

"Who will be there to listen if I let myself be wholly won by a deaf God?

"Whose work upon me I have felt only too much advancing fiber by fiber during these four years of prison?"

So it is perfectly clear: this man who counted lack of understanding among his attributes had understood perfectly. Then why did he deny it? If we look at his works, the question becomes far more insistent still. For the world of Claudel's dramas is the least conventional, the least reasonable, the least "theological" there is. This ambassador never staged monarchs or great personages who were not imperceptibly derisory: the King of Spain and his court in *Satin Slipper,* interrupted at each instant in their maneuvers by the movements of the floating landing they had elected domicile upon; Pope Pius, who goes to sleep in front of Coûfontaine (and it is this old man's somnolence which has the onus of representing on earth and the stage of the Théâtre-Français the Church's resistance to violence); the amputated Rodrigue who lets himself be taken in by the talk of a provocative actress sent by the King of Spain, and brings upon himself the ridicule of claiming unwonted powers before the court (and in what a tone of voice!), only to be given finally to two soldiers who do not even suceed in selling him.

The only characters Claudel takes completely seriously are those who are nothing but a simple passion, a sorrow, or an earthly possession. Mara is right in being jealous because she is ugly and awkward. Sygne is right in refusing at the last moment to make the sacrifice she nevertheless made, because "everything is exhausted" and no one can ask a human being to go any further. Turelure in his way was not wrong in pushing the monks of the abbey into paradise that summer of the Year I when the greengages were so good.

"We were going to open everything up, we were going to lie down all together, we were going to stroll along without constraint or breeches in the midst of a regenerated universe, we were going to set out across an earth freed of gods and tyrants!

"It is also the fault of all those old things which were not solid; it was too tempting to shake them a little bit to see what would happen!

Is it our fault if everything has fallen on us? I swear, I regret nothing."

We really have to know how to read to find God's unswerving hand

In this way the duel goes on between those who fear for what exists and those who want what does not or does not yet exist. To both groups liberal régimes oppose only a consummate art of diluting contradictions; putting problems obliquely; stifling action in procedures; creating favorable or unfavorable presumptions; taking the edge off the majorities themselves, when they do not behave properly, and leading them where they do not want to go; and manipulating minds without moving them—in a word, a juridical and artful form of violence.

Then was Gide right? Is our only choice between open violence and precarious compromise between violences? Must we be a-political, misanthropic?

* * *

All is not so simple or so dark. Misanthropy will always be wrong because in the last analysis the vices of politics derive from what is most valuable in men—their idea of truth. The man who has seen something and thinks it is true thinks it is true for everyone. If the others do not see it, it is because they are fanatics, do not judge it openly. In this way the free man makes his evidence the measure of all things, and there he is a fanatic at the moment he complains about the fanaticism of others. But after all, the reason why each man "meddles in others' business," why he substitutes himself for them, is also that he "puts himself in their place," that men do not exist side by side like pebbles, and that each lives in all.

So a day comes when the man who wanted to withdraw from the political game is brought back to it by precisely this taste for freedom he was cultivating to his advantage. Gide often said so—extreme individualism makes us sensitive to other individuals—and his *Journal* tells how he remained speechless when, taking a taxi to go see a sick man in the clinic on rue Boileau (which was luxurious then), and being surprised that the taxi-driver did not know the street, he got this simple answer: "We go to the Lariboisière."

We can play tricks on other people, inventing dreams that blot them out—the "real France," the ideal proletariat—we cannot refuse to listen to someone who is talking about his life. There is at least one subject other men are sovereign judges of: their lot, their happiness, or their misfortune. Each man is infallible on this score, and this restores to their correct proportions the commonplaces about voting Gide had no fear of echoing.

Now this ability goes a long way. Perhaps Gide's concierge did not have as subtle views about history as Gide did. So what? Voting is not writing a treatise on politics or universal history. It is saying yes or no to an action judged by its vital consequences, which are perfectly evident to each man, which are even evident to each man alone. The beginning of the Russian Revolution had grasped this quite clearly when it based the new power on the Soviets, on men taken in their jobs and the milieu of their lives. This real voting, this abrupt judgment which can be put in a single word, expresses what each man intends to make and not to make of his life. Even though they might be right as rain, those who "know" cannot put their lights (which are, moreover, flickering ones) in the place of this consentment or refusal. The majority is not always right, but in the long run no one can be right in opposition to it; and if someone evades the test indefinitely, it means that he is wrong. Here we touch rock-bottom. Not that the majority is oracular, but because it is the only check.

We still have to find out how to obtain this suffrage, how to protect it against diversions, and by what institutions; and this is not easy, for each man's sense of his life depends to an incredible degree upon ideologies. In a tense situation especially the abstract itself becomes concrete, and each man lives to such an extent in social symbols that it is difficult to find in him a private realm of his *own* certainties.

What is far worse is that there is a comedy of liberal societies which causes checks and balances to change into their opposites. Alain thought that checks and balances cannot be abused, that once and for all the role of citizens is to say no and that of those who are in power to push for tyranny. If each is fulfilling his office to the best of his ability, society and the human community are all that they can be. He had not foreseen that exchange of roles in which freedom and checks and balances serve to perpetuate tyrannies, while the interests of freedom move in the direction of those who are in power. All unchecked power makes one mad. That is true. But what are we to do when there is no longer any power at all, when only those who do the checking are left? The citizen against those who are in power is not always an equilibrium between tyranny and chaos; sometimes it is a mixture of the two—a society without action and without history.

The problem of suffrage is wholly before us. We have not even reached the point of catching a glimpse of what a society which had solved it would be like. But the problem is to get what is said and done communicated. So we already know that a worthwhile society will not be less but more free than our own. More instruction, more—and more precise—information, more concrete criticism, publicity given to the actual functioning of society and politics, all problems put in the most offensive terms—offensive as misfortune and all good reasoning are—here are the preliminary conditions for "transparent" social relations.

(July, 1955)

11 / On Indo-China

IN DECEMBER *Les Temps Modernes* published an editorial on Indo-China which could be judged incomplete: it did not define a policy; it expressed the sentiments in which one must be sought for. It said that we would be wrong *a priori* if, after eighty years, we were still hated as enemies, and that a military reconquest would be in a strict sense our shame. That a son of friends of ours who has just served in Indo-China should now write us that the soldiers out there are victims, and that it is harder to die than draft protests, seems natural to us. (When a man has risked his life, it is painful to recognize that it was for a dubious cause. But it is just for this reason that we must protest against a press which holds up dead soldiers as models in order to justify additional sacrifices.) That in the eyes of a colonel we disqualify ourselves by speaking of morality and honoring heroism wherever it is found is already more surprising. This colonel is straight out of the book, and we knew some of a different stripe during the War. But that a moral protest could provoke "a veritable stupor" [1] in a Christian like François Mauriac is what leaves us stupefied in turn.

You speak of mood, he says to us. And certainly morality exists, but it should not legislate without considering the case. We are also against abstract morality. That is why we do not go along with the anti-Communists, who judge communism without considering the U.S.S.R.'s problems. Still, values must be recognizable in their appearance at a given time. That is why, not recognizing those of Marxist humanism in today's communism, we are not Communists. In the Indo-China affair we have not opposed colonization with arguments of principle such as human equality or man's right to self-determination.

1. *Le Figaro,* February 4, 1947, "Le Philosophe et l'Indochine." We shall pass over the extremely provincial idea of guessing the author of a joint editorial. The funniest thing is that the handwriting expert's guess is wrong.

We have made the very concrete observation that after eighty years we are still badly tolerated "occupying authorities" in Indo-China,[2] that we have failed, and that a military solution would confirm our failure. We agree that pure and applied morality should be distinguished. But there must also be some relationship between them. When pure morality is only verbal generalities, it becomes a trick and an alibi. Then it must be caught in the act. It must be said, and we repeat it: "let us make peace or get out." When we enter the ways of relative morality, we must do so knowing what we ultimately want and resolved not to accept *anything whatsoever*. François Mauriac is confusing a sense of reality and a respect for it.

How dare you write, he continues, that the French image in Indo-China is the German image in France? The Germans pillaged Europe and we have established a "beneficent civilization" out there. We answer that if the Germans had stayed in France three-quarters of a century, they surely would have ended up by building factories here in which Frenchmen would have worked, roads and bridges we would have used—and even by distributing sulfur and sulfate to proprietors to care for hereditary vineyards. This would not have excused them for the hostages they executed. If the Italians had stayed in Abyssinia, they would have equipped the country. François Mauriac was indeed frivolous when he condemned the Ethiopian undertaking. He had only to wait for the time of roads and bridges. What are we saying? At least the strategic roads were already under way. French policy in Indo-China has not only failed to free the peasants from usury, but has not even tolerated the formation of an industrial bourgeoisie. Here is why we are still an occupying power out there. We are judged by what we have and have not done.

Finally, says François Mauriac, colonization is a kind of Crusade, which like all Crusades is ambiguous. Its violence is only "the corruption of a great idea." But the idea is in François Mauriac's mind or in our history books. The Vietnamese themselves have above all seen the "corruption" of it. It is in a precise sense scandalous that a Christian should show himself so incapable of getting outside himself and his "ideas," and should refuse to see himself even for an instant through the eyes of others. The least revolutionary among us have understood once and for all through the Spanish Civil War and the German Occupation that honor is sometimes in prisons. They have learned what the great "ideas" of those in power mean for the oppressed. But the war is over, the Germans are gone, everything is orderly again. We are the

2. "Out there," the editorial said, "we are Germans without a Gestapo or concentration camps—at least we want to think so." A futile hope. J. Cuisinier's article will show that we were still too optimistic.

ones in power now; so that it can only be honorable. Once again, the irregulars' point of view does not count.

As in the days of his sheltered childhood, François Mauriac is deaf to the cries of those who mix in killing and dying. Let us be patient. It is nothing but the corruption of a great idea "and literally a calling betrayed." We say that a Christian is not made to betray his vocation or to excuse those who betray it, and we are not the only ones who are saying it. A priest writes us: "I have just gotten back from Vietnam, where I spent seven years. Reading your note . . . on the subject of Vietnam did me good, and I am grateful to you for it. . . . I would not have written you if M. Mauriac's February 4 article in *le Figaro* had not by chance come to my attention. . . . Has he gotten old? Have his country's sufferings embittered him? What has the Christian become? . . . So long as so many Christians refuse to be there where they are expected, can we be surprised that others are claiming to take their place?"

Certainly François Mauriac repudiates colonialism "as it was practiced in the nineteenth century" (as if it had changed so much since then). He calls upon us "to discover before it is too late new bases for understanding and cooperation" with Vietnam. It cannot be said that his article is much help to us. How can he fail to realize that, seen from without, this article is precisely a moralizing cover for a violent solution? [3] A Vietnamese said to us: your system functions beautifully. You have your colonialists. And among your administrators, writers, and journalists, you have many men of good will. The former act, the latter speak and are the former's moral guarantee. Thus principles are saved—and colonization remains in fact just what it has always been. After an article written to give us a good conscience and justify our power in Indo-China, the conciliatory sentences at the end do not carry much weight. A civil servant from Indo-China lately said to us: "You were right; it is a matter of waking people up." François Mauriac's article is designed to put them to sleep. If they listen to it they will let things alone—until the rainy season comes, the Vietnamese troops get tired, the peasants get weary, and the Viet-Minh surrenders unconditionally. At this point we shall be able to negotiate without promising anything, and along with headquarters (which is in fact Communist), colonialism will liquidate as "Communist" the best-founded claims of the Indo-Chinese people.

It certainly is hard for a minister to open negotiations without reinforcing the Viet-Minh. That is why they are always saying that

3. We do not even know whether "before it is too late" means, as we hope it does, "before military repression wins out," or whether, as we fear it may, "before we are kicked out."

each word spoken in favor of the Vietnamese in the French press prolongs the struggle by reviving their hopes. But it must be realized that the other formula—"let us be victors today; tomorrow we shall be just"—comes down to ruling out reforms. There has been a double rule in Indo-China since the War. The logic of colonialism demands that "intruders" be eliminated. It will not reform itself in the hour of its triumph. To be for a military solution is to confirm the eighty-year-old French policy in Indo-China.

It is not surprising that a minister overtaken by events should rally to support this policy. But in a time when almost the whole press is unanimous, independent writers are not doing their job if they facilitate the operation. To the cynics who are carrying it out there should be granted that sort of grandeur which has been the statesman's since the world has been the world. But what shall we say of those good souls who associate themselves with it without having the courage to call Terror terror? Our time has the incomparable advantage over others of having given the public a glimpse into the wings of history and brought to light a few of its crude tricks. It is up to us to defend this privilege.

All this is so clear that we are "stupefied" to have to say it again, above all to François Mauriac, who had been so lucid on other occasions. What is happening to him then? This article is not clear. We sense that he is speaking of one thing and *also* thinking of another. What is the source of this fraudulent tone, which he never took when it was a question of morality or religion, and which he had long since lost in politics? Like the psychoanalyst's subject, he gives us the answer incidentally. Towards the end of his article, and as if he were passing to side-issues of the problem, our author asks: "Is it true or not that another power (the very one whose spirit animates the Viet-Minh) would be substituted for a France that failed?" And there we have it. No lengthy investigation is required to know that the French Communists, who are associated with the government, are co-responsibles for its colonial policy; that the Viet-Minh has not been given serious support by the U.S.S.R.; that in accordance with its general policy of prudence, the U.S.S.R. wants compromise and not a war which could involve Anglo-Saxon intervention; that the Viet-Minh's arms come from China, most frequently by way of a French firm; and that finally the Viet-Minh's Communist headquarters has headed up an Indo-Chinese nationalist movement which is amply motivated by the French policy in Indo-China, and which owes nothing to the Machiavellianism of the Kremlin. But none of this is important. It suffices for Ho-Chi-Minh to be a Communist and François Mauriac to have understood. There is nothing but a tentacle of the U.S.S.R. here.

This is a striking example of that *political nominalism* which is falsifying French public life. Whether it is a question of Indo-China or of something else, each man chooses a position according to whether it weakens or reinforces the U.S.S.R., and gets along as well as he can with his ideas. That is why there are no longer any political problems or any real political discussions. The Communists used to believe that by the logic of the proletarian movement the U.S.S.R. would be eminently served by revolutionary advances in the world. They might hesitate about tactics and wonder at a given moment if a proletarian offensive was opportune. But it was understood at least that the problem would be resolved by a serious analysis of the local situation, and by an evaluation of the world situation in which the national proletariats' pressure on their governments would enter into consideration. Today, they no longer have such confidence in the course of events; they no longer believe in a rational development of history, and in the connivance of the efficacious and the valuable. Their diplomacy, like that of all chancelleries, calculates the relationships of forces in terms of geographical and military conditions, and without taking into consideration class consciousness, which is indeed greatly weakened. On its side, anti-communism does not deal with any question in depth. It is so impoverished of ideas and so far from facts that it does not even rise to the level of the leftist maneuver, which is nevertheless easy under present circumstances. It falls back purely and simply upon the old conservatism, and in blind disapproval confuses Soviet diplomacy and spontaneous mass movements. In an affair like the Indo-Chinese one, where it is nevertheless clear that no problem will be solved by pursuing the phantom of the U.S.S.R., anti-communism sticks by the police chief's conception, according to which all problems are created by a few ringleaders.

We understand now what is happening to François Mauriac. When French patriotism blew in the direction of humanity, he knew how to judge those in power. But he only asked to be quit of such a tiring lucidity. The War had the inconvenience of obliging him to distinguish between the legal and the just. Let us, he thinks, forget these horrors. Do not reopen our old sores. The wound, for him, is not the Indo-Chinese affair; it is the dishonor of Vichy. From the moment our wounds heal, out there blood may well begin to flow.

(March, 1947)

12 / On Madagascar[1]

(INTERVIEW)

—As a philosopher and political thinker, do you have an opinion about the war in Algeria, and can you tell us what it is?

—I have an opinion and I do not hide it. But it is perhaps no longer a solution, even if it was one two years and a half ago. Nothing proves that a given problem is soluble at any time whatsoever, and it would be excessive to reproach us for not having any solution when the problem itself has been allowed to go to pot. I see only partial truths:

1st. I am unconditionally opposed to repression, and to torture in particular. The man who wrote *The Question*[2] knows what honor and real glory are; remember the words in the prison passageway when he runs into the Moslems who encourage him: ". . . *and in their eyes I grasped a solidarity, a friendship, and a confidence so total that I felt proud, precisely because I was a European, to have my place among them.*" The man who thought that and his fellows are literally saving honor, our honor and that of our ministers. It is said, and it is true, that torture is *the* answer to terrorism. This does not justify torture. We ought to have acted in such a way that terrorism would not have arisen;

2nd. But to me it seems impossible to deduce an Algerian policy from this judgment about torture. It does not suffice to know what one thinks of torture to know what one thinks of Algeria. Politics is not the contrary of morality, but it is never reduced to morality. The Pole Hlasko said recently that the political convictions of French writers did

1. My stay in Madagascar referred to here was in October and November of 1957. The text of the interview dates from January and February of 1958. It is put back to its actual date in this volume. Although it was scheduled for publication in *l'Express* on July 3, it did not appear until August 21, 1958.

2. Henri Alleeg has given an unforgettable account of French torture in Algeria in *The Question*.—Trans.

not interest him much because they were only moral attitudes. It seems to me that he was right.

—What do you call a moral attitude?

—For example the attitude of those who think that as a matter of principle white men had no business in the rest of the world; that they were wrong to go there; that their only duty and their only role at present is to get out; that the countries overseas, if left to themselves, will run into great difficulties, but that we do not have to worry about it; that it is up to them to face up to them and make whatever use they wish of a total freedom which must be granted them to begin with.

This feeling, which can be found in a great part of the non-Communist Left, is all of the properly revolutionary attitude which is left in it. Now the revolutionary attitude was a politics: it was thought that a ripe historical force ready to harvest the human heritage really existed in the world, that the colonial countries and the proletariats of advanced countries were an inseparable part of that struggle, and that the revolutionary policy was to combine the action of both.

Today it is fairly clear that the proletariat is not in power in the very countries in which the bourgeoisie has lost power; the very idea of a proletarian power has become problematical. Many men who no longer believe that the U.S.S.R. is such a proletarian power transfer the revolutionary ideology to colonized countries, *precisely because they no longer believe it.* Precisely because they can no longer be Communists, they do not envisage any compromise in colonial policy.

Yet it is clear that a revolutionary politics cannot be maintained without its pivot, that is, proletarian power. If there is no "universal class" and exercise of power by that class, the revolutionary spirit becomes pure morality or moral radicalism again. Revolutionary politics was a doing, a realism, the birth of a force. The non-Communist Left often retains only its negations. This phenomenon is a chapter in the great decline of the revolutionary idea.

—And what is the reason for this decline?

—Because its principal hypothesis, that of a revolutionary class, is not confirmed by the actual course of events. We have only to travel in one of the overseas countries to understand both what is fictitious in the revolutionary schema and how it nevertheless gets a wholly apparent justification from events. Take Madagascar for example, where I was a few months ago. One is struck first of all by the fact that the nationalist intellectuals of Tananarive are very far from what would make us assume a revolutionary conception of history. One of them said in my presence that the distinction between nobles and bourgeois was a permanent trait of Madagascan personality. Another one, that after independence it would be necessary to be concerned with keeping the population which is moving towards the cities in the villages. Still another, a Catholic, that it would be necessary to build a sort of feudal socialism. Another that Liberia was an example for all African peoples. Another, finally, that nothing was more important than the differences between Catholics and Protestants at Tananarive.

These intellectuals are very far from being ready for a possible revolution. The Marxist's answer to this will be that they constitute a nationalist bourgeoisie, and that this bourgeoisie will open the gates of power to the masses and to the improvised leaders the masses will give themselves. With all due consideration of the insufficiency of a short trip and of the possibility of unexpected events as well (in 1947 almost no one believed in an uprising), it must be admitted that in the country itself one does not at any time have the impression of a revolution hatching. That many Madagascans, above all in Tananarive, have had enough of French rule is one thing. That this foretells the accelerated growth of a proletariat in the Marxist sense is another. In Betsileo country, in the South, toward Tulear and Fort-Dauphin, and even at Issotry, the suburb of Tananarive, where the water of the rice paddies floods into the houses during the rainy season, and where one sees nondescript objects which are the most cruel symbols of destitution sold on hawkers' trays—the isolated traveler does not feel himself surrounded by anger. Even if all this explodes tomorrow, it will remain to be proved that it is a question of an eruption whose foundations have been laid by history. I know we have to look beneath appearances, but it would have to be shown that there is in "the depths" a revolutionary proletariat in the classical Marxian sense.

Here is why history nèvertheless gives the impression of flowing in the direction of communism: if the French pulled out of Madagascar immediately and completely, it is probable that the bourgeoisie I was speaking of a while ago, which is qualified but far too small in number, would try to head up the country, and that a part of the hill population would rise up against it (we attempt to play upon these hatreds, but they do exist, and we have not created them; after a lecture on the idea of race, I realized that the Merina in Tananarive found me really too little racist: they did not succeed in thinking of the hill Negroes as equals). In brief, the nationalist Madagascans willingly admit the departure of the French would be followed by bloody public disturbances. After which, since we have to live, men who had sprung forth from the masses would as a matter of fact impose their authority, put the country to work, and without capital and with the means at hand undertake the task of development. This would be very long and hard. I see no reason to say that this is history's immanent meaning, the solution it has prepared for the problems of destitution. Even if, contrary to the actual case, all the newly independent colonial countries ended up militarizing themselves and realizing a sort of communism, this would not mean at all that the Marxist philosophy of history is true, but that an authoritarian and non-bourgeois régime is the only possible outcome when political independence precedes economic maturity. If we restrict ourselves to what is observable, nothing in Madagascar makes us think of the classical schema of the colonial proletariat which tears through the stages of development without stopping, and sometimes outstrips the proletariats of the advanced countries in revolutionary maturity.

The apparent confirmation of the schema makes us inattentive to facts and problems Marxism treats as secondary or even passes over in silence. In talking to advanced intellectuals at Tananarive, one is struck for example by the little interest they show in problems of development or even in the study of Madagascan customs and society. One of them, who studied in a French university, told me it was almost impossible to make a connection between his Madagascan and his scientific personality, and furthermore, any study of Madagascan beliefs undertaken in the spirit of science would seem treason to his fellow Madagascans. Their rebellion against us is not intellectual (they love conversation in the French manner and practice it admirably); it is wholly emotional and moral.

One can reply that the rest would come with independence. I think that in reality independence would cruelly resolve but not solve the problem, which is to weld together a European way of thinking and what is still an archaic civilization. Perhaps communism masters this problem and others only by taking away its means of expression.

When Rabemanandjara [3] wanted to express the wishes of the Madagascans in a Parisian newspaper, he could only place end to end a eulogy to European techniques and a demand for an immediate relationship to nature which he said Madagascan civilization has always held the key to, without saying how this poetic relationship to nature was compatible with labor and production in the Western way.

Césaire [4] honors Negroes for not having invented the compass, and we know what he means: the compass, the steam engine, and the rest have too often served to cover up the facts and gestures of Frenchmen. But after all, taking sides purely and simply against the compass means dealing very superficially with the historical problem of development. Independence would not stop but accelerate the erosion of archaic structures. One can still reply that idealization of the archaic

3. Jacques Rabemanandjara, Madagascan political figure.—Trans.

4. Aimé Césaire, Martiniquan political figure, poet, essayist, and professor. —Trans.

past is a quest for security and hides revolutionary anguish. One can say this, and it is still the same recourse to a depth-history. If we stick to what is observable, nothing justifies our saying that immediate and unconditional independence would be the relieving of a worn-out imperialism by a nation ripe for living by itself. It would be more of a draft drawn on the unknown, a challenge to destiny. There is what the ideology of the revolution hides from the French Left.

—According to you, the traditional criticisms made of colonialism are unrealistic and, above all, have no present significance?

—Colonialism, whatever the assumption, is three-fourths finished. When the Europeans deported fifteen million African Negroes to America, when they dealt with the herds of the Argentine pampas as fat-and-hide quarries, when they developed itinerant sugar-cane growing in Brazil which left the soil exhausted and (with the contribution of tropical erosion) turned the country into a desert, or when French administration in Africa was still dominated by the great companies, there was a colonialism.

I think the same thing about the old facts I just spoke of that I think of all the infamies which are never lacking in historical undertakings, in Roman history as well as in that of the French monarchy. It is in this way that Nantes and Bordeaux accumulated the capital which was to make the Industrial Revolution possible. I do not approve of this blood, these sufferings, these horrors any more than I approve of the execution of Vercingetorix. I am saying that on condition that this stop, we do not have to make it a rule that the whites must go back where they came from, for in today's Africa they *are* something different than that colonialism.

You will see in the book Ballandier published, *Le Tiers Monde,* that since the law of August, 1946, French public investments in the countries south of the Sahara come to about a billion dollars, as much in ten years as during the previous forty years—the equivalent, it has been said, of an African Marshall Plan.

You will see in Germaine Tillion's book that out of 1,200,000 non-Moslems, there are in Algeria 19,000 colonials in the strict sense, 7,000 of whom are poor people, 300 rich, and a dozen very rich. The remaining Frenchmen in Algeria are the salaried people, engineers, and businessmen who represent three-quarters of the country's economic infrastracture. During this time 400,000 Algerian workers are working in France and feeding two million Algerians in Algeria itself.

I am not saying that the French industrial leaders hire them out of philanthropy. I am confirming the fact that this relation between Algeria and France has nothing to do with colonialism. Much more than vestiges of colonialism remain, above all in customs, ways of thinking, and even administrative practices. We can ponder over the modest level of the S.M.I.G. in a given region of Madagascar where a major private enterprise has been established which parenthetically takes credit for paying only slightly higher wages. We can no longer say that the system is *made for* exploitation; there is no longer, as it used to be called, any "colony of exploitation."

—Under these conditions, why do we see most of the overseas countries rising up for independence, or at least demanding it?

—Look at Ballandier's book again: a tenth of the world's population disposes of 80% of its revenues; Asia, which shelters half of humanity, possesses only a fifth of the world's revenue. Five hundred million men in the so-called advanced countries live with an annual income of from five hundred to a thousand dollars; four hundred million others (the U.S.S.R., Japan, two or three countries of Eastern Europe, and one or two South American republics) live with an annual income of from one hundred to five hundred dollars; the remainder—that is 1,500 million men—with less than one hundred dollars per year. Two-thirds of the world's population live in hunger; a German, an Englishman, an American in 1950 had five thousand units of energy per year at his disposal; an African or a Chinaman, one hundred and fifty; a Hindu or an Indonesian, less than one hundred.

To this is added, as you know, the high birth rate of the underdeveloped countries, in the order of forty to fifty per thousand—Europe's birthrate *before birth control* was only thirty to forty per thousand. Without birth control, it has been calculated that European women would have to get married towards thirty-five simply in order not to have more children in marriage than they now have. The intervention of medical techniques has lowered the mortality rate. This has been frequently pointed out, but the figures are striking. From 1946 to 1952, life expectancy in Ceylon went from 42.8 to 56.6; *France itself took fifty years, from 1880 to 1930, to go from the first to the second figure.* On the whole, towards the year 2000 the underdeveloped countries will probably have gone from 1,800 to 4,000 million inhabitants, the others from 900 to 1,150. All this and the decline of customary structures (in a word, what Germaine Tillion calls the "*clochardisation*" of three-quarters of the underdeveloped populations), and finally, progress in information and political consciousness amply explain the uprising of underdeveloped countries. The little that the colonizing countries have done for them (in Algeria in 1954, 95% of the men were illiterate in French) has hastened rather than retarded it.

All this does not absolve the whites' racism and the facts of exploitation, but the facts we are speaking about are of a wholly different class. Alfred Sauvy, who is above suspicion, recently wrote that the

Algerians' standard of living since the French arrival in Algeria has evolved in approximately the same way as that of the politically independent Arab countries. But as the colonized countries were not administering themselves, as the power there was a foreign power, it is natural that they impute their suffering to it.

—If the essence of the ills the colonized countries suffer from cannot be imputed to colonialism, is there no solution then?

—No short-run solution; independence is not one, and communism would not be one. It has been calculated that in order to raise the living standard 1%, 4% of the national income must be set aside in developed countries, and probably much more in underdeveloped countries. Taking the rate of population growth into consideration, from 12 to 20% of the national income would have to be set aside and invested in order to obtain a very poor result.

As for foreign aid, it is estimated that the developed countries (without even taking into account the discordancy between their demographic progression and that of the others) would have to give from 4 to 7% of their total income from the first year on in order to double the standard of living of the underdeveloped peoples in thirty-five years, that is, to bring their income up to 70,000 francs per year per man.

—Why do you say that communism would not be a solution?

—Because inside and outside the U.S.S.R. it has encountered the problems of underdevelopment. Now in the U.S.S.R., where resources were exceptional, it has overcome them, at least as far as the industrial sector is concerned (it seems there is still an agrarian problem). But as for the Peoples' Democracies, the reconversion of agricultural countries into industrial countries (for example, the annual integration of 700,000 persons into Hungarian industry) would have required, the Englishman Mandelbaum says, the investment of a fifth of the national income. Taking account of the characteristic defects of a purely authoritarian planning, and of all its human consequences, it is perhaps in the face of this inordinate effort that Poland and Hungary revolted.

—The problems you are bringing out—those who think about politics have not always seen them—do seem to be the essential problems which are going to govern our epoch, and which already dominate it. But as inordinate as they seem to us, we cannot face up to them without envisaging a way of dealing with them, or of trying, in no matter how small a way, to keep them in check. Have you nothing to suggest?

—I must certainly suggest something, but this is no statement of an immediate solution. I do not want Algeria, Black Africa, and Madagascar to become independent countries without delay; because political independence, which does not solve the problems of accelerated development, would give them on the other hand the means for permanent agitation on a world scale, and would aggravate the tension between the U.S.S.R. and America without either one being able to bring a solution to the problems of underdevelopment as long as they continue their arms race.

I want internally autonomous or federalist régimes immediately, as a transition toward independence, with calculated delays and stages. Since there is no short-run technical and economic solution, these countries must get the means of political expression so that their affairs may become really theirs, and their representatives may obtain from France the maximum it can do in the direction of a "handout economy."

—Do you think that such a policy, if it were resolute, would have a chance of being applied?

—The difficulties are evident. In Madagascar, under a colonially administered régime, many Madagascans think that nothing is changed. Today in Madagascar, under an internally autonomous régime, a Madagascan journalist insinuated in my presence that the administration deliberately set brush fires (which are forbidden) in order to have those alleged to be guilty condemned. I observed to the journalist from Tananarive who told me this that ten years ago he was in prison, and today is the editor-in-chief of a newspaper in Tananarive. Many Frenchmen, I should even say administrators, are openly or tacitly hostile to the colonial administration. One of them said to me: "We are teaching them to do without us." He was right. That is indeed the mission of French administrators under an internally autonomous régime.

But if it is a question of career, there is enough in this mission to fill a whole career, the task of teaching children and of training men is so great, and has been so long postponed. It must be added that certain administrators play the game with an openness, activeness and, moreover, a success which are admirable. I have seen some who by their character, their independence, and their talent had succeeded in imposing their moral authority on both sides after elections which had swept away the old managerial class. Even more: an administrator, a man of the Right, said regretfully to me: "When Deferre [5] was minister, we were harassed by application forms. They asked us to do the impossible, but they asked us." I think that many men who are hesitating or scheming would get to work if they felt a movement and an expectancy behind them.

5. Gaston Deferre, French Socialist mayor of Marseilles and Ministre de la France d'Outre Mer under Guy Mollet.—Trans.

—You do not want France to withdraw from Africa. Can you specify your essential reasons for this?

—I can state them frankly: because I think she was able to and still is able to do some good there, and because I would rather be a part of a country which does something in history than of a country which submits to it. At bottom, what annoys me in those of my fellows who speak too easily of independence is that the duties they propose for us are always abstentions.

I have seen people who honored Mendès-France highly for having signed the Geneva Agreements. At Geneva, he did what he could. What honors him is not Geneva but Tunis, the Carthage Agreements, which have nothing to do with the French policy in Morocco. On the one hand, an initiative; on the other, a mixture of weakness and sharp practice.

—You seem to believe that our values, the values of Western civilizations, are superior to those of the underdeveloped countries.

—Certainly not in respect to their moral value, and even less to their superior beauty, but, how shall I put it, in respect to their *historical* value. In landing at Orly in the morning twilight, after a month in Madagascar, how amazing it is to see so many roads, so many objects, so much patience, labor, knowledge; to make out in the switching on of lights so many individual lives arising in the morning. This great feverish and crushing arrangement of what is called developed humanity is, after all, what will one day enable all men on earth to eat. It has already made them exist in one another's eyes, instead of each proliferating in his country like trees. They have met in blood, fear, and hatred, and this is what must stop. I cannot seriously consider this encounter an evil. In any case, it is something settled; there can be no question of recreating archaism; we are all embarked and it is no small matter to have begun this game.

13 / On May 13, 1958

So THE ALGERIAN EXTREMISTS have risen up to put a government in power which is going to carry out the policy Mendès-France called for two-and-a-half years or more ago. The Algerian officers broke discipline in order to have a government which disciplines them again. Guy Mollet—a traitor to his socialism, then to the defense of the Republic, and tomorrow, I suppose, to General de Gaulle—has General de Gaulle's *esteem;* Robert Lacoste—who, as certain birds do to other birds' eggs, hatched out a rebellion at Algiers that he fled—has all his *friendship.*

The Socialist members of Parliament, who are unanimously against de Gaulle, wait until Coty has threatened them with civil war, then until General de Gaulle is too committed to retract, to find fault with him. They find fault with him under their breath, and procure (also under their breath) appeasements which bowl Deixonne over. Is politics always these stupidities, this laisser-faire, these fits of hysterics, these oaths immediately revoked—these oaths taken *in order to* negotiate their withdrawal? Or is this not the politics of decadence, and are we not condemned to parody and unreality by a more serious illness which will rot tomorrow's institutions as well as yesterday's?

General de Gaulle's appearance, we must not forget, is also the sequel to and so to speak the masterpiece of Molletism. I am not sure that it is the end of it. From Tamanrasset to Dunkirk, we see only Frenchmen who are daydreaming, creating intoxicating situations in order to forget the real problems, and going straight to a sort of political nothingness rather than a civil war. For once the parachutists in Paris had destroyed the "system" and put all the left-wing intellectuals in prison, we really cannot see what they would do with an entrenched and absent country, what they would say to Bourguiba, to the King of Morocco, to the F.L.N., to the men of Cairo. As for the "left-wing totalitarians," who will claim that even in the case of a victorious resistance by the working class the U.S.S.R. would risk an open conflict to uphold a Peoples' Democracy here? Yet such are the terrors men are trying to make Frenchmen live in. The characters of the drama are partly imaginary.

To begin with, the Algerian movement, of which nothing can be said politically: it is not even the outline of a politics. The extremists rose up to forget the Algerian problem they are beginning to discover; they make a scene before giving in, and when they have to speak of events, they only revive the slogans of the time prior to Guy Mollet.

But what counts is the Army. According to all that is known about it, it is once again living *military Servitude and Grandeur.* Existing on the fringe of the nation and always out of step with it—trained in self-denial and, as Vigny says, accepting everything including the "sinister functions" it comprises, having renounced freedom of thought and action—"it knows not what it does or what it is," but "needs to obey and place its will in the hands of others, like a heavy and importunate thing." Is it the State's slave or its queen? But it cannot be its slave when there is no more State. And what is one to do with power when one wants nothing? "The Army is blind and dumb. . . . It wants nothing and acts on springs. It is a big thing which is moved and which kills; but it is also a thing which suffers." Scapegoat; "simultaneously ferocious and humble martyr"; accustomed to scorning death (and thus life), men (and thus himself); through all this a stranger to the men who live in the century and at times "puerile" in the face of their life; on the other hand, free-spirited and, if he discovers men, capable of dedicating himself to them—the soldier has no special ties to the special interests, but he must not be asked to have a politics.

Now it is a soldier who is charged in this case with healing the ill. He certainly has a greater share of the grandeurs than of the servitudes of the Army, and seems, I must say, unscathed enough by the ravages of *passive obedience*. Is he by the disease of scorn? How misanthropic a man has to be to offer Guy Mollet and Robert Lacoste to Frenchmen as models! General de Gaulle may change the laws; he is not changing the life of France, because that is not the business of one man *alone,* because one man alone always has too simple an idea of the system. In his fashion, how well he plays the game, without a lie but also without an error! This rebellion which was inevitable "no matter what he could say . . . ," he writes to Vincent Auriol, and thus foreseen and advised against, but which he takes as a fact—which he "could not possibly approve of" while negotiations were going on, but which he makes use of—which he does not repudiate, but which he understands better than it understands itself, and which he is going to bring back to its true meaning—all this is extremely well done. It is work done upon men, the same kind of tough flexibility, of egalitarian scorn, which put General de Gaulle in power in 1944—and which was not enough to keep him there, not just because the "system" started up again, but also because if it suffices to manipulate men to acquire power, it is necessary, in order to keep it, to take an interest in things, have tendencies and a body of ideas about problems. There was never a movement behind de Gaulle in the government, because he had no policy, because he arbitrated without governing.

We seem to forget these days that the French Army and the National Assembly are not the world. What are we to do in relation to Tunisia and Morocco? How are we to deal with the F.L.N., which has never accepted integration, free elections, or a cease-fire, and has never spoken of anything but independence? If we wish to reduce the irreducibles by cutting off their supply of arms, will we keep Bourguiba's good-will for long? Does announcing peace in six months put us in a position of strength? There is something dreamlike in the productions at Algiers, in that way of suppressing obstacles with thought, of projecting the rapture of Frenchmen in Algeria into the adversary, as if the universe participated in and obeyed the drunkenness of the forum of Algiers. General de Gaulle is shut up in his solitude, as the crowd at Algiers is in its wrath, and Guy Mollet in his lobbyings. Where at this time is there an idea, where political imagination, and if there is no solution, what does this carnival mean? I deeply hope I am wrong, since I do not believe in the virtues of nothingness, but in maybe six months, maybe six weeks, we are going to find the expiration of our tenancy in even worse shape.

It is in these circumstances that Sirius calls upon his readers to say yes or no to de Gaulle, to give him their support if they wish deeply for his success, to put an end to "futile discussions," and to bring their vigilance to bear again upon the totalitarians of the Right and the Left. So here we are, brought in five days from the "lesser evil" to a sacred union. There is no longer any place for an opposition, even in agreement on presumed goals. We must be either for or against. But for or against what? The "totalitarians of the Right and the Left"? Doesn't this remind Sirius of anything? These are the very words of Pflimlin. This is the language of the "system." When we have seen the Communist Party and the C.G.T. so well-behaved, how can we help perceiving that it is also the language of political blackmail and myths? General de Gaulle has not even asked the French for the kind of support Sirius is insisting we give him. Since he was invested he has not even spoken to them. Wholly concerned with putting the system out of harm's way, he is no doubt keeping himself in reserve for Algiers. This is not reassuring. Between him and Algiers there is an account to settle. Him alone, and not us. He is alone, as he wanted it. His failure would be serious, but we cannot help him succeed, or play "double or nothing" on his undertaking as if there were nothing after him and after us.

Our role is to understand what has just ended and what is beginning. For my part, I would like to propose two inseparable reflections to my readers. The first is that no liberal policy will be possible overseas as long as the governments which would be disposed to effect it are deprived of the support of the Frenchmen who send one hundred and forty Communist deputies to Parliament. It is clear enough this time that the famous deduction of Communist votes cuts off from France a certain number of citizens (who are what they are, but certainly not extremists), covers the Right's operations in advance, presages the set purpose of capitulating, and is the first act of extortion from the civil war. Mendès-France deducted the Communist votes at the time he went to negotiate with Russia and China; he was right to do it then, if negotiation is not capitulation. The inventor of the "system" is still General de Gaulle, with his theme of the "separatists." The blackmailings and omnipotence of a minority Right, the trials of intentions, the general suspicion—in short, paranoid politics, paralysis of liberal governments, and erosion of powers—will continue as long as the mass of Communist electors continues to be like a foreign body in France.

Now it will continue to be so as long as the Communist Party does not present itself for what it is: a workers' party which presses with all its weight in what it believes to be the workers' direction—and it is right—but which has nothing in common, in theory or in practice, with revolutionary Marxism, and in addition is in no way charged with establishing a popular democracy in France. In this respect too, recent events are clear: it is hard to believe that a revolutionary State would have received General de Gaulle with the discreet favor the Soviet government has accorded him. Since communism is in fact won over to reforms and compromises, the point of honor of verbal bolshevism only serves to uphold the Right's propaganda. There is a tendency toward reformism and the "program" in the Communist Party. This tendency is slowly gaining ground; one day it will win out. As long as the Communist Party has not made its mutation, there will not be any democracy in France.

Our present is bounded by phantoms. This is no reason to add to them. It is not of restoring the Republic, above all the Republic we have had for the past two years, that we need to think. We must think of recreating it free of its rituals and obsessions, in the light.

(June 5, 1958)

14 / Tomorrow . . .

(INTERVIEW)

—HAVE THE EVENTS IN ALGIERS changed the idea you had formed of overseas problems?

I told you I was not in favor of a revolutionary policy, a "depth" policy. I am even less so today: it would risk extending to the French mainland the fascism which has appeared in Algeria. For it is a question of a fascism, that is more and more evident as information reaches us here.

It is not by chance that several months before the rebellion, the 5th Bureau of Algiers got an operating plan of the radio station. After Pflimlin took office, we heard colonels starting up paramilitary groups again while pretending to abandon them. It is no longer a question here of those malaises which now are standard in the Army: it is a question of a theory of terror, not only as a means of struggling at Algiers, but as a means of governing at home in France, and as a "philosophy" of history.

—Aren't people exaggerating when they attribute a whole policy to the "colonels"? Isn't their attitude inspired above all by the problems of war?

—You will soon be reading in the press the report of a lecture given June 7, at Algiers, by Colonel Trinquier; and there you will find, with some hesitations or precautions, the temptation to extend to the French mainland the means employed at Algiers to make the populace "commandable." This policy is clearly set forth in a book that I recently read: *La troisième guerre mondiale est commencée,* by Pierre Debray. War will no longer be, *is* no longer a visible war. It will be, or rather it is, a clandestine war. Since 1917 a will to subversion whose theory was provided by bolshevism has made its way across the world, developing punctually according to the Bolshevist calendar: "*We abandoned Tunisia and Morocco, when subversive action was still only at the second of the phases described by Trotsky. Here and now, in Algeria, the fourth phase has been reached. Who can reasonably claim that mainland France itself is only at the first one?"*

We are in the realm of the occult. All the history of communism since Trotsky, the actions and reactions, the ups and downs, the purges and turning-points, all that is verifiable, all the events are conjured away: there is only one substance of history, the advances of subversion. This abstract enemy is all around us and justifies a permanent suspicion, whether it is, of course, a question of the U.S.S.R. or the United States. But also of Germany, Italy, and three-fourths of France. The enemy is even within us if we hold back something in the struggle engaged against him. We must not, Pierre Debray says, draw back at integrating the Army and the police. The soldier, who has been changed into an instructor and administrator, must be made a militant or even an executioner. *"The soldier's job has been changed; that's all. We are waging a war which is imposed upon us, a war without rules, a war without 'honor,' a plebeian war."* If the soldier refuses any part of this role, *"the party of treason annexes him." "Whoever evades the choice condemns himself to acting, if not subjectively at least objectively, as a partisan of surrender."* So what the counter-Communists retain from their experience and readings is the apparatus of decadent communism, the guillotine of "objectively," formalism, Manichaeism, and thinking which is agglutinated or, by admixture, made even worse by them because their movement does not have even a perspective in view and is summed up in resistance to an invisible poison. The reason why these officers have adopted the word *subversion,* in spite of its Courtelinesque overtones, is that "revolution" could evoke a positive undertaking, and they are concerned with presenting the enemy as the power of negation.

Of course they have eyes and ears; they know there is a visible history; and in unguarded moments Pierre Debray remarks that Communists are politicians, that they subordinate war to politics, and that they can thus allow halts, stages, and delays in destruction. It is the F.L.N. which is the immediate negation, *"absolute war"*—and it cannot be otherwise, since there is no Algerian nation, *"no Algeria."* Was not Ramdane a *"great reader of Clausewitz"*? But the F.L.N.'s absolute war and physical violence only translate into clearer terms what is the sole essence of today's history, the "metaphysic" of phenomena—subversion. This poison, which is everywhere, can be resisted only through *"absolute counter-war."*

The conclusions are clear: a *"revolutionary legality"* must be created in mainland France, *"the mainland apparatus of Communist subversion"* destroyed, and censorship and the death penalty established for journalists. In Algeria, the proposed single electoral college is alleged to be a trick to bring about independence. After all, it would be absurd to wage war to make elections which could lead to independence possible. The only goal is to *"annihilate the fellagha." "Our surrenders in Morocco and Tunisia heavily mortgage the situation"*; the Sakhiet operation *"was wrong only in being too late and above all too timid."*

The ultimate meaning of this attitude can be debated. I cannot help thinking that the soldiers who leave the Tunisian frontier in order to come rebel at Algiers, and bring their wrath for the enemy to bear upon their fellow countrymen, really do not have much hope of beating the enemy any more. As Robert Lacoste said, it is not easy to fight on two fronts. Pierre Debray writes: *"Either the whole nation goes to war, or it is better to stop having our soldiers killed right now. . . . How can we help it? We have no taste for useless sacrifices."* I cannot help it either; and furthermore I have no authority to send anyone whatsoever to the sacrifice, useful or useless. So I will say only this: the soldiers I have known, who were very close to me, would have blushed to take that tone. Since Pierre Debray thinks about bolshevism so much, he ought to remember that it is often defeated armies which make revolutions.

But enough of psychology. What is important is that we have here an aggressive nihilism *which excludes all policy*. When the author tries to outline one—with a sigh of regret, for after all the *"most reasonable solution"* would perhaps be ideally to propose nothing at all to the Africans—he can only speak of *"intellectual audacity," "spectacular transformations,"* and a *"twentieth-century technical revolution"* whose nature he does not futher specify, and about which we know only that it will be the inverse of the 1917 one. The truth is that the conditions for a policy are suppressed by a thinking which is not even totalitarian but a monism of terror—anguish, failure, and shame asserted in despair and dressed out as policy.

All this is a fascism in the most precise sense of the term—revival and external imitation of the methods of revolutionary struggle, mimesis of revolutionary pathos, underestimation of the visible to the profit of the occult, and identification at a distance of adversaries with each other and of counter-bolshevism with its adversaries.

—What relationships do you see between these tendencies and those of the Paris government?

—There is no need to demonstrate at length that General de Gaulle's undertaking has no relationship to this state of mind. The single electoral college, which is a betrayal for the Fascists, was his first proposal in Algeria; the evacuation of Tunisia, which was a "surrender," his first act. General de Gaulle has in common with the Fascist officers only the polemic against the "system"; this has led him in recent years to refuse to take part when some republicans were trying to tear the Republic out of its political nothingness—and more recently to refuse to repudiate the movement at Algiers: if the "system" is Evil, all that tends to destroy it was relatively justified.

But what General de Gaulle wants to put in the place of the Fourth Republic has nothing to do with the colonels' aggressive nihilism. He is an old-style man and soldier—I mean with solid superstructures—*homo historicus*, and not the *homo psychologicus* of the new generation. The hidden realities he believes in are not the phantasms of subversion and counter-subversion but the archetype of a self-sustained France and the people, who at the other end of the field of history and from the depths of their daily life will say yes to France. The metaphysics of the arbitrator and the people, one above and the other beyond parties, is a completely different thing than Fascist activism.

—Do you think that the Paris government is in a position to bring the part of the Army you spoke of earlier round to its policy?

—Like everyone else, I just do not know. I doubt that it will succeed in doing so by persuasion. Sheer coercion would require a refusal of reinforcements and gasoline. The question is perhaps one of disassociating a part of the French populace and the Army from fascism. And here I am afraid that General de Gaulle's convictions about domestic politics (which are far less personal and original than he is himself) may blind him and prevent him from seeking the support of public opinion he would need. For after all, does he see and say exactly why the Fourth Republic was incapable of a reform policy like the one he is undertaking?

He thinks French politics lacks *continuity*. Is it continuity that the Fourth Republic lacked? Did not the governments which followed one another, with one exception, follow the same policy? Is it not, on the contrary, initiative, movement, and novelty that they continually lacked, without excepting the Suez affair, which figures as a convulsion and not an action, since they were not determined to carry it out to the end? Is it hoped that this continuity in inaction will be remedied by increasing the powers of the President of the Republic, which means in a sense decreasing correspondingly the powers of the President of the Council? When the President of the Republic is no longer de Gaulle, he will go back to being what he has always been: a man who has followed his long and honorable career and who tends more to customary solutions than to those which demand imagination, new knowledge, and initiative. And even when he is General de Gaulle, the question is to know whether the French problem is to find an arbitrator who gives each a little of what he asks for, or whether it is not instead to have a power which rules, that is, which draws along and transforms the country in action, instead of leaving it as it is and behind its back conceiving of a grand political design which the leaders do not try to convince it about but simply invite it to say yes to. I am afraid that between the arbitrator's secret mediation and the muffled response of the referendum, French politics will lack air as much as or more than before, and that France under this régime will continue to be what it is: a country advanced in understanding and retarded in social, political, and economic practice.

General de Gaulle also calls *party rule* into question. But since he does not propose the one-party system in exchange, he thus wants to "muster" or create union outside all parties, which assumes both that an opposition between parties answers to nothing in events, that it is by itself a cause of paralysis, and that it suffices to abolish it for all to be saved. Now the opposition between a Right-wing and a Left-wing policy is so little an illusion that up until now General de Gaulle has taken up the very policy of governments said to be Left-wing: Tunisian independence, elections in the single electoral college, reforms and equipping in Algeria—a policy the Right has never accepted except to the extent it remained verbal. What General de Gaulle does not admit to himself, or does not say to Frenchmen, is that if there are solutions they are all liberal. At bottom, almost everyone knows it, at Algiers as at Paris. I do not see annihilation of the fellagha being spoken about so much today at Algiers: and this is not only because they are to all intents and purposes won over, but also because the de Gaulle government's reason for being is to end the war by concessions, independence excluded. The Algiers movement (with the exception perhaps of its Fascist elements) did not put de Gaulle in power to "wage war" in Clemenceau's sense; they put him in power to make peace without admitting the failure of the war. The policy he is taking up is the one that the Left and the Center-Left were in agreement upon, and that the Communist Party itself was satisfied with when it voted plenary powers to the Mollet government. But this must not be said; to do so would mean depriving the Algiers movement of its consolation, which is to give in to a general; it would mean compromising the operation. The great dramas of French politics come down perhaps to making the Right swallow a liberal policy by accompanying it with an anti-parliamentarian gong-beat. Either free elections, a single electoral college, and social equality will remain dead letters, as has been the case up till now (social equality will remain a dead letter in any case, as the theory of underdevelopment clearly shows)—or General de Gaulle will succeed in bringing out of his words some new status for Algeria, but this is wholly contingent. For the moment, we are still at the stage of words, the same words the Left set in motion and the Right accepted only if they remained words. So it is indeed futile to call party rule into question at the moment one takes up the policy of one of the parties.

The fact remains that party rule could not put this policy into *practice;* it could only *talk about* it: this is the only argument which counts, but it does count. We still have to say why, and there is nothing very mysterious about it. It could not put a liberal policy into practice because, the Communist votes being excluded, it had to purchase those of the Right at the cost of a daily supervision which annihilated the governmental function. The party of independents announced that it would withdraw its ministers if the Tunisian airfields were evacuated. As everyone has pointed out, it accepts today what it rejected yesterday. So the parliamentary Right was not fighting from real positions; it was fighting against *surrender,* which like a ghost appeared and disappeared unpredictably. Only the oblique way was left for the government, but this way increased mistrust and still further reduced its margin of action. Edgar Faure establishing a policy of resistance for his resident minister in Morocco when he knew it could not be followed (or so he claimed later), organizing the demonstration of his impotence himself while he was waiting to demand it cynically—this episode was tremendously important. It led everyone, Frenchmen and Moslems, to think that the government's official positions could always be gotten around, bearing out the former in their neurosis of surrender and the latter in their intransigence.

After the speech to the Bey, the French colony was received at Tunis; after the Moroccan affair, we know how Guy Mollet was received in Algiers. The annihilation of the governmental function resulted from the fact that the government, simultaneously weak and rigid, could persevere in the war, perhaps to surrender in the end, but not in any case to give life to a serious political or diplomatic action.

It is not the diversity of parties and the "division of Frenchmen" which has kept the governments from putting a liberal policy into practice; it is the existence of a Right without ideas which has become the arbitrator of French politics by the subterfuge of deducting the Communist votes. By calling party rule into question, General de Gaulle is blaming democracy's passiveness for what should be blamed on the Right's passiveness. Now it is not a matter here of a futile search for past responsibilities. As the new régime being readied will be based upon this evaluation, I do not expect, for my part, anything good of it. It is a falsified democracy the legal coup d'Etat has judged, not democracy; and the remedy would be to seek in the opposite direction from the one they are seeking.

—But does not true or corrected democracy mean a Popular Front?

—Democracy was falsified by the Right's political indigence coupled with a reeling Communist policy: it is this combination which has gotten French politics assigned to unreality and condemned it to paralysis. If it were a question of a class struggle between the Communists and the Right, it would be really naive to denounce it. But that is not the case. Let us not forget that Pinay counts for something in Moroccan independence, and that the Communists put up with the repression of the Constantinians in 1946 and gave plenary powers to the Guy Mollet government. Between the Right and the C.P., there is no real opposition; for they are not fighting for one policy, both have many of them. *Both are no longer parties; they are "pressure groups."* They exercised joint pressures on the régime and together overturned ministries, but neither accepted responsibility for French political life. The independents did not assume their responsibility in French political life because they do not have any ideas: they have never been known to offer a view about the future or the present; their reason for being is to be in opposition—to communism, they say, but if they did not have that pretext they would look for another one.

As for the Communists, they can be asked to do almost anything except *take part* in an action. Even in the government, even in the midst of compromise, they remained indifferent to what they were doing; because their heart is not in it, because they did not intend to be judges of it, because they were not really committed to it. They are always repeating "Popular Front," but for them the Popular Front is not a formula for action. I can still see Ramadier between the Place de la Nation and the Place de la République, bothered by the heat, leaving the ranks of the demonstrators and marching along red-faced, no doubt towards a drug store, with the lost look of a completely exhausted man. A group of militants surround him like a fetish, fists raised, crying "Popular Front." This visibly worn-out man, who had for a moment regained in the Assembly the limelight of the old days, surrounded by gay and merciless young bucks—there is an image one never forgets. There will be no true or proper democracy as long as the Communists refuse to enter positively into the régime, as long as they disguise their practice of compromise under the disruptive, diversionist theses of "absolute pauperization." Yet they well know that there will be a People's Democracy in France only if the United States is defeated in an atomic war. What are they waiting for then? No one has the slightest idea; nor do they, I think.

—What are the chances for a true democracy?

—If the causes which have falsified it are as I have described them, there is little chance of a rebirth of a true democracy. I do not see what could enlighten the independents. I do not see how the worn-out headquarters which had succeeded in "mopping up" de-Stalinization would be capable of a political initiative, at the moment when the execution of Imre Nagy and his companions confirmed it in its profound wisdom. I do not see how it could put the problem of the conditions required for democracy and freedom before the country. Was the democracy of 1956–58 capable of living? There is the question which counts, and it is the one the Communists do not want to know about. So they will call upon the French to struggle for the reestablishment of this democracy which has destroyed itself.

—But what if the new Constitution is approved in the referendum?

—In the Assemblies which it will create, the goverments (whether presidential or not, armed or not with a right to dissolve the Assembly, which as a matter of principle cannot often be used) will find themselves confronted with the same dilemma: either the Popular Front, that is, an *a-politics*—the evacuation of countries overseas, a social policy which merely makes demands without doing anything about them, no management of capitalism, nothing organic, no action—or the "deduction of Communist votes," that is, the destruction of the governmental function by the Right.

—Then what is to be done?

—By the force of circumstances, the real questions can be asked only outside the Right and the Communist Party, with the hope that they, and the country along with them, will end up by taking an interest in them. When existing forces are confused, we must first of all speak to the point without looking for an immediate point of incidence.

The Fourth Republic will not be reborn: it is not worth regretting, having been only the shadow of a republic. The French crisis is a result of the fact that if there is a solution to our problems it is a liberal one, and there is no longer any theoretical or practical political freedom in France. We are living on the leftovers of eighteenth-century thought, and it has to be reconstructed from top to bottom.

Someone had me observe that Montesquieu sees freedom in the separation and balance of powers, and that before they can be separated or balanced, the powers must first exist. The problem today is to re-create them. Fifty years ago Alain could still define the Republic by checks and balances and the citizen's permanent polemic against those in power. But what do checks and balances mean when there is no longer any action to check and balance? The only task, in 1900 as two centuries before, was to organize criticism. Today it is necessary, in continuing the criticism, to reorganize the power. Many stupid things are said against "personal power" or "strong power": it is genuine strength and personality which those in power during the Fourth Republic lacked.

Our very notion of *opinion* has to be looked at again: it is based upon a philosophy of judgment and decision which is a little limited; the reality of a régime is not, any more than that of a man, an instantaneous series of opinions. There is no freedom in submission to each shiver of opinion. As Hegel said, freedom requires something substantial; it requires a State, which bears it and which it gives life to.

An analysis of Parliament would have to be undertaken from this point of view: we know almost nothing about its real functioning. I only know, as a result of having attended some sessions of the National Assembly, that there was no lack of intelligence or knowledge there, but that one felt the same uneasiness there as in a "crowd" where one is not introduced. At some moments, it was not without grandeur; at other times (I remember certain laughs of the initiated, certain veiled comments) it was bad company, or Mme Verdurin's salon. The high point of the régime was no doubt reached when the Communists voted for the Pflimlin government in order to compel it to include them, and the independents also voted for it out of fear of a Popular Front, yet Pflimlin was very quietly getting ready to pull out. Maybe this is parliamentary sublimity; I doubt that the nation appreciated it.

The reason why the Mendès-France government was momentarily able to lift French political life out of its anguish and boredom as *no* other government had since 1944, was that he conceived of government as an initiative which gathers support, and of action as a movement which cannot be constantly harassed but arranges meetings with the nation, organizes its own pedagogy, and demonstrates as it develops. This is living political power and not a fulguration on Mt. Sinai. But Mendès-France acted this way instinctively—because he is well-born, I would say—he never tried to give his practice a theoretical formulation. The problem is to find institutions which implant this practice of freedom in our customs.

This communication between the statesman and the nation, which is why it no longer submits to a destiny but recognizes itself in what is done in its name—there, I greatly fear, is something that General de Gaulle has never known or felt, except in the "great circumstances" of 1940 and 1944. As proof I need only the total *satisfecit* he gave to all the men of the system, to Pleven as much as and more than to Mendès-France. The spirit which always denies, he recently said. How wrong he is! What puts us on our guard is precisely *his* skepticism. It would take a lot to rob me of the respect I bear for General de Gaulle. But we owe him something other and better than devotion: we owe him our opinion. He is too young to be our father, and we are too old to act like children.

Are the politicians of the opposition better aware of the problem? One is flabbergasted at reading the reflections of commission members. One would like to say to them: it's all over; it is no longer a question of *making use of a government;* you have to create a régime. Oppose idea to idea, and since you can do it, speak to Frenchmen. One is stupefied to read in *Le Populaire,* concerning the recent elections and in the face of the *"stability of the electoral body,"* that *"the system is in good shape."* In order to face up to today's questions, it is not just the apparatus of the Communist Party which needs to say its prayers. Who can describe the comedy of the Socialist Party, whose whole structure, conceived of formerly as that of a workers' and Marxist party in order to subject elected officials to the militants' vigilance, is today one more means in the Secretary-General's hands of subjecting the parliamentary group to his maneuvers? But after all, many people know this better than I do. . . . Who am I to speak at such length about it? The officers prophesy; the professors sharpen their pens. Where are the counselors of the people, and have they nothing they can offer us but their regrets?

(July, 1958)

Index